D0852382

WONDERS OF THE WORLD

WONDERS OF THE WORLD

MetroBooks

CONTENTS

Writers: Rosemary Burton and Richard Cavendish
Copy Editor: Janet Tabinski

World and continental locator maps:
© The Automobile Association 1991.
Reference maps and endpapers:
© 1991, Rand McNally & Company.

Published by AA Publishing, a trading name of Automobile Association Developments Limited, whose registered office is Millstream, Maidenhead Road, Windsor, Berkshire SL4 5GD.
Registered number 1878835.

Typeset by Microset Graphics Ltd, Basingstoke, Hampshire.
Colour origination by Scantrans Pte Ltd, Singapore.
Printed and bound in Dubai by Oriental Press

Reprinted 1995, 1998, 1999, 2001

2002 MetroBooks
An Imprint of Friedman/Fairfax Publishers

This edition published by Metrobook , by arrangement with Automobile Association Developments Limited.

ISBN 1-58663-751-7

1 3 5 7 9 10 8 6 4 2
For bulk purchases and special sales, please contact:
Friedman/Fairfax Publishers
Attention: Sales Department
230 Fifth Avenue, Suite 700
New York, NY 10001
212/685-6610 FAX 212/685-3916

Visit our website:
www.metrobooks.com

A CIP catalogue record for this book is available from the British Library.

Title page
The pyramids at Giza, Egypt

This page
The Taj Mahal at sunset, India

THE HUNDRED WONDERS OF THE WORLD

A WONDER is something that arouses astonishment and awe. All the hundred wonders in this book are things to marvel at. All of them, also, are the work of human hands. Taken together they span 10,000 years of human history, from the earliest farming settlement at Jericho to the latest engineering prodigies in South America and Japan. They span the globe as well, and are arranged here by continents and, within that, in order of date.

Everywhere in the world there has always been a delight in the spectacular and an urge to burden the groaning earth with the tallest, heaviest, hugest constructions that skill and technology would allow, from Stonehenge to the Itaipu Dam. The C.N. Tower in Toronto, swaying slightly in the wind, rises more than one-third of a mile (535 m) into the sky. The Empire State Building in New York City enjoyed for more than 40 years the prestige of being the world's highest building, and like the Eiffel Tower and the soaring spires of medieval cathedrals, it shows what human beings can do when they aim at the skies.

MARVELS AND MYSTERY

Some wonders are marvels of engineering, the conquest of distance and the taming of nature: the Suez and Panama canals, the Trans-Siberian and the Canadian Pacific, the Aswan High Dam. Some are astonishing feats of construction without benefit of modern machinery: Stonehenge, the Great Wall of China, Great Zimbabwe, the Ethiopian rock churches. Some are in extraordinary, inaccessible places, like the Meteora monasteries in Greece.

There are parallels and resonances between achievements widely separated by geography and time: the Colosseum in Rome and the Superdome in New Orleans; the sea-girt gate of the Itsukushima Shrine in Japan and the Gateway Arch beside the Mississippi in St. Louis; the colossal statues of Egyptian pharoahs and the stone faces of American presidents hewn in Mount Rushmore. Wonder can imply an

element of the unknown and enigmatic, and mystery is indeed present in the shadow of the Great Pyramid, among the Maya temple-cities in the jungles of Yucatán, in the patterns on the desert floor at Nazca, in the Easter Island statues gazing mute at the Pacific.

PARADISE ON EARTH

Many vast constructions in stone and marble display the power of kings, from Persepolis to the Kremlin. By impressing on his subjects the ruler's awesome majesty, they serve the practical purpose of supporting his regime. Ironically, they can turn into gilded prisons – like the Forbidden City of the Chinese emperors in Beijing or the Potala Palace of the Dalai Lamas at Lhasa – in which the ruler becomes a puppet, cut off from real life.

Buildings like these may be attempts to create the perfect place, the earthly paradise. "If there is a paradise on earth," said Shah Jehan, who built the Red Fort in Delhi, "it is this, it is this, it is this." The Alhambra in Spain and the Topkapi Palace in Istanbul were designed with the same intention. In their 20th-century ways, William Randolph Hearst's great mansion at San Simeon and Walt Disney World in Florida are attempts to realize paradise on earth. At Versailles, Louis XIV's architects and landscape designers set out to build a palace of ideal proportions, which would demonstrate not only the Sun King's splendor, but also the order of the world.

The same is true of great religious buildings – cathedrals, mosques, temples – which are symbols of the divine order of things. The colossal "temple-mountains" of the East, like Borobudur in Java and Angkor Wat in Cambodia, are stone lessons on the true nature of the universe.

Hence the importance of orientation, of aligning a building with the order of the world. The Great Pyramid in Egypt was built so that its four sides accurately face north, east, south, and west. Across the other side of the earth 3,000 years later, the city of Teotihuacán in Mexico was laid out in the same fashion.

Sometimes orientation was organized to provide a spectacular symbolic effect. The massive burial mound of Newgrange in Ireland was constructed in such a way that, on the day of the winter solstice every year, a ray of sunlight shone down a long dark corridor to light up the innermost blackness of the tomb. At Chichén Itzá in Mexico, where the steps and terraces of the pyramid-temple represent the days and months of the year, at the spring and autumn equinoxes the patterns of sunlight and shadows make it look as if the serpent god is coiling and writhing his way out of the temple.

What this book demonstrates above all, as it steps from continent to continent, is the indefatigable ambition, skill, and creativity that human beings have displayed in every corner of the globe. The Hundred Wonders of the World are wonders of the human spirit.

The pyramid-temple of Quetzalcoatl, the plumed serpent, at Chichén Itzá, Mexico.

EUROPE

BETWEEN the massive Stone Age tomb of Newgrange in Ireland and the controversial Pompidou Center in Paris, there stretches a span of 5,000 years, filled with remarkable constructions and heroic feats of engineering. At Stonehenge, over a period of some 1,500 years, a great temple was raised with titanic labor and impressive skill. Its deities and rituals we can now only guess at, but its worn gray stones standing solitary on Salisbury Plain can still send an eerie shiver of recognition down the spine.

THE CLASSICS

In the 5th century B.C. one small city emerged as the leading center and beacon of Greek civilization in the eastern Mediterranean area. In that single century, the extraordinary flowering in Athens laid the foundations of Western culture in the tragedies of Aeschylus, Sophocles, and Euripides, the comedies of Aristophanes, the philosophy of Socrates, the writings of Herodotus and Thucydides, and the sculpture of Phidias. It also produced the Parthenon, the temple of the city's protecting goddess, which has stood ever since as a symbol of the glory that was Greece.

Rome was at that time an obscure little backwoods town in Italy of no apparent interest to civilized persons, but the Romans were flexing their muscles and beginning to bring their neighbors under their sway. By halfway through the 3rd century B.C., Rome controlled or dominated more than half the land surface of Italy. The Roman state and its formidable legions marched on to build up an enormous empire, which, by the 2nd century A.D., stretched from Britain across Europe and North Africa to Egypt, Mesopotamia, and the Caspian Sea. In Rome itself the Colosseum is a monument to both imperial grandeur and imperial savagery, and on the empire's northernmost border in Britain, Hadrian's Wall still bears witness to Roman ambition and military genius.

Rome weakened and fell, the Germanic tribes swept across Europe from beyond the Rhine, and in time a new Western European civilization emerged in the Middle Ages.

The glory that was Greece: the Parthenon against the Athens sky.

Christianity was its guiding light, and it evolved the soaring, God-directed style of architecture (later derisively called Gothic) that created cathedrals like Chartres. Meanwhile, in sun-drenched Granada, the Moorish culture of the Muslim conquerors of Spain was building a paradise on earth among the fountains and shaded courts of the Alhambra.

The genius of Greece and Rome took hold of Europe afresh in the Renaissance. In Rome, at the center of Western Christendom, the vast new church raised above the tomb of St. Peter heralded the grandiose style of the baroque. The merchant princes of Venice, who controlled European trade with the East, constructed their waterside palaces along the Grand Canal, while their northern equivalents in the Low Countries created the sumptuous Grand' Place in Brussels. Renaissance influence spread as far as Moscow, where the cathedral of St. Michael the Archangel was built in the citadel of the Kremlin.

As the modern nation-state strode onto the stage, rulers occupied palaces of a size and grandeur to support and assert their high place in the world. In Vienna the Hapsburg dynasty ruled an empire from the Hofburg. A Spanish Hapsburg created the palace-monastery

The Great Palace
The Kremlin
Trans-Siberian Railway
Hadrian's Wall
Newgrange
Pont Cysyllte Aqueduct
The Iron Bridge
Stonehenge
Windsor Castle
Grand' Place
Golden Lane
Versailles
Sacré-Coeur, Eiffel Tower, Pompidou Center
Chartres Cathedral
The Hofburg
Parliament Building
Neuschwanstein Castle
Kapellbrücke
The Grand Canal
Pont du Gard
Leaning Tower of Pisa
Diocletian's Palace
The Escorial
The Sagrada Família
The Colosseum, St. Peter's Basilica
Meteora Monasteries
The Alhambra
The Parthenon

of the Escorial outside Madrid. Versailles made a noble setting for the Sun King, Louis XIV, and his successors in France.

THE MACHINE WORLD

In 18th-century England a new age dawned with the Industrial Revolution. Its fitting symbol is the Iron Bridge across the River Severn. Erected in 1779, it was the first major construction in the world made of iron, and it ushered in an era that would transform the rural, agricultural economy of Western Europe into a predominantly industrial economy of machines, factories, teeming towns, and mass production of consumer goods. The Eiffel Tower in Paris and the rails of the Trans-Siberian Railway, stretching from Moscow to the far coast of Asia, are two symbols of the machine age.

The 19th-century reaction against the horrors of industrialism inspired nostalgic dreams of the past, expressed in stone. At Windsor Castle in England, a fortress and royal residence going back to Norman times was refashioned for King George IV in mock-feudal, baronial majesty. In Bavaria a romantic fairy-tale stronghold fit for a swan knight or a Grail hero was raised for King Ludwig at Neuschwanstein.

The modern movement in architecture has turned its back on dreams and the past. Its major creations have been outside Europe on the whole, but in Paris the Pompidou Center boldly challenges the achievements of the previous 5,000 years.

The revolutionary Pompidou Center turns the conventional building inside out.

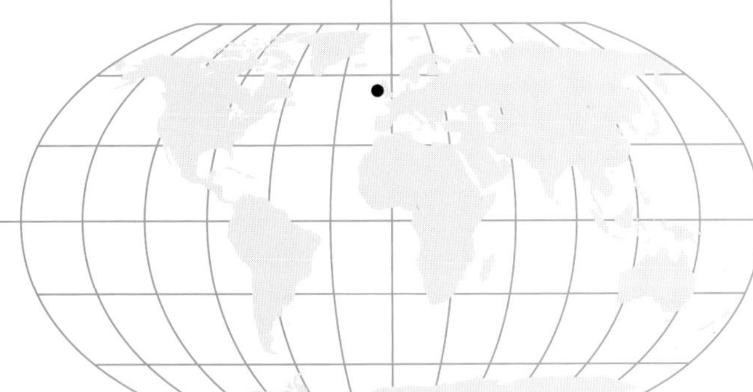

4th Millennium B.C. Ireland

NEWGRANGE

At the winter solstice the rising sun sends a beam of light into the dark heart of this mysterious grave.

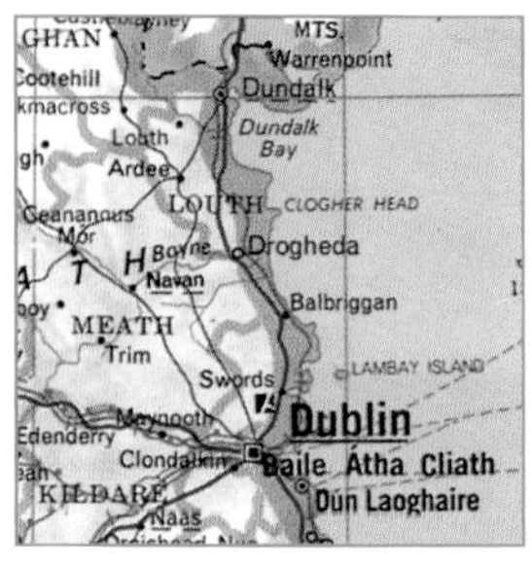

Newgrange, County Meath, Republic of Ireland, is on the north bank of the River Boyne less than 10 miles (16 km) from Drogheda and about 30 miles (48 km) north of Dublin. The best approach from Dublin by road is via the N2 to the village of Slane, which is 5 miles (8 km) east of Newgrange.

WHEN it was unearthed in 1699 by men looking for building stone, Newgrange was described as a cave. Since then it has been attributed to the Danes, regarded as a tomb of the kings of Tara belonging to the first centuries of the Christian era, and even seen as a remote descendant of the beehive tombs at Mycenae. In fact, it is far older than Mycenae, older even than Stonehenge or the Pyramids. Newgrange, celebrated in Irish literature as the Brugh (abode) of Boyne, is a megalithic passage grave dating back to 3200 B.C., and it offers clear evidence that a technically competent and sophisticated Neolithic society was flourishing

Right: the vast heap of stones and earth was faced with gleaming white quartz pebbles and was surrounded by a circle of tall standing stones, of which only those in front of the entrance are still in place.

Facing page: at the turn of the year, the sun lit up the inner chamber for about 17 minutes. The builders of this massive tomb evidently had a good grasp of the calendar.

in the Boyne Valley at this time.

A passage, 3 feet (91 cm) wide and 55 feet (16.7 m) long, lined and roofed with great monoliths, leads to a central chamber that has three arms. The height of the passage increases from under 5 feet (1.5 m) at the front to twice this at the chamber entrance. Both chamber and passage are covered by a cairn estimated to contain 220,507 U.S. tons (200,000 metric tons) of loose stones. The whole structure was sealed against water penetration and ringed by standing stones.

Newgrange poses many unanswered questions. Why did so elaborate a tomb apparently contain the remains of only five bodies? How were the huge slabs of stone transported to the site? (They were not quarried, but appear to have been deposited around the region by glacial movement.) How long did the work take, and how many people were involved? Some stones are decorated with distinctive geometric patterns, but why is the decoration sometimes hidden from view?

On another point there is greater certainty: the excavator of Newgrange, Professor O'Kelly, has shown that the tomb is oriented in such a way that the rising midwinter sun shines along the length of the passageway and into the chamber. It would have done the same, casting light on one decorated stone at the far end of the chamber, when Newgrange was built.

The entrance to the passageway was originally blocked by a stone, but sunlight enters through a slit carefully constructed in the roof above. The effect has been observed at the winter solstice and for about a week before and after this date. Something similar is known in Scotland's Orkney Islands at the chambered tomb of Maes Howe, which has been dated to before 2700 B.C., but in this case it is the *setting* midwinter sun that illuminates the tomb. The importance of the sun at Newgrange supports the theory, drawn from early Irish literature, that the tomb was associated with supernatural creatures, in particular the Dagda, or "good god" who was also known as a sun god.

The Boyne Valley Cemetery

NEWGRANGE stands in an area formed by a loop of the River Boyne that is strangely rich in prehistoric monuments. Within a mile or two are two other mounds, Knowth and Dowth, which are much the same size as Newgrange but are thought to have been made slightly later. The Knowth mound contains two passage graves, and many smaller ones lie outside. In the vicinity there are also several barrows and standing stones, and it would not be difficult to believe that the whole complex acquired some sort of mystic reputation over the centuries. Both Knowth and Dowth show signs of disturbance by later visitors, but Newgrange appears to have stayed sealed. This may mean that the latter was regarded with special respect or perhaps feared as a house of the dead. The discovery of objects outside the mound, including jewelry and coins from the 4th century A.D., suggests that Newgrange was considered a holy place and that there was a tradition of leaving offerings (albeit at a safe distance) to please the inhabitants.

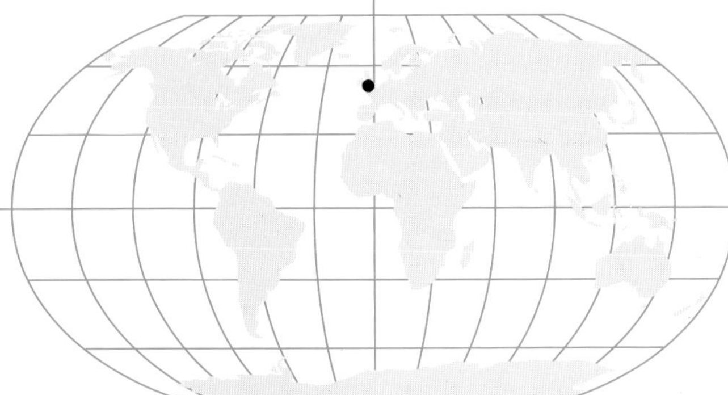

4th to 2nd Millennium B.C. England

STONEHENGE

"You may put a hundred questions to these rough-hewn giants as they bend in grim contemplation of their fallen companions." – HENRY JAMES

Stonehenge stands on Salisbury Plain 2 miles (3 km) west of Amesbury in Wiltshire at the junction of the A303 and the A344/A360. The nearest British Rail stations are at Salisbury and Grateley, both about 10 miles (16 km) away.

Seen from different angles and in different lights, the massive stones loom up mysteriously against the sky. There is no doubt about Stonehenge's timeless appeal, but its original purpose and meaning are still fiercely debated.

STONEHENGE remains a mystery. Theories about it range from the plausible to the absurd, and arguments have raged over its intended purpose. Inigo Jones, the 17th-century English architect, concluded that it was a primitive attempt to imitate Roman architecture; others are convinced that beings from outer space had a hand in it, perhaps using it as a landing place on their terrestrial excursions. It is unlikely that we will ever fully understand it, but for those who are moved by the atmosphere and beauty of the monument and its setting, that hardly matters.

There are several different building phases at Stonehenge, some more than a thousand years apart. First, around 3100 B.C., there was a circular ditch, with a "heelstone" outside it and, inside, a mound and a ring of holes used at some stage to hold cremated matter. Later, so-called bluestones were arranged in two concentric rings inside the ditch. These were eventually cleared away, and around 2100 B.C. (by which time the first phase could already have qualified as an ancient monument) the most familiar aspect of Stonehenge began to take shape. A ring of huge gray sandstone blocks with lintels above them was built. Within this circle was a horseshoe arrangement formed by a number of huge trilithons (two freestanding upright stones supporting a lintel). The bluestones appear to have been rearranged several times by different generations. Today, some of them form a separate horseshoe within the sandstone horseshoe, and a circle of bluestones stands inside the sandstone circle.

The bluestones themselves have caused much speculation. Their unusual composition has long been thought to mean that they could only have come from the Prescelly Mountains of south Wales, in which case they were probably transported by rafts along water routes. But recently geologists have challenged this theory, saying that the stones are too varied to have come from any one source and that it is more likely that a glacier carried them to the vicinity of Stonehenge from a number of different places.

Construction at Stonehenge was neither primitive nor haphazard, and the shaping of the stones reveals a remarkable understanding of perspective. Great claims have been made for the mathematical abilities of the builders, and the whole structure may have been some sort of astronomical observatory, possibly intended to predict eclipses of the moon. It is well known that Stonehenge becomes a place of pilgrimage at the time of the summer solstice (the axis of the horseshoes and an ancient approach road to the site are aligned with the path of the rising midsummer sun), and this fact has enhanced the supposed mystical significance of the place.

Stonehenge is also popularly associated with the Druids, who are believed to have taken a special interest in astronomical phenomena. But this theory takes no account of the great age of the monument – Druids belong to Celtic society, and if they did have anything to do with Stonehenge in later years, they certainly weren't around when it was built.

With the development of archaeology into a strict and ever more accurate science involving carbon-14 dating and the precise analysis of geological formations, the theory of Druidic origins has been discounted. For the present, Stonehenge and its ghostly resonances remain a mystery.

Avebury

A FEW miles from Stonehenge, at Avebury, also in Wiltshire, is a stone circle thought to be the largest in the world. One estimate gives a total of 247 standing stones forming the outer and inner rings, and there were perhaps another 97 pairs of such stones forming an associated avenue. A huge ditch around the outer stone circle measures some 70 feet (21 m) in width, and it encloses an area of nearly 30 acres (12 hectares). The outer circle of about a hundred stones surrounds two smaller circles, and each of the smaller circles had another stone or stones arranged within. Unlike the stone blocks at Stonehenge, these stones were not specially shaped and dressed; but, like Stonehenge, Avebury defies all attempts to solve its mysteries. Sun or moon worship, male or female fertility rites – the list of theories is a long one, with little hope of confirmation or refutation. The Avebury stones date from about 2600 B.C., but the area shows many signs of earlier activity and can be studied as an excellent example of Neolithic landscape.

Devizes and Salisbury both have museums of note, and the cities in themselves are highly rewarding places to visit while in the vicinity of Stonehenge.

Huge stones were hauled across country on rollers and heaved into position on ramps to build the impressive temple at Avebury.

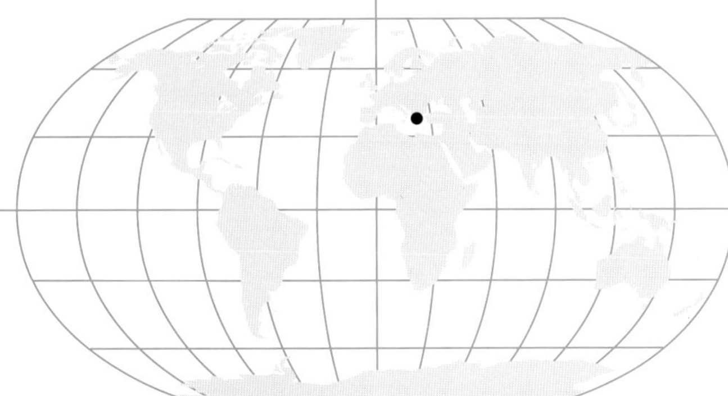

About 450 B.C. Greece

THE PARTHENON

"The most perfect monument of ancient art and even in ruins an imposing and soul-stirring object."
– BAEDEKER, 1889

The Parthenon stands on the Acropolis, the ancient city on a hill beneath which modern Athens sprawls. There will be no difficulty finding it. The sculpture from the Parthenon is distributed among a number of museums, including Athens' National Museum.

DESCRIPTIONS of the Parthenon have always been littered with superlatives. This temple to Athena Parthenos, the virgin protectress of Athens, is regarded as the supreme example of classical architecture, an artistic and sculptural masterpiece. The building belongs to the middle of the 5th century B.C. By then the Persians, who in 480 B.C. succeeded in storming Athens, had been decisively defeated, and the city, under the influence of the statesman Pericles, was brimming with pride and self-confidence. This mood was reflected in a lavish building program, and the money to finance it was available in the form of tribute exacted from Athens' allies. Classical civilization was at its height, and the new temple of Athena on the Acropolis would demonstrate that fact to the whole world.

The Parthenon is a temple in the Doric style, 228 feet (69.5 m) long and 100 feet (30.5 m) wide. The peristyle, or outer colonnade, enclosed an inner building, the *cella*, containing the shrine that housed a giant statue of the goddess made of gold and ivory. The peristyle had 46 columns – eight being visible across the front of the temple, 17 along the sides – each fluted, composed of a number of massive drums, and tapering toward the top. The columns were marble, as were the pediments and entablature they supported, but the roof of the temple was wooden. The building style had developed from that used for simple timber structures, and the Parthenon displays in stone all the elegance of those early solutions to engineering problems. But its simplicity of line and form is deceptive: the architect, an Ionian Greek called Iktinos, was nothing less than a master of perspective, calculating exactly how a building must be shaped if it is to please the human eye gazing up at it from below.

The Parthenon was built on the foundations of an earlier temple to Athena and once contained a colossal statue of the goddess by the great sculptor Phidias, carved in chryselephantine. Athena was a warlike deity,

Greek temples were simple buildings, usually rectangular in shape, with the statue of the deity at the east end. Large temples, like the Parthenon, had a peristyle, or verandah, of columns outside.

and she was also a patron of the arts and crafts.

If the Parthenon was a temple, it was also something of an art gallery, a perfect setting for a wealth of sculpture. The pediments and entablature were covered with figures visible from outside, but the celebrated "Parthenon frieze" (half of which was removed to London by Lord Elgin and bought by the British Museum in 1816) ran around the solid outer walls of the *cella* at a height of about 40 feet (12 m), where its detail would have been largely unappreciated.

The modern image of Greek temples as gleaming white buildings is a false one. The Parthenon was originally painted in colorful, not to say gaudy, fashion. In recent years the marble has suffered badly from the effects of Athens' smog and from the sheer number of tourists who crowd onto the Acropolis. In the past the building was adapted to many different uses, serving among other things as a Greek Orthodox church, a Roman Catholic church, and a mosque. In 1687 the Turkish army was using it as a gunpowder store when besieging Venetian forces succeeded in blowing it up. Dubious 19th-century restoration schemes were resisted, and today – despite the fact that so much of it is roped off and great quantities of its sculpture reside in foreign museums – the Parthenon is still a truly breathtaking sight.

The frieze was too high up for its details to be appreciated.

The Parthenon Frieze

THE birth of the goddess Athena was celebrated annually at Athens, and every four years there was a special ceremony involving a procession and the presentation of a new robe for the statue of the goddess. The Parthenon frieze – over 500 feet (152 m) in length – has long been thought to represent this procession, and many of the details support such an interpretation. Yet there are some anomalies. Professor John Boardman has recently suggested that the frieze shows the 192 Greek heroes who died fighting the Persians at the Battle of Marathon in 490 B.C. The presence of a whole assembly of gods, in addition to Athena, seems to show that this is a ceremony of greater than usual significance and that the actual heroes of Marathon are being presented to the gods of Olympus.

About half the panels of the Parthenon frieze can be seen at the British Museum (although there are repeated calls for the restoration of the so-called Elgin Marbles to Greece). The poet John Keats viewed the frieze soon after it came to London, and part of his "Ode on a Grecian Urn" seems to have been directly inspired by one of the panels:

> To what green altar,
> O mysterious priest,
> Lead'st thou that heifer
> lowing at the skies...

Evocative words from a poet whose culture owes an immeasurable debt to that of ancient Athens.

The heifer lowing at the skies: drawing of a frieze detail.

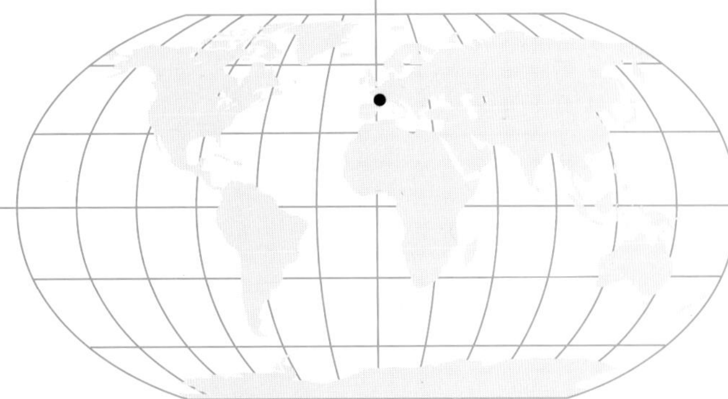

19 B.C. France

PONT DU GARD

A work of civil engineering that combines elegance with excellence and, in the process, becomes a work of art.

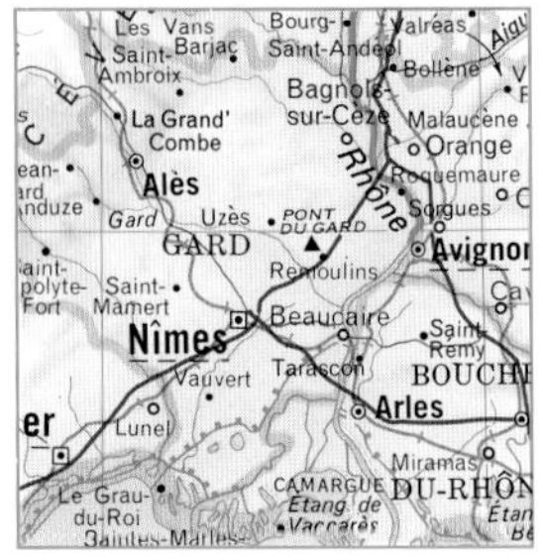

Northeast of Nîmes and about 10 miles (16 km) from Uzès and 2 miles (3 km) from Remoulins in Provence. The towns of Avignon and Arles are also near. The Pont du Gard actually carries traffic across the Gardon River (a road was built along the east side of the lowest tier in the 17th century) and forms part of the minor road D981.

Aqueducts were one of the major Roman contributions to civilization and hygienic living. Crossing the river, the Pont du Gard carried the water into Nîmes, where it was distributed to public baths, fountains and private homes.

THE Pont du Gard was built by the Romans for a specific, utilitarian purpose: to carry a supply of fresh water across the Gardon River to the city of Nîmes in southern France. Measuring 160 feet (49 m) high and 900 feet (274 m) long, it was part of a system of conduits and bridges that stretched for 30 miles (48 km) between Nîmes and the water source near Uzès. This is functional civil engineering, without ornament or frills, providing the solution to basic problems and doing so in a strikingly elegant way.

An inscription suggests that the Pont du Gard was built by the Roman general and proconsul Agrippa, a friend and ally of the emperor Augustus, and that it dates back to 19 B.C., but there are archaeologists who dispute this, arguing that a structure of such technical competence must belong to a later era. Nîmes itself developed around the sanctuary of a native water god who was believed to have healing powers. Under the Romans it became a town of some 500 acres (202 hectares) and 50,000 inhabitants and took its name, Nemausus, from that of the god. Calculations suggest that the aqueduct could supply 108 U.S. gallons/90 imperial gallons (409 liters) of water per person per day.

Despite its name, the Maison Carrée in Nîmes is not a "square house", but a rectangular Roman temple of the first century A.D.

The Pont du Gard has three tiers of arches, six at the bottom, 11 in the middle, and 35 along the top directly below the water channel. The blocks of stone were laid without mortar, and the rough knobs that stand out from the sides were used to attach wooden scaffolding. This feature, which might be considered rude and unfinished, may have been essential for maintenance work – as the water in the area is very hard, in time large quantities of mineral deposits would have accumulated in the water channel. Today, walking along the top of the Pont du Gard, you can look into the water channel, which has lost some of its covering stones. Overall, the aqueduct was built with a gradient of one in 3,000, resulting in a total drop of about 55 feet (17 m) between the water source and the outlet into the city.

It is surprising to discover that only one of the bottom six arches actually spans the river and that the arches in each tier are not identical. Nor does the Pont du Gard cross the river at a 90° angle – it curves slightly against the flow of the water.

What happened at the end of the aqueduct? In Nîmes it is still possible to see a well-preserved *castellum divisorium* – a circular tank about 20 feet (6 m) across. Water flowed from the aqueduct into the tank and was then channeled in five different directions by five pairs of pipes. Three openings in the bottom of the tank appear to have collected sediment, which could be cleared out when necessary.

Nîmes

NÎMES has a number of impressive Roman monuments, notably a huge amphitheater and the Maison Carrée, a temple standing on the edge of the original Roman forum and dedicated to Rome and Augustus in 16 B.C. This temple was used as the model for the State House in Richmond, Virginia.

Roman Waterworks

IN the first century A.D. a man called Frontinus was the superintendent of Rome's water supply. The technical handbook he wrote on the subject, *De Aquis*, goes into a great deal of mathematical detail about the dimensions of pipes and the construction of aqueducts, but also gives an amusing idea of some of the sharp practices he encountered. He tells of landowners who intercepted the public water supply running past their fields and diverted it to irrigate their crops. Confiscation of the land in question was a possible penalty for those caught in the act. Frontinus also reveals that a secret and elaborate network of pipes was detected beneath the pavements of Rome – an unauthorized system that drew water illegally from public sources and supplied it to private premises and shops.

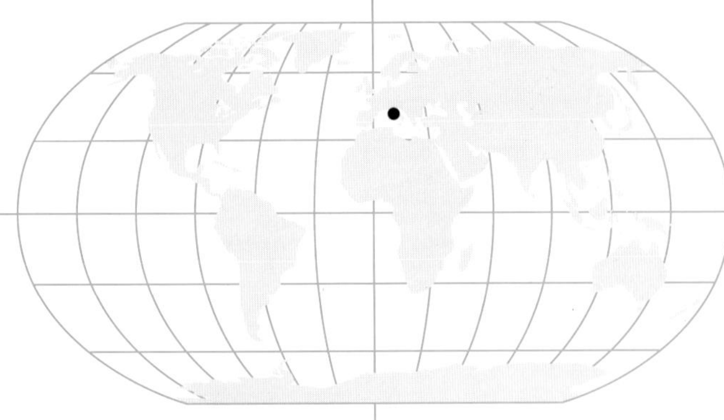

THE COLOSSEUM

It was opened with a ceremony that involved the exhibition of 5,000 wild beasts.

The Colosseum dominates its surroundings even today. It stands in the center of Rome at the east end of the Via dei Fori Imperiali. A short distance from the main Termini station, it also has its own station, Colosseo, on the Metropolitana railway.

THE amphitheater was a Roman invention, an elliptical arena surrounded by tiers of seats from which huge crowds could look safely down on spectacular displays of combat and carnage. Here gladiators fought and exotic animals were paraded, stared at, and then slaughtered. Rome had amphitheaters before the Colosseum, but after the great fire of A.D. 64 a new one was needed. Vespasian, who became emperor in A.D. 69, ordered construction of a massive permanent building that would bear his family name and be bigger and better than any other.

Known as the Flavian Amphitheater, the new arena was built on the bed of a lake that had belonged to his predecessor Nero's absurdly opulent Golden House. The choice of site was a wise one structurally, and it also demonstrated that an era of monstrous self-indulgence was at an end. Vespasian was seen to build on as grand a scale as Nero, but he did so as a public gesture, not for mere private pleasure. Ironically, Nero had his posthumous revenge: ever since the 8th century the Flavian Amphitheater has been known as the Colosseum, a title thought to come from the colossal statue of Nero that stood nearby. (Rather than demolish this, Vespasian had ordered a head transplant and renamed the statue Apollo.)

Nearly a third of a mile (1/2 km) in circumference and over 180 feet (55 m) high, the Colosseum was built of travertine stone, tufa, and brick. It was opened by Vespasian's successor, Titus, in A.D. 80 with a ceremony that involved the exhibition of 5,000 wild beasts. But even then, work was not complete, and it was only during the reign of the next emperor, Domitian, that the final tier was added.

The complexity of the building is remarkable, and its design reveals an ingenious response to the question of crowd control. Although some 50,000 people could be accommodated in the amphitheater, the system of staircases and corridors ensured trouble-free

Nowadays floodlit at night, the Colosseum has been one of Rome's principal sights ever since it was opened. Benvenuto Cellini, the brilliant 16th-century Italian artist, tried to conjure up spirits in the ruined stadium one night and gave himself a terrible fright.

progress to and from the banks of seating.

Still more important was the careful control of the animals. Here, too, the architects of the Colosseum displayed great skill, designing a network of passages and elevators that delivered wild and enraged creatures directly to the arena from their cages below stage. Much of this infrastructure can still be seen, as can sockets and brackets on the top story, which once held the masts from which a huge awning could be stretched over the open top of the amphitheater. This elaborate arrangement of canvas, pulleys, and ropes was operated by sailors recruited specially for the task.

With such advanced engineering and efficient crowd control, the Colosseum could be described as a building ahead of its time. Even the method of construction seems to have been surprisingly modern, not unlike that used in 20th-century steel- or concrete-framed high-rise buildings. Nearly 2,000 years after it was opened, the Colosseum remains an outstanding monument to Roman achievement, if also to the Roman predilection for gore.

In the 18th and 19th centuries it was considered essential to view the Colosseum by night. The building was ruined and creeper-clad and there was an outcry when the greenery was cleared away in the 1850s.

Christians and Lions

IN 1744 the Colosseum, which had become church property in the 13th century, was consecrated in memory of the Christians said to have died for their faith in front of crowds of baying Romans. The Colosseum has long been associated with Christian martyrdom (George Bernard Shaw's play *Androcles and the Lion* is a good example), but there is actually very little evidence to link the two. Nonetheless, a cross stands in the arena to this day.

Man against Beast and Man against Man

IN the Villa Borghese in Rome there are mosaics showing scenes of combat in the arena. Bulls, stags, lions, and even ostriches were considered fair game for the *bestiarius*, a man not unlike the modern matador. (Some surviving Roman amphitheaters are used today for bullfighting.) The Roman fascination with unfamiliar animals seems to date from the time when Carthaginian elephants were displayed in the city, long before the building of the Colosseum. Contests between gladiators were also part of a long tradition thought to have developed from Etruscan funeral ceremonies. Gladiatorial fights were sometimes highly professional affairs between trained and evenly matched men, sometimes pathetic displays involving unwilling captives.

Seating and access were most efficiently arranged. Spectators' ticket numbers showed which part of the stadium to enter.

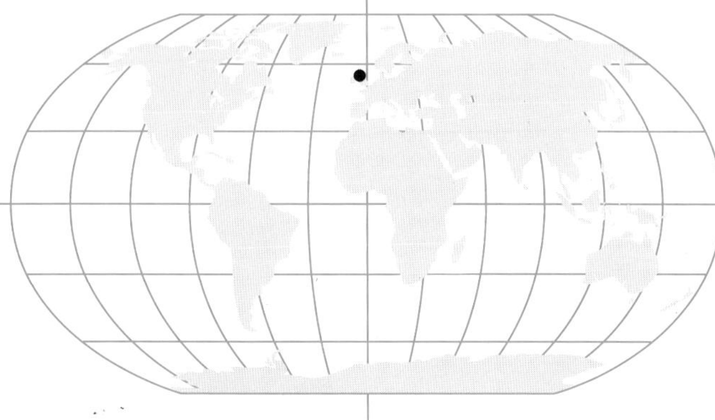

2nd Century A.D. England

HADRIAN'S WALL

A titanic barrier, scaling sheer crags amid some of Britain's most dramatic scenery.

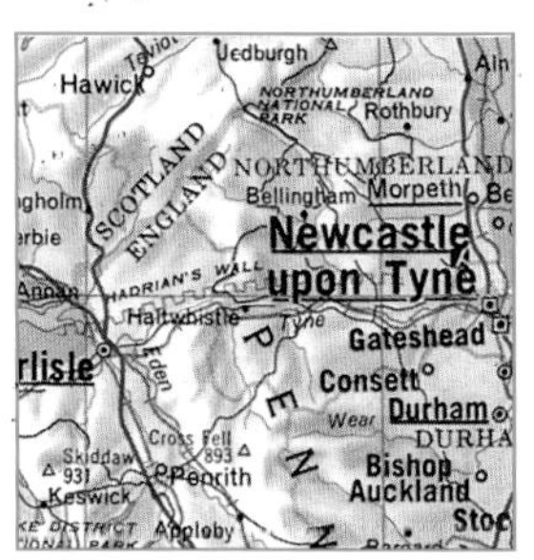

Stretching across Cumbria and Northumberland in northern England, Hadrian's Wall is not one site, but many. The best way to see it is on foot, starting from Carlisle or Newcastle, and allowing about two weeks. Housesteads Fort and the section of wall between there and Steel Rigg are the major showpieces, with good road connections from east or west. The B6318 is not the fastest road, but it follows the line of the wall for many miles. Newcastle and Carlisle are linked by the Tyne Valley railway, and in summer the Hadrian's Wall Bus Service connects with trains at Hexham and some other stations. A long-distance footpath along the wall is being planned for the future.

Museums

As well as the museums at various sites on Hadrian's Wall itself, there are others that should not be missed. The Museum of Antiquities in the Quadrangle of the University of Newcastle upon Tyne has a model of the whole wall, Tullie House Museum in Carlisle has a fine collection of inscriptions and many helpful displays, and the Roman Army Museum at Carvoran reveals much about the life of the soldier.

The wall swoops over the lonely hills near Housesteads, where the remains of a fort can be inspected. It had barracks for a thousand men, with efficient latrines and a hospital.

SEVENTY-FIVE miles (120 km) long, stretching across northern England from coast to coast, perhaps 15 feet (4.5 m) high, 8-10 feet (2.5-3 m) broad, and composed of roughly a million cubic yards (about ¾ million cu m) of stone, Hadrian's Wall was an astonishingly ambitious building project, even by the typically grandiose standards of the Roman Empire. Why was it built at all? Archaeologists and historians have argued about the wall for centuries, and debate continues with every new season of excavation. Hadrian's biographer makes a simple statement: the emperor built the wall to separate the Romans from the barbarians.

Several generations earlier, in A.D. 43, the Roman army had invaded Britain. Working its way north, the army eventually subdued troublesome native Caledonian tribes at the battle of Mons Graupius in northeast Scotland in A.D. 84. But Rome's triumph was short-lived, and by the time Hadrian arrived in A.D. 122, the forces had retreated to the Tyne Valley area, where they had already built the Stanegate road and a number of forts, which formed an 80-mile (128-km) frontier running from Corbridge to Carlisle in the west. Hadrian appears to have come to a pessimistic conclusion: the barbarians of North Britain could not be tamed, so he would build a permanent barrier, a complex military zone that would also be a symbol of Roman power, standing at the northwestern tip of his vast empire.

The wall was built a few miles north of the Stanegate and the Tyne Valley. Rivers had to be bridged and wild, inhospitable terrain negotiated. The project called for skilled engineers, surveyors, and stonemasons. The enormous manpower of the Roman army made it possible for work to be completed within seven or eight years, but there were several changes of plan during this time. The width of the wall varies, for example, and the western section was initially built of turf that was later replaced with stone.

The original wall incorporated milecastles (placed at intervals of one Roman mile, about 1,620 yards/1,481 m) and turrets (two, evenly spaced, between each pair of milecastles). The milecastles could accommodate a few men, but the majority of forces were garrisoned south of the wall. All this was soon changed. Fourteen new forts, including those that can still be seen at Housesteads, Chesters, and Birdoswald, were built on the line of the wall, and Hadrian's frontier became home for some 10,000 troops.

In addition to the wall with its milecastles, turrets, and forts, there were also roads, supply bases, and earthworks. The Vallum, a flat-bottomed ditch between two substantial mounds of earth, is still visible running south of and parallel to the wall, and it is possible to walk along the Military Way, a road whose path lies between the Vallum and the wall.

South of Hadrian's Wall on the Stanegate road, lie two particularly interesting sites – Corbridge and Vindolanda. Both have excellent museums and both have produced remarkable finds. The excavated remains are complex and reveal many changes of use and occupancy over several hundred years. A wooden chest, discovered at Corbridge in 1964, contained Roman armor dating from the 2nd century A.D. At Vindolanda a Roman milestone is still standing in its original position on the Stanegate. Modern reconstructions here help the visitor to appreciate what a formidable and effective obstacle the wall was when first built. The most famous discovery made at this site was a collection of wooden writing tablets dealing with military supplies and personal matters.

Over the centuries, Hadrian's Wall has been robbed of stone (the evidence can be seen in many buildings in the area) and, in some places, blasted out of existence to allow for quarrying. In the 18th century, long stretches of it were flattened to make way for a road (today's B6318). Despite these depredations, it remains magnificent, scaling sheer crags amid some of the most dramatic scenery in Britain.

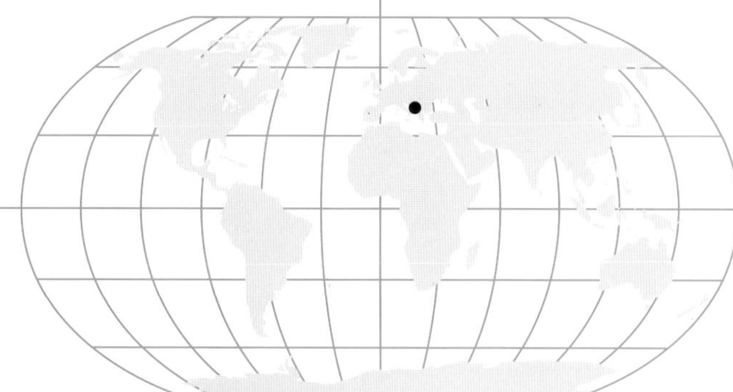

3rd Century A.D. Yugoslavia

DIOCLETIAN'S PALACE

"An extraordinary revelation of the continuity of history."
– *Rebecca West*

Diocletian's Palace is the ancient center of the city of Split. Air, rail, and road communications are all good, but the recommended way to approach the palace is by sea.

THE word *palace* scarcely does justice to the huge residence and retirement home that the Roman emperor Diocletian built on the Adriatic coast at the end of the 3rd century A.D. The walls, 7 feet (2.1 m) thick and 50-70 feet (15-21 m) high, enclose an area of nearly 9 acres (3.6 hectares). The rectangular plan is similar to that of a Roman fort, with massive gates, watchtowers, and two intersecting principal streets, which have remained important thoroughfares to this day.

When Diocletian died, his property was slowly colonized and gradually turned into a city. Today, much of its appeal lies in the way that buildings of different eras jostle together, butting up against the walls and columns of the original structure and creating a curious collage of architectural styles. Visiting the palace just before the Second World War, the English writer Rebecca West reported that a fifth of the population of Split lived within the walls – about 9,000 people "with houses set as closely as cells in a honeycomb filling every vacant space that was left by Diocletian's architects."

The palace faced the sea with a monumental colonnade. Within, supported by a substantial vaulted basement, which survives remarkably intact, were the imperial apartments, a great hall, and a vestibule crowned with a dome. The emperor's mausoleum, an octagonal

Right: part of the palace, near the medieval cathedral. Diocletian reformed the Roman imperial system and deliberately emphasized the grandeur of the office of emperor, a trend reflected in the splendor of the palace itself.

Facing page, above: view from the waterfront at Split, looking across to the palace, which after Diocletian's death slowly turned into a crowded city.

Facing page, below: massive Roman vaulting in the palace.

building surrounded by Corinthian columns, became the city's cathedral in the 7th century. Fine wooden doors and choir stalls were added in the 13th century, but otherwise the building has been very little altered structurally, and portraits of Diocletian and his wife Prisca survive on an internal frieze. Opposite the mausoleum, the temple of Jupiter, with its elegant doorway, is also well preserved; it became the cathedral baptistery. (The baths that Diocletian built in Rome had a similar destiny – a part of them forms the Church of Santa Maria degli Angeli.)

Diocletian built his palace on his home ground, but its grandeur is in surprising contrast to the conditions of his early life. He is thought to have been the son of a slave, and he rose to power through the imperial bodyguard. He became emperor in A.D. 284 and, faced with an unwieldy and chaotic realm, established the tetrarchy – a system of four rulers, two in the east (of which he was the superior one) and two in the west. No longer the sole focus of the empire, Rome was not even visited by Diocletian until A.D. 303.

His palace, where he eventually retired after abdicating, may have been intended to foster an image of the emperor as a remote, godlike figure, residing in splendor while cocooned behind impenetrable walls. He is remembered as a man who showed good sense in halting the decline of an ailing empire and as a persecutor of Christians whose mausoleum became a Christian cathedral.

Robert Adam and Diocletian's Palace

Two Egyptian sphinxes, various palaces in Romanesque, Gothic, and later styles, chapels, a campanile, and the remains of an 11th-century monastery – all this and more can be seen within the limestone walls of Diocletian's Palace. But when Robert Adam visited Split in 1757, it was with the intention of making an accurate record of the original building. After a year in Rome, the young Scottish architect was looking for a serious research project that would allow him to pursue his interest in Roman architecture and also help to win him work. He chose to study Diocletian's Palace and, with three other draughtsmen, produced measured drawings that formed the basis of a lavish book published seven years later.

Adam's work on the palace also inspired one of the most significant developments in 18th-century British architecture – the Adelphi. This complex of residences and offices facing the River Thames south of the Strand in London included a terrace of houses standing on a vaulted arcade rising from the riverside. Four Adam brothers were involved in the project (the word *adelphi* comes from the Greek for "brothers"), and enormous complications and expense nearly left them bankrupt. The dream of creating a new style of architecture based on a Roman model was vindicted by the eventual success of the scheme. Although most of the Adelphi was demolished in 1937, provoking howls of outrage that still echo today, Adam's elegant, uncluttered classical façades had a lasting influence on future architectural thinking.

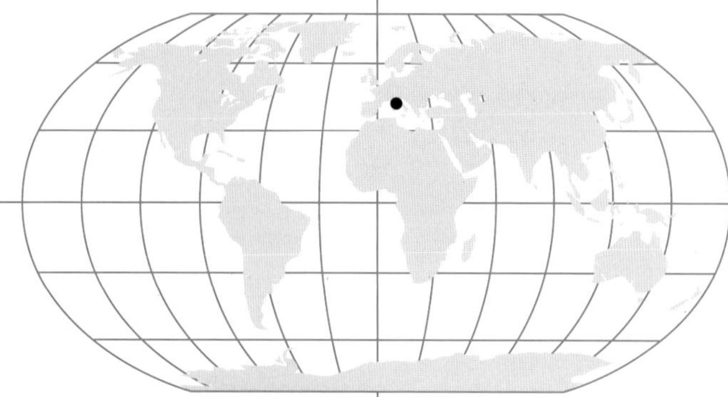

1173 Italy

LEANING TOWER OF PISA

A building that seems to defy gravity, reputedly the scene of an experiment that established one of the laws of physics.

Pisa has an international airport and excellent access by road. The city stands close to the mouth of the Arno River, 50 miles (80 km) west of Florence.

PISA'S famous Leaning Tower *(Torre Pendente)* is actually the campanile, or bell tower, of the city's cathedral, part of a magnificent ensemble of cathedral, bell tower, baptistery, and cemetery. If it stood upright, its fame would probably be limited mainly to historians of art and architecture. But because it is structurally flawed, its image is known throughout the world.

The tower is 179 feet (55 m) high. An inscription records that it was begun in 1174, but as the Pisan calendar was a year in advance of conventional dating, the true date was 1173. The original architects were Bonnano Pisano and William of Innsbruck, but they did not live to see the work completed – the tower had no bell chamber until the second half of the 14th century.

Some have suggested that the tower was always intended to lean and that this was a daring demonstration of the skill of the architects. The idea is scarcely believable, and it is much more likely that the designers knew they would be building on less than solid ground and made some allowance for this in their plans, constructing foundations that would tolerate a certain amount of subsidence.

Seeing the tower today, and experiencing the odd, disorienting sensation of being pulled to one side while climbing the 294 steps, one can only marvel at the fact that it still stands at all. With every year that passes, the angle of inclination and the fears for the future increase. At the beginning of the 20th century, the tower was 14 feet (4.3 m) out of perpendicular; now the figure is 15 feet (4.6 m) – and a large sum of money has recently been allocated to find a solution before it is too late.

The Leaning Tower is circular in plan and rises in eight tiers, including the bell chamber. The six central stages are surrounded by delicate arcading, which is thought possibly to have been influenced by Byzantine or Islamic architecture. The question of Islamic influences is an interesting one, and it is not clear whether the idea of freestanding bell towers for

Christian churches was inspired by the minarets of the Muslim world, or whether the minaret, from which the muezzin calls the faithful to prayer, developed from the campanile.

The Leaning Tower was built as the bell tower of Pisa's cathedral, which was begun a hundred years earlier, following a naval battle in 1063 in which the Pisans defeated the Saracens at Palermo. The style of architecture is known as Pisan Romanesque, and Islamic influence can once again be detected in the exterior bands of alternating red and white marble. There are arcades along the ground floor on the outside and the graceful entrance front has tiers of open arcades rising one above the other into the gable. The handsome dome over the crossing of the nave and the transepts was a later addition.

In 1564 the scientist Galileo was born in Pisa, and he is said to have made use of the Leaning Tower for one of his experiments, dropping objects from the top in order to demonstrate that the speed of their acceleration would be the same, regardless of weight. There is no doubt that Galileo proved this point, but whether he did so from the Leaning Tower is less certain. On the other hand, it would have offered an ideal setting for experiments with gravity, despite defying gravity itself.

The Baptistery

THE Baptistery is a circular building of marble begun in the middle of the 12th century in Romanesque style, but with some later work being Gothic. The pulpit dates from 1260 and has remarkable carvings depicting scenes from the life of Christ.

Campo Santo

THIS cemetery was begun in the late 12th or early 13th century, supposedly using earth brought by the shipload from Calvary. Elegant Gothic arcades are decorated with frescoes and, despite such themes as the Triumph of Death, Hell, and the Last Judgment, this is a place with an attractive and peaceful atmosphere.

Above: looking out past the bell in the Leaning Tower to the roof and unusual dome of the Baptistery.

Facing page: the Leaning Tower, with Pisa Cathedral next to it. When work began on the cathedral, Pisa was a rich trading city with close contacts with the Muslims in Sicily and in the Near East.

1238-1358 Spain

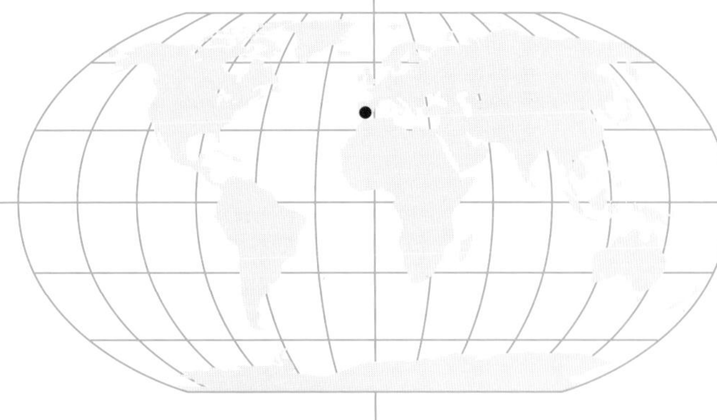

THE ALHAMBRA

For sheer decorative exuberance and display, the Alhambra, or Red Castle, in southern Spain has no equal.

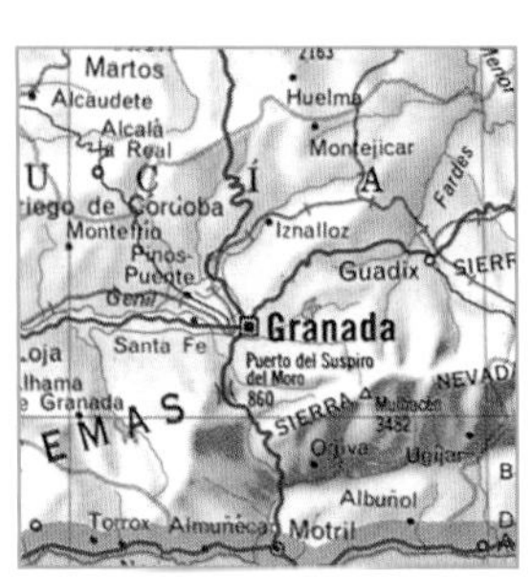

Granada is in the region of southern Spain known as Andalusia, less than 50 miles (80 km) from the Mediterranean coast, about 275 miles (443 km) from Madrid and 75 miles (121 km) from Málaga, both of which have airports. The Alhambra, towering over the eastern side of the town, is easily found.

The Court of the Lions, open to the sky in the interior of the palace, with the stone lions supporting the fountain in the middle. The surrounding arcade is of wood and plaster.

EXTERNALLY it is a rude congregation of towers and battlements, with no regularity of plan nor grace of architecture, and giving little promise of the grace and beauty which prevail within." This was the American writer Washington Irving's description of the Alhambra in 1829, and today the contrast is just as striking. Externally, this was a fortress, a defensive stronghold with 23 towers, built by the Moors at a time when Islamic power in Spain was threatened by Christian resurgence. Internally, it is an attempt to create paradise.

The Alhambra served the Nasrid dynasty of Granada as military headquarters, administrative center, and royal palace. It was begun by the founder of the dynasty, Muhammad I al Ghalib, in the middle of the 13th century, but the royal apartments date from the reigns of Yusuf I and Muhammad V in the second half of the 14th century. Courtyards, corridors, and water conduits combine to create a remarkable sequence of vistas. The decoration is sumptuous and ubiquitous, in the form of ceramic tiles, pierced stonework, carved foliage designs, and amazingly elaborate calligraphy. Some have seen this as the crowning achievement of Islamic decorative art in the West, delicate, elegant, and technically superb. Others suggest that the whole place has an air of decadence, an unmistakable whiff of a culture on the verge of decline.

Certainly there is something curiously insubstantial and other-worldly about the exuberant *muqarnas* vaults – riotous honeycomb-like structures suspended from wooden frames, which are themselves supported on slim columns. Verse inscriptions speak of the stars and the heavens, water runs in channels to symbolize the four rivers of the Islamic paradise, and both water and light are employed by the architects as essential components in the overall design.

The Alhambra's plan is one of gardens and courtyards, usually with apartments opening off each of four sides. The names themselves are evocative: the Court of Myrtles (planted in beds beside a long pool); the Hall of the Two Sisters (actually two white marble stones built into the floor); and the Court of the Lions (named after the antique fountain, supported by 12 stone lions, that stands at the center). The Hall of the Ambassadors was intended for official business – royal audiences and court procedures – but again the imagery is that of paradise. The chamber has a wooden ceiling 60 feet (18.3 m) above ground, and the carving is said to be an attempt to suggest the heavens.

By the mid-13th century Granada was the last major Moorish kingdom remaining in Spain. The Nasrid dynasty ruled it for 250 years under an unbroken succession of 25 sovereigns. They were notable patrons of art and learning, and attracted the great Muslim historian Ibn Khaldun to their highly civilized court.

The Nasrids finally left Granada in 1492. The emperor Charles V built his own palace within the Alhambra walls in the 16th century, but later the buildings suffered neglect, and a part of the Nasrid fortress was destroyed by Napoleon's forces. During the 19th century the romance of the place captured the imagination of such visitors as Victor Hugo, Theophile Gautier, and Washington Irving, whose *Tales of the Alhambra* was published in 1829. It was partly as a result of these authors' descriptions that efforts were made to halt the decay and to preserve the Alhambra.

Detail of the decoration, which is in the Moorish style of interlaced geometrical patterns and elaborate calligraphy.

The Generalife

THE Generalife was a summer palace of the Nasrid royal family, built in the 14th century and once directly linked to the Alhambra by a covered walkway across a ravine. The rectangular Patio de la Acequia, with its long, narrow pool, fountains, rosebushes, colonnades, and pavilions, is thought to be one of the oldest surviving Moorish gardens anywhere.

The Moors in Spain

MUSLIMS came from North Africa to Spain in the year 711 and conquered the Visigoth rulers who had their capital at Toledo. Islamic power was centered on Córdoba, just over a hundred miles (160 km) from Granada, which became first an emirate and later a caliphate. Here a remarkable mosque was built, begun in the 8th century and subsequently extended and embellished. The building was later converted into a Christian cathedral, but it still displays all the fundamental elements of Moorish architecture, with horseshoe arches, polychromatic brickwork, and carved floral designs and inscriptions taken from the Koran. The Muslims were driven out of Córdoba during the Christian reconquest in 1236. Many escaped to Granada, where the Nasrid dynasty was then established. Islamic rule continued until, after a period of civil war and a siege, the last Muslim ruler of Granada was driven into exile in 1492.

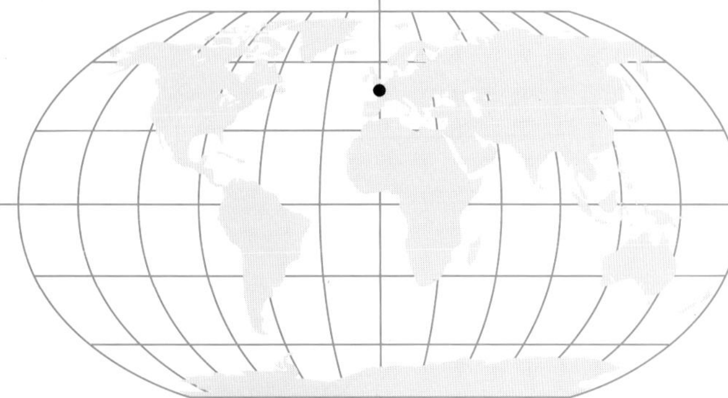

Consecrated 1260 France

CHARTRES CATHEDRAL

A beautiful church dedicated to the Virgin Mary stands on a site where the Druids once worshipped.

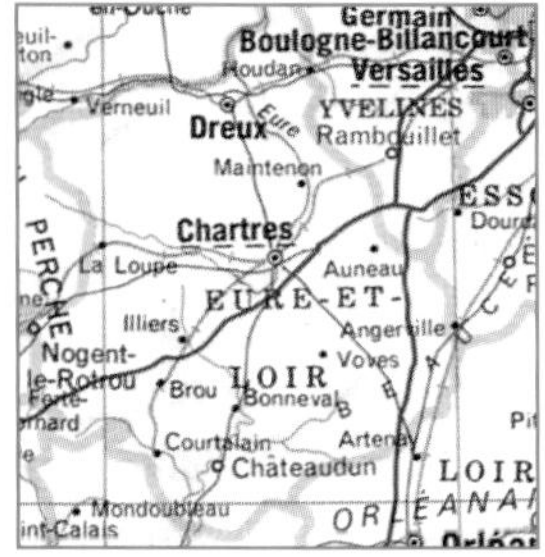

Chartres, capital of the *département* of Eure-et-Loir, is 55 miles (88 km) southwest of Paris. There are numerous guided tours from Paris, and the city is on the rail line from Paris to Le Mans and Brittany. Trains from Paris (Montparnasse).

DOMINATING the flat country for miles around, the Cathedral of Our Lady at Chartres is one of the supreme achievements of Gothic architecture and medieval Christian civilization. The church rises above the town on a site that was sacred long before the coming of Christianity: an important pagan Celtic sanctuary existed here, in Roman times and before, and the cathedral crypt, the biggest in France, is believed to occupy its site.

Well into the 18th century the cathedral possessed a deeply venerated wooden figure of the Virgin, pregnant with the baby Jesus, which was said to date far back to pagan times. It may have been an image of a Celtic mother goddess, adopted and Christianized, but it was burned during the French Revolution.

A succession of churches, built here from about A.D. 350, were ruined by fire, until in 1194 the whole building burned down, except for the west front and the crypt. Once more a church rose from the ashes, and it is this noble building, consecrated in 1260, that the visitor sees today.

Of the two eye-catching spires at the west end, both over 300 feet (91 m) high, the lower and simpler one dates from the 1130s, the taller and more elaborate one from 1513. Below are the three great doors of the western façade and a wealth of 12th-century statuary, with Christ in Glory at the center. A rose window depicts the Last Judgment. The entrances to the north and south transepts are adorned with 13th-century statues. Inside and out, the cathedral is home to more than 10,000 figures in stone and glass.

The church is famous especially for its superlative stained glass – close to 22,000 square feet (2,044 sq m) of it in all – with a wonderfully rich shade of deep blue that is at its loveliest in sunlight. There are exceptionally large and impressive rose windows in the north and south transepts, and another treasure is the 12th-century window known as Note Dame de la Belle Verrière (Our Lady of the Beautiful Glass). The glass has recently been treated for a

Facing page, above left: Christ with the symbols of the four evangelists, above the west door of the cathedral, which is home to thousands of figures in stone and glass. They portray Old and New Testament characters and scenes, saints and kings, and abstractions like the virtues and vices or the liberal arts.

Right: the first church in France to be dedicated to the Virgin Mary towers over the roofs and chimneys of the city.

mysterious "disease" from which it was suffering.

Marked on the floor of the nave is a maze, probably intended for penitents to negotiate painfully on their knees. The huge choir screen, with 40 carved scenes from the lives of the Virgin and Christ, was begun in 1514, but not completed for almost 200 years.

Pilgrims flocked to Chartres for centuries. Besides the ancient wooden Virgin, the cathedral possessed the head of St. Anne, Mary's mother, and a particularly famous relic, the *sainte chemise*, believed to be the garment the Virgin was wearing when she gave birth to Jesus. It is preserved in a reliquary.

Figures from the royal portal. The carvings at Chartres portray the medieval Christian view of the order of the universe.

Rose of France

MANY of the stained-glass windows at Chartres Cathedral are connected with the veneration of the Virgin Mary. The great rose window in honor of her in the north transept was given by the pious King Louis IX (St. Louis) and his queen, Blanche of Castile, and bears the royal arms of both France and Castile. It is known as the Rose of France.

The long history of devotion to the Virgin as the Mother of God, who mercifully intercedes with her Son for sinners, has created a wealth of symbolism. The almond and the bramble belong to her, and so do the apple and the lemon. The lily is the emblem of her purity, the violet of her humility. From the Song of Solomon and in reference to her unbroken virginity, she is "the garden enclosed," "the fountain sealed," "the closed gate." She is Queen of Heaven and, through a play on her name, she is Stella Maris, "the Star of the Sea." The Virgin is also closely linked with the rose. She is shown in medieval art in her beautiful garden of roses, her rosary is depicted as a garland of the flowers, and being free of original sin – the Immaculate Conception – she is "the rose without a thorn."

The church at Chartres was the first in France to be dedicated to the Virgin, and in the Middle Ages the city attracted throngs of pilgrims by holding four great fairs every year on her four principal feast days: her Nativity, the Annunciation, the Purification, and the Assumption.

HOUSES OF GOD

Christianity has expressed its beliefs and its understanding of the world in the architecture and symbolism of its churches

THE earliest churches began to go up in the 4th century A.D., when Christianity was adopted as the Roman Empire's official religion. Their architects modeled them on the basilica, a type of hall found in all Roman cities, which was used as both a law court and a meeting place for merchants.

Columned arcades inside divided the simple rectangular building into three sections: a wider and taller central area flanked by two narrower and lower ones. Hence the pattern familiar in churches ever since, of the central nave with an aisle on each side. The altar was usually placed at the east end, in an apse, and a porch was built at the opposite end, which was the entrance.

Later on, although basilican churches continued to be built for centuries, an alternative plan developed, in the shape of Christ's cross. In Eastern Europe the cross usually had four equal arms. In the West the western arm was longer than

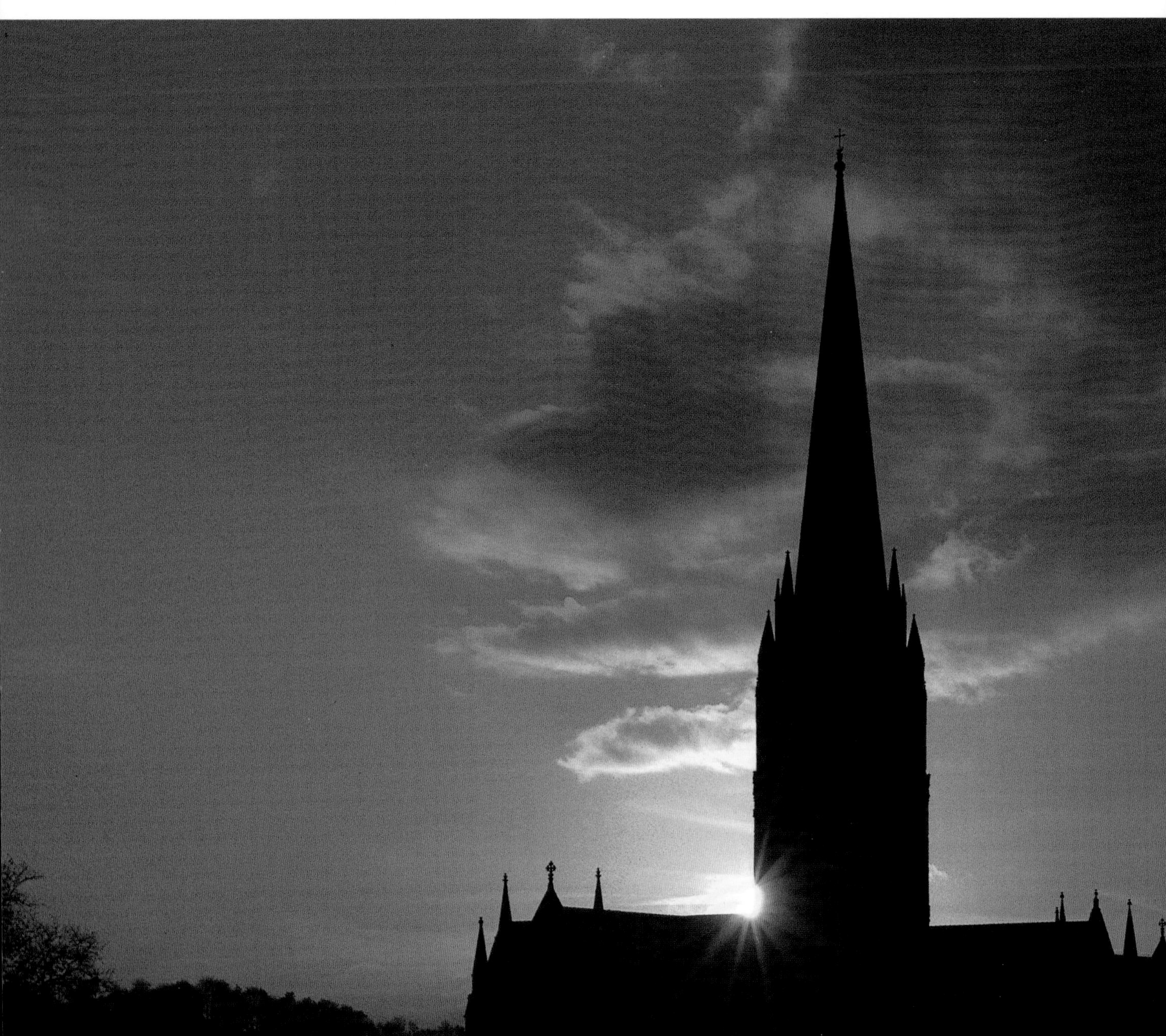

the other three, and this contained the nave, where the congregation stood during liturgies. "Nave" is from the Latin *navis* (ship) and relates to the symbol of the church as a ship that bears the faithful safely over the perilous sea of this world.

The eastern arm of the church contained the altar and the clergy, who conducted the services. The crosspiece on the plan formed the north and south transepts, and above the point of intersection was a tower. There were also towers at the western end in large churches.

In the 11th and 12th centuries, stone churches in the Romanesque style had massive walls, small windows and wooden roofs, supported on ponderous pillars and round arches.

SOARING TO GOD

In France in the 12th century, there emerged a strikingly different style that was to dominate Western architecture until well into the 16th century. Chartres Cathedral was an early and key example of it.

Gothic was the architecture of the pointed arch, which instead of taking the eye up over the round Romanesque curve and down to earth again, impelled the gaze upwards to the heights. With flying buttresses supporting lofty vaulted stone roofs, anonymous architects constructed some of the most beautiful buildings ever conceived. They were almost literally uplifting buildings, whose whole emphasis was on the vertical. The church and its slender spire seemed to defy gravity and carry the human spirit soaring heavenwards to God.

Windows grew steadily bigger and were filled with sinuous stone tracery and glowing stained glass, whose scenes and figures reminded the congregation – few of whom could read – of the stories and teachings of the Bible. In the great cathedrals like Chartres, stone carvings of episodes and characters in the history of God's world since the Creation helped to make a visible representation of the entire world as understood by medieval Christian thought. The church was the world in miniature, and high up in its vault the angels could be seen, playing musical instruments to create the harmony of heaven. The ceiling might be painted with stars to represent the sky.

AT THE WORLD'S CENTER

No one at the time called this architecture Gothic. That was a term of abuse, coined in the 16th century to characterize it as primitive and barbaric. The Renaissance had brought a profound admiration for classical Greece and Rome, including classical architecture, and a new confidence in the potential of the human being as the measure and master of all things. Churches now began to look like the temples of Roman deities, with pillared porticos surmounted by triangular pediments.

At the heart of Western Christianity, in Rome itself, the great new church of St. Peter's was designed by Donato Bramante in the early 1500s, basically an equal-armed cross with a dome of heroic proportions over the middle. Such a centrally planned church has a completely different symbolism from a Gothic one. In the latter the long arm of the nave leads the worshipper's eye and spirit towards the altar some distance away at the far end. But in a centrally planned church, the worshipper is placed symbolically at the center of the world, with all the divine beauty and harmony of the universe ranged around the human being. One church is God-directed, the other is human-oriented.

Salisbury Cathedral, with the tallest spire in England, is a sublime expression of the idea of ascent.

St Paul's Cathedral, London, built in the 17th century, is an inspiring example of the revival of classical architecture.

In the 17th and 18th centuries the classical style continued to hold sway, achieving its most extravagant expression in the great baroque churches with their temple porticos, their sumptuous curves and domes, their lavish grandeur of ornament and decoration.

The 19th century brought a revival of Gothic, a reaction against the implied paganism of the classical style. The war between the Gothic and the classical was waged all through the period, until both were abandoned by modern architects who turned away from the heritage of the past, but not before Antoni Gaudí had magically combined Gothic with Art Nouveau in Barcelona's fantastic Sagrada Familia church.

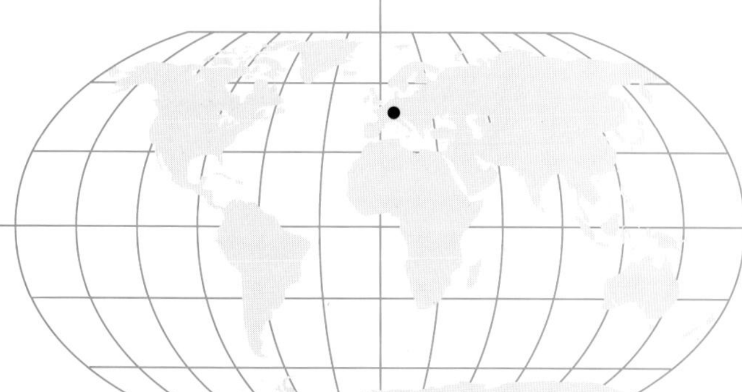

1333 Switzerland

KAPELLBRÜCKE

Europe's oldest wooden bridge helped to protect the town against attack.

Lucerne is in central Switzerland, 61 miles (98 km) southeast of Basel by the N2 superhighway. Trains from Basel. The nearest major airport is 42 miles (68 km) away at Zürich.

THE town of Lucerne, or Luzern as it is called locally (it is in the German-speaking part of Switzerland), is set scenically below the mountains at the northwestern corner of Lake Lucerne. The covered wooden bridge over the Reuss River, called the Kapellbrücke (Chapel Bridge), has become a symbol of the town. Constructed in 1333, it is the oldest wooden bridge in Europe. It is a little over 650 feet (198 m) long and runs diagonally across the river.

Towards the southern end is the octagonal, tile-roofed Wasserturm (water tower). This tower and the covered bridge itself were originally part of the medieval town's defenses. In its time the tower has served as a prison and torture chamber, as well as the town treasury. High up in the rafters of the bridge are 112

Right: looking across the river, along the length of the wooden bridge, with the Wasserturm in the foreground. At the far end is the chapel of St. Peter and in the background rise the towers of the 17th-century church of St. Maurice and St. Léger, the town's patron saints.

Facing page: floodlit at night, the Wasserturm shows to advantage.

triangular paintings dating from the early 17th century. Restored in the early 1900s, they depict the history of Lucerne and the brave deeds of the people of this area, which played a crucial part in the struggle for Swiss independence. They also illustrate the lives and legends of Lucerne's two patron saints, St. Léger and St. Maurice. Each picture has explanatory verses in German.

A little further west is another picturesque old covered bridge across the Reuss. This is the Spreuerbrücke (Mill Bridge), which dates from 1407 and is grimly adorned with 17th-century paintings of the Dance of Death.

Lucerne is a popular tourist center, with attractive gardens along the lake and much else to see. The oldest part of town, on the north bank of the Reuss, retains its medieval street plan. There's the 14th-century town wall with its watchtowers, the delightful old square called the Weinmarkt, the 17th-century town hall, and the twin-towered church of St. Léger and St. Maurice, consecrated in 1644.

The famous Löwendenkmal (Lion Monument) commemorates the heroic Swiss soldiers who lost their lives defending Louis XVI of France and his family against the revolutionary mob that stormed the Tuileries in Paris in 1792. The wounded lion lies dying in a niche carved out of a hillside. The monument, designed by the great Danish sculptor Bertel Thorwaldsen, was completed in 1821. Lucerne also boasts the biggest transport museum in Europe, a planetarium, a museum of the Ice Age with a glacier garden, and a museum of Swiss folk costumes. Delightful cruises by steamer traverse romantic Lake Lucerne, with its panoramic views of the surrounding mountains and forests.

Lucerne probably began as a fishing village. What made its fortune was the opening in the 13th century of the Alpine route through the St. Gotthard Pass between northern Italy and the Rhineland. The town grew and prospered with the traffic along this route and became a major commercial center. It was owned by the Hapsburg dynasty of Austria until, in the 14th century, the town opposed them and threw off their yoke. It has always been a stronghold of Roman Catholicism in Switzerland.

Wagnerian Idyll

JUST outside Lucerne, on a promontory above the lake, is the house where Richard Wagner lived from 1866 to 1872. Tribschen is now a museum devoted to the great composer, who wrote most of *Die Meistersinger* there and part of the *Ring* cycle. It was there, too, that the "Siegfried Idyll" was first played, on Christmas morning 1870, to Wagner's wife Cosima. The philosopher Friedrich Nietszche was a frequent visitor to the house, though his sister Elizabeth disliked the Wagners' style of decoration, complaining of an excess of pink satin and cupids.

Freedom and William Tell

SWITZERLAND was the first democratic state in Europe, and the cradle of Swiss democracy was the area around Lake Lucerne. In the Middle Ages, Switzerland was part of the Holy Roman Empire, but the small settlements isolated among the remote mountains and forests were inevitably largely self-governing. They resisted the efforts of the Hapsburg emperors to impose a more effective system of administration on them, and in 1291 the representatives of three forest states, or cantons, close to the lake signed a treaty of mutual assistance. This is regarded as the founding moment of the Swiss Confederation, which the town of Lucerne joined in 1332 to protect its commercial interests. Other communities joined the confederacy, and the Swiss eventually won their independence.

The area was the home of the legendary Swiss patriotic hero William Tell. According to tradition, Altdorf, about 20 miles (32 km) southeast of Lucerne, is where he shot an apple off his young son's head with a crossbow, and there is a statue of him in the main square.

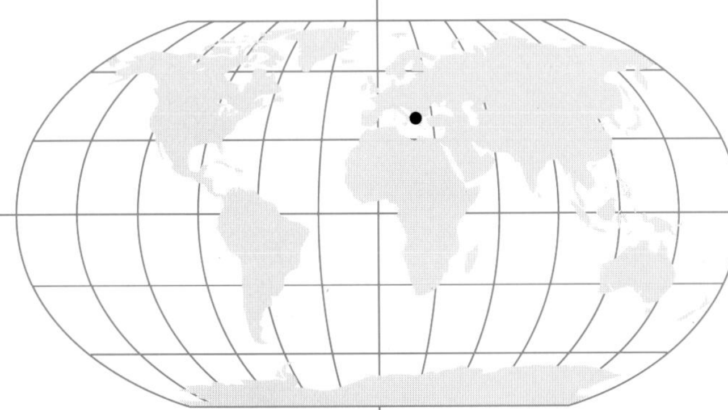

From about 1350 Greece

METEORA MONASTERIES

Hundreds of feet up on tall columns of rock, monks lived simple lives of devotion to God.

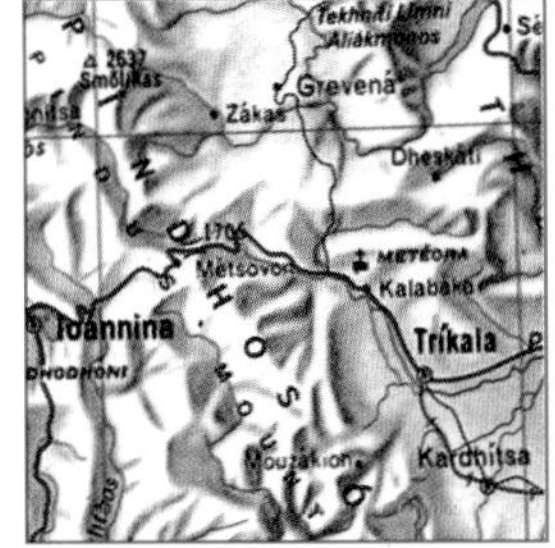

The monasteries are close to the small town of Kalambaka, some 265 miles (426 km) from Athens by road via Larisa. Regular bus service from Larisa. Trains from Athens and Salonika (Thessaloniki), which also have the nearest international airports. The monasteries are generally open in the morning, and again in the afternoon after siesta. Visitors are required to be decorously dressed.

METEORA means "in the air," and the monasteries are indeed up in the sky. Perched astonishingly atop sheer pillars and pinnacles of rock up to 1,800 feet (549 m) high on the edge of the Pindus Mountains, they look out over the valley of the Pinios River in Thessaly in central Greece. Until the 1920s, visitors either had to climb perilous and rickety

The Wild Horsemen

FROM ancient times the broad plains of Thessaly in central Greece were an important horse-breeding district, and in Greek mythology their inhabitants were pictured literally as horsemen. These were the centaurs, who had a human head and torso growing out of the body of a horse. With their lust and predilection for strong drink, they personified the animal urges in human nature, but among their numbers was a wise old shaman named Chiron, who taught the heroes Achilles and Jason in their youth.

The toil and difficulty of building these religious retreats, high on their pillars of rock, can only be imagined. They provided a simple lifestyle, secure against intrusion from the outside world.

ladders, 100 feet (30.5 m) or more long, fastened to the rock (these could be drawn up from above as a precaution against attack) or were hauled up by rope in a swaying net. The local straight-faced joke was that the rope was only mended if it broke.

Supplies are still hauled up in nets, but the monasteries began attracting tourists after the First World War, and especially after the 1960s, when a new road was built from the town of Kalambaka to make them easier to reach. Access now is by long flights of steps cut into the rock and across bridges over dizzying precipices. Many monks have moved away to regain privacy, and the sites today are more like museums than living communities.

Worshipping God in remote and barren places, far from the pleasures and preoccupations of ordinary daily life, was an element of Christianity from early on. Ascetics were already living in caves and on top of the rock pillars in this region in the 12th century, but the founder of the principal monastery, the Great Meteoron, arrived in about 1350. He was St. Athanasios, a monk from Mount Athos. According to legend, he was lifted up to the top of the pillar on which the monastery now stands by either an angel or an eagle. His pupil, Joasaph, a son of the king of Serbia, enlarged and enriched the foundation 30 or 40 years later.

The Rousanou monastery. The way up used to be by swaying net or rickety ladders.

Many more communities – over 30 in all – were founded in the 15th and 16th centuries after the Turks conquered Thessaly, but a long, slow decline set in during the 17th and 18th centuries and most of them have not survived. In the 19th century the monasteries attracted the attention of inquiring and indomitable travelers, and word of them began to spread.

Built of stone, with red-tiled roofs and wooden galleries projecting vertiginously over deep abysses, the monasteries had a cramped cell for each monk, a church, and a refectory for meals. Cisterns were cut in the rock to catch rainwater. The refectory at Agios Varlaam was restored as a museum in the 1960s. At the Great Meteoron you can see the simple kitchen with its clumsy bowls and ladles. In both, the churches are adorned with frescoes depicting hell and the grisly sufferings of martyrs, replete with hackings and beheadings, hammerings and nailings, stabbings, boilings, and skinnings alive. The deserted monastery of Agios Nikolaos has fine 16th-century frescoes by an artist from Crete named Theophanis.

The monasteries were strictly for men, but there were also nunneries. One of them, Agios Stephanos, is reached by a bridge over a terrifying chasm. Like all the communities, it commands the most breathtaking views.

The Life of Prayer

FROM late in the 3rd century A.D., Christian ascetics retreated into the deserts of Egypt and Syria to lead austere lives of prayer and meditation, away from people and close to God. They were also well away from the growing authority of the church. Their numbers increased in the 4th century when Christianity, now the official religion, became more identified with the power of the state.

The most famous of these early hermits was St. Antony of Egypt, celebrated for the attacks made on him by armies of evil spirits in grotesque and horrible forms, which furnished a lively theme for generations of painters. Another famous figure was St. Simeon Stylites, who spent 40 years perched on top of a 60-foot (18-m) pillar in the Syrian mountains.

Soon more organized communities grew up, where monks could lead a life of prayer. Since the 10th century the most important monastic center of the Orthodox Church has been the "holy mountain" of Mount Athos in northern Greece. It was a monk from Mount Athos, St. Athanasios, who founded the Great Meteoron.

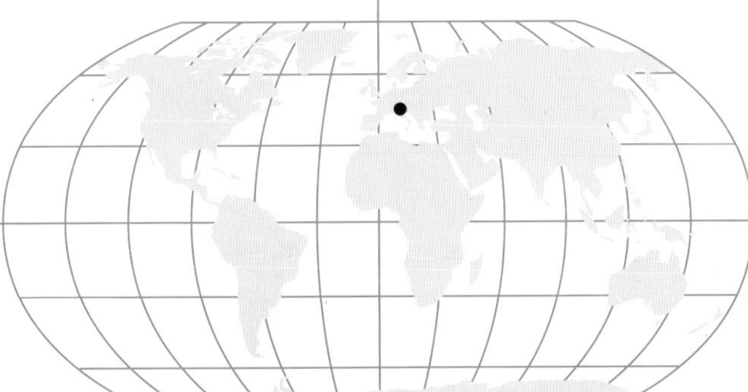

Mainly from the 15th Century Italy

THE GRAND CANAL

"The most beautiful street in the world"
– Philippe de Commynes

Venice can be approached by air, road, or rail, but nothing can compare with a first glimpse of the city from the deck of a boat. Within Venice, Vaporetto Route One runs up and down the Grand Canal.

At the height of summer, with thousands of tourists swarming on and off the *vaporetti* (water buses), or on a damp, gray winter morning, with fog rolling in from the lagoon – under whatever conditions you see it, the Grand Canal is magical. It is difficult not to be overwhelmed by Venice. Everywhere you turn, there is a building of note, a magnificent juxtaposition of brick and marble, an example of elegant Gothic tracery or outrageous baroque overstatement. And almost everywhere there is water, lapping the edges of the buildings, reflecting the splendor of the architecture, and serving as a thoroughfare for floating traffic of every kind. From its position among the lagoons at the head of the Adriatic, Venice built up one of the greatest commercial empires in history on the basis of its maritime trade. Water was its life and every year on Ascension Day this was affirmed when the Doge 'married' the sea by casting a gold ring into it, in the spectacular ceremony of the *Spozalizio del Mar*.

The Grand Canal is the main artery of Venice, snaking in a broad S shape for about 2$^{1}/_{2}$ miles (4 km) from the train station in the northwest of the city to the Punta della Salute in the southeast. The canal is crossed by only three bridges – one at the station, one at the Accademia art gallery, and the Rialto Bridge, the oldest and most celebrated of all. At other points gondolas, known as *traghetti*, act as ferries from one side of the canal to the other.

Venice is built on thousands of islands, which originally were little more than mud flats. The city rose on millions of wooden piles, and a unique style of architecture evolved to suit these maritime conditions. The palaces lining the Grand Canal display Venetian grandeur of every era, from the 13th century to the 20th.

The visitor could journey along the canal every day for a year, even for a lifetime, and still find something new to marvel at. The 16th-century Ca' d'Oro is perhaps the most celebrated palace of them all. Now an art

Looking across the Grand Canal to the double-domed magnificence of Santa Maria della Salute, designed in the 17th century by Baldassare Longhena, the grand apotheosis of Venetian baroque architecture.

gallery and open to the public again after years of restoration work, the building is a supreme example of Venetian Gothic architecture; it is said to owe its name to the fact that it was originally adorned with gilt. The Ca' d'Oro was completed before the middle of the 15th century. A slightly later and quite different building on the Grand Canal is the Palazzo Dario, with a façade studded with polychrome marble. In his book *The Stones of Venice*, the 19th-century English art critic and philosopher John Ruskin called this delightful palace an exquisite example of Venetian Early Renaissance domestic architecture.

At the southeastern end of the Grand Canal stands the Church of Santa Maria della Salute, designed by Longhena and built between 1630 and 1687 to commemorate deliverance from a plague that had afflicted the city. In November of each year a bridge of boats is constructed across the canal, allowing people to walk over to the church to celebrate its annual festival.

The Fondaco dei Turchi (built at the beginning of the 13th century but heavily restored), the Ca' Giustinian (mid-15th century), the Ca' Rezzonico (17th and 18th century, now a museum), the Ca' da Mosto (13th century) . . . the list of buildings to be seen along the Grand Canal is as long as the canal itself.

The gondola, symbol of the romance of the city, is artfully designed for shallow water, to carry the maximum of load with the minimum of draught.

The Gondola

THE gondola is a craft unique to Venice, and eight different types of wood are traditionally used in its construction. Its asymmetrical design allows it to be maneuvered easily by one person standing at the stern and using one oar. In the 18th century there were perhaps 14,000 gondolas in Venice. Now there are about 500.

Piazza San Marco

THE most beautiful street in the world leads to what Napoleon called the finest drawing room in Europe. St. Mark's Square (the one and only piazza in Venice) is bordered by buildings of different dates and styles, and yet the combined effect is so harmonious as to suggest that the ensemble might have been carefully planned. The 11th-century basilica of St. Mark is an astonishingly rich building with a profusion of fine mosaics and inlaid marble floors. It was originally the private chapel of the Doges of Venice, whose palace is another of the major sights of Venice. The Clock Tower, built at the end of the 15th century, has a surprisingly modern-looking digital display of the time, and two bronze figures strike a bell to announce the hour to crowds and pigeons in the square below.

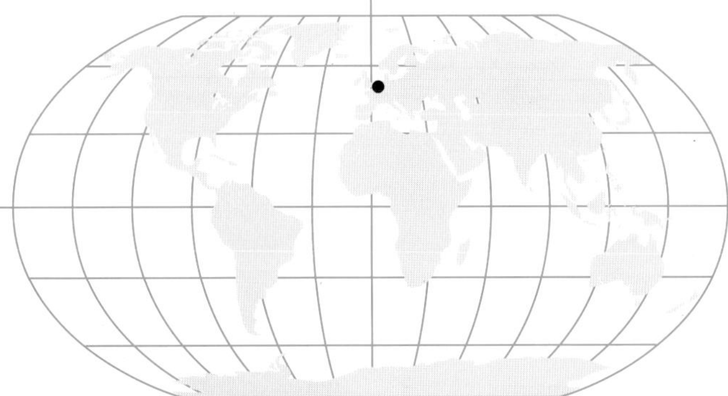

From 1402 Belgium

GRAND' PLACE

A magnificent square testifies to the wealth of the merchant guilds of medieval Brussels.

Brussels is the capital of Belgium and the hub of the Belgian superhighway network. The Grand' Place is at the heart of the city, on numerous bus routes. Nearest metro stations are Bourse and Gare Centrale. There are guided tours of the Hôtel de Ville (town hall).

THE 19th-century French writer Victor Hugo, who lived in Brussels for a time, described the Grand' Place as the most beautiful town square in Europe, and many would agree with him. With its stupendous town hall in Flemish Gothic, its elaborate royal palace, and the tall, gold-scrolled houses of the city's rich merchant guilds, it strikes the eye

Right: a riot of flamboyant baroque, spectacularly floodlit at night, the Grand' Place was rebuilt in the 1690s. The houses were used by the wealthy merchants of Brussels for business and social occasions.

Facing page: The House of the Boatmen, lavishly adorned in gold leaf, was rebuilt in 1697.

with a theatrical wealth of pinnacles and curlicues, ornate gables, statues, gargoyles, busts and trophies, medallions, heraldic beasts, columns and balustrades, like a set for a fabulously lavish opera.

There's a flower market every day in the square, and a caged-bird market on Sunday mornings. The Burgundian nobility once jousted here in tournaments, but the square began prosaically as the marketplace of the old town of Brussels, a village in the marshes along the Senne River that prospered on trade.

Work started on the town hall, the Hôtel de Ville, which occupies most of one side of the square, in 1402, and the bulk of it was completed by 1480. The dazzling 300-foot (91-m) spire, designed by Jan van Ruysbroek, architect to the Duke of Burgundy, dates from the 1450s. On top of it, doing duty as a weathervane while trampling the Devil underfoot, is a 16-foot (5-m) copper statue of St. Michael the Archangel. On the façade are more than 100 statues, 19th-century replacements of the originals. Inside are richly decorated rooms hung with Brussels tapestries and paintings. The two fountains in the inner courtyard represent Belgium's principal rivers, the Scheldt and the Meuse.

On the opposite side, the Maison du Roi, despite its name, was never a royal residence, but was used by the governors appointed by the Spanish rulers of the Low Countries. Completely rebuilt between 1873 and 1895 in the original lavishly ornate 16th-century style, it is now home to a museum of the city's history. One of the most engaging exhibits displays more than 300 costumes which over the centuries have been presented as gifts to Manneken Pis, the city's mascot.

The guild houses were used by the Brussels merchant princes for business meetings and entertaining. They were built of wood originally, but in 1695 the square was badly damaged when Brussels was besieged by a French army that bombarded it for 36 hours, destroying 16 churches and thousands of houses. The city's merchants promptly poured out money like water to rebuild in the most flamboyant and ostentatious baroque.

The houses have names bestowed on them by popular fancy, usually based on the decorative features. Le Renard (The Fox), Number 7, has a golden fox over the doorway. Victor Hugo lived at Number 26, Le Pigeon (The Dove). An equestrian statue gallantly surmounts Number 10, L'Arbre d'Or (The Golden Tree). Number 5, La Louve (The She-Wolf), belonged to the Guild of Archers and has above the door a relief of Romulus and Remus being suckled by a wolf. On top of the gable is a giant golden phoenix, a suitable emblem of Brussels reborn.

Manneken Pis

On the Rue de L'Etuve, not too far from the grandeur of the Grand' Place, is the little bronze figure of a small boy cherubically making water into the marble basin of a fountain. The 2-foot (61-cm) statue dates from the 19th century, but replaces much older figures. There are numerous legends about Manneken Pis, one of which says he was caught naughtily bedewing the front steps of a wicked fairy, who retaliated by turning him to stone.

Manneken Pis is held in great affection and is dressed up in special costumes on great occasions. His first costume was presented to him in 1698 by the Elector of Bavaria, it is said, and in 1747 Louis XV of France sent him a suit of brocade embroidered in gold. Many other outfits have been given to him since then, and more than 300 of them are displayed in the Maison du Roi.

Lace for a Queen

Brussels is famous for its lace, and striking examples of antique and contemporary lace-making can be admired in the Costume Museum on the Rue de la Violette, near the Grand' Place. There are also many shops in this area selling lace.

Lace first became fashionable in the 16th century, and different towns in the Low Countries evolved their own varying local styles. In the 18th century there were 10,000 lace-makers in Brussels, producing the most exquisite and subtle pieces for kings and queens, aristocrats, and the rich of Europe. Some superb examples can be seen in Brussels' churches, most notably the gorgeous lace headdress of the Virgin in the beautiful Church of Notre Dame du Sablon, on the Rue de la Régence.

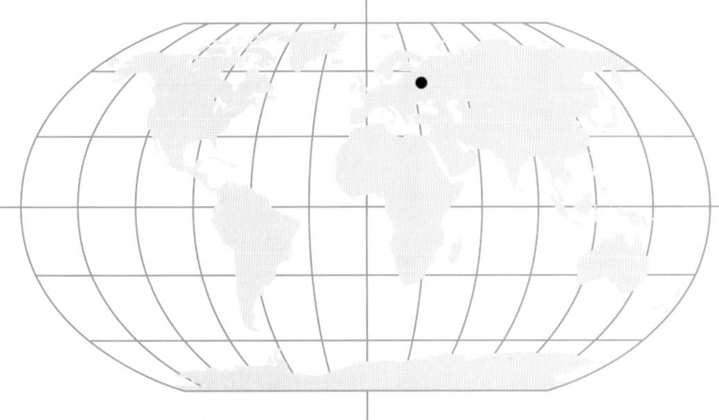

Mainly from 1475 USSR

THE KREMLIN

Splendidly towered, golden-domed, and battlemented, the citadel of the Russian czars rises above the Moscow River.

Visits to the Kremlin begin at the Trinity (Troitskaya) Gate, midway along the northern wall. Metro station on Karl Marx Boulevard. Visitors to Moscow should check arrangements in advance with Intourist, the Soviet state tourism agency.

Right: the Kremlin seen from across the river, with the Water Tower to the left. Water was raised from the river and carried by an aqueduct to the buildings and gardens. The tower was rebuilt in 1817. At the far end is the bell tower of Ivan the Great.

Facing page: the Cathedral of the Assumption was built for Czar Ivan III and completed in 1479.

IVAN the Terrible, the first man who could justly claim to be Czar of All the Russias, was crowned in the Kremlin in Moscow in 1547. There is a kremlin, or fortress, in many an ancient Russian city, but from that moment the citadel in Moscow has been *the* Kremlin.

The stronghold was the nucleus around which Moscow grew after its foundation in the 12th century. Triangular in shape, it covers 69 acres (28 hectares) of ground beside the Moscow River. Inside are the palaces of the czars and a constellation of churches. After the Revolution of 1917 the Kremlin became the headquarters of the Soviet government.

The towering walls were rebuilt in brick late in the 15th century. Standing up to 60 feet (18.3 m) high, they run for more than a mile (1.6 km) and are broken by 20 towers, some with tent-shaped steeples above the gates. The main entrance is the Spassky Gate, which faces Red Square. The soaring bell tower of Ivan the Great, 266 feet (81 m) high, was completed in 1600 by Czar Boris Godunov. A watchtower, it commanded a view for 20 miles (32 km) around. At its foot is the world's largest bell, the monstrous Czar Kolokol, cast in the 1730s and weighing more than 224 U.S. tons (203 metric tons). Nearby lurks another monster, the Czar Cannon, with a 35-inch (89-cm) caliber, made in 1586 and tipping the scales at 44.8 U.S. tons (40.6 metric tons). The bell has never been rung, and the cannon has never been fired.

In the late 15th century Ivan III commissioned Italian architects to rebuild the Kremlin as capital of the Third Rome. The Granovitaya Palata, completed in 1491, with the splendid Renaissance throne room, is still used for state occasions. The Cathedral of the Assumption, built in the 1470s, was the crowning place of the czars. Near the main entrance stands the carved walnut throne of Ivan the Terrible, made in 1551. The Cathedral of the Annunciation, rebuilt in the 1560s, was known as "the golden-domed" because its entire roof was gilded. The Cathedral of St. Michael the Archangel, where the czars were buried, is in the Russian style, but with Italian Renaissance influence. All three churches contain impressive frescoes and icons, and there are lesser churches close by.

The Great Kremlin Palace, subsequently the meeting place of the Supreme Soviet, was completed in 1849. From it there is access to the czars' private apartments in the 17th-century Terem Palace. The treasures amassed by the imperial family over the centuries are displayed in the Armory. They range from weapons and armor to crowns and regalia, magnificent thrones, jewels, vestments, carriages, delectable snuffboxes, and Fabergé Easter eggs. The Palace of the Patriarchs of the Russian Orthodox Church, which dates from the 1650s, now houses a museum of 17th-century Russian art and culture.

Also in the Kremlin is the building used for Party conferences, completed in 1961 and specially sunk into the ground so as not to detract from the older buildings. Immediately outside is Red Square, with the mausoleum where the body of Lenin was put on display after his death. Stalin's body was displayed there from 1953 until 1961. In the square is the gorgeous and fantastic Cathedral of St. Basil with its writhing onion domes. Built on the orders of Ivan the Terrible in the 1550s, it has been a symbol of Russia ever since.

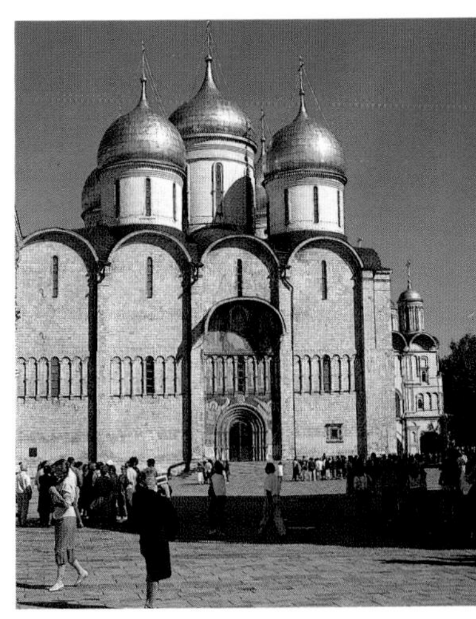

Autocrat of All the Russias

IN 1453 the city of Constantinople, or Byzantium, fell to the Turks, marking the end of the Eastern Roman Empire and the long reign of Byzantium as the Second Rome. Far to the north, in Russia, the Grand Dukes of Muscovy proclaimed themselves the spiritual heirs of Byzantium and protectors of the Eastern Orthodox Church, with their capital of Moscow as the Third Rome.

The claim was given teeth by the formidable Ivan IV, known in Russian as *Groznyi*, "the Awesome," which Western writers rendered as "the Terrible." Inheriting the Grand Duchy as a baby of three, he took the reins of government into his hands at 14. At 16 he was crowned czar (Caesar), and his conquests established a Russian empire ruled from Moscow. He certainly had a savage temper, and he killed his son in a rage in 1581, three years before his own death. It is said that when St. Basil's Cathedral was finished, the czar had the architect blinded so that he could never create a rival.

Unburied Caesar

THE Soviet government made its headquarters in Moscow in March 1918, and since then the USSR has been ruled from the Kremlin. Vladimir Ilyich Lenin himself moved into the 18th-century Senate building, where he lived austerely on the top floor. The clock on his study wall was kept at 8:15, the time when, desperately ill, he left the room for the last time. He died in 1924, and his embalmed body was displayed in a wooden pyramid in Red Square, which in 1930 was replaced by a granite mausoleum.

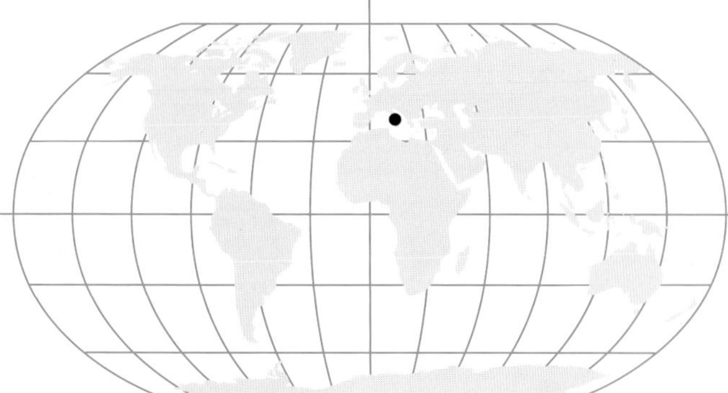

From 1506 Italy

ST. PETER'S BASILICA

St. Peter's is a vast church built over a humble tomb. Almost all the celebrated architects of 16th-century Italy had a hand in its construction.

On the right bank of the Tiber River, west of the center of Rome. The direct approach is along the Via della Conciliazione. Technically, the church is not in Rome at all, but in a separate state, Vatican City.

THE Church of St. Peter covers an area of some 240,000 square feet (22,300 sq m) and, until 1990, when it was surpassed by an even bigger cathedral in Africa, it was the largest Christian church in the world. Its dimensions are awe-inspiring, but even more remarkable, given the saga of its construction, is the fact that it was ever completed at all.

The vast church we see today had its origin in the tomb of a man martyred for his faith in the first century A.D. – the apostle Peter, crucified by Nero and buried in a public cemetery in about A.D. 64. Peter's tomb became a place of pilgrimage, and the Christian emperor Constantine built a basilica around it, which stood for a thousand years. When the structure began to crumble, Pope Nicholas V planned a grandiose replacement, but died in 1455 before work was under way. For the next 170 years, work on the new St. Peter's was regularly interrupted as yet another pope or architect died and one scheme was replaced by another.

Bramante began to construct a church with a huge dome in 1506. When he died in 1514, Raphael took over, but after his death in 1520, a different scheme was adopted, the dome was abandoned, and some Gothic elements were introduced. Michelangelo, taking the job over at the age of 71 – "for the love of God, the Blessed Virgin, and St. Peter" – reinstated the dome, but he too died before work was

The Pietà

MICHELANGELO'S statue of the mourning Virgin Mary holding the dead body of her son – the *Pietà* – is the only known piece that bears his signature. The marble he required – flawless, with a glowing, milky translucence – was quarried high in the mountains of Tuscany, and an access road was specially built to transport it. The Virgin's nose, damaged by a vandal in 1972, has been skillfully restored.

Right: Bernini's grand Piazza of St. Peter, with its central obelisk, makes a fitting setting for the grandeur of the mother church of Roman Catholic Christendom. Michelangelo designed the tremendous dome.

Facing page: the sumptuously ornate interior scales the heights of baroque splendor.

completed. The subsequent design of nave, façade, and portico was ill-advised and ruined the view of the dome for the approaching visitor.

The church was finally consecrated on November 18, 1626, by Pope Urban VIII. The piazza in front of St. Peter's was built much more swiftly, between 1656 and 1667. The work of Bernini, it has 284 Tuscan columns arranged four deep with statues of saints above. Inside St. Peter's, Bernini constructed something that has been less universally admired – the huge bronze baldacchino set canopy-like over the papal altar and supported on serpentine columns 95 feet (29 m) high.

It is possible to inspect St. Peter's literally from top to bottom, to look down on Rome from a balcony attached to the lantern on top of the dome, and to descend beneath the high altar and view the excavations of the cemetery that stood beneath Constantine's original basilica. One monument discovered here may well mark the site of St. Peter's grave, although there is not sufficient archaeological evidence to allow anyone to argue conclusively for or against such an interpretation.

Built on a massive scale and heavily ornate in much of its internal decoration, St. Peter's is, for some visitors, overly elaborate and even oppressive. The initial impression on walking into the building, which stretches ahead of you for a distance of 620 feet (189 m), is sometimes one of bewilderment – there is simply too much to take in, and it cannot all be appreciated at once. Unqualified admiration may not be everyone's verdict, but as a whole it certainly excites wonder.

The Vatican

St. Peter's stands in Vatican City, an autonomous state recognized as being independent of Italy in 1929. Its head of state is the pope, and the Vatican has its own currency, a newspaper, a train station, and an entitlement to diplomatic representation abroad. Swiss Guards, in distinctive colorful uniforms, act as the state police force.

The buildings of the Vatican, constructed with ever increasing grandeur during the 14th, 15th, and 16th centuries, house half a million books and what is said to be the biggest collection of ancient art anywhere in the world. It would take months to see everything, and those visitors who attempt to see it all in one visit are embarking on a perilous course likely to end in extreme exhaustion.

The Sistine Chapel, built for Pope Sixtus IV around 1473, is part of the complex of rooms and galleries open to the public, and it is celebrated throughout the world for its frescoes by Michelangelo. Painted between 1508 and 1512, those on the ceiling depict biblical scenes before the Flood. Twenty years after these were completed, the artist went on to paint the Last Judgment on the chapel's east wall.

Mainly from 1533 Austria

THE HOFBURG

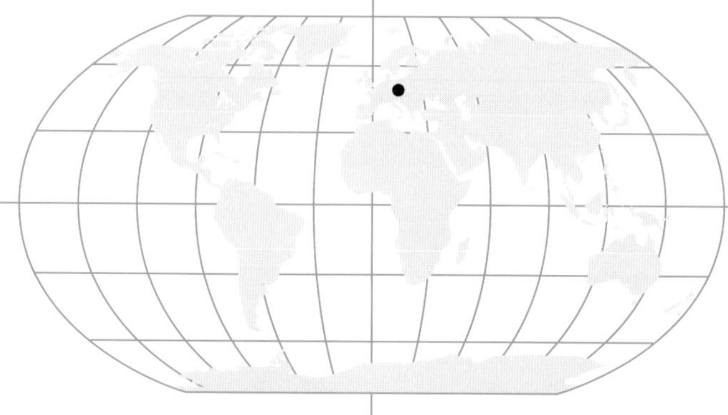

The white Lipizzaner stallions parade in the elegant riding school of the palace of the Hapsburgs.

The Hofburg stands, or rather sprawls, on the eastern side of the Ringstrasse, the handsome boulevard that encircles the oldest part of Vienna. Visits begin from the Michaelerplatz.

Airs Above the Ground

ONE of Vienna's enduringly popular attractions is the elegant Spanish Riding School in the Hofburg, where the white Lipizzaner stallions, adorned with gold ribbons and still trained as in the 17th century, go through their gravity-defying repertoire of levade, courbette, and capriole to the music of quadrille and gavotte.

City of Music

THE Hofburg's collection of musical instruments is a reminder that no city in the world can boast of remotely as many great composers as Vienna. Christoph Gluck wrote operas for the Hapsburg court in the 18th century. Mozart and Haydn both lived and composed in Vienna. Beethoven settled in Vienna in 1792, and Schubert lived and died here.

Above: "your carriage awaits" in front of the palace.

Right: the horses tread their stately measures in the world's most elegant riding school. The riders need almost as much schooling as the horses.

Facing page: the equestrian monument to Prince Eugene in front of the Outer Gate.

NOT so much a palace as a jumble of buildings of periods and styles from the 13th century to the 19th, the Hofburg was the Vienna residence and court of the Hapsburg dynasty, Holy Roman Emperors and subsequently rulers of the Austro-Hungarian Empire. The massive muddle – as courtyard follows courtyard and wing succeeds to wing – has been compared to the Hapsburgs' ramshackle empire itself, but it contains much beauty and many remarkable treasures, from Beethoven's piano to the feather robes and headdress of Moctezuma of Mexico.

Parts of the Hofburg are used as government offices, while other areas have been turned into museums for the gigantic collections that generations of Hapsburgs amassed. The oldest part of the palace is the Schweizerhof, named after the Swiss guard that garrisoned it, but it was not until after 1533, when Emperor Ferdinand I made the castle his home, that it became a regular royal residence. In the imperial apartments you can see the huge stoves that were needed to heat the rooms, the imperial audience chamber, and the simple, austere bedroom of Emperor Franz Josef, who died in 1916 after a reign of almost 80 years. There is also the gymnasium where his wife, the wayward and fascinating Empress Elizabeth, kept herself in trim. And in the chapel the world famous and highly acclaimed Vienna Boys Choir sings Mass on Sunday mornings.

The imperial treasury houses a collection of objects extending back for a thousand years to the gem-studded imperial crown, which is believed to date from the 10th century. Here are the robes and accoutrements of the fabulous Order of the Golden Fleece, the sumptuous ecclesiastical vestments, the jewels and reliquaries inherited from the Dukes of Burgundy. Here too is one of the great relics of Christendom, the Holy Lance, reputedly the one that pierced Christ's side on the cross.

Century by century the Hapsburgs kept adding to the palace. Ferdinand I built a handsome Renaissance wing, which was later turned into stables. Part of it is now an art gallery. The Amalienburg, where Empress Elizabeth lived when in residence, was begun in 1575. The president of Austria now occupies a 17th-century wing.

The beautiful library was built in the 1720s

to house 90,000 volumes that the family acquired. "A cathedral of books," it has been called, with its elegant columned hall with trompe l'oeil frescoes in the dome. Books on theology and law were bound in blue, scientific books in yellow, all others in red. The famous columned and chandeliered Spanish Riding School, where the white Lipazzaner horses show off their curious antique paces, was completed in 1735.

In the Albertina is one of the world's greatest collections of graphic art, with more than a million items. Dürer's *Praying Hands* is here. Nearby is the court's parish church, the Augustinerkirche, originally part of an Augustinian friary. Here, by proxy, the ill-fated Marie Antoinette was married to the future Louis XVI, and Marie-Louise to Napoleon. Here are interred the hearts of the Hapsburgs, each in its urn, ruling only the silence now.

On the lighter side, the city hummed to the waltzes and operettas of Johann Strauss and Franz Lehar, but the procession of heavyweights was far from over. Brahms and Bruckner both settled in Vienna in the 1860s. Gustav Mahler was director of the court opera in the 1890s. Arnold Schönberg and Alban Berg were both born in Vienna before the end of the century.

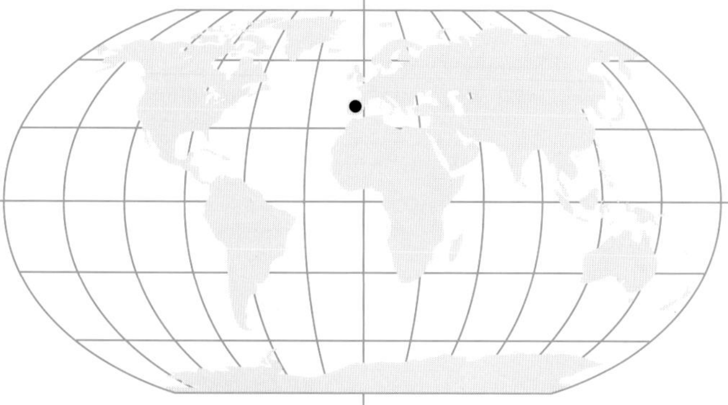

1563-1584 Spain

THE ESCORIAL

The building is said to have 10 miles (16 km) of corridors and nearly a hundred staircases. In Spain it is called the eighth wonder of the world.

The Escorial is about 25 miles (40 km) northwest of Madrid in the Sierra de Guadarrama foothills. From Madrid take the NVI road towards Corunna, turning off on the C505 at Las Rosas, or stay on the NVI to Guadarrama and take the El Escorial exit. Trains from Madrid to San Lorenzo de El Escorial station.

MONASTERIES and royal palaces are normally entirely separate institutions. A king on his travels might demand hospitality from an abbot, and a member of a royal family concerned about his immortal soul might pay to have monks pray for him. Philip II of Spain chose to create a monastery that was also a palace – the Escorial.

On August 10, 1557, Philip's forces defeated the French at St. Quentin in Flanders. The date

Right: the south front of the Escorial. Built of yellowish-gray granite, with plain façades and angle towers, the palace mirrors the reserved, austere temperament of Philip II. There are said to be 2,500 windows, but attempts to count them rarely agree.

Facing page: allegorical paintings cover the ceiling of Philip II's library.

was significant – it was the feast day of St. Lawrence and, curiously, the church at St. Quentin, dedicated to St. Lawrence, had been destroyed during the battle. Philip, a devout man, vowed that St. Lawrence would have a new church. The huge Escorial complex is said to have been laid out on a grid pattern as a symbol of the way the saint died, martyred on a gridiron. The monastery was to belong to the Hieronymite order, followers of St. Augustine and St. Jerome who traditionally led a life of contemplation and prayer.

Known in Spain as the eighth wonder of the world, the Escorial has something of the appearance of a fortress. A vast rectangular structure, its outer walls measure 680 by 530 feet (207 by 153 m), and the sheer regularity of the façades is too austere for some tastes. Attempts to count the doors and windows seldom produce the same results, but the numbers are something in the region of 1,250 (doors) and 2,500 (windows). Two chief architects were involved. Juan Bautista of Toledo made the first plans in 1559 and seems to have drawn on his experiences in Rome, working on St. Peter's, in designing the church. Juan de Herrera completed the project after Juan Bautista's death.

The Escorial was built between 1563 and 1584, and the king himself took an active interest in its progress. The royal apartments were designed in such a way that he could enter the church from his own room, and, as a sick old man, he had a view of the high altar from his bed. Philip's palace, attached to the east end of the church and jutting out beyond the rest of the complex, has been called the handle of St. Lawrence's gridiron. Philip's successors, seeking more opulent and spacious accommodation and not so insistent on views of the high altar, constructed further royal apartments on the north side of the church. South of the church is a two-story cloister. The central courtyard here is known as the Patio of the Evangelists because of its statues.

As well as palace and monastery, the Escorial was to serve as a mausoleum for the kings of Spain, and this "pantheon" lies below the huge high altar of the church. It was not completed until long after Philip II's death. The library, however, housed in a long gallery over the western entrance to the Escorial, was something that Philip did see completed. A valuable collection of books and manuscripts can be seen in a room decorated with allegorical paintings of subjects such as philosophy, theology, music, and geometry.

Philip's Seat

Philip II involved himself in the building of the Escorial, and he is said to have sought out a place in the hills from which he could watch the work progressing. Philip's Seat (Silla de Felipe) can be reached by a winding, narrow road branching off the main road at the front of the palace. It is quite a climb, and accurate directions are needed. The reward is a magnificent view of the palace.

Art and Architecture

Philip II favored a restrained, rather than an overly elaborate architectural style for the Escorial, but he furnished his palace with remarkable works of art. Today a visit to the monastery-palace is also a visit to a richly endowed gallery. The New Museums at the Escorial are particularly noted for work by Titian. El Greco, Veronese, Tintoretto, and Velasquez are also represented. A panel of Hieronymus Bosch's *Garden of Earthly Delights* can be seen here, and a workshop replica of Bosch's *Hay Wain* triptych is in Philip's own apartments. The palace also has a fine collection of tapestries, some based on designs by Goya and Rubens. The twin chapterhouses of the monastery are used to display paintings and artifacts, and the Escorial has its own architectural museum.

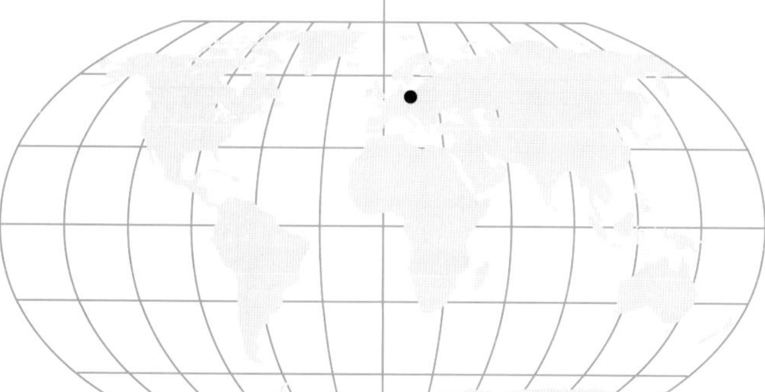

Late 16th Century Czechoslovakia

GOLDEN LANE

With their gnomelike air, the houses might be the workshops of industrious dwarfs.

Prague's Golden Lane (Zlata Ulicka in Czech) is between the walls of Hradcany Castle and the Old Castellan's Lodging. Visitors enter the castle from the west, in Hradcany Square (Hradcanske Namesti). Nearest Metro stations are Hradcanska and Malostranska.

Right: according to legend, Emperor Rudolf II installed his alchemists in the diminutive houses, where like a legion of goblins they worked and experimented to make the fabled Stone of the Philosophers.

Facing page: the main entrance door of the cathedral of St Vitus, the church that dominates the Hradcany palace complex.

GOLDEN Lane was formerly known as the Street of the Alchemists. Nestling against the walls of Hradcany Castle, it is a narrow, cobblestoned street of small houses that look as if they were designed by the Brothers Grimm. Color-washed in pastel shades, they have diminutive doors and windows, low roofs, and what seems to be an excessive supply of chimneys – all contributing to an elfin effect. The street is now a tourist attraction, and many of the houses have become small shops.

In the 1590s, in the time of Rudolf II, the Hapsburg emperor who lived mainly in Prague, the houses were occupied by guards from the castle. Later it became a goldsmiths' center, and a legend grew up that the emperor had installed his own alchemists there, laboring earnestly over furnaces and stills to make gold and the elixir of life. The story gained credence from the fact that Rudolf II was indeed passionately interested in alchemy.

At one end of the street is a tower called the Daliborka. It was built as a prison in 1496, and the story goes that it was named after its first prisoner, a young man called Dalibor of Kozojedy, who had made the mistake of siding with the peasants against the landowners in his country district. Imprisoned in chains, he taught himself to play the violin, which he did so sweetly that people used to gather below the tower to listen. Eventually the day came when they waited in vain: Dalibor and his violin had both been silenced. The 19th-century Czech composer Bedřich Smetana based his opera *Dalibor* on the story.

Franz Kafka, author of *The Castle* and other enigmatically menacing novels, lived in Golden Lane for a few months, between November 1916 and March 1917. His favorite sister, Ottla, rented Number 22 for him, and there he wrote many of the stories later included in *Ein Landarzt* (A Country Doctor), a collection that was published in 1919. Kafka was unusually happy in Golden Lane and liked to walk along the steep streets around the castle late at night.

Prague is by general consent one of the most enchanting cities in the world. It is set on the Vltava River, and the ground rising steeply from the river's west bank is crowned by the great Hradcany castle-palace complex, long the home of rulers of Bohemia (now known as Czechoslovakia) and more recently the official residence of the president.

Originally built in wood in the 9th century, the castle was rebuilt in stone in the 12th. It was rebuilt again when Prague became the capital of the Holy Roman Empire under Charles IV, King of Bohemia, who was crowned emperor in Rome in 1355. There was more rebuilding in later centuries, down to the 18th, when the New Palace at the western end of the complex was constructed for Empress Maria Theresa. Notable rooms in the Old Palace include the Vladislav Hall and the Versailles-style Hall of Mirrors. The whole complex is dominated by the tower and spires of the Cathedral of St. Vitus, built by Charles IV and extended between 1877 and 1929. Inside is the famous Chapel of St. Wenceslas, covered with paintings and precious stones. With its towering main steeple, the cathedral is the largest and most important of Prague's churches. It is the burial place of Czech kings and emperors, and their consorts. Among them are Charles IV, Ferdinand I and Maximilian II. The cathedral also contains the tin coffin of Rudolf II.

Good King Wenceslas

ST. Wenceslas, the patron saint of Bohemia, was a Christian ruler of the country early in the 10th century. There was a pagan revolt against him, and he was murdered by the followers of his brother Boleslav in the year 929. Boleslav had his remains interred in the Church of St. Vitus in Prague, where they attracted pilgrims, and Wenceslas became a symbol of the Czech nation. In English-speaking countries the saint is familiar as the "Good King Wenceslas" of the Christmas carol written by J.M. Neale in the 19th century. The carol's story, however, grew up long after the real Wenceslas's day and is not based on any incident in his life.

The Philosopher's Stone

RUDOLF II was deeply preoccupied with matters that in his time were on the border of science and the occult: alchemy and chemistry, astrology and astronomy. Born in Vienna in 1552, he was crowned king of Bohemia in 1575 and succeeded his father, Maximilian II, as Holy Roman Emperor the following year. He suffered from severe bouts of depression, which made him incapable of doing so much as signing state papers and which put his sanity in doubt. He shut himself away in his favorite residence, the castle in Prague, and devoted his time largely to alchemical experiments, while his court poet was ordered to write verse in praise of the fabled Philosopher's Stone, which turned base metals to gold and prolonged human life indefinitely. It was rumored that the emperor had discovered it himself, but in 1606 his family declared him incapable of ruling and tried to install his brother in his place. After several years of internecine strife, Rudolf died in Prague in 1612.

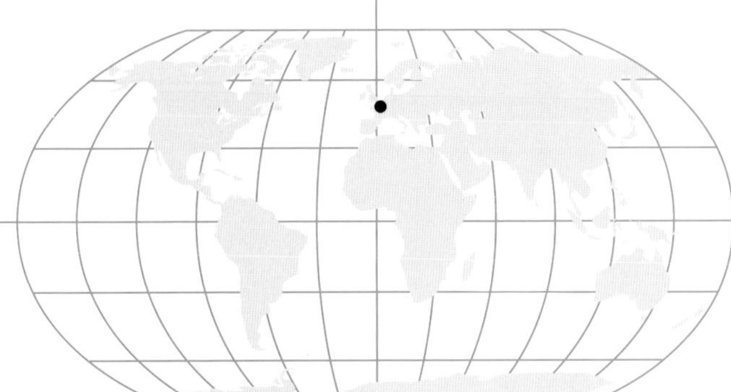

From 1661 France

VERSAILLES

Many attempts have been made to copy Versailles, but it remains the inimitable creation of King Louis XIV: a palace fit for a Sun King.

Versailles is easily reached by train or by road from Paris. There is far too much to be seen in one visit, and although some areas can be inspected at any time, for others it is necessary to join a guided tour. By train from Paris, take RER Line C5 to Versailles Rive Gauche.

Right: the classical order and regularity of the architecture of the palace was intended to convey a sense of the harmony and dignity of France under Louis XIV, just as the immense size and splendor demonstrated the king's power and grandeur.

Facing page, above: surmounted by eagles, the royal badge and the royal crown, the gate gives a foretaste of the magnificence beyond.

Facing page, below: Apollo drives the chariot of the sun up out of one of the lakes in the grounds.

VERSAILLES, less than 15 miles (24 km) from Paris, was chosen by King Louis XIII as the site for a modest chateau that would serve him as a base for his hunting expeditions. His son, Louis XIV, also enjoyed hunting but had somewhat more elaborate plans for the estate. Dissatisfied with the other palaces available (including the Louvre and the Tuileries), he decided, in 1660, to turn Versailles into a vast royal enclave. Everything was to be the ultimate in magnificence, and he would build on such a scale that eventually the whole

French court could be accommodated.

Work began in 1661, and in the course of two years Louis XIV, who came to be known as the Sun King, spent a vast amount of money, provoking anguished protests from the treasury. In fact, building was to continue for decades, involving many thousands of workmen and ever-increasing expense. The original architect was Louis Le Vau, succeeded by Jules Hardouin Mansart, who worked on Versailles for 30 years. André Le Notre was responsible for the landscaping, and his grand design for the gardens so surpassed the original chateau that it was decided to turn it into a far more sumptuous palace.

The gardens of Versailles, furnished with countless fountains, sculptures, and grottoes, provided the major attraction for Parisian nobility during the early years of the Sun King's reign, and in 1664, 1668, and 1674 these became the backdrop for elaborate artistic extravaganzas, featuring operas by Lully and plays by Molière and Racine. In a sense the whole place was like a stage set, and the tradition was continued by Louis XIV's successors, most notoriously by Marie Antoinette. She had her own theater built within the grounds and created a rustic hamlet, staffed by shepherds and other yokels, where she and her friends could play at being peasants.

The gardens of Versailles cover 250 acres (101 hectares), with numerous planned vistas, promenades, and parterres, and a "Grand Canal" with its own "Little Venice." The dimensions of the palace itself are awesome: the garden frontage is 2,100 feet (640 m) long and has at its center the Hall of Mirrors, a gallery 235 feet (72 m) long, 35 feet (10.6 m) wide, and 42 feet (12.8 m) high. Seventeen windows look out over the gardens, and these are matched by huge mirrors on the opposite wall. The paintings here, the work of Charles Le Brun, present a flattering account of the reign of Louis XIV between 1661 and 1678.

This artistic celebration of the king helped to enhance the aura of royalty that Louis XIV was so determined to cultivate. Versailles became his permanent residence in 1682, and the entire French court was soon established there. Complex rituals developed, and precise rules of etiquette were observed. Considerable personal advancement was possible if one found favor with the king, so hopeful courtiers would come to Versailles and wait, sometimes in vain, for an opportunity to witness the *Levée* or the *Coucher* – the rising, or the retiring to bed, of the monarch.

Louis XIV died in 1715. Louis XV engaged the architect Gabriel to carry out further work, including the building of an opera salon and the palace known as the Petit Trianon. Under Louis XVI a fine library was added and Marie Antoinette took over the Petit Trianon. But reality was about to intrude on the stage set. In October of 1789 the French Revolution reached Versailles and the palace was invaded.

The Gardens

THE gardens of Versailles were designed to house a wealth of sculpture. The Water Parterre, in front of the Hall of Mirrors, has two lakes, each boasting four statues representing rivers of France: the Loire and Loiret by Regnaudin, the Saône and the Rhône by Tuby, the Marne and the Seine by Le Hongre, and the Garonne and the Dordogne by Coysevox. There are some impressive animal groups, numerous figures from classical mythology, including Bacchus, Apollo, Mercury, and Silenus, and a few works that appear to be faithful copies of ancient originals, such as a Venus by Coysevox and a Knife Grinder by Foggini. The fountain known as the Bath of the Nymphs, by François Girardon, takes its name from a bas-relief modeled in lead. A magnificent work by Tuby, also in lead, depicts Apollo, god of the sun, driving his horses and chariot out of a lake, and the Fountain of Enceladus, dating from 1676, is a powerful work in which the sculptor, Gaspard Marsy, portrays the tortured figure of the Titan Enceladus virtually buried beneath rocks.

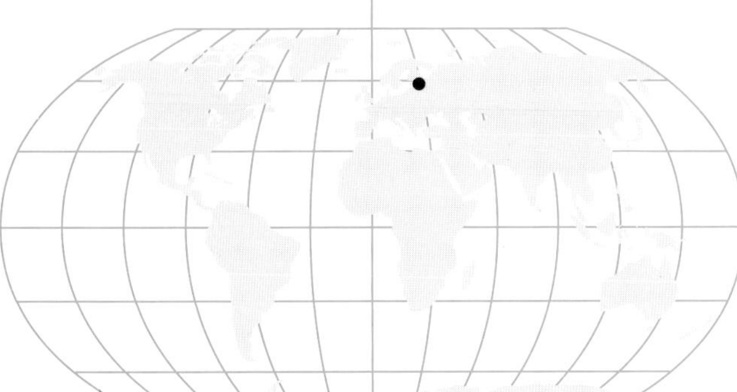

From 1714 USSR

THE GREAT PALACE

Astounding waterworks dazzle the eye on the grounds of the Great Palace of the Russian imperial family outside Leningrad.

Petrodvorets is 18 miles (29 km) west of Leningrad on the shore of the Gulf of Finland. The palace can be reached by road or by train from Baltic Station in Leningrad, or by hydrofoil from Makarov Quay.

CZAR Peter the Great founded his new capital city of St. Petersburg (later called Leningrad) in 1703. An energetic and determined Westernizer, he set out to create outside the city a complex to rival Versailles. He planned the layout himself and assembled an army of soldiers and serfs to dig canals and channels for the dizzying array of waterworks, which require some 9,007 U.S. gallons/7,500 imperial gallons (34,095 liters) of water per second.

In the 300-acre (21-hectare) park are regiments of cascades and fountains, some of them intended to go off unexpectedly and drench unsuspecting visitors. They culminate in the Great Cascade, which descends seven vast steps, with fountains shooting up from each step and gilded statues of classical gods and heroes on either side. Set on a rock in a capacious basin of water is a statue of the Old Testament hero Samson, wrenching apart the jaws of a lion, from which a jet of water hurls itself 66 feet (20 m) into the air. All around is a riot of leaping, sparkling water, with grottoes and figures of dolphins, water nymphs and Tritons triumphantly blowing horns, in a wildly spectacular celebration of the Russion defeat of the "lion" of Sweden at Poltava on St. Samson's Day in 1709.

The palace complex and park at Peterhof – now called Petrodvorets (Peter's Palace) – was severely damaged during World War II and has been magnificently restored since 1945. Immediately behind the Great Cascade is the Great Palace, on a terrace looking out over the Gulf of Finland, the arm of the Baltic Sea on which Leningrad is situated. Begun in 1714 for Peter the Great, the palace was substantially enlarged and altered for his daughter, Empress Elizabeth, and later czars and czarinas changed it in their turn – among them Catherine the Great, who was living here when she set in motion the coup that was successfully to overthrow her estranged husband, Peter III, and put her in power.

Czar Peter's oak-paneled study has been restored. Other rooms are resplendent in gilt, crystal, and bronze, and some of the rooms the imperial family occupied are hung in green and white silk. The portrait room is lined with more than 350 paintings.

Out in the park are smaller buildings,

Right: Samson forces the jaws of the lion apart at the center of the Great Palace's most spectacular water feature. In the background is the charming 18th-century palace itself.

Facing page: looking away from the palace, across the Great Cascade to the canal with its subsidiary fountains. In the distance is the Gulf of Finland.

including Monplaisir, on the Gulf shore, where Czar Peter lived while the Great Palace was being built. It was completed in 1722, but it too was enlarged for Empress Elizabeth. The famous Lacquer Room, hung with lacquered papier-mâché plates showing Chinese scenes in gold on a black background, has been superbly recreated. In Peter's time house rules were hung up for the czar's guests, including a prohibition on going to bed in one's riding boots. The Hermitage, also built for Peter, is a dining pavilion on the upper floor. Part of the table can be lowered bodily to the ground floor, to be cleared and reset by the servants.

Peter's principal landscape architect in the early stages at Peterhof was a Frenchman, Alexandre Le Blond. Empress Elizabeth employed her Italian court architect Bartolomeo Rastrelli here, and Jeger Velten redecorated many rooms for Catherine the Great in the 1770s. Nicholas I extended the park in the 19th century.

Imperial Grandeur

WITHIN easy reach of Leningrad are two other imperial palace complexes of exceptional splendor. Pushkin, 17 miles (27 km) to the south, is better known as Tsarskoe Selo, and was mainly laid out in the 18th century for Empress Elizabeth and Catherine the Great. Rich families from St. Petersburg (Leningrad) built houses here, and it is said to have been the first town in Europe entirely lit by electricity. It was renamed Pushkin in 1937 on the centenary of the poet's birth.

The major building is the Yekaterinsky (Catherine) Palace, or Summer Palace, created in the most sumptuous baroque by Rastrelli for Empress Elizabeth. The interiors were redone in the Robert Adam manner for Catherine the Great by a Scots architect, Charles Cameron. The war-damaged palace and park have been restored, except for the fabulous Amber Room, whose walls were entirely covered with amber. There's a museum to Pushkin, who went to school here.

The Alexandrovsky Palace, built in the 1790s, was the favorite home of the ill-fated last czar, Nicholas II, who was murdered with his family in 1918. They knew many happy times here. The palace is not open to visitors. Two miles (3 km) from Pushkin is Pavlovsk, where yet another palace of astonishing grandeur is set in a breathtaking park of 1,500 acres (607 hectares). It was created by Charles Cameron for Catherine the Great's son, Czar Paul I.

1779 England

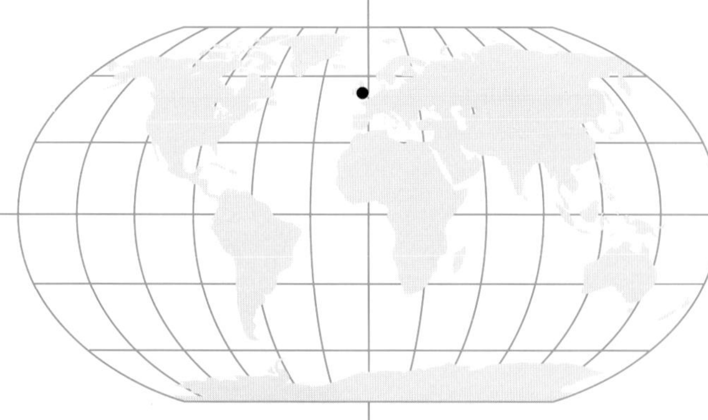

THE IRON BRIDGE

"It is one arch, a hundred feet broad, 52 high and 18 wide; all of cast iron, weighing many hundred tons. I doubt whether the Colossus of Rhodes weighed more."
—JOHN WESLEY

Ironbridge is in the county of Shropshire, on the B4373 and B4380 roads, south of the M54 highway and the town of Telford. Buses from Telford town center. The museum complex covers an area of 6 square miles (15.5 sq km), and a shuttle bus does the round of the sites in the peak summer months.

THE first major structure of its kind in the world, the Iron Bridge over the River Severn at Coalbrookdale in England has a classical gracefulness of proportion entirely appropriate to the 18th century, but it was also a portent of things to come. It was a daring project in its day and a tribute to the nerve as well as the skill of the ironmasters who conceived it.

The project was broached in 1773 by an architect and bridge designer from Shrewsbury named Thomas Farnolls Pritchard to one of his clients, John Wilkinson, who owned ironworks in the area and in Wales. The formidable Wilkinson was such an enthusiast for iron that he was nicknamed "Iron-Mad" Wilkinson. He wore an iron hat, made the first iron boats, was buried in an iron coffin, and commemorated by an iron obelisk. He evidently helped to get things moving, and the youthful Abraham Darby, the leading Coalbrookdale iron magnate, was drawn in. Other prominent supporters included Wilkinson's partner Edward Blakeway, afterwards one of the founders of the Coalport china factory, and two of the Guest dynasty who later founded the famous Dowlais ironworks at Merthyr Tydfil in south Wales.

After some false starts, the Darby works began casting the ribs and deck members of the bridge in 1777. The main ribs weighed 5.6 U.S. tons (5.1 metric tons) apiece. The design was apparently by Pritchard, who died later that year, but the bridge probably owed as much or more to the skill and experience of Darby and his men. The bridge was prefabricated and then fitted together like a piece of carpentry, with interlocking joints and wedges, not bolted together. It was erected over a period of several months in 1779 without interrupting the busy traffic of barges on the river. The road approaches still had to be completed and the deck surfaced, and the bridge was finally opened to traffic on New Year's Day in 1781.

The bridge has an elegant single span of

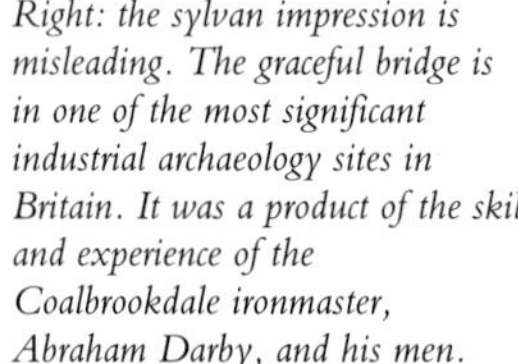

Right: the sylvan impression is misleading. The graceful bridge is in one of the most significant industrial archaeology sites in Britain. It was a product of the skill and experience of the Coalbrookdale ironmaster, Abraham Darby, and his men.

Facing page: the prefabricated bridge was put in place over several months in 1779 without disturbing the barge traffic on the River Severn.

100½ feet (30.6 m) and weighs just over 423 U.S. tons (384 metric tons). It aroused lively interest and curiosity in its own time, as it still does. People came to look at it, artists painted it, and it was as powerful an advertizement for the ironmasters and their new technology as they no doubt intended it to be.

A weekly market sprang up at the northern end of the bridge and has flourished there on Fridays ever since. A small town developed, called Ironbridge. In 1795 the fact that the bridge survived a fearsome flood on the Severn unharmed, while every stone bridge on the river was damaged, made a strong impression, and the Coalbrookdale works began to get more orders for iron bridges.

The bridge was restored in the 1970s and is today the centerpiece of the Ironbridge Gorge complex of museums, which is a World Heritage Site. The complex includes the Coalbrookdale Museum of Iron, a china museum in the old Coalport factory, a decorative tile museum in the former Craven Dunnill factory, and a recreated 1890s industrial township at Blists Hill. Points of interest include the furnace where Abraham Darby I smelted iron with coke, later rebuilt and used to cast the Iron Bridge members, and the Hay Inclined Plane on the Shropshire Canal, used to transfer boats to different levels.

Nursery of Industry

COALBROOKDALE was an industrial center long before the Iron Bridge spanned the Severn. There was a bloomery furnace here in the 16th century or earlier, producing pieces of wrought iron ("blooms"). In 1708 a Quaker manufacturer of iron cooking pots named Abraham Darby leased a furnace in Coalbrookdale, and in the following year succeeded in smelting iron using coke for fuel in place of charcoal. This was a major innovation in the industry that would make the Darby family's fortune. The original furnace itself can be seen at Coalbrookdale today in the Museum of Iron.

Abraham Darby died in 1717, leaving as his heir a six-year-old boy, Abraham Darby II. When he took over, the son expanded the business. Early phases of the development of railroads occurred at Coalbrookdale in his time, with the making of the first iron rails and trucks. When he died in 1763 he was succeeded by his son, Abraham Darby III, a teenager, who was later to build the Iron Bridge. He died young in 1789, aged only 39.

In 1802 the great engineer Richard Trevithick, who had close connections with the Darby family, built the world's first steam locomotive at the Coalbrookdale works. Under Abraham Darby IV, the last Quaker of the dynasty, the works rolled the plates for the *Great Britain*, the world's first iron oceangoing ship. In 1851, as the largest foundry complex in Britain, it made the magnificent ornamental gates for the Great Exhibition of 1851 in London, which can still be seen in Kensington Gardens today.

AGE OF IRON

The Industrial Revolution brought with it iron bridges, iron railroads, iron buildings and the iron regime of factories.

THE first Iron Age began at some unknown but distant date in prehistory when human beings discovered how to make iron from iron ore in the ground and use it to manufacture weapons and implements that were superior to those made of bronze. For long centuries in Europe the ore was made into wrought iron in charcoal-fired furnaces, with bellows worked by human labor, animal power, or water power.

In France, somewhere about the year 1400, the introduction of the blast furnace made it possible to smelt the ore into cast iron in larger quantities. The bellows were usually driven by waterwheels. The molten metal was poured into molds that looked like a sow with her piglets, hence "pig iron." Ironworks could exist only where there was close at hand a supply of iron ore, timber to make charcoal from, and a stream to supply power.

NIGHT AND DAY

The second Iron Age began in England in 1709 when Abraham Darby devised a way of smelting iron with coke instead of charcoal. This gave the industry a new and more efficient source of fuel, but it still depended on fickle flows of water for power. The savior appeared in the form of steam.

The first successful steam engine was built by Thomas Newcomen, an ironmonger from Devonshire, and installed in 1712 at a coal mine in Dudley in the English Midlands, to pump water out of the levels. It mustered about 5½ horsepower. Bigger and better steam engines were rapidly developed, notably by James Watt, who invented one that could turn a shaft, and so drive machinery.

Meanwhile, the textile industry was being revolutionized by the invention of spinning and weaving machinery, which transformed what had been a craft carried out by skilled operatives working in their own homes into an unskilled drudgery carried out by men, women, and children working on production lines in mills. The age of the factory was dawning. In 1771 the pioneer textile tycoon and Lancashire ex-barber Richard Arkwright opened his cotton mill at Cromford in Derbyshire, where the spinning machines clattered and rattled all day and all night as the work force of women and children labored in 12-hour shifts six days a week.

Arkwright's mill was powered by waterwheels, but soon steam engines in mines, foundries, and factories were turning Britain into the world's workshop. If steam was the power that drove the Industrial Revolution, its key metals were iron and its derivative, steel. Powerful iron locomotives driven by steam thundered, whistling and screaming, across country on vibrating iron rails, as the railroads introduced unprecedented speed of communication, trade, and delivery of factory-made, mass-produced products. The greatest of the railroad engineers, Isambard Kingdom Brunel, decided to extend his London-to-Bristol rail line on to New York by constructing an oceangoing, steam-driven iron ship of unheard-of speed and carrying capacity. He built the *SS Great Britain* in a Bristol dock, where she can be seen again today. Brunel went on to design more iron ocean greyhounds of ever more grandiose dimensions.

Engineers usurped the functions of architects in the 19th century as designers of a whole category of important constructions: factories, warehouses, docks, railroads – all of which employed iron. Iron bridges leaped over previously uncrossable gulfs. Iron vaults of previously impossible spans roofed over train stations. In 1851 the largest building the world had ever seen, the Crystal Palace erected for the Great Exhibition in London, was constructed of prefabricated sections of iron and glass. Iron girders provided the skeletons of taller and taller constructions, as dramatically demonstrated by the Eiffel Tower in Paris.

AT HOME AND ABROAD

Domestic life was transformed too. Houses were equipped with iron kitchen stoves, pots and pans, fire grates, tables, hat stands, garden seats and ornaments, vases, letter boxes, boot scrapers, and window frames. The streets bristled with iron gates and railings, lampposts, mileposts, drinking fountains, horse troughs, and bollards. Iron gravestones sprouted in church-yards. Enameled iron advertising signs lauded products on the sides of houses and the walls of train stations.

The age of iron had begun to spread out from Britain well before 1850. By 1809 there were steam-powered factories in the Ruhr Valley in Germany, which would become one of the major industrial areas of the world. Industrialization followed in the coalfield areas of France and Belgium, and along the eastern seaboard of the United States of America. Steam railroads invaded the Continent, and steamships ploughed the oceans of the world. In 1869 the first transcontinental railroad in North America was completed with the junction of the Union Pacific line from the east and the Central Pacific line from California. A new phase of the Industrial Revolution was about to open, based on steel, chemicals, and electricity, with Germany and the United States in the lead.

Contemporary illustrations from the age of iron and steam.
Facing page: the Butterley Ironworks.
Above: a paddlewheeler driven partly by steam and partly by sail.
Below: belching smoke, an early steam locomotive draws its freight on iron rails through the Primrose Hill Tunnel.

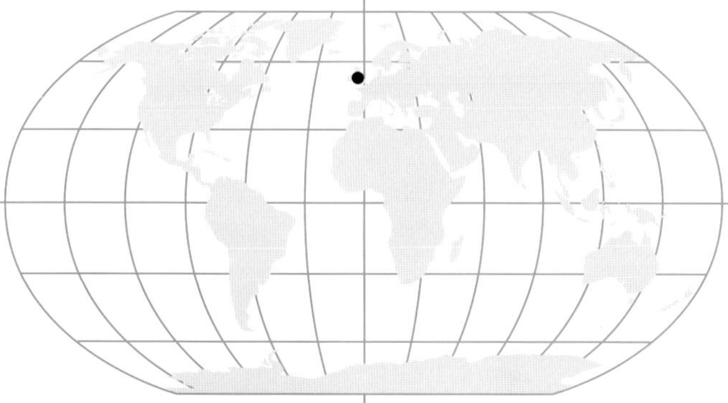

1805 Wales

PONT CYSYLLTE AQUEDUCT

"It is awe-inspiring nowadays to cross the aqueduct; in 1805 when it was first opened, it must have seemed miraculous." – L. T. C. Rolt

The aqueduct is just north of the A5 road between Llangollen and Chirk, at Froncysyllte, $3^1/_2$ miles (5.6 km) east of Llangollen. The Shropshire Union Canal is still in use for pleasure boating, and there are boat trips across the aqueduct for parties from Llangollen. Those with a good head for heights can walk across it on the towpath.

On November 26, 1805, thousands of spectators gathered in the romantically beautiful Vale of Llangollen to witness the ceremonial opening of what was already regarded as one of the Wonders of Wales, the great aqueduct carrying the Ellesmere Canal high above and across the River Dee on 19 graceful stone arches. Cheers welled up as a procession of boats moved in stately fashion across the sky. In one of them the band of the Shropshire Volunteers played vigorously. The others were occupied by canal company directors and managers, engineers, and their families. A detachment of artillery fired an echoing salute of 15 rounds. Later, as the procession turned and recrossed the aqueduct,

The Ladies of Llangollen

The small town of Llangollen clusters around a medieval bridge over the Dee that was one of the seven traditional Wonders of Wales. Since 1947 the town has played host in July every year to the International Musical Eisteddfod (not to be confused with the major Welsh cultural festival, the National Eisteddfod), which attracts folk singers, choirs, and dancers from all over the world.

On the southern outskirts of the town is the glitteringly ornate black-and-white half-timbered mansion called Plas Newydd, which early in the

Right: the graceful aqueduct across the Dee carrying the canal boats over the valley. To reduce their weight, the arches are hollow inside, from just over halfway up.

Facing page, above: looking along the aqueduct. Boats still use it and you can walk across on the towpath.

Facing page, below: the black-and-white face of Plas Newydd.

the guns boomed out once more.

The ceremony formally inaugurated what is now generally considered the greatest monument of the Canal Age. The Ellesmere Canal (now called the Shropshire Union Canal) was proposed early in the 1790s to link the River Severn at Shrewsbury with the Dee at Chester and the Mersey at Ellesmere Port. In 1793 a 36-year-old Scottish engineer named Thomas Telford was put in charge of it, with strong support from the leading ironmaster, John Wilkinson.

By far the most difficult problem was to carry the canal across the deep valley of the Dee outside Llangollen. Telford boldly hurled the waterway over the valley in a cast-iron trough, 1,000 feet (305 m) long and 127 feet (38 m) above the river, supported on stone arches. Sir Walter Scott called the aqueduct the greatest work of art he had ever seen. To this day it remains a breathtaking spectacle, and it is a hair-raising experience to cross it in a boat (not recommended to anyone with a fear of heights), for it is still in use.

The canal company, startled almost out of its wits by the prospect of its narrowboats trundling through the sky 120 feet (36 m) up, gritted its teeth and approved. The total length of the aqueduct as built is 1,007 feet (307 m). The iron trough in which the boats move is 11 feet 10 inches (3.6 m) wide, but this width is reduced by an iron towpath, 4 feet 8 inches (1.4 m) wide, set above the trough on one side and supported on brackets and columns. The stone piers of the aqueduct each span 53 feet (16.2 m) and are hollow inside from 70 feet (21 m) up. The canal approaches the aqueduct from the south on a massive embankment of earth, rising to 97 feet (30 m) high, the biggest built in Britain up to that time and a major engineering feat in itself. The canal also negotiates two tunnels and another aqueduct, across the River Ceiriog at Chirk, before reaching the crossing of the Dee.

The Chirk aqueduct, which can be seen from the A5 road, has 10 spans of 40 feet (12 m) each and is 70 feet (21 m) above the river. The ironwork for both aqueducts was carried out with rigorous efficiency by Telford's friend and fellow Freemason, William Hazeldine, at his local works.

The Pont Cysyllte aqueduct deservedly made Telford's reputation. He went on to works on a still grander scale – the construction of the Caledonian Canal in Scotland and the world's first major suspension bridge, across the Menai Strait in Wales.

19th century was the home of the celebrated Ladies of Llangollen, Lady Eleanor Butler and Sarah Ponsonby. These aristocratic bluestockings had run away from their homes to set up house together. Many famous people of the time, including Wordsworth, Sir Walter Scott, and the Duke of Wellington, visited them and brought respectful offerings for their curio collection, especially pieces of carved oak, which the ladies particularly liked. The remarkable heavy carved paneling in the house today was installed by a later owner.

From the grounds there is a fine view of the Hill of Bran, north of the town. Sticking up from it, fanglike, are the ruins of Castell Dinas Bran, a medieval stronghold on the site of a hill fort going back to Celtic times.

1824-1828 England

WINDSOR CASTLE

"The most romantic castle in the world."
– SAMUEL PEPYS

Windsor is 21 miles (34 km) west of London, off the M4 highway, which commands an impressive view of the castle in the distance. Green Line buses from London, trains from Paddington and Waterloo.

Windsor and the Garter

WINDSOR Castle has been the focus of the Order of the Garter, the senior English order of chivalry, ever since the Garter was founded. In June every year the knights assemble at Windsor for a special service in St. George's Chapel. In their dark blue velvet robes and white-plumed hats, they walk in solemn procession with the queen and other members of the royal family, accompanied by heralds in a golden and scarlet splendor of blazonry.

The ceremony has 650 years of history behind it. The order was founded in 1348 by King Edward III, who had earlier toyed with the idea of creating a new Order of the Round Table in emulation of the legendary King Arthur. The garter was "a symbol of amity," and the new order was to uphold the highest ideals of chivalry. The king himself was a member, and so was his son,

Above right: the castle seen from the spacious grounds of Windsor Great Park, with the Round Tower to the left. The architect, Jeffry Wyattville, was knighted in 1828 and was granted residence in Windsor Castle for life.

Facing page: on sentry duty is a smartly uniformed guardsman.

WINDSOR Castle has been the principal country residence of the monarchs of England for nearly nine centuries. Rising majestically above the River Thames in a formidable panoply of towers and battlements, turrets and machicolations, it owes its appearance today principally to Sir Jeffry Wyattville, the architect who reconstructed the castle for King George IV in the 1820s. The intention, which was successfully achieved, was to create an overwhelming impression of medieval royal splendor. No major alterations have been made since.

George IV's secondary intention was to secure himself greater privacy. In his father George III's time, people wandered about the place more or less at will, gaping at the royal family, strolling on the terraces, and flying kites in the park.

The castle's history goes back to the 11th century and William the Conqueror, who built a wooden fortress on the site, on a ridge above the Thames, to control what was then the main route into London from the west. In the following century the castle was rebuilt in stone. It was reconstructed in the 13th century, and again in the 14th, by King Edward III, who was born here. In the 17th century yet another overhaul was carried out for Charles II.

The basic plan of the castle has survived all these rebuildings. At the center is the circular keep, the Round Tower, which Wyattville heightened. On either side is a "ward" or courtyard, with the whole surrounded by a defensive wall. The eastern courtyard is called the Upper Ward, the western one the Lower Ward. The private apartments of the present monarch, Queen Elizabeth II, are on the eastern side of Upper Ward; these are not open to visitors.

On the northern side are the state apartments, which are open when the queen is not officially in residence. Used for entertaining and impressing distinguished guests, they contain notable paintings, furniture, and treasures, which include Henry VIII's armor and the bullet that killed Nelson. The impressive main staircase was built for Queen Victoria in 1866 and is dominated by a statue of George IV by Sir Francis Chantrey. Most of

the rooms were designed by Wyattville for George IV, but three rooms, designed for Charles II, have also survived.

Near the entrance to the state apartments is the famous dollhouse designed by Sir Edwin Lutyens and presented to Queen Mary in 1923. It has 40 rooms, running hot and cold water in five bathrooms, working elevators, and electric lights. The house was furnished and decorated by leading craftspeople of the day.

The principal building in the Lower Ward is St. George's Chapel, where the banners of the Knights of the Garter hang above their stalls in the choir. Many kings are buried here, including Henry VIII, Charles I, and George IV. Lutyens designed the tomb of George V and Queen Mary.

The Albert Memorial Chapel was converted by Queen Victoria into a monument to her beloved husband, the Prince Consort, who died at Windsor in 1861. It contains the amazingly elaborate tomb by Sir Alfred Gilbert of the Duke of Clarence, who died in 1892. Queen Victoria and Prince Albert themselves are buried in the beautiful Royal Mausoleum in the grounds.

the redoubtable Black Prince.

The order's heavenly patron was St. George, and its chapel was the one already built in the castle in the previous century. The chapel acquired famous relics, including St. George's heart and a piece of the True Cross, which pilgrims came to venerate. Between 1475 and 1528 it was rebuilt like a miniature cathedral in a soaring loveliness of late Gothic. Each knight has his stall in the choir, where hang his helmet and crest, sword and banner.

1869-1886 Germany

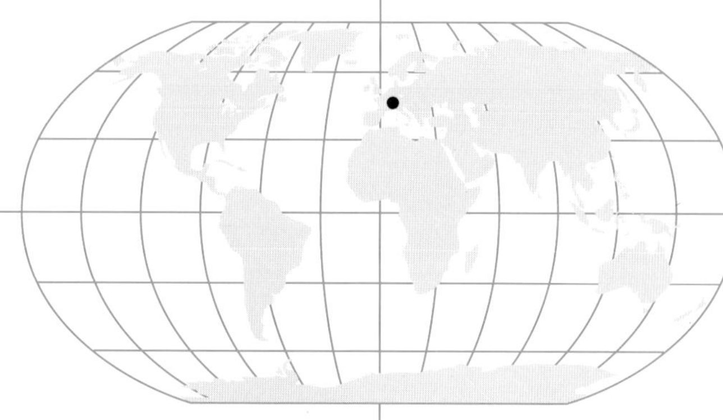

NEUSCHWANSTEIN CASTLE

A stage designer's dream castle brought to life at the whim of a king.

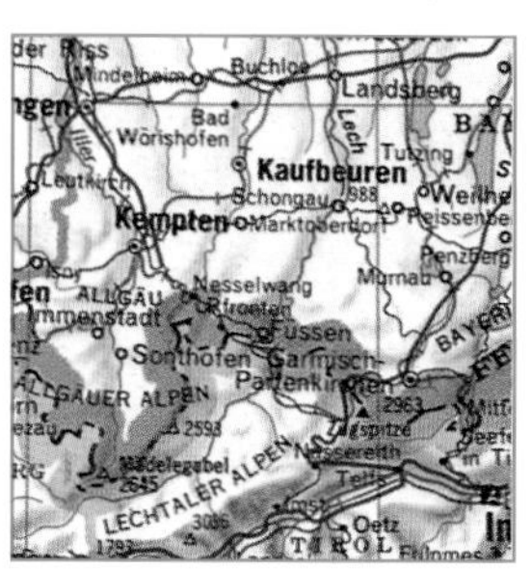

The castles of Neuschwanstein and Hohenschwangau are in the Bavarian Alps near the town of Füssen and close to the Austrian border. The "Romantische Strasse" from Füssen to Wurzburg passes close to both castles. Cars can be left at Hohenschwangau, but the approach to Neuschwanstein is on foot. A walk of about a mile (1.5 km) is involved.

NEUSCHWANSTEIN is fantasy made real – a fairy-tale castle festooned with balconies and turrets, rising high above the trees in the Bavarian Alps. Vast and substantial, it took 17 years to build. It is also utterly improbable, a piece of stage design (the work of a leading Munich scene painter called Christian Jank) invented by King Ludwig II of Bavaria as a backdrop against which he might act out the stuff of German romantic legend.

Ludwig had grown up in the nearby castle of Hohenschwangau, a medieval fortress restored by his father, Maximilian II, and decorated with wall paintings depicting, among other subjects, the Lohengrin legend. He appears to have identified with Lohengrin, the Knight of the Swan, and he developed an obsession with German mythology. A performance of Wagner's opera *Lohengrin* in 1861 left him enchanted, and when he succeeded to the throne three years later at the age of 18, one of his first acts was to summon Wagner for an audience. Now, with money at his disposal and all the power of a king, he became Wagner's patron, paid his debts, and promised to endow the theater and festival that the composer yearned for. Wagner would create German legend on stage on a grand scale and enact struggles between good and evil in front of an audience. Meanwhile, Ludwig would create a fantastic castle worthy in every way of the ancient German knights.

This sort of thing was of limited appeal in Germany at the end of the 19th century. Ludwig was called the Mad King and seen as a man with no grasp of reality. Despite his love of dressing up and a curious lifestyle (sleeping all day, and reputedly entertaining the ghost of Louis XIV at the dinner table), Bismarck credited him, in his youth, with being clear-headed – although towards the end of his life his madness was not in doubt.

Fifteen men are said to have worked for four and a half years just carving the king's bed. The interior of the castle is a riot of different architectural styles, a Moorish-Gothic-baroque

Right: outrageously and operatically romantic, Ludwig II of Bavaria's fairyland stronghold rises among the snowy peaks of the Alps like a dream of the Middle Ages.

Facing page: Ludwig's palace at Linderhof was another attempt to bring the world of German medieval legends to vivid life.

confection that incorporates stalactites, a throne room of outrageous Byzantine decadence, and a huge Singers' Hall elaborately lit and intended for Wagnerian performances.

Ludwig's taste for the medieval did not prevent him installing modern technology. The castle had an advanced heating system involving the circulation of warm air, and a kitchen in which there was hot and cold running water.

Despite his fairy-tale palace, the king failed to live happily ever after. In 1886, only three months after he had moved in, he was declared unfit to rule. He drowned himself almost immediately afterwards.

Linderhof

NEUSCHWANSTEIN was only one of Ludwig's extravagant palaces. Two others can be seen, and he had plans for many more. This palace near Oberammergau stands in a magnificent park equipped with a temple of Venus and a Moorish kiosk that Ludwig bought while visiting at the Paris Exhibition of 1867. Linderhof was built between 1869 and 1879, and here too the stage designer Jank was employed. Here in the kiosk the king had installed an outrageous peacock throne, and he is said even to have dined on peacock from time to time and to have requested supplies of the bird from the Shah of Persia. Most astonishing of all is the Linderhof Venusberg Grotto, an artificial cave complete with lake, stalagmites, and stalactites and decorated with a huge painting of a scene from *Tannhauser.* A swan-shaped boat floated on the lake, and a hefty singer, one Madame Scheffzky, is said to have overbalanced this in an attempt to provoke Ludwig into a chivalrous rescue attempt. He merely summoned a footman and saw to it that the woman did not sing for him again.

Herrenchiemsee

LUDWIG bought an island in Chiemsee Lake in 1873 with the idea of creating his own version of Versailles. He built a bigger and, to his mind, better Hall of Mirrors and a more sumptuous version of Louis XIV's Versailles bedroom, supposedly reserved for the use of that long-dead monarch. The gardens were in the French style too, but after seven years' work the money ran out and the palace was never completed.

1874-1919 France

SACRÉ-COEUR

This 19th-century church is forever associated with a 19th-century colony of writers and artists.

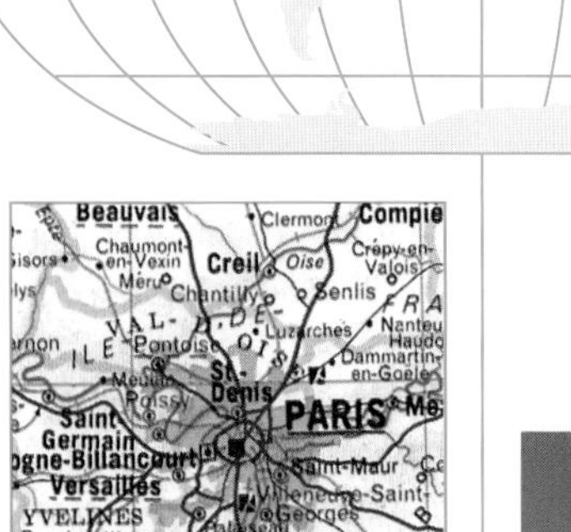

Sacré-Coeur is visible over a wide area of Paris. It lies north of the ring road formed by the Boulevard de Clichy and the Boulevard de Rochechouart and within walking distance of several Metro stations.

Montmartre

THE name Montmartre may be derived from Mons Martyrum – the Martyr's Mount – a reference to the belief that St. Denis, the first Bishop of Paris, died for his faith here in A.D. 270. More probably it comes from Mons Martis, after a Roman temple of Mars. Because of its relative height, the area was once used as a site for windmills, some of which later gave their names to famous music halls such as the Moulin de la Galette. Montmartre has long been celebrated for its night life and for the artists and writers who painted its streets and gathered in cafés such as the Lapin Agile. Utrillo is the artist particularly associated with the area. Van Gogh lived for a while on the Rue Lepic, and Toulouse-Lautrec painted the Moulin de la Galette. Picasso worked in a building known as le Bateau-Lavoir on the Place Emile-Goudeau, which became a center for avant-garde art and literature.

Above right: with its shining white dome and cupolas, the church reflects the influence of the Byzantine style.

Facing page: the church has been a magnet to pilgrims since the moment it was built, drawn by its dedication to the Sacred Heart of Jesus as a symbol of redemptive love.

SACRÉ-COEUR (the Church of the Sacred Heart) stands on the hill, or *Butte*, of Montmartre north of the center of Paris, but it was inspired by another church, the Cathedral of St. Front, far away to the southwest in Périgueux.

St. Front was an unusual Byzantine-style church built at the end of the 12th century, and with its five domes it bore some resemblance to St. Mark's in Venice. During the 19th century St. Front's was heavily restored, and one of the architects responsible for that restoration, Paul Abadie, kept that church in mind when he was appointed to build Sacré-Coeur in 1874. There are those who complain that Abadie ruined St. Front and produced a far from elegant building in Sacré-Coeur.

The project was undertaken with state support and was something of a symbolic gesture of renewed confidence after France's defeat in the Franco-Prussian War of 1870-71. The postwar uprising known as the Paris Commune, in which the Archbishop of Paris was killed, had its origins in Montmartre, so the building of the church also marked the suppression of this movement. The church was built, with the approval of the Roman Catholic hierarchy, as a symbol of national repentance.

Stone for the new basilica came from Château-Landon, south of Paris, and this gives the building its characteristic white sheen. Progress was slow at first. Old quarries beneath the site, from which gypsum had been extracted to make plaster of paris, complicated the construction of the foundations. The building was being used for worship by 1891, but it was not finally completed until 1919.

The large dome, rather more Oriental than European in appearance, is about 260 feet (79 m) high, and visitors can climb to the top for a spectacular view of Paris and of the interior of the church. The campanile, towering a further hundred feet (30 m) or so above the dome, houses one of the world's largest bells, 10 feet (3 m) high and weighing 21.3 U.S. tons (19.3 metric tons). The gift of the province of Savoy in 1895, it is known as the Savoyarde.

The interior of the church has much decorative mosaic work, but the original stained glass was destroyed during the Second World War. The mosaics above the chancel are on the theme of devotion to the Sacred Heart. The monumental façade, approached by flights of steps, was designed to display sculptures of Christ and the woman of Samaria, and of Mary at the house of Simon. The crypt, extending beneath the whole church, is open to visitors and serves as an exhibition space for religious art.

The terrace outside the church, at the top of the steps, commands an excellent view. Descending steeply from there are the flights of steps and narrow streets of the Butte. Of the medieval abbey of Montmartre, all that is left is the Church of St. Pierre. Restored in the 19th century, it has a romantic churchyard. The Place du Tertre is the "village square" of Montmartre, with some pleasant 18th-century houses. The Montmartre Museum on the Rue de Cortot has a store of pictures, photographs, relics, and memories of the Bohemian life of the area, with its artists, musicians, and writers, its cafés and nightclubs. But Sacré-Coeur remains the crowning glory of present-day Montmartre.

Museums

THE Montmartre Museum, on the Rue St. Vincent, and the wax museum known as the Historial, on the Rue Poulbot, help to recreate the history of the area. There is also a Museum of Jewish Art on the Rue des Saules and a Gustave Moreau Museum on the Rue de la Rochefoucauld.

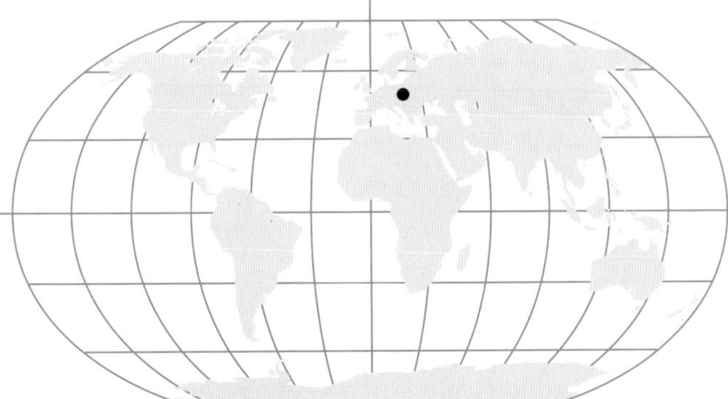

1884-1902 Hungary

PARLIAMENT BUILDING

A massive statement of Hungarian national identity and pride gazes majestically across the Danube.

The Parliament Building is in Pest, on the eastern side of the Danube River opposite Buda, the other half of the Hungarian capital of Budapest. There are regular guided tours. Nearest Metro station Kossuth Ter.

Right: the mighty dome rears up, floodlit, into the night sky. The architect, Imre Steindl, was a specialist in the restoration of historic buildings and a pupil of the Austrian church architect Friedrich Schmitt, a craftsman in Gothic.

Facing page: one of the largest legislative buildings in the world is an expression of Hungarian nationalism.

IN 1867, after centuries as part of the empire of the Hapsburgs, the ancient kingdom of Hungary was recognized as an independent state in its own right, though it continued to have the same sovereign as Austria in the person of Emperor Franz Josef, who was crowned king of Hungary in Budapest that year. The new state of Hungary had a separate parliament, and in 1880 permission was granted to construct a new home for it in Budapest. Under the architect Imre Steindl, work began in 1884 and by 1896 was sufficiently advanced for the building to be used in the celebration of a thousand years since the Magyar conquest of Hungary. It was finally completed in 1902.

Reaching high above the Danube, the Parliament Building is an edifice of tremendous size and grandeur, and one of the most imposing exercises in 19th-century Gothic in the world. The building expresses the high ambitions for the newly independent kingdom, nationalistic pride in its heroic Christian past, and the cosmopolitanism of its capital. At the same time, it testifies to the wealth created by Hungary's industrial boom at that time.

Resplendently towered and pinnacled, the building rises to a colossal dome between two tall Gothic towers. The dome is exactly 96 meters (315 ft.) high, a deliberate allusion to the Magyar conquest in the year 896. The building is approximately 880 feet (268 m) long and 380 feet (116 m) wide, and inside are 10 courtyards, 29 staircases and hundreds of rooms.

The major theme is Hungarian national identity. The exterior is adorned with statues of Hungarian rulers, princes of Transylvania, and famous warriors of yore, and above the windows are the coats of arms of kings and princes. In front of the building is an equestrian statue of Ferenc Rakoczi II, the Transylvanian prince who led a rebellion against the Hapsburgs early in the 18th century. At the northern end is a group of figures centered around a statue of Lajos Kossuth, who led the revolution of 1848 against Hapsburg authority and was briefly regent of Hungary.

At the center of the building is a huge 16-sided hall under the dome. To either side is a grand hall for the two houses of the Hungarian parliament: the upper house (which was abolished in 1945) to the north, the lower house (now the National Assembly) to the south. The main entrance is in the center of the eastern façade, with steps leading up to it between bronze lions.

Inside, beneath ceiling frescoes, the grand staircase rises. There is a bust of the architect, Imre Steindl, off the first landing. A circular corridor surrounds the central hall, in which there are more statues of important figures in Hungarian history. Among them are Arpad, the leader of the Magyar horsemen who overran Hungary at the end of the 9th century and afterwards conquered Transylvania; St. Stephen, who as King Stephen I established the Hungarian kingdom and presided over the conversion to Christianity; and the famous soldier Janos Hunyadi, who routed the Turks at Belgrade in 1456. This great room, intended for official receptions and occasions of state, sums up the spirit of the building.

Buda and Pest

BUDA and Pest were originally two separate towns on opposite banks of the Danube. They formally merged in 1872 as a single city, which until the Communist takeover after the Second World War had a reputation for Parisian smartness, elegance, and charm. There is a fine view of the city from Castle Hill in Buda, which can be reached by cable car. Among enjoyable and interesting things for the visitor to see are the restored royal palace, residence of the viceroys of the Hapsburgs and of Admiral Horthy between the First and Second World Wars; the restored and much-loved Chain Bridge across the Danube, a symbol of the city, originally opened in 1849; the 19th-century St. Stephen's Church whose dome is, again, exactly 96 meters (315 ft.) high; the old Jewish quarter in Pest, with its museum; and the National History Museum.

Oh Danube So Brown

THE Danube River is not blue, whatever the famous waltz may say, but muddy brown. The second longest river in Europe (only the Volga is longer), it flows for a total of 1,775 miles (2,857 km) from the mountains of the Black Forest in Germany by way of Vienna, Budapest, and Belgrade, through the Carpathian Mountains at the Iron Gates, and along the Bulgarian-Romanian frontier, and finally out through its sprawling delta to the Black Sea. The river has more than 300 tributaries, drains an area of well over 300,000 square miles (776,940 sq km), and has always been a major trade route between western and eastern Europe.

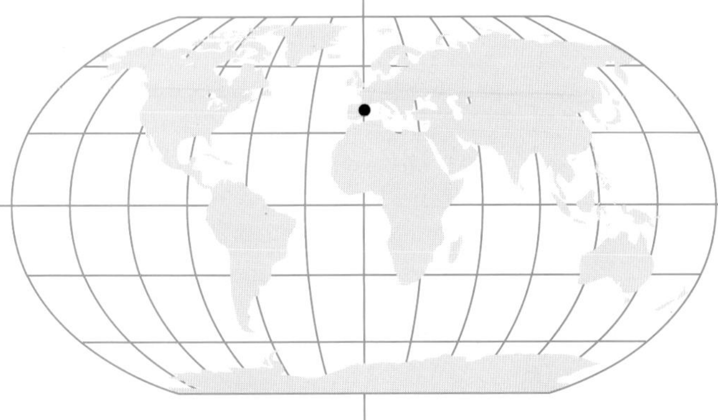

From 1884 Spain

THE SAGRADA FAMILIA

This far from traditional building was intended to inspire a return to the orthodox teachings of the Roman Catholic Church.

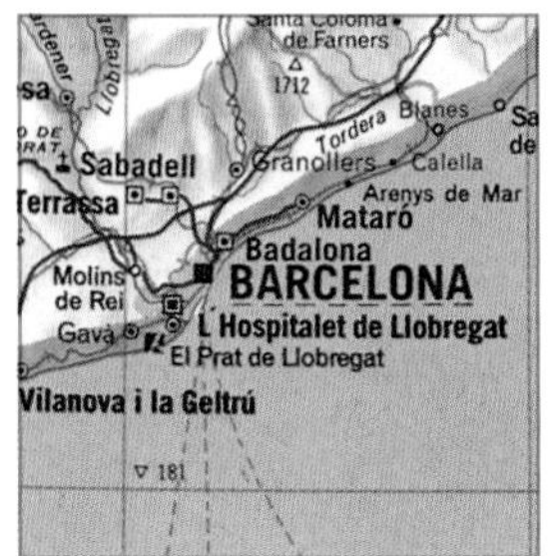

North of the center of Barcelona, at the intersection of the Paseo del Emperador and the Calle de Mallorca.

WORK on the Sagrada Familia basilica (the Church of the Holy Family) began in 1884, and it continues to this day. Intended as a symbol of the living Roman Catholic faith, the church was to be the center of a complex of buildings, including schools and educational workshops. The unfinished building is known throughout the world as a major work of the architect Antoni Gaudí.

It is a building that can hardly fail to take the visitor by surprise. Huge and exuberant, its Nativity façade takes a familiar and conventional subject of Christian art and, with no sacrifice of respect or reverence, presents it in a thoroughly original, almost surreal setting. Gaudí's work reveals a certain amount of Moorish influence, and he is known to have been familiar with the Pre-Raphaelite movement and the writings of John Ruskin and William Morris. He has some affinities with Art Nouveau, but his was an unquestionably unique approach to architecture. He treated building as an organic process – stone takes on a living form, and decoration grows out of it in the way that a plant might grow. He made rough sketches rather than accurate plans of the projects on which he worked, and he preferred to be on site, watching something take shape and altering it at will rather than leaving others to execute a specific design.

This method of work explains why the Sagrada Familia remains incomplete. Gaudí took over the project in 1891 at a very early stage and devoted enormous energy to it, rejecting all other commissions after 1914. When he died, run over by a tram in 1926, it was impossible for anyone else to continue building in the way that he would have done.

It is known that Gaudí intended the church to have three monumental façades, depicting the Nativity, the Passion, and the Resurrection, and that each was to have four huge towers of the type that were completed above the Nativity façade in the 1950s. The architect was a perfectionist; for his representation of the Flight into Egypt, for example, he is said to have found a working donkey and, with the owner's permission, to have made plaster casts of this animal because its weary appearance was exactly the image he wanted for his sculpture. It is unlikely that the church would have remained the color of the original stone if Gaudí had lived to complete it. He was inspired by the colors as well as the forms of natural things, and much of his work displays a riotous use of different tones, textures, and surfaces.

The architect was an accomplished artist and craftsman. He designed furniture and fashioned iron gates and railings that astonish the eye. Among his buildings in Barcelona, the Casa Batllo and Casa Mila – both containing private apartments – are particularly striking.

There have been arguments about the wisdom of attempting to complete Gaudí's work – some say that it is like adding arms to the *Venus de Milo*, or that the concept should have been abandoned, or the Nativity façade turned into an altarpiece in its own right. But an entirely new Passion façade has now been built, obscuring some of Gaudí's original design. On the other hand, the remarkable vision of the architect is all the more striking when seen in conjunction with subsequent attempts to complete the building.

Guell Park

EUSEBIO Guell, Gaudí's patron and a rich industrialist, wanted the architect to build a whole suburb northwest of downtown Barcelona. The plan was never completed, but Gaudí did create a remarkable park in an area that had been without water or plants. Here it is possible to see what Gaudí could achieve by reusing ceramic tiles. A huge curving bench is decorated with colorful mosaic work, and a great dragon – looking more friendly than menacing and also created out of colored tiles – clutches playfully at a wall near the entrance. The park also contains two very unusual entrance pavilions with mosaic-tiled roofs and a central square supported on columns that represent his idiosyncratic version of Doric style.

Above right: Gaudí delighted in color and lively ornament, as can be seen from this lively dragon in Guell Park.

Facing page: though Gaudí was conventional in his religion, he was wildly surrealistic in the way he expressed it in the Sagrada Familia cathedral.

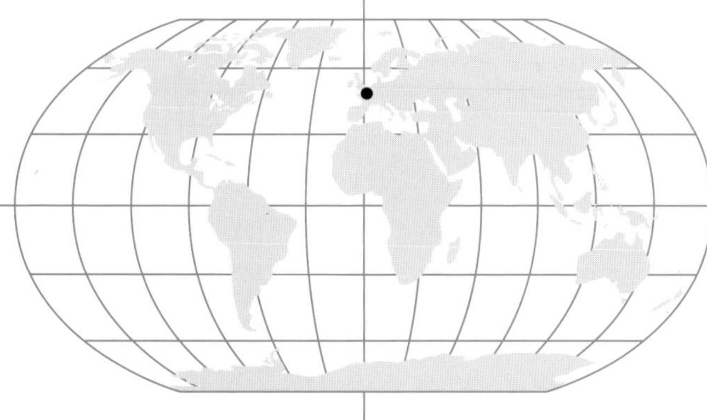

1889 France

THE EIFFEL TOWER

A daring display of 19th-century engineering skill which became the symbol of Paris throughout the world.

The Eiffel Tower stands by the Seine River, opposite the Trocadero Palace, by the Pont d'Iéna. It is visible far and wide throughout the city of Paris.

Uses of the Tower

GUSTAVE Eiffel was a serious scientist who recoiled from the idea that his tower was a mere ornament. He installed meteorological equipment at the top in order to investigate weather conditions at altitude and compare readings with those taken on the ground. He also used the tower to conduct experiments in aerodynamics and constructed a wind tunnel at the base. Pioneering work in radio transmission was done in the tower, and it housed the country's first radio and TV stations.

Protests

WHEN the Eiffel Tower began to rise, a group of writers and artists signed a letter protesting about the effect that it would have on the Paris skyline and claiming that it was an insult to the city's great buildings. Some later came to appreciate the tower, but the author Guy de Maupassant is said to have frequented one of the platform restaurants because

Right: the tower is brightly lit at night. Eiffel had earlier designed the framework for the Statue of Liberty.

Facing page: Eiffel first made his name building iron bridges.

FOR a hundred years the Eiffel Tower has been synonymous with Paris, an instantly recognizable silhouette known throughout the world. It can also be seen as a symbol of the industrial age, a daring demonstration of the heights to which man could aspire given the knowledge and engineering skills of the late 19th century.

As new building techniques were developed and the pace of change accelerated, various people in various lands formed the ambition to build something a thousand feet (305 m) high. Some tried and failed; most people would have regarded the notion as absurd. But in France, the engineer Gustave Eiffel believed that he could do it. Eiffel and Company produced plans for a "300-meter tower" at the end of 1884, and these were largely the work of Eiffel's head of research, Maurice Koechlin. In 1886 a competition was announced for design schemes for the 1889 Paris Exposition, which was to be a grand exhibition of industrial progress. The organizing committee expressed the wish that those who tendered would include plans for an iron tower 1,000 feet tall. It appears that the rules of the competition may have been written with Eiffel's tower in mind. Over a hundred schemes were submitted, but it was Eiffel who was chosen to create the world's tallest structure – in little more than two years.

The base of the Eiffel Tower forms a square enclosing an area of 4 acres (1.6 hectares). The entire structure weighs about 11,760 U.S. tons (10,668 metric tons), and $2^1/_2$ million rivets are said to have been used in the construction. Over 18,000 separate components were used, many of them prefabricated and produced with the aid of precise technical drawings. The tallest tower in the world was built by a team of some 250 men at a speed that was considered phenomenal.

Eiffel had built a number of railroad bridges and had a reputation for solving the most technically challenging problems. The speed of construction of the tower was possible only because of his ability to plan ahead and do so with the utmost precision. The 16 piers on which the tower stands (four to each leg of the base) incorporated hydraulic jacks to allow for exact alignment when the first platform came to be built. Only very minor adjustment was necessary, but without this facility it might never have been possible to complete the building.

Later this first platform housed a restaurant, and during the 1889 Exposition, it became *the* place to eat. The newspaper *Le Figaro* had its own office on the second platform, at a height of 380 feet (116 m).

The tower was built in 26 months, and it held the title of tallest building in the world until the construction of the Chrysler Building in New York City in 1929. Two million people visited it during the Exposition, traveling to the first, second, and third platforms by elevator. There are also steps to the very top, a total of 1,671. Proclaimed a historic monument in 1964, the Eiffel Tower attracts some 3 million visitors a year, unfailingly fascinating generation after generation.

it was the only place in Paris from which he did not have a view of the thing. At one point, building work was halted because of the fears of local residents that their lives and property were in danger: a mathematician had claimed that the whole structure would collapse before it reached 750 feet (229 m). Eiffel, who was already bearing the majority of the cost of the project, agreed to continue entirely at his own risk.

1891-1905 USSR

TRANS-SIBERIAN RAILWAY

The longest train journey in the world straddles the continents of Europe and Asia.

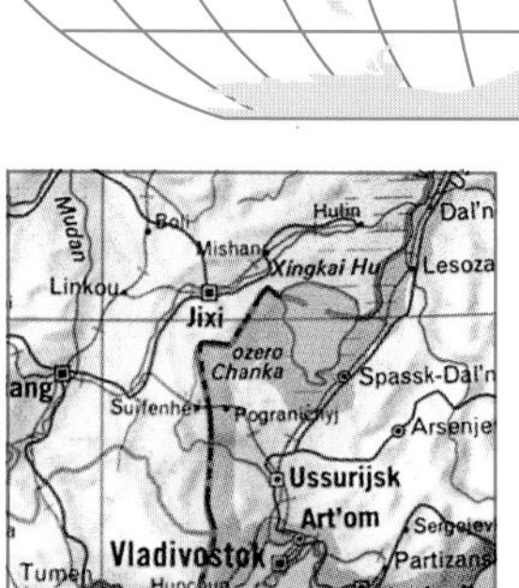

The Trans-Siberian expresses leave Moscow from Yarolslavl Station, a remarkable Art Nouveau edifice of 1904 designed by Fedor Shekhtel, like an entrance to fairyland with a weird, steeply pitched roof. At the other end, foreign visitors were not allowed into Vladivostok – until recently, at least – and had to end (or start) their journeys at Nakhodka, 50 miles (80 km) farther north.

TRAVELING in the Soviet Union in the 1960s, the distinguished writer Laurens van der Post remarked that railroads were increasingly dishonored everywhere in the world except in the Soviet Union and Japan. There they remained "not only a vital means of transport, but also a thing of wonder in the popular imagination."

That the Great Siberian Railway, as the Trans-Siberian is known in the Soviet Union, should be considered a thing of wonder is hardly surprising. By far the longest line in the world on which a regular service operates, it was built between 1891 and 1905. The single track ran a distance of 4,608 miles (7,416 km) between Moscow and Vladivostok on the Sea of Japan. A second track was added later.

Work began simultaneously at both the Moscow and the Vladivostok ends. The western arm reached Irkutsk in 1898. At this point passengers had to be ferried the 40 miles (65 km) across Lake Baikal – frozen during the long Siberian winter – in a 4,704-U.S.-ton (4,267-metric-ton) icebreaker, which was built in England and transported to Siberia in sections. The rail line was subsequently constructed around the southern end of the lake to cut out the ferry passage. A journey that, a hundred years ago, would have taken three months in a horse-drawn carriage had been reduced to two weeks, later to one week.

A new eastern section, 2,250 miles (3,621 km) long, has been completed from Taishet to Komsomolsk. For strategic reasons this runs well to the north of the original Trans-Siberian line and much farther away from the border with China.

Above: the trains for Siberia leave Moscow from the Yaroslavl Station, a splendid edifice of 1904 with a towering gateway emblematic of the riches and mysterious wonders of the far-off "Sleeping Land."

Right: the line was originally built as a single track, but has since been widened and electrified.

Facing page: the Baikal Express and the Peking Express stand side by side in Siberia. The modern engines lack the endearing glamor of the old steam locomotives.

The timetable is in Moscow time, as are the clocks at the stations along the route, but the train passes through eight time zones, making the east coast seven hours ahead of Moscow time. The train crosses rivers and negotiates mountain ranges and vast, sweeping plains blanketed with snow in winter, passing lakes, cornfields, and villages, domed and spired churches, as well as towns that the railroad itself has largely created.

The line was built to an unusually broad gauge of 5 feet (1.5 m). In the early days there were separate carriages for Ladies, Clergy and Smokers. Most of the rolling stock today is of 1940s vintage, with sleeping cars and a dining car that is open all day; the latter doubles as a shop, used by people from the towns and villages on the route. Starting from Moscow, the train crosses the Volga River and then heads southeast to the Ural Mountains where, 1,100 miles (1,770 km) out from Moscow, it crosses from Europe into Asia. From Sverdlovsk, a major industrial town in the Urals, the line goes on to Omsk and

Novosibirsk, across the Ob River, busy with cargo boats and barges, to Krasnoyarsk on the Yenisey. Then to Irkutsk, past the high mountains south of Lake Baikal, over the edge of the Gobi Desert and beside the Shilka River to Khabarovsk and Vladivostok.

The Sleeping Land

THE Trans-Siberian was built primarily to allow exploitation of the gold and rich mineral resources of Siberia. It was constructed in part by the forced labor of political prisoners and was used from the beginning to transport criminals and enemies of the czarist regime into exile. Under Stalinism the Siberian *gulags*, or labor camps, became notorious. The railroad also made possible the substantial peasant migration to Siberia and the industrialization of this huge region of the earth, which covers close to five million square miles (12,949,000 sq km) and measures more than 4,000 miles (6,437 km) across from west to east and close to 2,000 miles (3,219 km) from north to south.

Siberia's name means "Sleeping Land" in the Tatar language, and it is full of wonders. Mammoths are preserved whole in ice. Tigers prowl the remoter areas, and wolves roam the steppes. Vast reserves of oil, coal, and iron lie beneath the surface of the land, and sinister monsters are believed to lurk in the depths of its lakes. As late as the 1940s, it is said, a previously completely unknown tribe of people was discovered by exploring geologists. There are seals in Lake Baikal, far inland in the middle of Asia, and no one knows how they got there. Siberian winters last seven or eight months, and temperatures almost down to -90°F (-68°C) have been recorded in the far north.

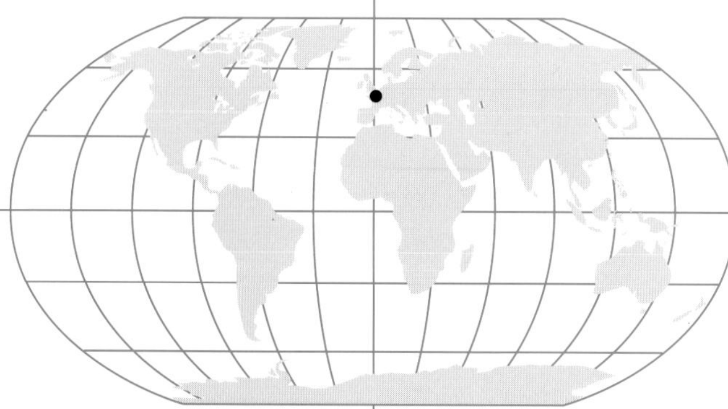

1977 France

THE POMPIDOU CENTER

The first and most famous example of high-tech architecture.

On the right bank of the Seine River, in the Beaubourg area of Paris, on the Rue du Renard. Rambuteau is the nearest Metro station.

The High-Tech Style

THE Pompidou Center has been criticized by those who consider the display of ducts and pipes on the outside as ugly and unnecessary. Some would argue that the building has nothing to do with architecture at all and that it is purely an example of engineering – a view that suggests that engineering is an inferior activity and one that has little to do with art. Ironically, the Pompidou Center is, in a sense, closer to the spirit of classical architecture than a modern pastiche of a Georgian building. Just as a Greek temple proudly

Above right: looking more like an oil refinery than the usual notion of an arts and culture complex, the building displays its structure for all to see, and has its pipes and cables on the outside to make for easier maintenance.

Facing page: at night, with the escalator snaking up the wall.

GALLERIES, museums, libraries, concert halls – such places have long been regarded as almost sacrosanct, holy temples of the Muses that could only be suitably housed in sturdy classical buildings. In Paris in the 1970s a new, multipurpose cultural center was built that swept away many of the old assumptions about the arts and marked an architectural turning point.

The Centre National d'Art et de Culture Georges Pompidou is not a building that is easy to forget. With its huge array of different-colored pipes traveling up the sides and an escalator snaking along the front, it has been likened to a factory or, more often, an oil refinery, but the appearance is not the result of a desire to be iconoclastic. Given the pace of change in modern technology, the architects

saw no point in burying heating ducts and water pipes, electrical cables and air-conditioning services under floors and within walls. Far better to take what amounted to the guts of the building and put them on the outside where they could be maintained and upgraded much more easily.

Some have condemned this approach as ugly. Others welcome it as a bold and brilliant idea, one that gives the interior of the building much more flexibility than would normally be the case. When the competition was announced for the design of a single building that would serve as a library, a modern art museum, a showplace for industrial design, and a musical research establishment, 681 different projects were submitted by architects from 49 different countries. The winners, Renzo Piano and Richard Rogers, were the ones deemed by the judges to have produced the most satisfactory means of reconciling these different activities.

The Pompidou Center, in the Beaubourg area of Paris, is often referred to simply as Beaubourg. The site was cleared in the 1930s and remained derelict land until 1971, when excavation for the winning scheme started. Today the center is noted not just for what goes on inside, but also for the jugglers, acrobats, fire eaters, and many other performers who entertain the crowds in the square outside. This area in front of the Pompidou Center was another inspired move by the winning architects: of all the schemes submitted, theirs was the only one that left half of the site free in order to create a new public open space in the center of Paris.

As well as providing Paris with a much-needed reference library and flexible exhibition space, the center has a movie theater and concert hall, an area for children, and bars and restaurants. When it first opened in 1977, it attracted 45,000 visitors a day and soon became the favorite attraction in Paris, even more popular than the Eiffel Tower. Although not built exactly as the architects intended (fire regulations and constraints of cost and time made some of the more ambitious ideas, such as movable floors, impractical), it has inspired a good many imitations. In 1977 it was described by the *Architectural Review* as reflecting "the supreme moment of technological euphoria in Western society." Today, by comparison, such euphoria appears to have run dry.

displayed the columns that held up the roof, so the Pompidou Center displays the metal skeleton from which it is suspended and refuses to conceal the service equipment that allows it to function. The divisions between architecture and engineering may have grown more blurred as technology has grown more complex, but, to take two examples from this book, the Pont du Gard and the Eiffel Tower both demonstrate that a skilled and logical approach to structural needs can result in buildings of elegance and artistic merit.

IRCAM

THE Institute for Research and Coordination in Acoustics and Music is a complex of advanced acoustic laboratories built entirely below ground as part of the Pompidou Center development. Designed to offer optimum conditions for acoustic research, it has a performance space open to the public, and it is possible to watch work going on by means of a special viewing window.

ASIA

Extending from the Mediterranean to the Pacific, Asia is the largest of the world's continents, covering about one-third of the land surface of the globe. The monuments of its past civilizations include what is probably the biggest construction job ever undertaken – the Great Wall of China.

The first steps on the road to civilization were taken in the Near East. Ten thousand years ago the human species consisted of small groups of hunter-gatherers who moved from place to place to find food. Then some of the nomads began to settle down in places where they lived partly by growing crops. One of the earliest sites so far discovered is ancient Jericho, whose inhabitants still lived in the Stone Age. They reaped their wheat and barley with stone sickles and ate out of stone bowls. The invention of writing was yet to come, but from this point on, development was rapid.

THE GREAT KINGS

Towns grew into cities, and cities into kingdoms and mighty empires. In Mesopotamia the Babylonian and then the Assyrian kings held sway. The Persian Empire was founded in the 6th century B.C. by Cyrus the Great, whose successors' realm stretched from the Mediterranean to the Indus River, embracing Egypt, modern Turkey, Mesopotamia, and modern Iran. The Great Kings of Persia ruled in a blazing splendor of marble, ivory, and gold, the better to overawe both their own subjects and foreign envoys. The audience chamber of Darius the Great at Persepolis was built to hold 10,000 people and the stairways were built on such a magnificent scale that they could be ascended by a rider on horseback.

Far to the east in the 3rd century B.C. in China, a new empire was established by Qin Shihuangdi, who founded a regime that would endure for more than 2,000 years. It is to him that we owe the Great Wall of China, and many thousands of his subjects their deaths. The famous army of terra-cotta warriors, discovered in 1974, was set to guard his tomb, which itself has not been opened, but which may well contain amazing treasures.

Above: the Great Kings of Persia ruled in breathtaking splendor at Persepolis.
Below: great palaces were also built for gods, as at the Meenakshi Temple in India.

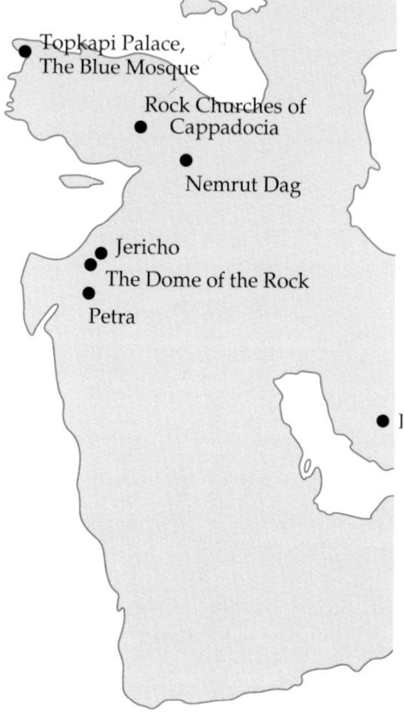

GODS ON EARTH

Religion has left its visible mark all across Asia, from the weird Christian rock churches of Turkey, like something dreamed up by Hieronymus Bosch, to the graceful Shinto shrines of Japan. In between are domed mosques, sky-piercing minarets and pagodas, Hindu and Buddhist temples replete with exuberant carvings and many-armed gods. Islam was on the march through Asia from the 7th century on, and its monuments range from the Dome of the Rock in Jerusalem to the seraglio of the Ottoman sultans in Istanbul and the beautiful Taj Mahal in Agra.

Buddhism grew up originally in India, but it virtually died out in its homeland. It had its greatest influence abroad, in Sri Lanka, Southeast Asia, Indonesia, China, and Japan, where at the popular level it blended with older native cults. The largest wooden building in the world was built at Nara in Japan to house an enormous image of the Buddha, but it is utterly dwarfed by the largest Buddhist temple in the world, which is Borobudur in Java. Hinduism, too, was exported from India to Southeast Asia and Indonesia, and not far away from Borobudur is an impressive temple to the Hindu god Shiva. The immense temple complex at Angkor Wat in Cambodia, built by the Khmer emperors, honored another Hindu god, Vishnu.

These colossal "temple-mountains" were attempts to realize in stone the legendary world mountain of Indian mythology, on which the whole universe rested. They were built by kings who regarded themselves as earthly incarnations of Indian deities. Similarly, the Dalai Lamas, the spiritual and political rulers of Tibet, holding sway from the vast Potala Palace at Lhasa, were believed to be successive incarnations on earth of Avalokitesvara, a great figure of Buddhist belief who was, in effect, the national god of

Trans-Siberian Railway
Vladivostock
The Great Wall,
The Forbidden City
Hall of the
Great Buddha
Itsukushima
Shrine
Seto Ohashi
Bridge
The Terra-cotta
Warriors
The Court House
Potala Palace
Persepolis
The Red Fort
The Taj Mahal
Angkor Wat
Meenakshi
Temple
Borobudur

The emperors of Japan, again, were venerated for centuries as gods walking in the world. The imperial dynasty claimed descent from the Shinto sun goddess, Amaterasu, who had entrusted them with the right to rule. Emperor Hirohito formally repudiated this doctrine in 1946.

In China the emperor, if not strictly speaking divine, was certainly closer to being so than any other mortal. As the Son of Heaven he ruled with the Mandate of Heaven, the god-given right to his throne, and it was believed that he could as readily promote or demote the celestial bureaucrats who ran the civil service in the sky as he did their equivalent mandarins on earth. So holy were the Chinese emperors that from the 15th century on they retreated from the contaminating presence of ordinary people behind the walls of the Forbidden City in Beijing (Peking); entry was forbidden to commoners and foreigners on pain of death, except by special permission. The effect, ironically, was to cut the emperors off from the real world and so turn them into figureheads, puppets of ambitious ministers, eunuchs, or concubines.

In this century one of the most remarkable and controversial creations of modern architecture has been built in Asia – Le Corbusier's new city at Chandigarh in India. The Japanese, meanwhile, have massive engineering works to their credit. The latest is the Seto Ohashi Bridge, gliding for some 7 miles (11 km) over the tranquil waters of the Inland Sea.

A bronze lion on guard in the Forbidden City, the palace of the Chinese emperors.

9th Millenium B.C. Israel

JERICHO

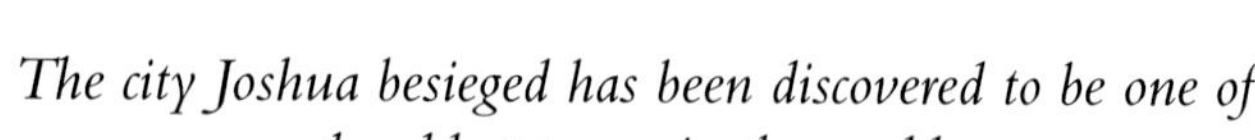

The city Joshua besieged has been discovered to be one of the oldest towns in the world.

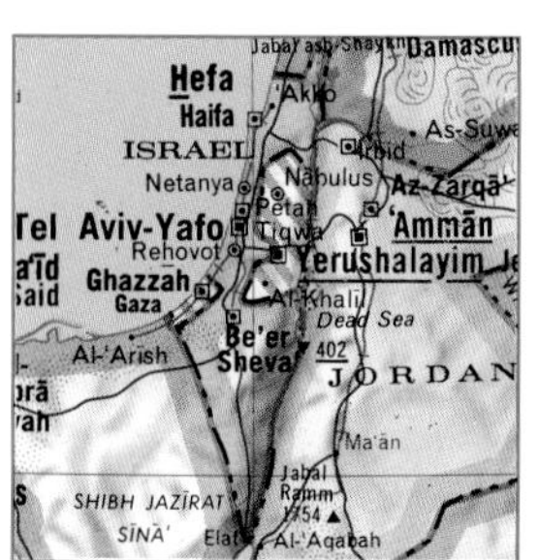

Jericho, on Route 90, lies northeast of Jerusalem and north of the Dead Sea. Regular bus service from East Jerusalem. Tours from Jerusalem and Tel Aviv.

The Place of Skulls

AMONG fascinating discoveries at ancient Jericho in the 1950s were human skulls that had been turned into portrait heads. Noses and other features had been built up on each skull in plaster, not in a stylized way, but apparently to make a realistic portrait of an individual person. Seashells were used for the eyes. It is at least a strong possibility that there was a cult of the ancestors in Jericho, in which leading members of the community were venerated for a time after their deaths.

Civilization needed defense, apparently, and the Stone Age town had strong walls, with this circular stone tower just inside them. Later on, a moat was dug in front of it.

JERICHO is famous for the story in the Bible that tells of the wall of the city falling down when it was besieged by the invading Israelites, led by Joshua. According to the Book of Joshua (chapter 6), the Ark of the Covenant, the portable shrine that was the dwelling place of Yahweh, was carried seven times around the city to the sonorous blowing of ram's-horn trumpets. On the seventh circuit, when the trumpets blew, all the Israelites shouted with a great shout, "and the wall of the city fell down flat, so that the people went up into the city, every man straight before him, and they took the city."

Archaeologists excavating the site of ancient Jericho in the 1930s thought they had uncovered the very wall that had fallen flat. It has turned out, however, that these remains were a thousand years too old for Joshua's period in the 13th century B.C.

The site of the Old Testament city is the mound called, in Arabic, Tel es-Sultan, a mile (1.5 km) outside modern Jericho. Excavations here in the 1950s, directed by the British archaeologist Kathleen Kenyon, discovered that Jericho is not merely older than Joshua, but is one of the oldest towns in the world. Indeed, it claims to be *the* oldest, though most archaeologists would be reluctant to make the assertion as flatly as that.

Far back in the Middle Stone Age, about 9000 B.C., nomadic hunters camped here and seem to have had some kind of shrine or place of worship on the site. By about 8000 B.C. there was a permanent town here. The houses, made of mud bricks supported by wooden posts, are among the earliest permanent dwellings ever discovered. The town was protected by a formidable wall, half a mile (800 m) long, with a massive circular stone tower, 30 feet (9 m) in diameter and still standing 30 feet (9 m) high.

Plentiful water from the local springs and a gentle climate made Jericho an attractive site long after the Stone Age, and the Umayad Caliph Hisham had a winter palace here.

Above: this orange tree mosaic with gazelles being attacked by a lion is a famous piece of craftsmanship in the palace.

Left: part of the palace ruins. It had two mosques and a set of bath-houses.

It was also clear that the townspeople, unlike the earlier nomads, lived at least partly by agriculture. Grains of cultivated varieties of wheat and barley were found, as well as the remains of digging sticks and the flint blades of sickles for reaping. There are underground springs here, which create a green oasis in the surrounding barren waste of the valley of the River Jordan. The townspeople of Jericho had probably discovered how to irrigate their land. So this was evidently one of the places where a decisive step was taken in the history of civilization, with the transition from the wandering life of the hunter to the settled life of the farmer.

The first city was apparently destroyed by fire, and in about 7000 B.C. a second, bigger city was built on its ruins. Much later on, there was a long succession of walled towns on the site. In the 1st century B.C. the Roman puppet ruler of Judaea, Herod the Great, built a Roman-style palace a mile (1.5 km) to the south, in which he died in 4 B.C. Part of it was uncovered by excavations in the 1950s. Later still, in the 8th century A.D., Caliph Hisham built a luxurious palace nearby.

Mount of Temptation

SEVERAL sites revered in Jewish, Christian, and Muslim tradition are close to Jericho. Near the mound of Tel es-Sultan is Elisha's Spring, whose waters the prophet purified at the request of the people of the city, as related in the Second Book of Kings (chapter 2). Immediately to the west of Jericho is the Mount of Temptation, with an Eastern Orthodox monastery built here in the 19th century by Russian monks. Tradition has it that Jesus was baptized at a ford in the Jordan some 6 miles (10 km) east of Jericho, and then retired here to fast for 40 days and 40 nights. Then the Devil came and tempted him, taking him up to the mountain peak and showing him "all the kingdoms of the world and the glory of them" (Matthew, chapter 4).

To the south of Jericho, off the road to Jerusalem, is the mosque of Nabi Musa, built in the 13th century at the place where, according to Muslim tradition, Moses was buried "in the land of Moab" (Deuteronomy, chapter 34). There is a Muslim pilgrimage here every year.

From 522 B.C. Iran

PERSEPOLIS

"Is it not passing brave to be a king,
And ride in triumph through Persepolis?"
– CHRISTOPHER MARLOWE, *Tamburlaine the Great*

At the time of writing, entry to Iran is restricted and only those with business visas are allowed to fly to Tehran. There are said to be plans to encourage tourism in the future, but the situation is uncertain. However, Tehran has an international airport, and there are domestic flights from Tehran to Shiraz taking about 70 minutes. Persepolis is a further 50 minutes' drive from Shiraz.

THE ruins of Persepolis that survive today, massive though they are, give only the barest hint of the wealth of this ancient seat of government. The Greek historian Plutarch throws some light on the matter when he says that Alexander the Great, who conquered Persepolis around 330 B.C., needed 10,000 mules and 5,000 camels to carry all the treasures away. The treasures belonged to the Achaemenid dynasty of kings, and Persepolis was just one of their three royal capitals. The city was founded by Darius the Great at the start of his reign in 522 B.C. and was occupied only in the spring and autumn of each year. Summers were spent in the hills at Ecbatana, winters at Susa. Persepolis continued to grow under successive rulers until it was destroyed by fire shortly after Alexander's arrival. According to one version of events, Alexander burned the place in revenge for the Persian sack of the Athenian Acropolis, but there is no evidence that the destruction was deliberate.

Scientific excavation of Persepolis, begun in the 1930s, revealed a huge royal enclave standing on a limestone platform on a mountain spur. The platform measures 975 feet by 1,470 feet (297 m by 448 m) and contains a sophisticated network of drainage channels, an underground water system that suggests the layout was carefully planned. The vast stairways that form the approach to the complex also appear to be the result of careful calculation – they could be ascended on horseback.

An inscription at the top of the stairway records that the entrance hall was the work of Darius' successor, Xerxes I, and this is one of a number of inscriptions given in three languages: Elamite, Babylonian, and Old Persian. Inscriptions of a different sort have been scratched on some of the walls – the names of more recent visitors, including Henry Morton Stanley, reporter for the New York *Herald Tribune* in the late 1860s. He was the man who made his name by tracking down Dr. Livingstone in Africa.

Persepolis was designed for royal ceremonies. The king and his family entourage had their private quarters here, but the most important rooms were the audience chambers, particularly the Apadana, or Audience Hall, of Darius the Great, 200 feet (61 m) square, with six rows of columns 60 feet (18 m) high and estimated to

Right: empty and silent under the sky, the vast ruins of the palace bear witness to the departed grandeur of the Great Kings.

Facing page: carved reliefs on the palace walls emphasized the Great King's power by showing emissaries bringing tribute from the far reaches of his empire.

have held 10,000 people. Xerxes' Throne Room, known as the Hall of a Hundred Columns, was even bigger, 240 feet (73 m) square. Limestone is the predominant material in evidence today, but once there were wooden columns and roofs and lavish decoration, with bright paint, fine tiles, gold and silver, ivory, and marble.

The great surviving glory of Persepolis is the sculpture. Extensive bas-relief friezes show figures in procession along walls and stairways, in imitation of the nobles and foreign delegations who sought audiences with the king or attended festivals at which they offered the required tribute. On the approach to Darius' Audience Hall, the right- and left-hand sides of the same figures can be seen on different walls, and one of the staircases has 23 panels in which different peoples of the Achaemenid empire can be identified – Bactrians, for example, leading a Bactrian camel, and Indians wearing *dhotis* and carrying two-headed axes. In the smaller, private rooms, a more personal side of life is portrayed, showing royal bath attendants carrying towels, perfumes – and a fly whisk.

Naqsh-i Rustam

This cliff near Persepolis has a number of monuments belonging to the Achaemenid and the later Sassanian dynasties. Four tombs are cut into the rock, and the inscription on one identifies it as that of Darius the Great. The others are thought to be the tombs of his successors, Xerxes I, Artaxerxes I, and Darius II. The tombs are carved to suggest the façade of the palace, and bas-reliefs show figures supporting a king on a throne while he apparently worships the Zoroastrian god Ahura Mazda. In front of these tombs stands the Cube of Zoroaster, a building 40 feet (12 m) high with a single inner chamber and an outside stairway. It is thought to date from the time of Darius the Great and may have been a fire temple.

The Sassanian dynasty ruled Persia from A.D. 224 to 628, and from this period there are eight monumental rock carvings at Naqsh-i Rustam. One shows the investiture of the first Sassanian king, Ardashir I; another, in which King Shahpur I is shown on horseback in triumph over a toga-clad figure with raised arms, is thought to represent the surrender of the Roman emperor Valerian, who was captured by the Persians in A.D. 260. The presence of the tombs, the rock carvings, and a number of fire altars scattered around the area suggests that the cliff had particular religious significance. In pre-Islamic Persia, religion focused on Zoroaster, an elusive figure belonging to the first millennium B.C., and on the winged spirit of Ahura Mazda, who is sometimes linked with Mithras, the god of light and a favorite deity of Roman soldiers.

About 300 B.C. Jordan

PETRA

Neither rose-red nor a city, nor half as old as time, but still remarkable.

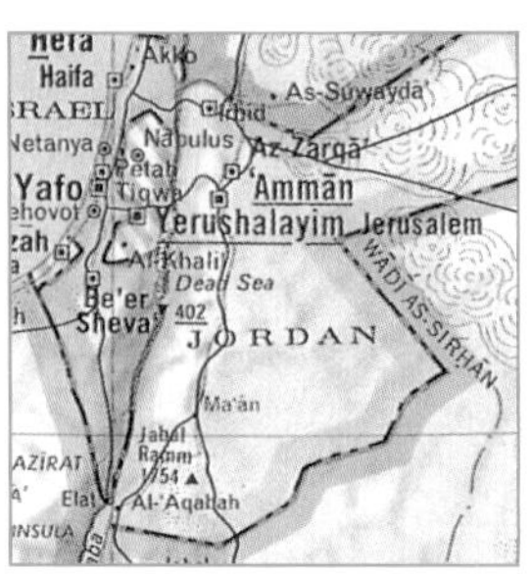

From the international airport at Amman, the drive to Petra takes about three hours. Alternatively, it is possible to fly from Amman to Aqaba and then drive for two hours via Wadi Rum. The approach to Petra along the Siq is usually done on horseback and takes about half an hour.

The Deir

A CLIMB of about half an hour from the center of Petra leads to the Deir, variously described as a monastery or a temple. Here is another huge rock-cut façade similar to the Treasury – 130 feet (40 m) high and 150 feet (46 m) wide with a doorway that, at 26 feet (8 m), dwarfs anyone standing in it. Inside there is one large chamber and, approached by steps at the far end, a niche that may have held an image of a god. According to one theory, the Deir was the scene of important religious festivals, the flat area in front of it being specially leveled to accommodate large groups of pilgrims or worshippers.

Above right: history passed Petra by for centuries, but it was once the hub of caravan routes between the Persian Gulf and the Red Sea.

Facing page: the famous Treasury is probably the tomb of one of the last Nabataean rulers.

MENTION Petra and chances are that someone will respond with the familiar quotation: "A rose-red city – half as old as time." The words come from a poem by the 19th-century Englishman J.W. Burgon. Unfortunately, the description is inaccurate, as Burgon himself conceded when he visited the place some years later. Petra is not so much rose-red as salmon-colored. It is not really a city either, but more of a monumental cemetery – any houses here were probably made of mud and they have disappeared. It is a place that poses many unanswered questions, and this air of mystery makes an already spectacular site all the more fascinating.

In the 6th century B.C. a nomadic tribe, the Nabataeans, gained control of a rift valley area between Aqaba and the Dead Sea on the eastern side of Wadi Arabah in Jordan. (A wadi is a ravine or dry river valley that may flood at certain times of the year.) Gaining control over important existing trade routes, the Nabataeans became powerful and wealthy. Petra is their legacy, a complex of monuments once believed to be houses but now recognized as tombs, cut into the rock in an inaccessible area 3,000 feet (914 m) above sea level. Some have remarkable classical detailing, others have a distinctive Nabataean "crow-step" decoration and reveal the influence of Egyptian and Assyrian building styles. All the emphasis is on the façades; inside, the bare chambers are usually completely free of ornament.

Petra became part of the Roman Empire in A.D. 106, acquiring a forum, baths, a theater, and all the usual elements of Roman civilization. Trade patterns changed with the rise of Palmyra and obscurity followed. For centuries Petra was known only to local tribesmen, who had little difficulty in warding off inquisitive strangers.

Rediscovery came in 1812 when the Swiss

explorer John Burckhardt, fluent in Arabic and dressed as a Muslim, persuaded a local guide that he wished to sacrifice a goat at a tomb, near which there was rumored to be a buried city. Burckhardt was escorted along the Siq – the deep, narrow cleft in the rocks through which visitors approach the site today – and he came upon the dramatic view of a building whose façade was 90 feet (27 m) wide and 130 feet (40 m) tall. This is the Treasury, or el-Kasneh, and it is perhaps Petra's most famous monument, though its design is classical rather than Nabataean. The urn that tops the façade is believed to have once contained treasure belonging to a pharaoh; many earlier visitors to the site took pot shots at it in the hope of dislodging the riches within.

Beyond the Treasury the valley opens out, revealing numerous rock-cut tombs in soft pink sandstone banded with many other colors. Where the carving has been exposed to the wind, it is eroded sometimes beyond recognition. Enough archaeological evidence has been found to suggest that originally Petra was neither rose-red nor salmon-pink, but clad in stucco decoration that would have given a very different impression from that of today. On the other hand, the experience of venturing along the narrow, shady Siq and suddenly catching sight of the Treasury's sunlit façade has doubtless been an amazing one in any era.

The High Place

ANOTHER steep climb leads to the Attuf Ridge on which there are two obelisks on a man-made plateau and, a little farther up the hillside, another flattened area measuring some 200 feet by 60 feet (61 m by 18 m). This "High Place" has been interpreted as a setting for ritual sacrifice with a high altar on which offerings were made. The Nabataeans are believed to have worshipped two gods, Dusares and Al Uzza. The altar at the High Place is equipped with drainage channels, presumably for blood, and there is some evidence that the Nabataeans performed human sacrifice.

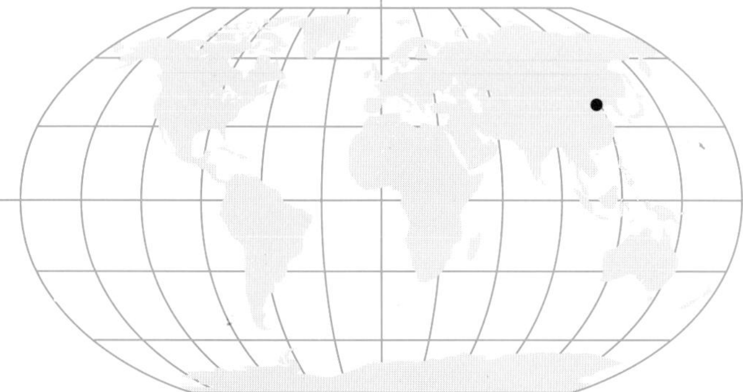

Late 3rd Century B.C. China

THE GREAT WALL

The largest construction ever built by human hands cost many thousands of lives.

The easiest but most commercialized section of the wall to visit from Beijing (Peking) is at Badaling Pass, 47 miles (76 km) northwest. Buses from Dongzhimen bus station. Also trains and helicopter tours from Beijing. Another section at Mutianyu, to the northeast and less crowded, was restored in the 1980s and is also reached by bus from Beijing.

Visitors stroll peacefully along the top of the Great Wall today, where once the soldiers of the Son of Heaven marched along 10 abreast in warlike array.

Left: the wall swoops over the mountains at Mutianyu like a roller-coaster.

Above: watchtower at Badaling.

THE Great Wall of China is one of the most remarkable feats of engineering of all time, and one of the most murderous. It was constructed in 10 years or so after 220 B.C. by the first man to rule a united China, the savagely formidable despot Qin Shihuangdi. Sections of defensive wall had been built earlier by the various quarreling minor kingdoms of northern China. Qin Shihuangdi conscripted an army of peasants, soldiers, convicts, and political prisoners to rebuild and connect the earlier sections in a single barrier through the mountains on his northern frontier. The wall was a bulwark against the warlike nomadic horsemen of the Mongolian plains to the north, and probably also a titanic assertion of the emperor's own power and glory.

Qin Shihuangdi put his most successful general, Meng Tian, in charge of the project. The wall snaked its way up and down the mountains, through desert country, through marshes. It was built of earth faced with brick on stone foundations. From the watchtowers, smoke signals – and bonfires at night – sent information cross-country with unprecedented speed.

It is said that 300,000 people toiled and struggled to build the wall, and the organization and supply of such an enormous work force was itself an astonishing achievement. Legend says that Qin Shihuangdi was told by a wizard that the wall would not stand unless *wan* – or 10,000 – were buried in it. The emperor found a man named Wan and had him killed and interred in the wall. In sober fact, it seems that many thousands who labored on it died in the task, and their bodies did indeed go to cement the wall. It has been called the world's longest graveyard and the Wall of Tears.

The Great Wall was effective when properly manned, but over subsequent centuries it was neglected, abandoned, and then rebuilt several times over. The Sui dynasty began reconstructing it in A.D. 607, when it is said that no fewer than a million laborers were forced to work on it and that half of them perished. The wall took its final shape under the Ming dynasty, with a major rebuilding in the 15th century. Sections of it have been recently restored, for tourists.

The wall runs from near the Bo Hai Sea northeast of Beijing across northern China and into the Gobi Desert. Figures for its total length vary by hundreds or even thousands of miles, because of the numerous rebuildings. The wall twists and turns on itself, there are parallel walls in some places, and numerous offshoots that may or may not be counted. A recent official figure is 3,946 miles (6,350 km), but in 1990 a Chinese was reported to have walked the whole length and ended with his pedometers indicating a total distance of 4,163 miles (6,700 km) .

The wall was as much a great highway as a barrier. At the top, it was 18 feet (5.5 m) wide, enough to allow infantry to march along it 10 abreast or cavalrymen to ride five abreast. It still stands an average 30 feet (9 m) high, with the watchtowers rising to 40 feet (12 m), immensely impressive after long centuries and relentless weather.

The Ming Tombs

MANY visitors to the Great Wall at Badaling also go to see the Ming tombs in their tranquil valley. The Ming dynasty ruled China from 1368 to 1644, and 13 of the Ming emperors rest here. The positions of the tombs were selected by the principles of Chinese geomancy, which sited buildings to ensure that they would be surrounded by favorable supernatural influences.

A succession of great gates marks the Spirit Way, which each emperor's funeral procession followed. At the Great Red Gate, everyone had to dismount and proceed further on foot, as the central arch of the gate was never used except by the emperor's coffin itself. Just beyond it is a stele (an upright slab of stone) 30 feet (9 m) high, resting on the back of a huge stone tortoise, a symbol of both the universe and immortality. The road passes between 15th-century statues of animals – lions, horses, camels, and others – that are bringers of good fortune. Then come human figures, providing the dead ruler with an honor guard.

The Spirit Way goes on through the Dragon and the Phoenix Gate to the tombs themselves. The largest and best-preserved tomb, with its courtyards and gates, is that of Emperor Yongle, who died in 1424; 16 concubines were buried alive with him. Also well worth seeing is the monumental tomb of Emperor Wanti, who was interred here in 1620 in a deep marble vault 90 feet (27 m) below ground. There is an exhibition of treasures discovered in the tomb during archaeological work in the 1950s.

210 B.C. China

THE TERRA-COTTA WARRIORS

For 2,000 years a life-size replica army has kept a silent watch over an emperor's tomb.

The discovery of the terra-cotta army has made Xi'an a popular tourist center. The city is some 720 miles (1,159 km) southwest of Beijing (Peking), from which it can be reached by air or train. Also direct flights from Hong Kong. The necropolis itself lies 19 miles (31 km) east of Xi'an, 3 miles (5 km) east of the town of Lintong. Bus service from Xi'an.

Above: the infantry soldiers wear their hair tied up in a roll on top of their heads.

Right: the figures standing in their ranks in one of the pits during excavation. Some of the horses can be seen. Skillfully carved to look like real individuals, the figures make a complete division of the emperor's army.

Facing page, left and right: more of the life-size figures. They have yielded invaluable information about the uniforms, weapons, and equipment of the Qin armies that fought to create the Chinese empire.

IN 1974 peasants digging a well near the town of Lintong in China found themselves, to their astonishment, uncovering life-size figures of soldiers and horses. This chance discovery led to one of the most exciting archaeological investigations of the century, in which were unearthed thousands of terra-cotta figures: an army buried close to Qin Shihuangdi, the first emperor of China and the builder of the Great Wall, no doubt assembled to fight his battles in death.

Nearly 8,000 figures have been found so far, in three underground halls or pits. Infantry, archers, crossbowmen, cavalry, and chariots with their horses – all were drawn up in battle formation. Standing around 5½ to 6 feet (1.6 to 1.7 m) tall, they have individual faces and expressions. Some are standing, some kneel with sword drawn, apparently to withstand attack. Some are in armor, but most of the soldiers wear tunics belted at the waist, leggings, and square-toed shoes. The torsos are hollow, but the arms and legs are solid. Their weapons – spears, swords, bows – are real, and the horses have bronze bridles. Each infantryman's hair is pulled up on top of his head and tied in a roll. Cavalrymen wear a cap held on with a chinstrap.

The figures were originally painted in bright colors, but the paint has worn off in the 2,000 years they have been silently standing guard. Close to 6,000 of them were found in the first pit, a subterranean hall 16 feet (4.9 m) deep and measuring roughly 750 feet by 200 feet (229 m by 61 m). They were infantry, archers, and chariots. In a second, smaller pit were hundreds more – cavalry, chariots, and archers. The third pit contained only 68 figures, evidently the commanders and their staff.

The first pit, with many of the figures, is open to visitors. Video films of the excavations are shown in the museum at the site, with more figures and two miniature bronze chariots, half life-size, with their horses and charioteers. Discovered in 1980, they are precisely the type of conveyance the emperor and his court officials and concubines would have used.

Qin Shihuangdi died in 210 B.C. His tomb, close by, is under a mound about 140 feet (43 m) high, which has not been opened as yet.

No one knows where the entrance is; it may well be that those who built it were killed and buried in it to make sure the secret was kept. It is believed that many of the emperor's officials, servants, and women were buried alive with him to serve him in death. The tomb complex was constructed by forced labor over many years before he died.

The discovery in 1974 was not the first of its kind, or the last. In the museum at Xianyang, not far away, are more than 2,500 terra-cotta miniatures, up to about 2 feet (60 cm) high, of infantry and cavalry, discovered in 1965 at a tomb of the Han dynasty (which succeeded the Qin emperors). In 1990 Chinese archaeologists were reported to be uncovering another Han tomb near Xi'an, containing thousands more small figures of men, boys, and horses in a labyrinth of pits and tunnels. They were equipped with bronze and iron weapons and wooden carts.

Heavenly Peace

THE ancient and historic city of Xi'an, capital of Shaanxi Province, is in the valley of the Wei River, not far to the west of its confluence with the Yellow River (Huang He). This was the home ground of Qin Shihuangdi, and Xi'an was the capital of imperial China for more than a thousand years. Under the Tang dynasty (between 618 and 907) it was the largest city in the world and rejoiced in the beautiful name of Chang'an, meaning Heavenly Peace. It was on the Silk Road, the great caravan route along which bales of silk and Chinese tea were carried across central Asia and on through Afghanistan to Persia and Syria, eventually to reach Europe. Many Indian, Persian, and Arab traders lived and bartered in Chang'an.

The 14th-century walls still surround the old city, with the 75-foot (23-m) Bell Tower at its center, built in 1384 and recently restored. The Great Wild Goose Pagoda towers up seven stories high. It was here in the 7th century that the first Buddhist texts were brought from India and translated into Chinese. The Great Mosque is Muslim in worship but Chinese in architecture, with exquisite courtyards and gardens. The Shaanxi Provincial Museum has one of the best collections in China, with jade and bronzes, sculptures including a statue of a rhinoceros weighing 11 U.S. tons (10 metric tons) from the tomb of the founder of the Tang dynasty, Confucian and Buddhist tablets, Buddhist sculptures, and a great array of silk fabrics, tiles, maps, mirrors, and ceramics.

QIN AND HAN: THE FOUNDATION OF CHINA

These early dynasties founded an empire that lasted into the 20th century.

Painting from the tomb of one of the Han emperors.

THE history of the huge area of the world which its inhabitants call the Middle Kingdom goes far back beyond the 3rd century B.C. into the remote mists of prehistory, but it was the Qin and Han dynasties that founded medieval and modern China. The name China itself comes from Qin (which is pronounced, more or less, "chin").

The Great Wall and the terra-cotta army guarding his tomb are the best-known legacies of one of the most ruthless and effective tyrants in history, a Chinese equivalent of Russia's Ivan the Terrible. Qin Shihuangdi was born in 259 B.C. and succeeded to his father's kingdom as a boy of 13, though it was rumored that he was the queen's bastard son by a merchant. A terrifying autocrat, he mastered the various warring kingdoms along the Yellow River and to the south to create an empire in 221 B.C.

Qin Shihuangdi was a great builder and ruthlessly used the forced labor of peasants, prisoners of war, and political prisoners to construct roads and canals as well as the Great Wall. He survived several assassination attempts. He standardized Chinese script and Chinese coins, weights, and measures.

THE ENDURING EMPIRE

From his capital at Xianyang, west of Xi'an, the emperor ran his realm through a powerful civil service, with savage punishments for anyone who fell afoul of the system. He was responsible for the notorious "burning of the books" in 213 B.C., when all copies of learned writings were destroyed except those in the imperial library. It is said that 460 scholars found to have evaded this order were burned alive. When the imperial library itself was burned down in the disorder after the emperor's death, the loss to China's intellectual life was severe.

Qin Shihuangdi left his harsh stamp

on China. The imperial system he instituted lasted through recurrent changes of dynasty from 221 B.C. until 1911, when it was finally toppled after more than 2,000 years, the longest surviving political regime in history.

After the terror of the emperor's presence was removed by his death in 210 B.C., his weakling successors could not keep control. The empire itself survived, however. The Qin dynasty was dethroned in 206 B.C. by a peasant rebellion, whose leader established himself as the first emperor of the Han dynasty. Helped, perhaps, in his bid by reputedly having exactly 72 moles on his left thigh, a highly mystic and potent number.

The Han dynasty lasted for 400 years until A.D. 220. The Han emperors expanded the empire to the south until they held at least nominal control of almost all the territory of modern China. They conquered what is now North Korea and opened up the Silk Road, the great trade route across Asia to Europe, along which silk reached Rome. It was in their time, too, that Confucianism and the civil service became fundamental and closely linked components of Chinese life.

THE CELESTIAL BUREAUCRACY

Confucius himself had lived long before the Han dynasty, around 500 B.C. His writings had all perished in the burning of the books (or so it had been supposed), but now hidden manuscripts came to light and lost books were written down relying on the memories of aged scholars. The Five Classics, a group of books attributed to Confucius, gained great influence.

The Confucian philosophy, as reconstructed in the Han period at least, provided an admirable blueprint for a society run by an all-powerful bureaucracy. It taught respect for authority, respect for one's elders, respect for the educated classes. It valued precedent and tradition, politeness and formality, calmness and detachment. It approved of keeping in one's appointed place in society, accepting one's lot, not striving vulgarly to get ahead.

It is hardly surprising that in the strictly regulated society of China, with its minutely stratified hierarchy of officialdom living by rule book and red tape, Confucius was venerated as a minor god. The bureaucracy was so encompassing that it was projected into the realm of the gods in the sky, where a hierarchy of celestial officials was believed to run the universe in the best mandarin tradition. The emperor, the autocrat at the head of the system on earth, was credited with power over the celestial bureaucracy as well. He promoted or demoted the minor godlings as he chose.

It is from the people of the Han dynasty that the Chinese today generally regard themselves as descended, and they call themselves Han. By the end of the Han period, after 450 years of imperial rule, a unified and centralized state, managed by a privileged, highly educated civil service under a remote autocrat, had become the accepted system in China. It has remained so virtually ever since.

The Great Wall, built to protect China from nomads to the north, was also an enduring symbol of imperial power.

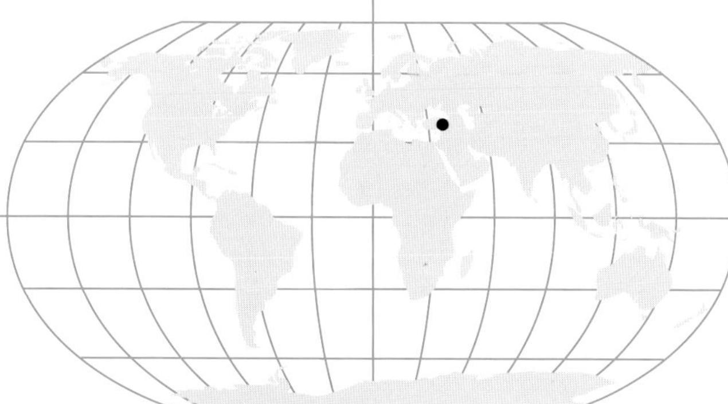

62 B.C. Turkey

NEMRUT DAG

The grandiose monument of an insignificant king who ranked himself among the immortals.

NEMRUT Dağ is a mountain rising to over 7,000 feet (2,134 m) above sea level in southeastern Anatolia. On the summit, Antiochus I, king of the area known as the Commagene from 69 to 34 B.C., built an extraordinary monument to commemorate (according to an inscription) his own glory and that of the gods. Of mixed Persian and Greek descent, he ruled a kingdom that lived profitably on trade between Syria and Persia.

Mountaintops are the traditional homes of immortals in many mythologies, and Antiochus made Nemrut Dağ the home for colossal statues of gods – and included himself among them. A tumulus, formed of heaps of loose stones, sits on the mountain peak guarded on

Because of the altitude, Nemrut Dağ is best visited in June, July, and August, and careful planning is necessary. There are domestic airports with connections from the capital, Ankara, at Elâziğ and Diyarbakır, both a good distance from Nemrut Dağ. The town of Adyaman is a popular base for car and minibus trips to the site, and it is also possible to travel from here by helicopter. Kahta, on Route 360, is a nearer base with limited accommodation, and car trips lasting a day can be arranged from Sanliurfa.

Commagene

COMMAGENE was originally part of the Seleucid Empire. It became an independent state in the middle of the 2nd century B.C. and, under Antiochus I, enjoyed good relations with Rome until the king allied himself with Rome's enemy, the Parthians. Mark Antony deposed Antiochus in 38 B.C., and after that the state of Commagene was considered untrustworthy. It was finally incorporated in the Roman province of Syria by the Emperor Vespasian in A.D. 72.

Right: an eagle stands guard on the hill, which was the highest peak in Antiochus's kingdom, and so was the closest point to the sky and the realm of the gods.

Facing page: "Look on my works, ye mighty, and despair." All the heads of the gods and the heroes have fallen.

the east and west sides by two lions, two eagles, and 30-foot (9-m) statues of Hercules, Zeus-Oromasdes (associated with the Persian god Ahura Mazda), Tyche (the Greek goddess of fortune), Apollo-Mithras, and Antiochus himself. The figures are seated and, over the intervening centuries, have all lost their heads; these lie around the site in a state of surreal detachment. The identity of the statues is revealed by inscriptions, and the same is true of the bas-relief figures depicted on a number of upright stone slabs that once formed a long frieze. These show the ancestors of Antiochus, both Macedonians and Persians, and altars for incense-burning appear to have been arranged in front of each one.

The same statues and the same ancestors appear on both sides of the tumulus, which is 160 feet (49 m) tall and 500 feet (152 m) in diameter, but the statues on the east terrace are much better preserved, and they are clearly not carved from monoliths, but composed of separate layers of stone. The vast heads are a curious amalgam of Greek facial features with

Persian headdresses and hairstyling. Antiochus seems to have been in no doubt that he belonged with the immortals, for he is depicted shaking the hands of Apollo, Zeus, and Hercules in bas-reliefs well preserved on the west terrace. Here, too, a large slab depicting a lion has aroused special interest because it shows an arrangement of stars and the planets Jupiter, Mercury, and Mars identified as a specific astronomical conjunction that occurred on July 7, 62 B.C. The significance of the date is not certain, but it may mark the beginning of building at Nemrut Dağ.

An altar survives on the eastern side of the tumulus, and there is evidence for a walled passageway between the two terraces and for an entrance into this passage from a mountain path below. It is likely that the whole complex was the scene of regular religious ceremonies. After centuries of obscurity, Nemrut Dağ was only rediscovered in 1881 by Karl Sester, a German engineer. Subsequent excavations have failed to reveal the tomb of Antiochus, but this is believed to be the site of his burial. The absence of any mortal remains hardly matters – the man's hubris is convincingly preserved in the colossal statues he left behind.

Arsameia on Nymphaios

THE arrangement of statues, altars, and tumulus on Nemrut Dağ is known by the technical term *hierotheseion*. A similar complex (but with no surviving colossal statues) has been discovered nearby at Arsameia on Nymphaios, and this is the hierotheseion of Antiochus's father, Mithridates I. Again, there are inscriptions that reveal something of the nature of the site, and again Antiochus I is featured in a bas-relief, shaking hands with a god. Particularly intriguing is a long tunnel that descends 500 feet (152 m) into the rock. Man-made, and with steps at some points, it is high enough to let a person stand upright, but it comes to a dead end. By the entrance there is a very long inscription carved in stone, but it reveals nothing about the tunnel. A relief in the same area shows a Commagene king, presumably Mithridates, elaborately dressed and shaking hands with a naked god who carries a club and a lion skin, the hallmarks of Hercules.

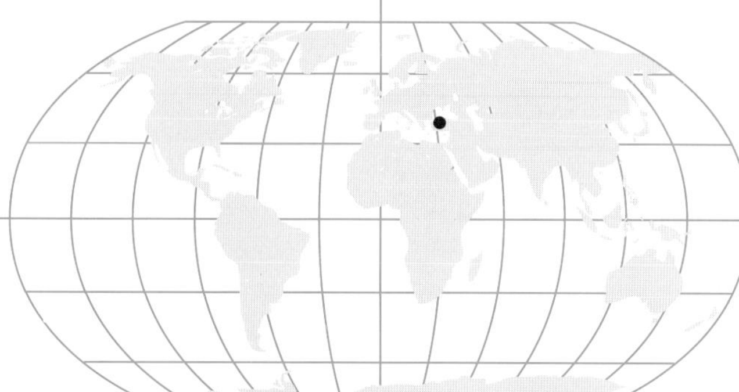

From A.D. 412 Turkey

THE ROCK CHURCHES OF CAPPADOCIA

A vast exhibition of Byzantine art can be seen on the walls of hundreds of rock-cut churches.

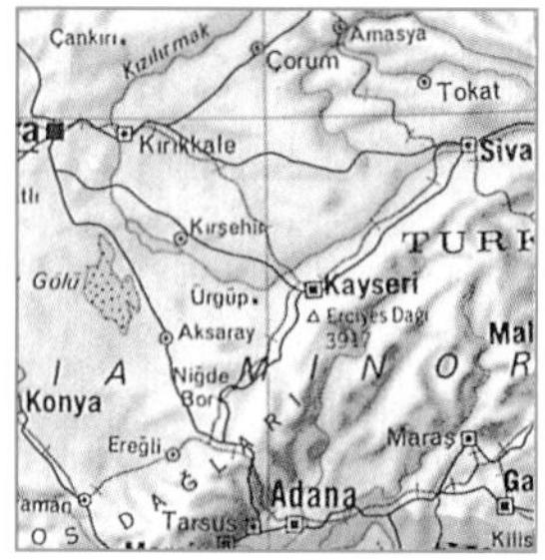

The nearest airport is at Kayseri, to which there are domestic flights from Istanbul and Ankara. The towns of Nevşehir and Ürgüp are good bases from which to explore the churches; to do so thoroughly it would be necessary to stay for three or four nights and have the use of a car. Organized excursions to Göreme are available from Ürgüp, Nevşehir, and even Ankara.

Kaymaklı and Derinkuyu

THESE two underground cities, a short distance south of the Göreme Valley, are still under archaeological investigation. It is possible that they were connected by a yet-to-be-discovered tunnel. The date of the cities is uncertain; they may go back to the second millennium B.C. and the Hittite Empire. Kaymaklı is a dark, rambling labyrinth of tunnels and chambers on four levels, where surviving storage jars and wells help the modern visitor to imagine how people lived here long ago. The city of Derinkuyu has eight subterranean levels. Here, too, there are storage facilities for food and drink and accommodation for perhaps 20,000 people.

Above: in the Göreme Valley are some 350 churches and chapels cut into living rock. Most of them date from the 10th and 11th centuries, but some are very much older. Troglodyte communities lived here in rooms hollowed out in the rock.

Right: some of the churches have elaborate frescoes.

CAPPADOCIA is the ancient name for a region of central Anatolia where the landscape also has an ancient, not to say other-worldly, appearance. Volcanic activity thousands of years ago created layers of ash, mud, and lava. Subsequent weathering eroded the softer material and left the more resistant stone standing in curious formations sometimes described as fairy chimneys. This barren, pale, inhospitable-looking region has been likened to a lunar landscape, but it was at one time surprisingly heavily populated.

Once under Hittite and then Persian rule, Cappadocia became a part of the Roman Empire in A.D. 17. The early Christian tendency to seek solitude and asceticism as a means to better communion with God is well known. The Göreme Valley in Cappadocia appealed to those who sought such a way of life, particularly when it was discovered that the curious pinnacles and "chimneys" could be hollowed out to provide shelters, even elaborate complexes of rooms and corridors. Cells were created by hermits, and cooperative communities were formed – but above all the Christians made churches, some only modest cells, others more elaborate structures with vaults and domes. In the Göreme area there are said to be 365 of them; in Cappadocia as a whole, there are many more.

Some estimates suggest that there were once whole cities here, communities of thousands of people seeking refuge from 7th-century Arab persecutions and finding it in underground networks of caves. Once the immediate danger was over, new and more elaborate churches were built in accordance with Byzantine traditions, all carefully hollowed out of the rock

and heavily decorated. In some, the decoration is entirely nonfigurative. This dates from the time of the iconoclastic dispute when, in the 8th and 9th centuries, there was argument within the Eastern Church as to whether it was permissible to portray God and Christ in the shape of mortals. In some of the Cappadocian churches, a decision to do so seems to have been made while the controversy still raged, but it was not until 842 that the matter was resolved. The earlier, more primitive geometrical decoration is painted straight onto the bare rock interiors. Later, as the technique became more advanced, the rock walls were plastered before being painted.

The Dark Church (Karanlık Kilise) at Göreme has some of the highest-quality frescoes, their colors conserved by the absence of daylight. This 11th-century church is attached to a refectory and appears to have been part of an underground monastery. A number of other churches are close to refectories, which suggests communal living; it is possible to see impressive remains of a convent that was built on six levels, with a chapel in the middle, cells above, and kitchen and refectory below.

In the Snake Church (Yılanı Kilise), frescoes depict a dragon (or snake) killed by St. George, and in the Church of the Apple (Elmalı Kilise) the walls and dome are covered with 11th-century paintings of scenes from the life of Christ – and these are just two among many. The Christian community existed here in strength until the fall of the Byzantine Empire, and some of the churches were still in use at the beginning of the 20th century.

Erosion by wind and water has sculpted a weird, surrealist landscape. Some features look as if they were carved by human hands while others, like the rock churches, actually were.

The Cappadocian Fathers

THIS region is associated with the work of three important figures in the early history of Christianity. Basil of Caesarea came to be known as St. Basil the Great. Having chosen the life of a hermit, he was called from his retreat to campaign against the growing 4th-century Arian heresy, which denied the divinity of Christ. Basil became Bishop of Caesarea and drew up his own monastic rule, a set of instructions and principles by which monasteries were to be governed. The Rule of St. Basil was widely adopted in the Eastern Church and remains the basis of Eastern monasticism to this day. Basil's brother, St. Gregory, Bishop of Nyssa in Cappadocia, joined him in opposing the Arians. Both he and another St. Gregory – of Nazianzus, also in Cappadocia – produced important works of theological scholarship.

692 Israel

THE DOME OF THE ROCK

One of Islam's holiest shrines is in the world's oldest Islamic building.

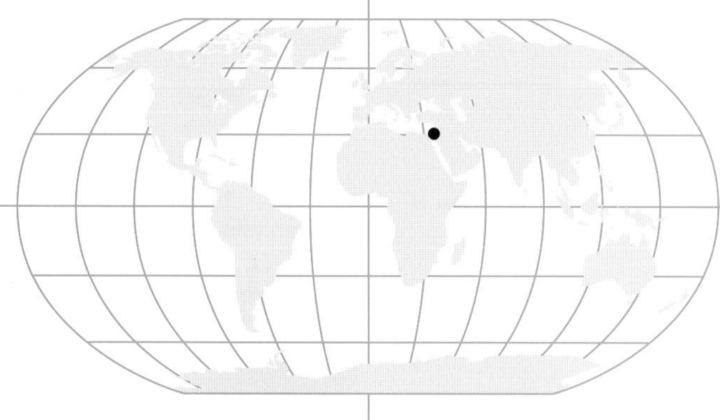

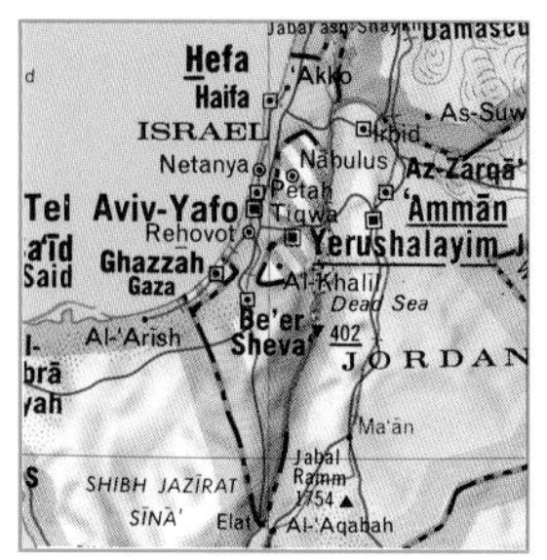

The Ben Gurion International Airport is 30 miles (48 km) northwest of Jerusalem. The Dome of the Rock is on the Temple Mount in the Old City of Jerusalem, east of the modern city center, about a mile (1.5 km) from the train station. It is easily reached by car and public transportation.

El Aqsa Mosque

THE mosque standing at the southern end of the Temple Mount was a place of Muslim worship before the construction of the Dome of the Rock. Rebuilt many times, it is a large rectangular structure with a dome, and is capable of holding 3,000 people.

Right: topped by the crescent badge of Islam and gleaming in the sunlight, the golden dome is a symbol of the sacred rock on which it stands, by ancient tradition at the heart and center of the world.

Facing page: the Wailing Wall is part of the massive platform of the former Temple.

THE Dome of the Rock is an Islamic shrine of supreme importance, but it stands on a site that was significant long before the advent of Islam. When King David captured Jerusalem at the beginning of the first millennium B.C., he tried to take a census, which incurred the wrath of God. A plague was the consequence and, to make amends, David built an altar on the rock in Jerusalem that was venerated as the place where Abraham had prepared to sacrifice his son Isaac. This rock, the summit of Mount Moriah, was considered by many people to be the center of the world.

It was here that David's son Solomon later built the great Temple in which the Ark of the Covenant was kept; it is still possible to see a small part of the platform on which the Temple stood. The Temple was rebuilt after the destruction of the city by Nebuchadrezzar in the 6th century B.C., and both platform and Temple were extended by King Herod during the first century B.C.

In the 7th century A.D. the Arab conqueror of Jerusalem, Umar ibn-Khatib, uncovered the original rock and built a mosque nearby. The caliph Abd el-Malik later determined that the city should become a place of pilgrimage for Muslims. This, after all, was the scene of Muhammad's Night Ride, when he was awoken by the angel Gabriel, brought to Jerusalem on a winged horse, and allowed to ascend from the summit of Mount Moriah for an audience with God, who entrusted the Prophet with the commandments of the Islamic faith. The Dome of the Rock marks the place where Muhammad ascended from the earth, and pilgrims can see his footprint and three hairs from his beard.

The building was constructed between 688 and 692, perhaps in a deliberate attempt to draw pilgrims away from Mecca. It is the oldest surviving Islamic building anywhere, and yet it has been called "un-Islamic" because its design shows some influence from early Christian architecture.

The dome, said to have been made originally of gold, is an outward symbol of the sacred rock that it shelters. Sixty-five feet (20 m) in diameter and 110 feet (34 m) high, it rests on a drum supported on stone columns. An outer arcade has an octagonal plan echoed by the outer walls of the building. The rock sits at the center of the building, and the arcades around it allow processions of pilgrims to move freely around the object of veneration.

Inside, there is sumptuous patterned mosaic work showing clear Byzantine influence. Calligraphy was already an important element of Islamic design at the time the shrine was built, and there are bands of inscriptions inside the building, some painted around the interior of the magnificently decorated dome. The exterior was originally covered with glass mosaic, but this was replaced during the 16th century with Islamic tiles.

The builder of the Dome of the Rock, the caliph Abd el-Malik of the Umayyad dynasty, is commemorated inside, but a later caliph belonging to the Abbasid dynasty tried to claim the building as his own creation by altering this inscription. He changed the name, but, with a remarkable display of incompetence, forgot to alter the date, so credit for the Dome of the Rock remains with Abd el-Malik. The Temple Mount, on which the Dome of the Rock stands, is a place where three religious faiths exist side by side.

The Wailing Wall

IN A.D. 66 there was a Jewish uprising against Rome, and four years later the Roman army destroyed Jerusalem. Jews were killed or enslaved, and those who survived were forbidden to return to the site of the Temple of Solomon. Later, a concession was made that allowed the faithful to return once a year to the scene of devastation to weep over the stones. The tradition continues to this day, and the Wailing Wall (actually the Western Wall, *Kotel Maaravi* in Hebrew) is one of Judaism's most poignant symbols. The wall, which remained in Jordanian hands from 1948 until the Six-Day War of 1967, is part of the platform of the enlarged Temple dating from the time of King Herod. Built of huge dressed stone blocks over 4 feet (1.2 m) high, it gives a memorable indication of the vast scale of the Temple.

The Via Dolorosa

THE Via Dolorosa is the route along which Christ carried his cross to Calvary. On a higher level now, after 2,000 years, the road runs along the northern edge of the Temple Mount from the site of the Roman procurator's headquarters where he was condemned to death. Many believers find the experience of walking the Via Dolorosa an overwhelming one.

752 Japan

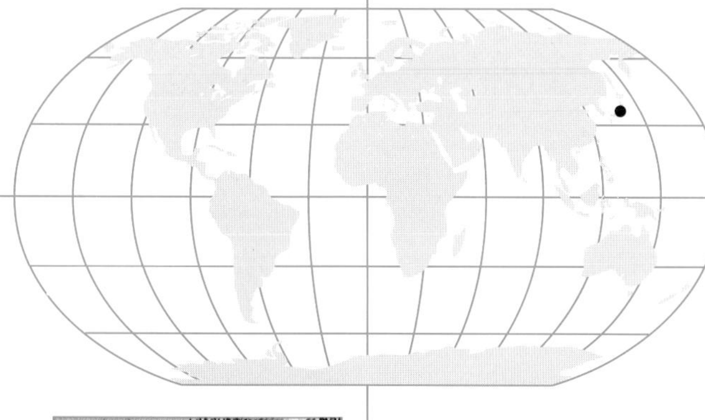

HALL OF THE GREAT BUDDHA

A gigantic image of Buddha, weighing hundreds of tons, raises a massive hand in blessing.

Nara is reached by train from Kyoto and Osaka (which has an air link with Tokyo). The Todaiji Temple and the other shrines and temples are in Nara Park, on the east side of town. Frequent buses from the Central Station, or a fairly short walk. Guided tours from Nara to all principal points of interest.

THE Daibutsuden, or Hall of the Great Buddha, in the Todaiji Temple, though only about two-thirds of its original size, is the largest wooden building in the world. Burned down and rebuilt several times, it now measures 187 by 166 feet (57 by 51 m) and stands 160 feet (49 m) high. It was constructed in the 8th century on the orders of Emperor Shomu to house one of the largest bronze statues in the world.

The Great Buddha is one of the most famous sights in Japan and is the biggest Buddha figure in the country. It was designed by a Korean sculptor, known in Japan as Kimimaro, and was cast from 489 U.S. tons (444 metric tons) of bronze. The seated figure is a towering 53 feet (16 m) high. The face is nearly 16 feet (4.9 m) long and 10 feet (3 m) wide, and the colossal ears alone are 8 feet (2.4 m) in length. The Buddha's right hand is raised with the palm facing outwards, a gesture of blessing that symbolizes the conferring of peace of mind upon the beholder, and the left hand's posture means the granting of wishes.

The Buddha is seated on a pedestal 68 feet (21 m) in circumference, formed of 56 bronze lotus petals, each close to 10 feet (3 m) high. Behind the head is a gilded wooden halo, on which are pictures of the Buddha's 16 incarnations. This was added in the 17th century, as were the two attendant statues, of the merciful goddess Kannon and the deity of good fortune. Behind the Buddha, to the right, is a wooden pillar with a small hole in it, which people try to crawl through: according to popular belief, those who do so are assured of paradise.

Also in the hall are figures of celestial guardians and a model of the original hall. The building was dedicated in 752 in a ceremony of the utmost splendor attended by the emperor and empress, the imperial court, thousands of priests, and delegations from all over Japan and from China and Korea. Some of the robes, sacred vessels, jewelry, and other treasures involved have been preserved ever since in what may well be the world's oldest museum, the temple treasury (occasionally open to the public), which had a remarkable built-in air-conditioning system. It was constructed with such skill and precision that in humid weather

Right: Buddhism became part of the apparatus of the Japanese state in the 8th century and the Todaiji Temple was the power center of the Kegon sect, which had been introduced into Japan from China.

Facing page, left: the Great Buddha. This vast image reflected the power of the Japanese emperors and the regular order and harmony of Japanese society.

Facing page, right: the Kasuga Shrine. The native Shinto cults were not suppressed, but continued to thrive alongside Buddhism.

the building's wooden beams expanded to seal it and keep the damp air out, while in dry conditions they contracted to open up cracks for ventilation. This is how screens and delicate objects of paper and silk have survived for 11 centuries. The Todaiji is the main temple of the Kegon sect of Japanese Buddhism, founded in the 8th century. Other buildings in the temple complex include pagodas and two 8th-century halls, the priests' living quarters, teahouses in a landscaped garden, and a small museum of Chinese and Korean crafts. The temple precinct is entered through a massive two-story gate, rebuilt in 1199 and supported on 18 wooden pillars 68 feet (21 m) high. In niches on the gate are two formidable 26-foot (8-m) statues of ferocious guardian beings called Deva Kings. In the surrounding Nara Park are numerous other historic temples and shrines, in an area that is close to the spiritual and emotional heart of Japanese life.

Nara

NARA, at the heart of the area where Japanese civilization first developed, was the imperial capital for most of the 8th century. The temples and shrines in the 1,300 acres (526 hectares) of Nara Park, with its ancient trees, its refreshing streams, and the sacred deer that have been kept safe here for centuries, are a legacy from a brilliant period of Japanese culture.

The Kofukiji Temple, calmly reflected in the water of a pool, has impressive halls, statues, and art treasures, and two graceful pagodas (the taller, five-story one is the second highest in Japan). The temple was founded by the Fujiwara family, a dynasty of ministers that ruled the country from the 8th century to the 12th. In the Nara National Museum are temple sculptures and paintings, and objects from the Todaiji Temple treasury. The 8th-century Shin Yakushiji Temple contains a statue of the Healing Buddha (Yakushi Nyorai), guarded by threatening figures of divine protectors.

During the Nara period, the emperors made Buddhism the state religion. But this decision was later reversed, and the older, native religion of Shinto continued to thrive. In the park is a great Shinto monument, also built by the Fujiwara family, the Kasuga Shrine. Approached through a succession of gates, it is surrounded by thousands of lanterns in stone, metal, and wood. They are lit twice a year, to dazzling effect. To the east is Mount Kasuga, traditionally the home of the Shinto deities; in the Kasuga Wakamiya Shrine, ritual dances are performed in honor of the sun goddess, Amaterasu, the most important native deity in the Land of the Rising Sun and the ancestress of the emperors.

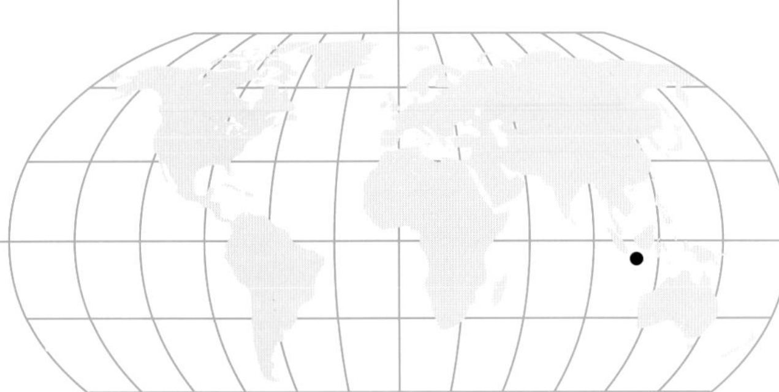

About 800 Indonesia

BOROBUDUR

The largest Buddhist shrine on earth is a textbook of Buddhist teachings in stone.

Borobudur is 26 miles (42 km) northwest of Yogyakarta, the principal city of this part of central Java. Regular bus service from Yogyakarta to Muntilan and Borobudur. Yogyakarta itself can be reached by air or train from Jakarta, the capital of Indonesia, which is in western Java.

Lord of the Dance

THE area of central Java in which Borobudur stands is historically and culturally the island's heartland. Among its tall mountains (there are still active volcanoes) there is a great wealth of archaeological remains. There are Buddhist and Hindu temples, ancient mosques, Portuguese castles, and the palaces of Muslim sultans. With Indian influences powerful in Indonesia from the 8th century on, there were Buddhist and Hindu kingdoms whose rulers claimed to be earthly incarnations of Indian gods.

The temple complex of

Right: statues and bell-shaped shrines on the highest terrace. Set among the mountains, the huge monument is in the style of Indian art, which was the dominating influence on Java in this period.

Facing page, above: there are more than 500 figures of seated Buddhas at Borobudur and an array of carvings conveying Buddhist teachings.

Facing page, below: the temple is an image of the World Mountain of Indian mythology.

THE builders of the colossal temple of Borobudur attempted to construct on the soil of Java a convincing facsimile of the fabulous Mount Meru of Indian mythology, the giant golden peak on which the entire universe rests. The result, still looming immense after 20 centuries with its fantastic multiplicity of pinnacles and images and carvings of Buddha, is said to be the largest monument in the whole southern hemisphere.

Seen from the air, Borobudur (the name means "many Buddhas") can be recognized as a huge three-dimensional mandala, or ritual diagram of the universe, combining symbols of heaven and earth. Built on and over a hill, it is a step pyramid of receding terraces, rising to some 1,310 feet (400 m) and estimated to contain more than 2 million cubic feet (56,634 cu m) of stone. The five lower terraces are square, to represent the earthly, material world. Above them are three circular terraces, representing the spiritual realm. The pilgrim makes the slow climb up the levels from the material to the spiritual.

On the upper terraces are rows of *stupas*, or bell-shaped shrines, each with a meditative Buddha inside, the hands in differing symbolic postures conveying different aspects of Buddhist teaching. At the top of the whole construction, in the center of the highest terrace and commanding a stupendous view of the surrounding mountains, is a single shrine 50 feet (15 m) in diameter, which represents the final goal of nirvana, spiritual freedom or heaven.

Visitors should follow the processional path, climbing the steps to each terrace, and then, turning always to the left (to go in the other direction is to turn towards evil), walk all the way around the monument at each level before going up to the next terrace. The walk, just over 3 miles (5 km) all told, passes one of the largest assemblages of Buddhist art in existence. There are 1,500 panels carved in relief with scenes of the Buddha's life and teachings, adding up to an encyclopedia of Buddhist doctrines in stone. Hundreds of other panels depict scenes of everyday life – work on the land, family life, storm-tossed ships, dancers, monkeys, martial arts – that make up another

textbook in stone about Java in the 9th century. These carvings were painted in bright colors originally. The whole monument is in the style of Indian art.

Borobudur was built by the Sailendra dynasty of kings around the year 800. It may have taken 75 years or more to construct and must have required an enormous work force and the services of many sculptors and craftspeople. It was apparently abandoned about 200 years later, being left to molder quietly away and be swallowed by the jungle. Long afterwards, when an English expeditionary force occupied Java during the Napoleonic Wars, one of the army officers rediscovered Borobudur. The vegetation was gradually cleared away, and a major restoration by Dutch archaeologists began in 1907. In the 1970s and 1980s another major restoration project was carried out with assistance from UNESCO.

Prambanan, 11 miles (17 km) northeast of Yogyakarta, was built in the 9th and 10th centuries and, like Borobudur, is covered with bas-reliefs in stone, in this case vividly depicting scenes from an Indian epic tale, the *Ramayana*. There are delightful carvings of mythical beasts and frolicking monkeys, trees of heaven, and the cosmic dance of the Hindu god Shiva, creator and destroyer of worlds.

The principal temple, 20-sided and about 160 feet (49 m) high, is dedicated to Shiva and contains a 10-foot (3-m) statue of the god with four arms. In another chamber is a figure of his consort, the goddess Durga, known here as "the slender virgin," her breasts worn shiny over the centuries by the touch of pious hands. Shiva's temple is flanked by two others, to the Hindu gods Vishnu and Brahma. There were once more than 200 smaller temples in the complex.

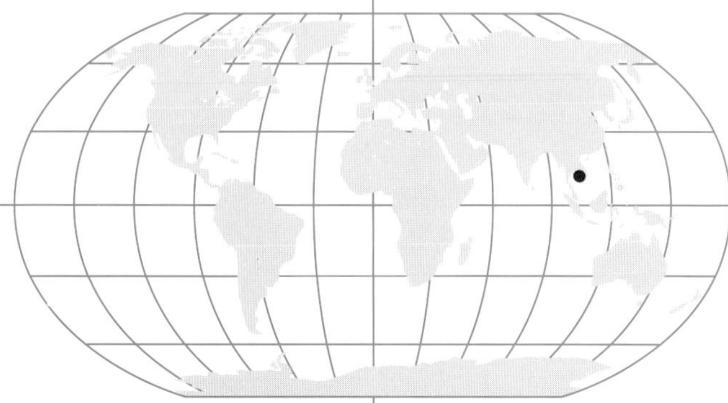

About 1150 Cambodia

ANGKOR WAT

The largest and most celebrated temple in the largest temple complex in the world.

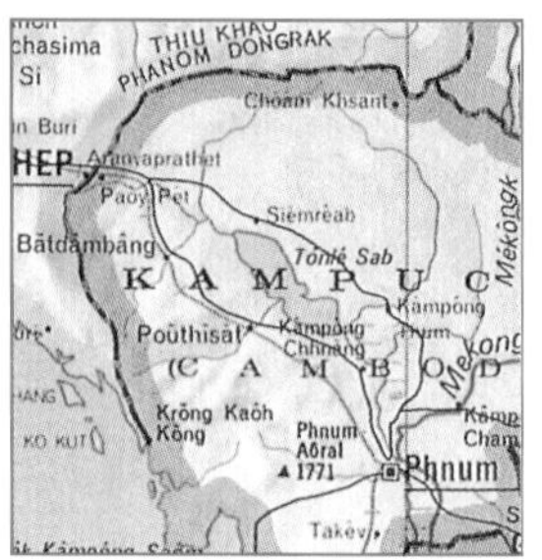

Vietnam withdrew from Cambodia (Kampuchea) in September 1989. Since then, attempts have been made to implement a peace plan, but with only slow progress. The country can hardly be regarded as a tourist destination at the time of writing. Angkor is in northwestern Cambodia, 4 miles north of the town of Siemreab.

Return to the Jungle

ANGKOR Wat is just one of hundreds of religious buildings in the territory of the Khmer kings. For 600 years the whole area was virtually lost in the jungle, and now parts of it are being reclaimed by nature. The remoter districts are considered dangerous, possibly littered with land mines, and some of the major temples are crumbling as maturing trees push their way through the stonework. There is still much to be seen, but some suspect that the stone buildings will eventually collapse, following the humbler wooden structures of the Khmer people into oblivion.

Right: the colossal temple, a marvel of gigantic symmetry with its soaring towers, was surrounded by moats which represented the ocean surrounding the sacred mountain in Indian myths.

THE most stunning example of Hindu architecture in the world is to be seen not in India, the birthplace of that religion, but in Cambodia, where a 12th-century god-king called Suyarvarman II built the huge temple of Angkor Wat. Dedicated to the Hindu god Vishnu, it doubles as a sanctuary and funeral monument for Suyarvarman himself. The Khmer rulers of Cambodia, who presided over a considerable kingdom from the 10th to 13th centuries A.D., considered themselves to be earthly incarnations of Vishnu. Angkor Wat was a sort of heavenly palace where the spirit of the king might roam.

The temple is surrounded by a moat, and large reservoirs lie outside the walls. The plan, geometrical and elegant, is on an enormous scale. An outer wall encloses an area of some 100,000 square yards (83,610 sq m). The visitor, approaching through a gate in the outer wall, beholds the whole building rising steadily up on a succession of platforms. The heart of the shrine, capped by a tower over 200 feet (61 m) high, is reached by way of further gateways, steps, and open courtyards. It is surrounded by four more lower towers, which mark the sites of additional sanctuaries.

The lavish sculptural decoration of Angkor Wat contrasts with the strictly geometrical plan. Scenes from Hindu epics are depicted vividly in carved stone, exuberant gods and goddesses cavort in erotic poses, and real figures from Khmer history march in low relief along the walls of colonnades in friezes that stretch for hundreds of feet. A favorite and much repeated image is that of the Asparas, or Khmer dancing girl-goddesses.

Angkor Wat is a supreme achievement showing an advanced appreciation of mass, space, and geometrical composition. The building techniques and style were limited – stone is used as if the material had the properties of wood, and the arch and the dome were unknown – but the overall effect cannot fail to be awe-inspiring.

Vishnu, the Hindu god who represents stability and preservation, has had his powers severely taxed at Angkor Wat. In 1973 the French archaeologists who used to supervise the site were forced to leave as war escalated and the vast complex of temples became a Khmer Rouge hideout (there may be as many as 200 temples in an area of 100 square miles [260 sq km], with Angkor Wat at the center). Today the temples are scarred with bullet holes and, with the Khmer Rouge policy of turning Cambodia into an entirely secular state, many of the sculptures of gods and goddesses have been decapitated. After 20 years of neglect, conservation work is beginning again, but there are fears that this will be crude restoration that could even produce farther damage. War and political uncertainty have already left their mark, and lack of money is another problem facing those who want to see Angkor Wat treated as respectfully as a unique example of Cambodia's religious, historical, and architectural heritage deserves.

Angkor Thom

KHMER art shows both Hindu and Buddhist influences, and the two religions appear to have been treated with equal respect. Angkor Thom, a Khmer city built by King Jayarvarman VII at the beginning of the 13th century, stands near to Angkor Wat but has at its heart a Buddhist monument, the Bayon. Again the king was honored in conjunction with a god, and again there were towers, rectangular galleries, and a central elevated shrine. Vivid and realistic bas-reliefs depict rulers riding in state on elephants surrounded by crowds of people, and the familiar dancing girls are also to be seen. Here the deity is the Lokesvara, the Buddha who has attained the state of nirvana, and the towers of Angkor Thom are crowned with massive smiling faces, four to each tower, representing this state of blissful serenity.

Above: huge and enigmatic, the stone face of the Bodhisattva Avalokiteshvara, one of the great beings of the Buddhist faith, gazes out from the Bayon at the heart of Angkor Thom.

Below: war scenes carved on the Bayon. Thai armies many times pillaged Angkor.

12th Century Japan

ITSUKUSHIMA SHRINE

A towering portico guards one of the most venerable shrines in Japan.

The island of Miyajima is in the Inland Sea, west of Hiroshima. Ferries and sightseeing boats from Hiroshima. Frequent trains and buses from Hiroshima to Miyajimaguchi, then by boat to the island. Hiroshima itself has fast air and rail connections with Tokyo.

Phoenix From the Ashes

THE name of Hiroshima is as indelibly etched on history as the shadows of its inhabitants were imprinted on walls and stairways when the first atom bomb was dropped on the city. At 8:15 on the morning of August 6, 1945, an area 4 miles (6.5 km) in diameter was instantly laid flat. Figures for the loss of life start at 250,000 and go up from there.

Since 1949 Hiroshima has been completely rebuilt, and it is now a thriving city of about 1 million inhabitants. Only the charred and battered skeleton of the Chamber of Commerce building, which somehow

EVERYWHERE in the world, gateways have a special symbolic and psychological significance. They are crossing points between two different zones or states of mind: the public and the private, the vulnerable and the protected, the known and the mysterious, the profane and the holy. Japan's most famous gateway, and one of the most beautiful in the world, is the red wooden *torii*, or portal, of the Itsukushima Shrine on the island of Miyajima. The largest in the country, it stands in the water of a small bay, its two main pillars rising 53 feet (16 m) and supporting a curved lintel 76 feet (23 m) long. Beyond it are the buildings of the shrine, with their white walls and red timbers, constructed on wooden piles in the bay so that at high tide they seem to be magically floating on the water in which their outlines are softly reflected. Behind them are the island's mountains.

Aligned exactly with the axis of the shrine beyond it, the gate was built in 1875. The shrine itself, however, is far older and is one of the most venerated in Japan. It has been restored several times since. The entire island was considered so sacred that for centuries no one was permitted to be born on it or to die on it. Pregnant women and the very old or ill had to go across to the mainland. No dogs were allowed on the island either, and still are not. They would annoy the deer, which nudge visitors for scraps and tidbits.

Most taboos were relaxed in the 19th century, but there is still no cemetery on Miyajima. The dead are taken to the mainland to be disposed of, and the relatives must be

Right and facing page: mirrored in the water, the torii *of the island shrine is the largest in Japan. Gateways of this kind are features of Shinto shrines and mark the entry to a sacred area. The fact that the word for them is close to the word for 'bird'* (tori) *in Japanese inspired the idea that they were meant as birds' perches.*

ritually cleansed of the pollution of death before returning to the island.

The principal shrine is dedicated to three Shinto goddesses, daughters of the powerful storm god Susano, one of the major native Japanese deities. The shrine has various buildings (not all of which are open to the public), including halls of prayer, purification, and offerings. There is a stage for the performance of the Shinto traditional dances, with two music pavilions. There is a separate shrine for the god Okinonushi, a son of Susano, and another for the god Tenjin. He was a real person originally, an imperial minister who died in 903. He was afterwards venerated as the divine protector of scholars and the god of calligraphy.

The buildings in the bay are linked to each other by covered gangways and to the shore by a red wooden bridge. At night, when the stone lanterns are lit, the scene is enchanting. Just offshore on another platform is the oldest Noh theater in Japan, built in 1568 and later restored.

Beside the bay stands a pagoda and next to it a modern, earthquake-proof building, the treasury, which houses hundreds of priceless objects – painted scrolls, masks and fans, armor and porcelain. On a small hill are a five-story pagoda and the Hall of a Thousand Mats, which is said to have been built of the wood of a single camphor tree. Mount Misen, the island's highest point at 1,740 feet (530 m), commands marvelous views.

remained standing at the center of the destruction, has been left as it was. It is now called the Atom Dome. The Park of Peace, where the center of the city used to be, is dedicated to "no more Hiroshimas." Peopled with statues and monuments, the park also contains the Peace Memorial Museum, one of the grimmest and most moving collections in the world. The memorial cenotaph, designed by the same architect, Tange Kenzo, is shaped like the A-frame houses in which the prehistoric inhabitants of Japan lived long centuries ago. Inside is a chest containing the names of all who died, and through the arch can be seen the Atom Dome. A peace flame burns in front of the cenotaph.

It is possible to regain some sense of tranquillity by visiting the beautiful Shukkeien Garden, originally laid out in the 17th century, with its pine trees, winding streams, and shimmering carp, its diminutive bridges and teahouses. The garden was completely destroyed in 1945, but was lovingly rebuilt and opened again in 1951.

1421 China

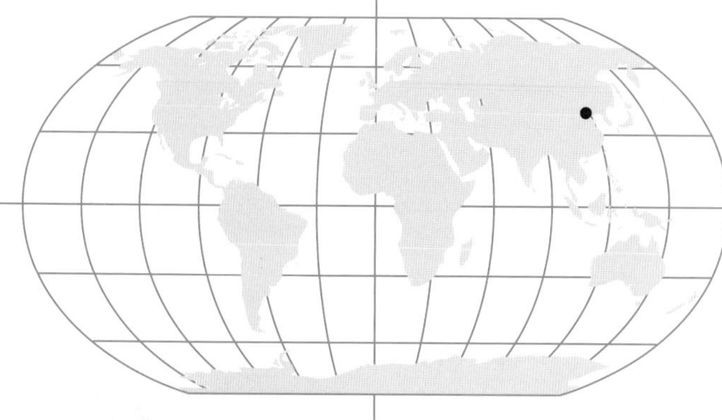

THE FORBIDDEN CITY

From the Dragon Throne in the Hall of Supreme Harmony, the emperors of China held sway.

The Forbidden City, or Gugong (Imperial Palace), is at the center of Beijing (Peking), north of Tiananmen Square. Visitors usually go in through the Wumen Gate, the main south entrance, and leave by the Shenwumen Gate on the north side. Buses serve both gates. Numerous guided tours.

Altar of Heaven

BEIJING was given its present name, which simply means "northern capital," by Emperor Yongle in the 15th century. It had been an important town long before that, but in the 13th century it was sacked by

Right: the Gate of Supreme Harmony. The Forbidden City was planned to express the order, unity, and harmony of the universe, as reflected in China itself, under the wise and serene dominion of the Son of Heaven, the emperor. Hence the names of the halls and gates.

Facing page, left: the imperial throne in the Hall of Supreme Harmony, which was reserved for great occasions of state.

Facing page, right: the Temple of Heaven, where the emperor was the leading figure in rituals to preserve order and peace in the universe.

CUT off by its moat and purple wall, banned to all ordinary mortals, roofed in the yellow tiles allowed only to emperors, the Forbidden City at the heart of Beijing was a city within a city – the center of the Chinese empire and, in their eyes, the center of the entire world. The Ming and Qing dynasties lived and ruled here until the fall of the empire in 1911.

Beijing's history goes back to early times, but the Forbidden City itself was created by Emperor Yongle of the Ming dynasty, who moved his capital here from Nanking in 1421. Enormous labor went into building a palace complex appropriate to the seat of imperial majesty. The Forbidden City was pillaged when the Manchus toppled the Ming dynasty in 1644, but the Manchu emperors, who installed themselves on the Dragon Throne as the Qing dynasty, restored it to its glory. New temples and palaces were built and lakes and gardens of ravishing loveliness laid out, and by the 18th century the city reached the height of its splendor.

The Forbidden City is square in shape, on an axis running due north and south, surrounded by a broad moat and a 30-foot (9-m) wall. Inside, arranged symmetrically, are palaces, gates, courtyards, streams, and gardens. There are 9,000 rooms altogether, formerly occupied by the emperor and his womenfolk – his mother, wives, and concubines – and an army of eunuchs and servants. Life was regulated by an elaborate code of rules, etiquette, and taboos. Eventually the Forbidden City became a golden cage in which the emperor and his retinue hid from the real world outside.

All the major buildings face south, so that the Forbidden City turns its back on hostile supernatural influences from the north as well as the cold winds from Siberia. The main gate is the southern one, the massive Meridian (Wumen) Gate, from which the emperor formally reviewed his troops. Beyond it is a courtyard crossed by a stream, the River of Gold, itself crossed by five marble bridges, which represent the five virtues and lead to the elegant Gate of Supreme Harmony. Beyond this gate is a vast courtyard, said to have been designed to hold 90,000 people. At the far side,

raised on a high marble terrace, is the largest building in the Forbidden City, the Hall of Supreme Harmony, where the emperor sat enthroned in majesty on great state occasions, surrounded by clouds of incense and regiments of kowtowing officials and dignitaries, to the gentle susurration of golden bells.

Beyond this again lie two more grand ceremonial chambers, the Hall of Perfect Harmony and the Hall of Preserving Harmony. Farther north, on a more human scale, is the warren of rooms where the emperor and his family and retinue lived. In various rooms are displayed some of the impressive and beautiful treasures that the emperors accumulated – including a notable collection of clocks and automata – yet these are but a shadow of the former glory. The Japanese looted the Forbidden City in the 1930s, and the Nationalists took much away with them to Taiwan in 1949.

At the northern end of the complex, the imperial gardens are charmingly landscaped and set with trees and statues, pavilions, rock gardens, pools, and waterfalls. Appropriately, this arbor of peace is entered through the Gate of Earthly Tranquillity.

the Mongol horde of Genghis Khan. The oldest buildings in Beijing today date from the subsequent rebuilding, from 1267, by Kublai Khan, the Mongol emperor who made it his winter capital. Emperor Yongle built the Forbidden City inside the Imperial City, which was also square in shape and surrounded by its own walls. In 1648 the new Qing emperor ordered the Chinese inhabitants out, to make room for his Manchu and Mongol supporters, and moved them to the south, the area later called the Chinese City.

There is much to see in Beijing today besides the Forbidden City. To the south of it is the vast expanse of Tiananmen Square, whose name (ironically, in view of recent events) means Square of the Gate of Heavenly Peace. Mao Tse-tung proclaimed the People's Republic of China here in 1949. The People's Culture Palace occupies the former Temple of the Imperial Ancestors. Not far away, in its 540-acre (220-hectare) park, is the Temple of Heaven, where the emperors carried out the rituals believed to preserve the order and harmony of the universe, offering sacrifice at the circular, three-tiered Altar of Heaven.

North of the Forbidden City is the beautiful Behai Park with the Bridge of Perfect Wisdom. In the northwest outskirts of Beijing is the Summer Palace. The imperial summer residence was looted by British and French troops in 1860. A new palace was built in 1888, and here can be found the Hall of Jade Billows and the Garden of Virtuous Harmony, the lake with its marble boat, and a delectable view from the Hill of Longevity.

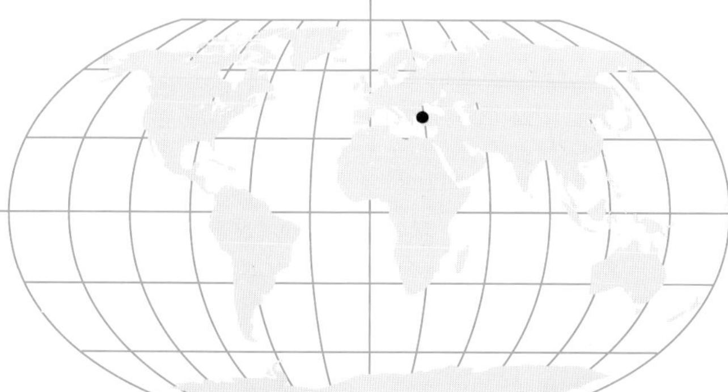

From 1468 Turkey

TOPKAPI PALACE

At the heart of the Ottoman Empire, politics, pleasure, and intrigue combined in a setting close to paradise.

Istanbul has an international airport. Topkapi is in the area of Istanbul that lies south of the Galata Bridge and west of the Bosphorus. Sirkeci train station is nearby. The district is known as Sultan Ahmet, and this is also the name of the nearest bus stop.

Right: the Gate of Majesty, Topkapi Palace, the "city" of the Ottoman sultans for 400 years. Beyond lies "the house of bliss", the residence of the immensely powerful ruler whose titles hailed him as the lord of both worlds and the shadow of God on earth.

Facing page, above: the Harem was home to as many as 4,000 women, who lived attended by black eunuchs in a gilded hothouse rife with political and sexual intrigue.

Facing page, below: mosaic decoration on the palace walls.

THE Topkapi Seraglio was once the nerve center of the Ottoman Empire. Literally "the cannon gate palace" (a 19th-century name; at first it was "the new palace"), it stands on the site of the Greek city of Byzantium, later called Constantinople, then Istanbul, overlooking the Golden Horn, the Bosphorus, and the Sea of Marmara. The setting is unrivaled, as is the palace itself.

As a description, "palace" is hardly adequate. Topkapi is a vast, sprawling city, altered and adapted over the centuries. Fires in 1574, 1665, and 1856 caused serious damage, and successive sultans attached new buildings to the complex when the need arose. Today Topkapi is a museum housing such a quantity and variety of riches that it is necessary to return again and again even to begin to appreciate what it offers.

Mehmet II, the Turkish conqueror of Christian Constantinople, built government offices here and made the city, renamed Istanbul, the new capital of the Ottoman

Empire in 1472. Topkapi was originally only a center of administration, not a royal residence, although Mehmet II's Çinili Kiosk – an elegantly tiled pavilion that still stands near the seraglio – was clearly built as a place for recreation. At first, the seraglio housed the government officials who formed the council known as the Divan; it was also the site of the treasury, the Palace School (a sort of elite training college for the civil service), and official workshops, warehouses, stables, and bakeries. It was not until the 1540s that Roxelana, a former slave who became the wife of Sultan Süleyman the Magnificent, arranged the seraglio to become the home of the sultan

and his female entourage. The Harem, policed by a group of black eunuchs, was the home of the wives, mistresses, and female relatives of the sultan. These women of the court led a secluded, even claustrophobic life, but some of them exercised remarkable power.

The guided tours available nowadays take in only a fraction of the 300 rooms, but leave no doubt as to the splendor of this palace-within-a-palace. Secret doors and passages, fountains set into walls of rooms (to foil eavesdroppers by drowning the sound of conversation), silks and brocades, fine decorative tiles, and furniture and paintings of many different eras combine to create an atmosphere of luxury tinged with mystery and intrigue – for in the midst of this luxury there was always fear. The sultan's lavish bath complex, with its dressing room and massage room, looks inviting, but the grille around the bath was designed to keep assassins at bay.

Fountains and running water, gardens and ornamental pavilions abound at Topkapi, and, as so often in Islamic architecture, there is the suggestion of an earthly paradise. Ahmet III, a sultan known for his devotion to tulips, created a special tulip garden in the grounds and even appointed a minister in charge of flowers. And if that is the stuff of fairy tales, the colossal jewels and wealth of precious metals here seem to belong to an equally unreal world. Diamonds, emeralds, and rubies, valued elsewhere for their rarity, are commonplace within Topkapi.

The Topkapi Courts

THE Topkapi Seraglio is arranged around a succession of courts. The first is used as a parking lot, so a tour of the palace proper starts with the second court. On the right-hand side of this are the extensive palace kitchens, with many domes and chimneys, which once employed over a thousand cooks. The kitchens now house an exceptional collection of Chinese porcelain, while the old treasury displays a collection of armor. The second court also gives access to the Divan, or council chamber, and to the Harem, which should on no account be missed. In the third court, holy relics of the Prophet Muhammad are displayed in the Pavilion of the Holy Mantle, the sultan's audience chamber can be seen, and the new treasury buildings contain amazing exhibits, including the Topkapi dagger with its jewel-encrusted handle. The Baghdad Kiosk, built to celebrate the capture of that city by Sultan Murat IV in 1638, is an exquisite pavilion with fine views over Istanbul. Ahmet III's tulip garden can also be seen here.

Haghia Eirene

THE church of Haghia Eirene stands on the edge of the original first court of Topkapi. There was a Christian church here at the beginning of the 4th century, and parts of the present building date back to the 6th century. A simple brick structure with a domed apse and some early mosaics, it was once used as a Turkish arsenal. Haghia Eirene, which means "church of holy peace," is now a museum and concert hall, but the building retains an impressively peaceful atmosphere.

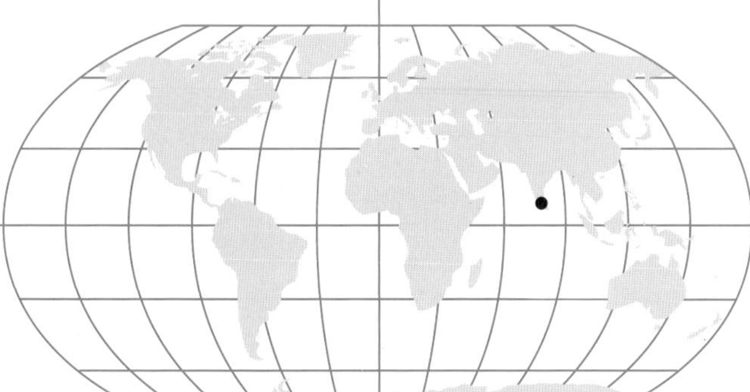

From about 1550 India

MEENAKSHI TEMPLE

A temple fascinating for its carvings and its history, but also as a living and vibrant center of pilgrimage.

The temple is situated at Madurai in the South Indian state of Tamil Nadu about 300 miles (483 km) from Madras. The city has an airport only 3 miles (5 km) away, with flights arriving from Madras, Cochin, and Bangalore. The journey by train from Madras takes about eight hours, and the station is very close to the temple. There are also long-distance bus services from Madras.

Other Monuments in Madurai

MADURAI has a number of other temples, including Tiruparamkundram Temple about 6 miles (10 km) from the city center. Like a vast sculpture, this building is cut out of solid rock. Back in Madurai, near the Meenakshi Temple, is the palace of the man who built it, Tirumala Nayak. There is a museum here, and occasional concerts and dance displays. The city also has its own museum, where there are exhibitions of craft work produced by small-scale village industries. Dedicated to the memory of Mahatma Gandhi, it also displays the *dhoti* (loin cloth) he was wearing when he was assassinated.

Right: the temple is one of the most sumptuous in southern India. Meenakshi means "fish-eye" and the princess was said to have long fish-shaped eyes and a fishy smell, which left her when she met Sundareshwara, "lord of beauty".

Facing page: the Raja Gate, one of the grand gateways.

MEENAKSHI was a princess who, at birth, was discovered to have three breasts. Advice was sought from various holy men, who announced that the extra breast would disappear when she met her future husband. This duly happened when the princess encountered the god Shiva, and eight days later, in the town of Madurai, she was married to the god, who took the guise of Lord Sundareshwara.

That is the story that is told to explain the origin of this Hindu temple complex, which has shrines dedicated to Meenakshi and Lord Sundareshwara and which is one of the most spectacular places of pilgrimage anywhere.

The temple precinct measures about 850 feet by 730 feet (259 m by 223 m). Nine *gopurams* (monumental gateways covered in sculpture) can be seen, rising up to 200 feet (61 m). Four are in the outer precinct walls; the others, marking earlier boundaries of the temple complex, are inside. Many of the buildings date from the time of the local ruler Tirumala Nayak (1623-55), but the shrine is said to have been founded in the 12th century, and the extraordinary Hall of a Thousand Pillars (by some counts only 997) dates from the mid-16th century. Every pillar is said to be different, and it would take months to study the thousands of sculptures – men and women, gods, goddesses, and musicians among them – carved in high relief on the columns. This hall is now a museum, a use that detracts slightly from the splendor of the place, but the site as a whole is

very far from being a thing of the past. This is a living temple to which thousands of people come on pilgrimage. The visitors, as well as the traders who set up shop to sell them everything from spices to plastic models of Lord Shiva, are an essential part of the whole colorful scene.

The temple attracts pilgrims by day and night, and there are many processions to be seen and much musical celebration. A large reservoir known as the Tank of the Golden Lily, which provides water for ritual washing, has stepped sides and a colonnade covered with paintings depicting 64 miracles performed by Shiva in Madurai.

The profusion of carved columns, corridors, halls, and shrines can be overpowering, but the temple observes certain rules that can be seen again and again in Indian religious buildings. The main axis of the complex is east-west, and the shrine of the god (in this case Sundareshwara) is aligned likewise. The inner sanctuary of the god is designed to allow the performance of *puja*, which involves walking in a clockwise direction around the deity. The pilgrim must also experience *darshan*, a ceremonial viewing of the deity. On special festival days, and when a large donation is given to the temple funds, images of the gods are carried in golden chariots around the temple complex, and echoing the numerous carvings of the Hindu elephant god Ganesh is the temple's own elephant. By climbing the steps of the tall south *gopuram* and looking down on the scene below, the visitor can better grasp this continuous display of color, music, and life that animates the Meenakshi Temple.

Teppam Festival

In January or February of each year, Madurai celebrates the festival known as Teppam. The images of Lord Sundareshwara and Meenakshi are taken from the temple and placed on rafts, which are then floated on the waters of the Mariammam Theppakkulam Tank, a huge artificial lake on the eastern edge of the city. A temple on an island in the middle of the lake was built at the same time as the Meenakshi Temple. This "Float Festival" attracts large numbers of pilgrims.

THE BLUE MOSQUE

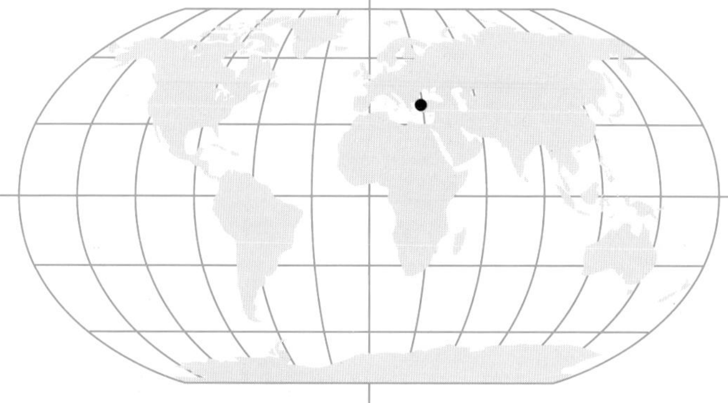

In a city of countless mosques, this is the most famous.

The mosque has given its official name to the area in which it stands: Sultan Ahmet. This is the old quarter of the city of Istanbul, south of the Galata Bridge and west of the Bosphorus. Sirkeci Station, served by trains from Europe rather than Asia, is a short distance away. Sultan Ahmet is also the name of the nearest bus stop.

Haghia Sophia

THE building that stands opposite the Blue Mosque, a short walk away through gardens, is the even more celebrated Haghia Sophia, the Church of Holy Wisdom. Built during the 6th century on the site of earlier churches, it is a vast domed basilica, the mother church of the Byzantine Empire until Constantinople fell to the Turks in 1453. At this point it was transformed into a mosque, and seen from outside, with its dome and four minarets, it looks as if it has never been anything else. The mosaics inside, uncovered and restored since the building was declared a museum in the 1930s, tell a different story. Subjects include Christ enthroned, with the inscription "I am the light of the world," and the archangels Michael and

Right: inside the mosque, the prevailingly blue and green tiles are gloriously lit from 260 windows and the main dome is supported by huge pillars.

Facing page: the mosque is specially admired for its tumbling cascade of domes. It stands on the site of the palace of the Byzantine emperors.

OFFICIALLY, the Blue Mosque is the Mosque of Sultan Ahmet I. It owes its more popular name to the 20,000 tiles, predominantly blue, used to decorate the interior.

Work on the mosque began in 1609 on the instructions of the 19-year-old sultan, who, according to one story, was anxious to appease Allah for some youthful misdemeanors. He had also been required to sign a treaty recognizing the ruler of the Hapsburg Empire as his equal, and this too may have called for some renewed demonstration of religious faith and special dedication to Islam.

The architect of the mosque was one Mehmet Aga, and his masterpiece took seven years to complete. All the standard features of mosque design can be seen, but the Blue Mosque is unusual in having six minarets – one at each of the four corners, as might be expected, and another two, slightly shorter, at the outer edge of the courtyard. According to one rather fanciful story, the young sultan offended the authorities at Mecca, the very center of the Islamic religion, and was required to pay for the construction of a seventh minaret for the mosque there, ensuring that it would have no rivals.

The mosque courtyard can be approached from three gateways that lead into an outer colonnade of granite columns. Beyond the colonnade, which has a roof composed of 30 small domes, a hexagonal fountain stands in the middle of the courtyard. Such fountains are familiar features, and their purpose is practical: enabling the faithful to wash before entering the mosque. To the east of the mosque courtyard stands the *medrese*, or college (educational centers are often found within a mosque complex).

The mosque itself presents a pleasing roofscape of domes – a large central one

surrounded by four half-domes, and a further four small domes beyond these. Inside, this arrangement of domes can be fully appreciated, with four huge elephant-foot columns supporting the whole structure. The dazzling effect of the thousands of tiles might be overpowering if it were not for the spaciousness of the interior and the remarkable light that streams in through the 260 windows.

The *mihrab* (the niche facing towards Mecca) and the *mimber* (the pulpit) are carved from white marble, and the floor is covered in thick carpets, mostly deep red, but it is the complex blue of the tiles that makes the greatest impact. There are numerous shades of blue, but also there are many other colors to be seen on closer inspection. This elegant ceramic work is the product of the famous Iznik factories, which achieved tremendous success during the 16th century, exporting their wares far and wide. Insistent that this new mosque should have nothing but the best, Sultan Ahmet is said to have forbidden the potteries to produce tiles for any building other than his. The strain of producing on such a scale was enormous, and the Iznik potteries never really recovered. The sultan for whom they labored also had a sad end. Ahmet died of typhus at the age of 27, shortly after the opening of his great new mosque.

Gabriel. If blue is the overwhelming color of Sultan Ahmet's mosque, here the dominant tone is gold. The rich effect is enhanced by the use of polychrome marble and other colored stone in pavements and wall decoration.

Museums

THE Blue Mosque attracts large numbers of tourists, but many overlook the appealing Carpet Museum, housed in a former royal pavilion, and the Kilim Museum. Both are well worth a visit.

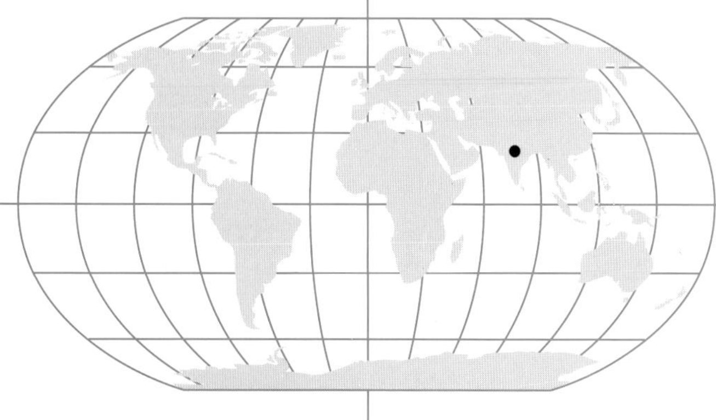

1632-1654 India

THE TAJ MAHAL

An emperor's memorial for his beloved wife – inimitable and unforgettable.

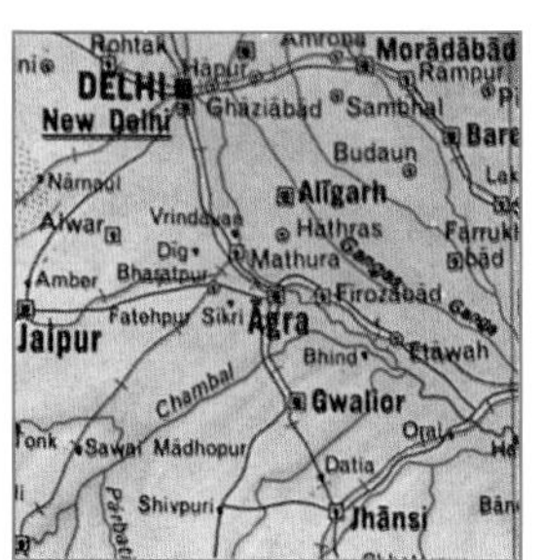

Beside the Jumna River in Agra, in the state of Uttar Pradesh, Agra is about 120 miles (193 km) from Delhi. There is an airport, with domestic flights from several Indian cities; by road the journey from Delhi takes about three hours, and the Taj Express train service takes a little longer.

Above: visitors to a building that symbolizes India.

Right: the building seems to change its personality with different tones of light and times of day. Below the lovely swell of the dome are four cupolas and below these again, the niches in the marble walls.

Facing page: the pearl-shaped dome is an Islamic symbol of both womanhood and paradise. The dome is heaven and the square building below is earth.

IN 1631 the wife of the Moghul emperor of India died giving birth to her 14th child. She was 36 years old and had been married for 18 years. Her husband, Shah Jehan, had lost not only a beloved wife but also a shrewd political adviser and is said to have been in mourning for two years (according to one account, his hair turned white with grief). He vowed to build a tomb worthy of his wife's memory, something utterly without equal anywhere in the world, and few would deny that he succeeded. Arjumand Banu, otherwise known as Mumtaz Mahal ("the Chosen One of the Palace"), has as her memorial an astonishing building which bears an abbreviation of her name: the Taj Mahal.

So many superlatives have been used to describe this building that most visitors approach it with fears that they will be disappointed. The silhouette, familiar from countless photographs, crops up again and again – as the emblem of a restaurant or the trademark of a manufacturer of chutneys and spices, indeed, wherever someone wants to suggest India with one instantly recognizable image. And yet disappointment is rare. The Taj can be seen again and again and can still surprise, such is its ability to take on a different character according to the time of day and the nature of the light. Although a tomb, the building lacks the cold monumentality one might expect; instead, it seems to float between heaven and earth – the proportions, the remarkable symmetry, the surrounding gardens, and the reflections in water all combining to create something that leaves countless visitors at a loss for words.

The Taj Mahal was built by an estimated 20,000 workers and took 22 years to complete. A Frenchman and a Venetian are said to have had some part in its construction, but no single architect's name is recorded with any certainty – as befits a building intended to be associated with the name of its occupant only.

It is made of marble (brought from quarries 200 miles [322 km] away), but it is by no

means the pure white building that some photographs suggest. Thousands of precious and semiprecious stones are inlaid in the marble surfaces, and black marble is used for calligraphic decoration. There is also remarkable craftsmanship in the pierced marble screens, which cast dramatic shadows when the sun strikes them. Once, there were silver doors and, inside, a gold railing and a cloth of pearls over the queen's cenotaph (this stands directly above the actual burial place). Thieves made off with such precious items, and many have tried to extract the inlaid jewels from their settings, but the magnificence remains overwhelming.

The building is set in landscaped grounds and is approached through a massive and magnificent gateway, symbolically an entrance to paradise. Surmounted by domed pavilions, it originally had a door of solid silver studded with hundreds of silver nails. This was plundered and the present door is of brass.

There seems to be little truth in the story that Shah Jehan intended to build himself an identical black marble monument on the other side of the Jumna River. His son Aurangzeb proclaimed himself emperor in 1658 and held his father under house arrest in the fort at Agra for nine years until his death. From the fort, Shah Jehan had a view of the Taj Mahal in the distance. Later, he too was buried there.

Moghul Architecture

The Taj Mahal represents the high point of Moghul architectural achievement. This style of monumental tomb, standing on a plinth, furnished with minarets, and approached with the same reverence as a mosque, can be seen developing and declining in northern India. Humayun's Tomb, in Delhi, was begun in 1564. It is a clear ancestor of the Taj, solid and imposing rather than delicate and ethereal. In the 1670s Aurangzeb built an imitation of the Taj Mahal for his wife at Aurangabad, but it lacks the grace and proportion of the original. Another tomb in Delhi, that of Safdar Jang, begun in 1753, has been called "the last flicker of the lamp of Moghul architecture," but it is not a building one would go out of one's way to see. There is a standard pattern for these monuments – a large, onion-shaped dome, water channels, a garden divided into four sections, a plinth, and minarets – but the builders of the Taj managed to combine these in a way that created something unique.

Tomb Robbers

The activities of the thieves who made off with the precious metals of the Taj look negligible when compared with a scheme hatched by Lord William Bentinck, Governor General of Bengal. In the 1830s he proposed to dismantle the Taj, which was neglected and overgrown, and ship the marble to London where it could be sold. The plan was abandoned when marble stripped from the Red Fort at Delhi (see page 116-117) failed to find a buyer. Later, Lord Curzon, who became Viceroy of India in 1900, had the Taj Mahal restored.

ISLAM IN ASIA

**"Iram indeed is gone with all its Rose,
And Jamshyd's seven-ringed Cup where no one knows;
But still the Vine her ancient Ruby yields,
And still a Garden by the Water blows."**

- EDWARD FITZGERALD, The Rubaiyat of Omar Khayyam

Tiles in the Topkapi Palace, Istanbul. Islam impelled Muslim artists towards intricate and stylized patterns of decoration.

THE Prophet Muhammad died in 632 at Medina in Arabia, which today ranks second only to Mecca among the revered cities of Islam. In an extraordinary unleashing of energy, his followers stormed out of the deserts of Arabia, riding swift camels and horses, to conquer the world for Allah with the war cry of *Allahu akbar* ("God is most great").

Muhammad was followed as leader by caliphs, or successors. The ferocious Caliph Umar took Damascus and Jerusalem, the third holiest city of Islam, where one of his successors built the Dome of the Rock (see page 94-95), the great mosque where Solomon's Temple once stood. The Arab armies meanwhile pressed on across the Euphrates and Tigris rivers to subdue Persia. Persepolis fell in 648, Samarkand in 710, and Islam stood at the edge of India. Within a hundred years of the Prophet's death, his followers ruled an area larger than the Roman Empire at its peak: from Spain and Morocco in the west, across North Africa to Egypt, Arabia, Palestine, Syria, Mesopotamia, and Persia. They saw in their success the hand of God.

An important factor in the speed and the acceptance of the conquest was that Arab rule was often less oppressive than the regimes it replaced. Adherents of other religions were usually allowed to practice their own faith undisturbed, though they had to pay a special tax. Most of the conquered were converted to Islam, however, partly for obvious reasons of practical advantage, but also because Islam was an impressive and attractive religion in its own right. The converts in time outnumbered the Arabs and took over the religion.

From 750 to 936, the Abbasid dynasty ruled Islam from Baghdad, while Muslim civilization came to its first golden flowering in architecture, poetry, philosophy, and art. Harun al-Raschid, the caliph of the *Arabian Nights,* dining off gold and silver plates, toying with the scented beauties of his harem, served by an army of officials, eunuchs, and slaves, was the richest potentate on earth. But the empire could not hold together indefinitely, and different ruling dynasties took power in different parts of the Muslim world.

MOSQUE AND MINARET

The principal everyday duty of the Muslim is to pray to God. This is done five times a day, at home or wherever the believer happens to be, but preferably in a mosque, or "place of prostration," which is a building organized for prayer.

The mosque spread all across Asia as the characteristic mark of a Muslim population, as the church marked a Christian one. Its basic shape, a central rectangular space beneath a dome, owes something to Eastern Orthodox churches. There are no pews or seats. The congregation stands in rows behind the prayer leader, the *imam*, all facing a recess in one wall, the *mihrab*, which shows the direction of Mecca. A mosque is traditionally a masculine preserve, and if women go to one, they are usually hidden behind screens.

The faithful are summoned to prayer by the *muezzin*, calling out from a minaret of the mosque, and the tall, slender outline of the minaret became a characteristic feature of Islamic architecture. Islam forbade the depiction in mosques of human, animal, or natural forms, which compelled Muslim artists to evolve graceful, intricate patterns of geometrical shapes, stylized foliage, and Arabic lettering.

GRANDEUR AND LUXURY

In the 11th century, expansion began again with the Muslim conquest of the Punjab in northern India. The Seljuk Turks succeeded the Abbasids to build a new empire in western Asia, and their successors in turn, the Ottoman Turks, conquered all of what is now Turkey, took Constantinople by storm in 1453, and extended their sway into the Balkans. The great Byzantine Church of Holy Wisdom (Haghia Sophia – see page 110-111) in Constantinople was turned into a mosque and the city was renamed Istanbul. From it, Süleyman the Magnificent ruled a territory stretching from the Balkans and Egypt to Persia. In Istanbul today, the Blue Mosque and the Topkapi Palace testify to the grandeur and luxury of the Ottoman sultans. Meanwhile, Muslim traders and missionaries had exported Islam to Malaysia, Indonesia, and China.

In India in 1526, a Turkish adventurer named Babur swept down upon the northern plains from Afghanistan to found another great empire, the dominion of the Moghuls, which became the dominant political power in the subcontinent. The Taj Mahal, its white walls studded with crystal and lapis lazuli, chalcedony and carnelian, bears ravishing witness to another rich and gorgeous flowering of Islamic civilization.

Both the Ottoman and the Moghul regimes fell into decline and eventually collapsed. The Ottoman Empire split up into the Muslim states of today's Near East. In India, after a period of British rule, the independent Muslim state of Pakistan was established in 1947. Meanwhile, a fundamentalist revival was gathering strength in reaction against Western culture and influences. Today, Islam is Asia's most dynamic religion.

The Taj Mahal at sunset, the most precious jewel of Muslim civilization in India.

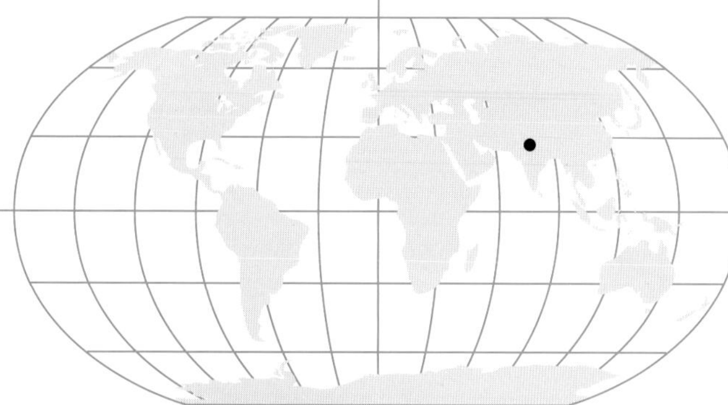

1638-1648 India

THE RED FORT

If there was paradise on earth in the mid-17th century, it was here.

In the northeastern zone of the city of Delhi (the area known as Old Delhi) near Chandni Chowk and not far from the main train station. Delhi has an international airport with connections from many cities in India.

THE Red Fort, or Lal Qila, takes its name from the red sandstone used to build its vast walls, but the various palaces and audience chambers inside were made of more precious materials. This fort, constructed for the Moghul Emperor Shah Jehan between 1638 and 1648, was celebrated for its opulence – the marble, the silver and gold, the lavish use of jewels. Inevitably, much of this wealth has disappeared over the years, and some of the original

Jama Masjid

THIS enormous mosque, also built on the orders of Shah Jehan, is the largest in India. It stands near the Red Fort in the heart of the bustling city of Old Delhi. The mosque, erected between 1644 and 1658, uses the red sandstone familiar from the fort, with white marble decoration. There are three domes and two minarets 130 feet (40 m) tall with a spectacular view from the top. The eastern gateway was reserved for the use of the emperor, who also had his own private gallery.

A 17th-century traveler said the Red Fort was "superior to the palaces promised in heaven". Fountains splashed in its courtyards and its gardens were lovely with cypresses.

buildings have been destroyed. What survives, however, still gives a powerful impression of the Moghul Empire at its height.

After the death of his wife, for whom he built the Taj Mahal, Shah Jehan intended to transfer the imperial capital from Agra to Delhi, or rather to a new city called Shahjehanabad, where the emperor built the Red Fort, which was virtually a royal city in itself.

Standard features of any Moghul court were two audience chambers – the Diwan-i-am and the Diwan-i-khas. The first was for public audiences with the ruler, the second for private audiences, and both survive at the Red Fort. The Diwan-i-am is a large hall raised on a plinth and opening on three sides onto courtyards. Large numbers of people could gather here, and petitions could be heard by the emperor in public. The Diwan-i-khas was the place for private consultations between the emperor and his officials or foreign ambassadors. Once it had a spacious courtyard, a marble pavement, and a ceiling made of silver. Shah Jehan had the famous "peacock throne" made for the Diwan-i-khas – an outrageously rich construction that took seven years to build and was studded with jewels by the bucket-load. The throne was carried off to Persia in 1739, but an inscription in the Diwan-i-khas records Shah Jehan's opinion of the place: "If there is a paradise on earth, it is this, it is this, it is this."

There were once six royal palaces (*mahals*) within the Red Fort. The Mumtaz Mahal is today a museum. Another is the Rang Mahal (literally "painted palace"), but the painting, like the silver ceiling, disappeared long ago. The Khas Mahal is a set of three private apartments for the emperor, rooms for eating, for sleeping, and for worship. Shah Jehan's son and successor, Aurangzeb, built the exquisite Moti Masjid, or Pearl Mosque, within the fort. The mosque and its courtyard are relatively small but have a sense of airy spaciousness, and the use of black marble inlay in a predominantly white marble building is very effective.

An arcade of shops can still be seen leading into the fort from the impressive Lahore Gate, and the royal baths also survive, but after the Indian Mutiny in 1857, much of the fort was swept away to make room for military barracks. James Fergusson, a noted 19th-century writer on Indian architecture, described the demolition as "a deliberate act of unnecessary vandalism."

The small Pearl Mosque in white marble with black pinnacles was added in 1663 as a royal chapel.

Lord Curzon

Lord Curzon, Viceroy of India at the beginning of the 20th century, arranged for restoration work to take place at the Red Fort. After the Mutiny in 1857, the British had removed some inlaid marble panels from the Diwan-i-am and sent them to London. One of the subjects depicted was the story of Orpheus from Greek mythology, which suggested that this was the work of a European. These marble panels, which suffered the indignity of being used as table tops, were eventually exhibited in the Victoria and Albert Museum. Curzon managed to retrieve them and had them restored to their original position. He also attended to the Red Fort's ornamental gardens, which had suffered total neglect.

Chandni Chowk

This seething crossroads was first designed as a bazaar area in 1648 by a daughter of Shah Jehan. Today, it is still a busy commercial center where narrow, winding streets are packed with all manner of shops and sidewalk traders.

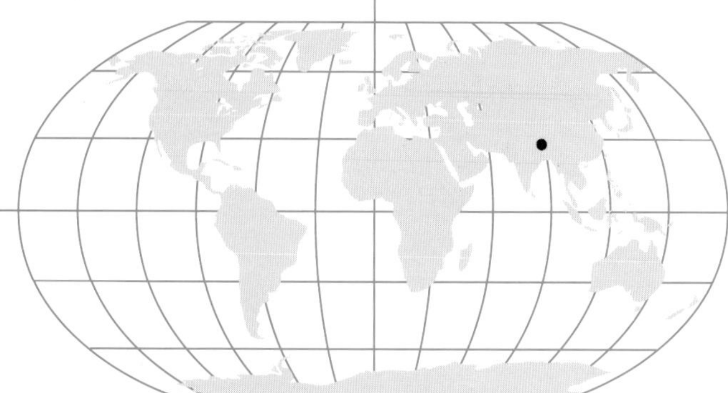

1694 Tibet

POTALA PALACE

The Palace of the Dalai Lamas dominates Tibet's holy city of Lhasa.

Gonggar Airport, 60 miles (97 km) outside Lhasa, can be reached from Chengdu and Beijing in China. By road the route is from Kathmandu in Nepal, which has air connections with New York, London, Hong Kong, and many Asian and European cities. A rail line to Lhasa from China is planned, but will not be built for some years.

A LANDMARK for miles in every direction, the Potala Palace towers up 13 stories high like a great cliff, with its white walls, regiments of windows, and serried roofs at different levels. It stands on a rocky outcrop called Marpori ("the Red Hill") some 300 feet (91 m) above the city.

The name Potala is derived from a Sanskrit word meaning "Buddha's mountain." Songtsen Gampo, Buddhist king of Tibet in the 7th century A.D., built a palace on this spot. He also founded the great Jokhang Temple in the town, to which legions of pilgrims are drawn as by a gigantic spiritual magnet. Centuries later, in 1645, the fifth Dalai Lama, then the ruler of Tibet, ordered work to begin on a palace for himself where the royal residence had once stood. It was not finished when he died in 1682, so his demise was kept secret until the building was completed in 1694. It remained the Tibetan seat of government right up until the 1950s.

Built of earth, stone, and wood, the Potala was constructed without benefit of the wheel, which had not yet been introduced into Tibet. All the stone and materials had to be carried on donkeys or the backs of human laborers. The vast edifice has more than 1,000 rooms and is said to contain 10,000 shrines and no fewer than 20,000 statues. Now preserved as a museum, it was the winter residence of the Dalai Lamas until the present holder of the office – the 14th – escaped to India in 1959. Their private quarters were high up near the top of the building, where they lived in isolation from the mass of the people. From the rooftop itself, monks would blow their brass horns, 13 feet (4 m) long, to signal the times for prayer.

The main bulk of the building contained government offices, the living quarters of the Dalai Lamas' numerous household staff, all of whom were monks, and also a monastic training school. There were meditation halls, libraries, armories, granaries and storerooms, torture chambers, and a dungeon known ominously as the Cave of Scorpions. The many chapels and shrines are rich in sculptures, mural paintings, embroidered silk hangings, incense burners, and ritual objects. Candles burn in the shrines, and Tibetan pilgrims bring yak butter

Right: towering up on its hill in the thin Himalayan air, the forbidding palace was built for the fifth Dalai Lama, who made himself the spiritual and political ruler of Tibet in the 17th century. It turned into a prison for some of his successors.

Facing page: a washing line hangs incongruously in the domestic quarters up on the roof.

to fuel them and drive away the darkness of ignorance. Also to be seen are the mausoleums of the fifth Dalai Lama and all his successors from the seventh to the 13th. Their *stupas*, or tomb chests, gleam with gold and precious stones. The solid-silver *stupa* of the 13th Dalai Lama, who died in 1933, stands over 70 feet (21 m) high and is studded with gems.

Lhasa lies 11,975 feet (3,650 m) up in the Himalayas, and the air is thin. Until the Chinese occupation in 1951, Buddhist monks made up a substantial percentage of the population. Pilgrims flock to the Jokhang Temple, which contains a famous jewel-encrusted Buddha statue given to Songtsen Gampo by his Chinese wife. Just west of the town is the Norbuglingka, or Jewel Palace, the summer residence of the Dalai Lamas since the 18th century. There, fine murals and the private rooms of the present Dalai Lama can be seen.

Ocean of Wisdom

TIBETAN Buddhism developed as an offshoot of the Buddhism of northern India and Nepal, which blended with the native Tibetan nature religion, called Bon, to produce a religious system with its own distinct character. Within it there were various sects, one of which converted the khan, or chief, of the Mongolians to Buddhism in the 16th century. The khan conferred on the head of the sect the title of Dalai Lama, signifying "ocean of wisdom." The "great fifth" Dalai Lama became ruler of Tibet.

One unusual feature of Tibetan Buddhism is the practice of succession by reincarnation. When each of the Dalai Lamas dies, a search is made, which might take several years, for the child in whom he is reborn. Sometimes the old Dalai Lama leaves a hint about where to look. The child might be revealed by signs and portents, by some recollection of his previous life, and very often by his ability to pick out from a selection of objects those that had been his as the previous Dalai Lama. This happened with the present Dalai Lama, born in 1935. He was declared the successor at the age of four.

Once found, the new Dalai Lama is taken to Lhasa to be trained and takes up the duties of his office at 18. During his minority, a regent rules for him. In practice, many Dalai Lamas never escaped from under their regent's thumb, and several of them were murdered when they became a threat to the regent's position.

1955 India

THE CITY OF CHANDIGARH

A new building for a new city, where modern art and color were judged to be in contempt of court.

There are daily flights to Chandigarh from Delhi. By bus the journey from the capital takes about five hours to cover the distance of some 160 miles (257 km) along the Great Trunk Road. There is also a train station with services from Delhi, but it is some distance from the center of the city. Chandigarh itself is divided into numerous sectors and is not easily seen on foot. The Court House is in Sector 1, the bus station and tourist office in Sector 17.

Right: a machine for working in – the Secretariat Building at Chandigarh. Le Corbusier was in his sixties when he began work on the new city. He had long dreamed of such an opportunity and had planned a projected city of 3 million people as far back as 1922.

Facing page, left: the Gandhi Bhawan memorial library, in the shape of a lotus blossom, was designed by Le Corbusier's cousin, Pierre Jeanneret.

Facing page, right: the High Court has a concrete grill across the front to shield those inside from the full glare of the sun.

THE Swiss architect Le Corbusier (1887-1965) has been described as a rare and original genius by some, and blamed for all that went wrong with 20th-century architecture by others. His real name was Charles-Edouard Jeanneret, but he called himself Le Corbusier. In 1950, after many disappointments and failures, he was finally given the opportunity to realize his ambition of designing an entire city. The invitation came not from Europe, or anywhere in the West, but from India. The northern state of Punjab had lost its capital, Lahore, to Pakistan following the partition of the subcontinent in 1947, and the authorities now wished to build a new capital for the part of Punjab that remained within India. This was to be the first new city in India since Jaipur was laid out in 1728. A site had been chosen and work had already begun, but the death of one of the leading architects in a plane crash resulted in the invitation to Le Corbusier. The intention was that he should design only the major government buildings, but in effect he revised the whole scheme.

The site lies below the Siwalik Hills and between two rivers. A large artificial lake was created, with a pleasant walk beside it, and the city was stocked with flowering trees. It is divided into sectors separated by wide boulevards. Many of the major buildings are raised up on pillars. Le Corbusier designed the huge Secretariat, the Assembly Hall and the Court House, but the planned governor's palace never materialised.

Le Corbusier envisaged a wide main axis road with the Secretariat on one side and the Court House on the other, and this is how the city was laid out. The buildings and roads have been fiercely criticized for their lack of human scale and proportion – ironically, because Le Corbusier employed his own system of measurement known as Modular, which was based on the principle of man as the measure of all things. Chandigarh has also come under fire for being a city designed for the automobile in a country where very few people own them. It is as if, the critics say, the architect planned Chandigarh without troubling to visit India or find out anything about Indian life.

The building that has attracted most attention is Le Corbusier's Court House, which contains a High Court and eight lower courts. The High Court is literally higher than the others, rising three stories to their two. The eight lower courts are all provided with separate entrances, and the divisions between them are clearly visible on the façade of the building, which is covered with a geometrical *brise-soleil.* This "sun-break" is something that Le Corbusier had first experimented with in the 1930s. Forming a deep grille across the front of the building, it is intended to shelter the occupants from the full strength of the sun, and it was a device that seemed particularly appropriate to the Indian climate.

Other attractions at Chandigarh include a rose garden and a weird and whimsical rock garden, near the lake. It was assembled out of all sorts of bits of junk, entirely without official knowledge, by one of the civil servants.

Other Work of Le Corbusier

VISITORS to Chandigarh will see the other buildings of the capital and judge for themselves whether the city is a disaster or a triumph – although it is perhaps still too early to say. The same may be true of Le Corbusier himself, who has been called a much misunderstood genius and a man way ahead of his time. In Ahmedabad, in the state of Gujarat, also in North India, he designed private villas for a couple of wealthy clients, a cultural center, and a headquarters building for the local mill-owners association. In Europe one of his most celebrated buildings is the church of Notre Dame du Haut, at Ronchamp, which belongs to the same era as Chandigarh (1950-55). In Marseilles, his Unité d'Habitation, dating from just after the Second World War, is an exciting design for a block of flats arranged as if several streets, including a street of shops, have been placed on top of one another. The effect is something like that of a great ship (there is even a suggestion of funnels on the flat roof). Other notable buildings in France include the Villa Savoye, near Paris, and the monastery of Sainte Marie de la Tourette, near Lyons.

The Open Hand

THE image of an open hand is one that appears in a number of Le Corbusier's sketches, and at Chandigarh in 1985, 20 years after his death, a great sculpture of such a hand was unveiled. Following Le Corbusier's design, it turns in the wind like a weather vane.

1988 Japan

THE SETO OHASHI BRIDGE

A triumph of modern engineering soars across the beautiful Inland Sea.

The Seto Ohashi Bridge carries General National Highway Number 30, with 11 bus stops en route. Toll for cars. The bridge also carries the Honshi-Bisa rail line, with three specially constructed new stations: Kimi, Kaminocho, and Kojima.

JAPAN consists of four main islands and numerous smaller ones. With the opening on April 10, 1988, of the Seto Ohashi Bridge, at that time the country's biggest civil engineering project, all four of the main islands were for the first time connected together by rail. It then became possible to speed from the Siberian cold of Hokkaido in the north across Honshu to the semitropical harbors of Kyushu and the pilgrim-haunted temples of Shikoku in the south. The new bridge crosses the Seto, or Inland Sea, between the main islands of Honshu and Shikoku, one of the most picturesquely beautiful stretches of water in the world.

The toll bridge glides elegantly across five small islands on its way between the towns of Kurashiki on Honshu and Sakaide on Shikoku for a total distance of 7 1/2 miles (12 km). It is, in fact, more accurate to use the plural, as this tremendous feat of engineering links together three suspension bridges, two cable-stayed bridges, one truss bridge, and five viaducts. The two cable-stayed bridges, each 2,600 feet (792 m) long, are the longest of their kind in the world.

The longest of the suspension bridges, the South Bisan Bridge, has a main span of 3,610 feet (1,100 m), which makes it the fifth-longest suspension bridge in the world. Its two main steel towers stand 637 feet (194 m) high, which is substantially taller than the Great Pyramid and about two-thirds the height of the Eiffel Tower. The amount of cable used in it would go three times around the globe. It stands 213 feet (65 m) above the water at high tide, to allow clear passage to tankers and liners in the Inland Sea.

The Seto Ohashi Bridge is a two-decker structure for road and rail, with the upper deck carrying a four-lane expressway and the lower carrying trains, including the Shinkansen flyers. The bridge took 10 years to build at a cost of 17 lives and over 1 trillion yen (roughly $9 1/2 billion, or £5 billion). The labor force at its maximum was about 5,000, and 67 million hours were spent on the construction. The whole bridge is designed to withstand an earthquake of 8.5 on the Richter scale, for although the Inland Sea is renowned for its sheltered tranquillity, the area is also notorious for temblors.

With the Speed of a Bullet

JAPAN'S surging postwar economic boom has been reflected in audacious civil engineering projects, with the construction of railroads, tunnels, and bridges. In 1964 the world was amazed by the opening of Japanese National Railways' new Shinkansen line,

Right: seen from the air, the bridge island-hops its way over the beautiful Inland Sea. It had to be specially designed to stand up to earthquakes, for which the area is notorious.

Facing page: the bridge seen from water level. The main span was built high enough to allow clear passage to ships.

Big as it is, the bridge will in time be dwarfed by a still larger one. Under construction since 1988 and planned for completion in 1998 is another two-tiered road-rail link between Honshu and Shikoku. The monster Akashi Kaikyo Bridge is to have a main span of 5,840 feet (1,780 m), which will make it the longest suspension bridge in the world.

The effect of these developments on Shikoku is likely to be considerable. The smallest of the four main islands, it was also the most secluded, attracting pilgrims rather than tourists. The pilgrims went to visit the island's 88 main temples, which on foot might take two months. The temples are linked with a famous Buddhist saint, Kobo Daishi, who was born on Shikoku in 774 and founded the Shingon sect of Japanese Buddhism. Now, however, his quiet island is fated to be transformed by the arrival of commercial tourism.

running 320 miles (515 km) between Tokyo and Osaka. The line was specially designed for 15,875-horsepower engines to haul 16-car trains each weighing 970 U.S. tons (880 metric tons) at speeds well above 100 miles per hour (160 km/h). The system was automatically controlled, and the line was the first major one in the world to need no signals along the track. The second generation of Shinkansen engines, 23,600 horsepower, hauls trains weighing 1,025 U.S. tons (930 metric tons).

By 1976 Shinkansen was running 100 "bullet trains" a day at scheduled speeds of over 90 m.p.h. (145 km/h) and reaching 130 m.p.h. (209 km/h) on the fastest stretch. In 1981 Shinkansen lost its "world's fastest train" title when the French started running high-speed trains at 160 m.p.h. (257 km/h) on the line between Paris and Lyons.

The connecting of Japan's four main islands by rail was another remarkable achievement. In the southwest, trains run between the islands of Kyushu and Honshu through two undersea rail tunnels (with a third one for cars). The Seto Ohashi Bridge now links Shikoku and Honshu by rail and road. In the north, March 1988 saw the opening of the astonishing Seikal rail tunnel between Honshu and Hokkaido. The longest in the world, it has a total length of $33\frac{1}{2}$ miles (54 km), of which $14\frac{1}{2}$ miles (23 km) is beneath the sea, descending to 328 feet (100 m) below the seabed. It took 24 years, and many lives, to build.

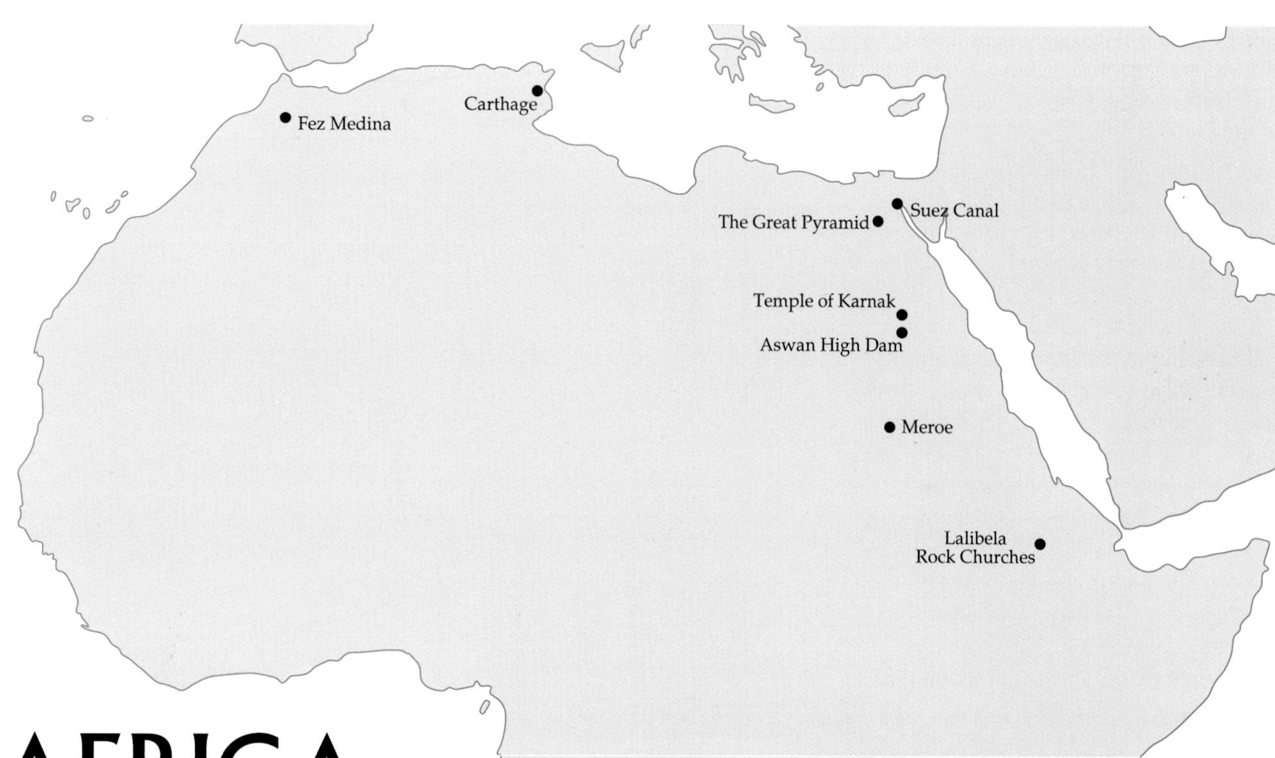

AFRICA

At Luxor a vast figure of Ramses II holds his little daughter between his knees.

AFRICA ranks behind Asia as the second largest of the continents, occupying about one-fifth of the globe's land surface. It is also the probable cradle of the human species. The earliest human, or humanlike, beings of whom traces have been discovered lived in Africa millions of years ago and from Africa, it seems, spread out to cover the earth. It is an indication of what has happened since that the continent today is home to a rich diversity of peoples who speak at least 800 totally distinct languages.

The first human beings lived by hunting and gathering, but by 5000 B.C. there were farming communities in Egypt, in the fertile valley of the Nile. To the west, the Sahara was not yet a desert, and there is evidence of cattle-breeding in what is now a barren wilderness. By about 3000 B.C. there was a unified kingdom of Egypt, in which a major civilization developed. It survived for 2,000 years and more, until the land of the pharaohs was conquered by foreign powers from Asia – the Assyrians in the 7th century B.C., the Persians in the 6th.

CARTHAGE AND CLEOPATRA

Meanwhile, the Phoenicians, based in Syria and Lebanon, had made their living at sea. Their major ports were Tyre and Sidon, and they built up a commercial empire in the

Mediterranean. Their galleys probed west along the North African coast, rowing or sailing by day and beaching on shore each night, and in this way they developed a string of trading posts. They founded a colony at Carthage in modern Tunisia (the traditional date is 814 B.C.), which became a formidable power in its own right.

In 334 B.C. Alexander the Great conquered Egypt, was hailed as a god by the Egyptian priests, went on to seize the whole Persian Empire, and died when he was still only 32 years old. After his death, his empire split. Egypt went to one of his Greek generals, Ptolemy, who established a new dynasty on the pharaohs' throne. The Carthaginians had profitable trade routes across the Sahara down to western Africa, even before the introduction of the camel, "the ship of the desert," from western Asia in about 100 B.C. Their western Mediterranean empire flourished until they collided with the burgeoning power of Rome. After three major wars, the Romans smashed Carthage in 146 B.C.

In the next century the bewitching Cleopatra, Ptolemaic queen of Egypt, backed the wrong man. She committed suicide after she and her lover, Mark Antony, were defeated by the future Roman emperor Augustus in 31 B.C. Rome took over Egypt and ruled the whole North African coast. Christianity, which became the Roman Empire's official religion in the 4th century A.D., occupied the same territory, and a Christian archbishop had his see in Carthage. The city was subsequently the capital of a kingdom of the Vandals, a Germanic people from beyond the Rhine, then was part of the Byzantine Empire. In the 7th century Carthage fell to the Arabs and Islam.

Layer upon layer of history built up at Carthage over the centuries. A grim archaeological find there was the discovery of the remains of thousands of small children, burned in sacrifice to the Carthaginian fertility goddess Tanit and her consort Baal Hammon.

WHITE AND BLACK IVORY

South of Egypt the powerful kingdom of Kush had grown up long before, with its capital at Meroe, where excavations have uncovered the palaces and temples of a prosperous city with a mixed Caucasian and Negro population. Egyptian culture was strong, and Meroe was a channel through which Egyptian influence penetrated further south into black Africa.

Early in the 4th century A.D., Meroe was overrun by Ethiopian armies from further south. The Ethiopian Orthodox Church would eventually create the fantastic rock churches at Lalibela, hidden deep among the mountains.

The Arabs conquered Egypt in 641 and swept in a torrent across North Africa. Mosques raised their domes to the African sky in walled cities like Fez in Morocco, seat of a university founded as far back as 859. To this day it keeps its ancient battlements, its venerable mosque, its narrow, crowded, clamorous streets. Until the 19th century, it was the only place in the world where fez hats were made.

Arab merchants pressed far south into Africa to trade in ivory, gold, and slaves. South of the Sahara, powerful kingdoms rose and fell. At Great Zimbabwe the stone ruins cover more than 60 acres (24 hectares), with walls 30 feet (9.1 m) high and 15 feet (4.6 m) thick.

From the 15th century, however, Africa was a magnet for European trade and imperialism, led by the Portuguese. The Spanish followed. The Dutch founded Cape Colony in 1652. A flourishing trade in slaves developed between the West African kingdoms and the New World, until the British government abolished the slave trade in 1807. In the 19th century the whole of Africa was carved up among the major European powers, and the Suez Canal was built by a French engineer backed by French money. Even in this century, when the African countries have gained independence, the Aswan High Dam in Egypt was designed by Germans and built by Russians.

Remains of rock churches at Lalibela in the mountain fastnesses of Ethiopia.

The Temple wall in Great Zimbabwe is a relic of the might of a vanished kingdom.

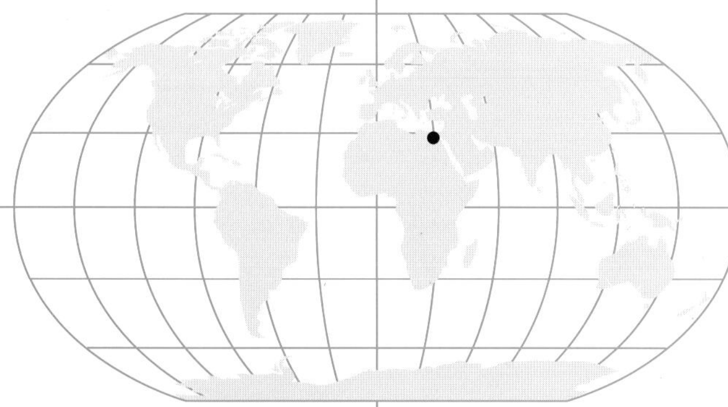

About 2560 B.C. Egypt

THE GREAT PYRAMID

Massive and mysterious, the Great Pyramid has withstood time for 45 centuries.

The Great Pyramid lies 6 miles (10 km) southwest of Cairo, outside the suburb of Giza. Buses from Tahrir Square in Cairo, or shared taxis. Visitors can go out into the desert by camel, horse, or carriage for a better view. Regular sound-and-light shows.

Riddle of the Sphinx

A SYMBOL of mystery and enigma down the ages, the Sphinx was built by Pharaoh Khafre (the head was apparently a portrait of him). Looking a mere kitten in proportion to the vast bulk of the pyramids looming behind it, the Sphinx is in fact a sizeable object, a recumbent lion with a human head, 66 feet (20 m) high and 240 feet (73 m) long. At its maximum the face is 13¾ feet (4.2 m) wide. It was made out of a knoll of rock left in place when the stone was quarried for the Great Pyramid.

Presumably the Sphinx is a guardian of the necropolis behind it, but no one knows for certain. The head has a royal headdress and the royal symbol of a cobra on the forehead, but its nose is partly missing and the beard has gone entirely. Originally it was probably plastered over and painted, apparently red.

In front of it is a stele, or

Above: the face of the Sphinx, an early essay in portraiture.

Right: the Sphinx at night, with the Great Pyramid behind.

Facing page: the planet's best-known group of buildings.

STANDING at the edge of the desert, to the west of the River Nile, the Great Pyramid was built for Pharaoh Khufu (the Greek form of his name was Cheops) in the 26th century B.C. Two later kings of the 4th dynasty – Khafre (Chephren) and Menkaure (Mykerinos) – built pyramids close by. The three together form what is possibly the world's most instantly recognizable group of buildings, regarded for centuries with fascination and awe.

Awe is justified. The Great Pyramid stands 450 feet (137 m) high. It is constructed of more than 2¼ million blocks of limestone, quarried nearby, weighing on average over 2¾ U.S. tons (2½ metric tons) each. The largest blocks weigh over 16¾ U.S. tons (15¼ metric tons), and the granite roof slabs over the King's Chamber inside weigh up to 56 U.S. tons (50¾ metric tons). The whole huge bulk of nearly 7 million U.S. tons (over 6 million metric tons) was erected without the assistance of modern machinery, but with the use of ramps, levers, rollers, and ox-drawn sledges to move the stone blocks.

Despite this, the pyramid was constructed with uncanny and fanatical accuracy. It stands on an artificially flattened site that deviates from a perfectly level plane by only a little more than half an inch (less than 2 cm). The base of the pyramid is remarkably close to being a perfect square, within a few inches, and so the four corners are almost perfect right angles. It was carefully aligned with the cardinal points of the compass, with the four sides facing due north, east, south, and west – again with only a tiny deviation from the most exact pinpoint accuracy.

Why it was vital to achieve such perfection no one knows, but evidently it was. For that matter, no one knows for certain why the pyramid was built in the first place. The generally accepted theory is that it was the pharaoh's tomb, which may well be true, but it is odd that no corpse was ever found in it, or in the other pyramids either. When an official party broke into the Great Pyramid in the 9th century A.D. and with great difficulty forced their way into the King's Chamber, they found the great stone coffin empty, but no sign of

previous disturbance.

There is an entrance to the north side from which a low, narrow passage leads the cramped and crouching visitor to a long passage called the Grand Gallery, 153 feet (46.6 m) long. It leads to what is usually called the King's Chamber, 140 feet (42.7 m) above ground level, with the empty granite sarcophagus. There are two other chambers inside the pyramid, both empty. Just outside the pyramid, in a long pit, a cedar boat was found in 1954. Partly dismantled, it was 143 feet (43.6 m) long and can be seen today in the Solar Barque Museum on the site. Other boats were evidently buried close by and may have been intended for the dead ruler's voyages in the afterlife.

The three pyramids are part of a complex that includes temples, miniature pyramids thought to have been provided for the pharaohs' wives, and the tombs of priests and officials. This city of the dead is guarded by the watchful Sphinx, gazing out over the desert sands.

upright slab of granite, on which is recorded the curious experience of a pharaoh of the 15th century B.C., Thutmose IV, who was out hunting gazelles one day when he sat down to rest in the Sphinx's shade. He fell asleep and had a dream that promised him the throne of Egypt if he cleared the sand from the monument. He did, and duly gained the throne. Various other pharoahs put up steles here, and apparently the monument was a place of pilgrimage.

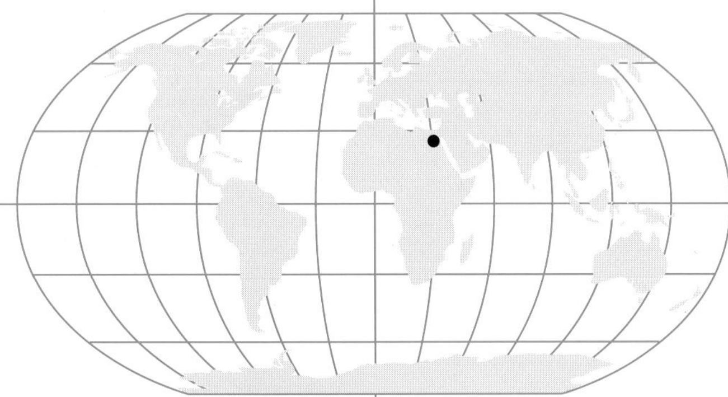

Mainly from the 16th Century B.C. Egypt

TEMPLE OF KARNAK

The golden statue of the god in his sacred boat stood in the temple's innermost sanctuary.

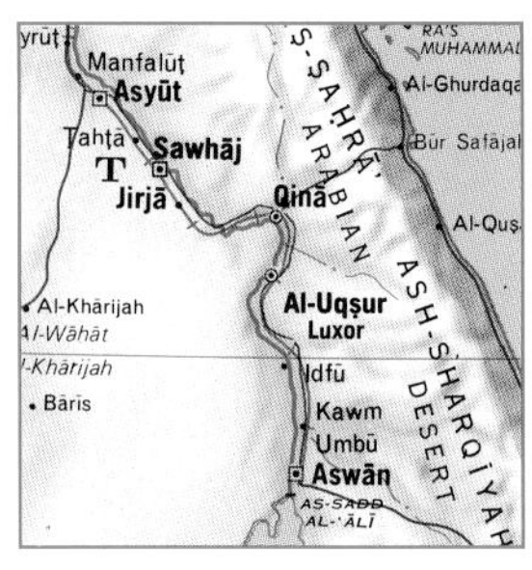

Luxor is some 400 miles (644 km) downriver from Cairo and 125 miles (201 km) north of Aswan. Flights from Cairo and Aswan. Trains from Ramses Station, Cairo, also buses from Cairo. Many Nile cruises take in Luxor and the Temple of Karnak.

THE city that the Greeks called Thebes, capital of Egypt for some 1,500 years in the period that historians call the New Kingdom, stood approximately where the town of Luxor is today, on the east bank of the Nile. Nothing is left of the city itself, but the mighty ruins of the Temple of Karnak still overawe today's visitors. With its imposing gates, its courts and halls, its forests of pillars, its carvings and statues and obelisks, it was the largest temple complex in ancient Egypt.

The principal temple here was sacred to the

King of Kings

NOT far from Luxor, on the west side of the Nile, two enormous seated figures of Pharaoh Amenohotep III stand solitary in a field. Known as the Colossi of Memnon, they once stood at the entrance to his temple. More than 50 feet (15 m) high, they have graffiti scrawled on them by such eminent visitors as the Roman emperor Hadrian's court poet.

Right: the ruined temples, seen across the sacred lake, which was supplied with water running underground from the Nile. Sacred geese were kept here and sacred boats sailed the lake.

Facing page: inside, the temple was a forest of pillars, which symbolized the palm trees that, in Egyptian mythology, grew on the Island of Creation, where the world began.

god Amun, lord of the winds and the air. He was represented as a human figure with a double feather crown, and his special animal was the ram. A minor local god originally, he was made Egypt's national god by the New Kingdom pharaohs, from the 16th century B.C. on, and identified with Re, the sun god. He was worshipped here with his consort, the goddess Mut, and their son, the moon god Khons.

Amun's little temple at Karnak was enlarged by Thutmose I at the beginning of the New Kingdom. His successors expanded it again and again. Different areas are entered through huge portals known as pylons, consisting of a doorway flanked by massive towers. There are 10 of these at Karnak. As the worshipper penetrated into the temple, he passed from the bright sunlight of the outside world into the deepening darkness of the great halls toward the mystery of the innermost shrine, which contained the image of the god. This shrine

was barred to all except the king and the priests.

The complex was approached along two avenues of ram-headed sphinxes, one leading from the Nile and the other from Luxor. The vast front pylon of the main temple still stands 143 feet (43.6 m) high and 370 feet (113 m) wide, with walls 49 feet (15 m) thick. Beyond this is the Great Court, surrounded by a colonnade, with subsidiary temples opening off it. The second pylon opens into the Great Pillared Hall, which alone covers an area one-third the size of St. Peter's in Rome. Open to the sky now, its roof originally rested 80 feet (24 m) above the ground on 140 pillars arranged in 16 rows, their capitals in the form of papyrus flowers and buds.

A third pylon leads to the central court, beyond which three more pylons lead to the inner sanctuary where the golden statue of the god stood in his sacred boat. To the south, through four more pylons, lies the temple of Mut, not yet fully excavated, but almost as large as her consort's. Also in the complex are temples of Khons and other gods. The gardens in which the buildings were set vanished long ago, but there is a fine view of the complex from across the sacred lake.

The temple of Luxor itself, also dedicated to Amun-Re and also built and added to over centuries, is smaller but very impressive. Christians used it as a church, and there is a mosque inside part of it today. There is a fine colonnade of papyrus columns, colossal statues of Ramses II, and lively carvings in relief.

Valley of the Kings

WITH their capital at Thebes, most of the New Kingdom pharaohs were buried in the desert to the west of the Nile, in the Valley of the Kings, where more than 60 tombs have so far been discovered. Only a small number are open to visitors. By far the most famous of them is the tomb of Tutankhamen, which created a sensation when it was opened in 1923. The most astonishing wealth of treasure was revealed – a coffin of solid gold, golden diadems and masks, jewels, statues, chariots, weapons, ornaments, paintings – in such profusion that it took three years to clear out the tomb. The youthful pharaoh, who was only 18 when he died in 1352 B.C., still rests inside his sarcophagus in the tomb, but almost all the treasures are in the Egyptian Museum in Cairo.

Who knows what fabulous riches may have surrounded more important rulers before the tomb robbers got in? Today the tombs are particularly interesting for their mural paintings, which include scenes of the afterlife from the Book of the Dead, scenes of the sun god's night journey through the underworld in a boat, and animal-headed gods and goddesses. The tomb of Ramses III has delightful scenes from daily life in ancient Egypt.

THE LAND OF THE PHARAOHS

A rich and enigmatic civilization developed in the valley of the Nile.

Afterlife frescoes in Seti I's tomb in the Valley of the Kings.

EGYPT has been described as a land with length, but no breadth. Although approximately the size of France, the habitable part of it is confined to a narrow corridor along the River Nile. The rest, on either side of the corridor, is desert.

In the Nile Valley there grew up one of the great ancient civilizations, whose remains have been preserved over centuries by the Egyptian climate. The sheer size of its monuments compels awe. The Great Pyramid, for instance, covers an area close to 13 acres (5 hectares), into which five of the biggest cathedrals in Europe could be fitted without the slightest difficulty. Also compelling is the mysteriousness of ancient Egypt: the tombs with their mummified corpses wrapped in linen bandages, the peculiar animal-headed gods, the temple walls and pillars covered with hieroglyphs or "sacred signs" that form one of the earliest systems of writing.

THE THREE KINGDOMS

The economy of Egypt always depended on the Nile and the sun. Every year, normally in July, the great river flowed over its banks onto the land on either side, spreading over it a rich black mud in which the crops grew, nourished by the sun's heat. Hence the Egyptian name of the country, *kemi*, "the black land." When the flood failed, everyone faced famine and disaster. Much of the apparatus of the Egyptian state religion was directed to performing the rituals that would preserve the proper order of things so that the life-giving flood would occur in due season. The main role in these rituals was taken by the pharaoh, who was king and chief priest in one, and whose remote ancestors had been primitive rain-making chieftains.

Somewhere about 3000 B.C. Egypt was welded into a single, unified state with its capital at Memphis, south of the Nile Delta. From this point on, its history is divided by Egyptologists into three main periods ("kingdoms"), with intermediate periods between them. The Old Kingdom, from the 27th to the 22nd century B.C., was the major period of pyramid building, culminating in the Great Pyramid and its companions at Giza, which are now about 4,500 years old. The shape of the pyramid, pointing upwards, may have symbolized the ascent of the deceased pharaoh to join his father, the sun god, in the sky.

The Middle Kingdom, from the 21st to the 17th century B.C., was another period of prosperity, but the golden age of ancient Egypt came with the New Kingdom, from the 16th to the 11th century. The capital was moved to Thebes (modern Luxor). The immense wealth of the pharaohs was spent on the construction of gigantic temples, adorned with statues, obelisks, sphinxes, vivid reliefs, and wall paintings. The Temple of Karnak at Thebes was the largest of all. The pharaohs were buried in the Valley of the Kings, interred with amazing quantities of treasures revealed to an astonished world when Tutankhamen's tomb was discovered in the 1920s.

Ramses II – who is often identified as the pharaoh of the Exodus, though this is uncertain – built the rock temples at Abu Simbel and raised four colossal statues of himself enthroned, gazing out over the barren wilderness of the desert in a triumphant statement of overwhelming power. It seems that, as examination of his mummified body has suggested, he probably suffered agonizing toothaches – a thought that brings him down to size.

THE NEXT WORLD

A fundamental focus of ancient Egyptian religion was the belief in a life after death. Extraordinarily elaborate procedures of mummification – too expensive for ordinary people, who had to do without – went to ensuring that a dead person would go safely to a new life in the land of the dead, a life very much like the one in this world. In the tombs lively paintings depict scenes of life in the afterworld. Miniature figures of servants were placed in tombs to serve their owner beyond death, and supplies of furniture, clothes, and weapons were placed in them with the same purpose. Food was provided too – bread, dried fish, and joints of lamb. It was not only people who were embalmed. Cemeteries have been discovered containing thousands of mummified cats, dogs, falcons, baboons, and crocodiles.

The Egyptian gods and goddesses are present everywhere, in statues, carvings, and paintings. Many of them are depicted with the heads of animals. The sky god Horus has the head of a hawk, the love goddess Hathor the ears and horns of a cow. The meaning of this has defied all attempts to fathom it, but no other people has so closely identified animals with the divine. It is yet another enigma of ancient Egypt.

The temple of the great goddess Isis, moved from Philae.

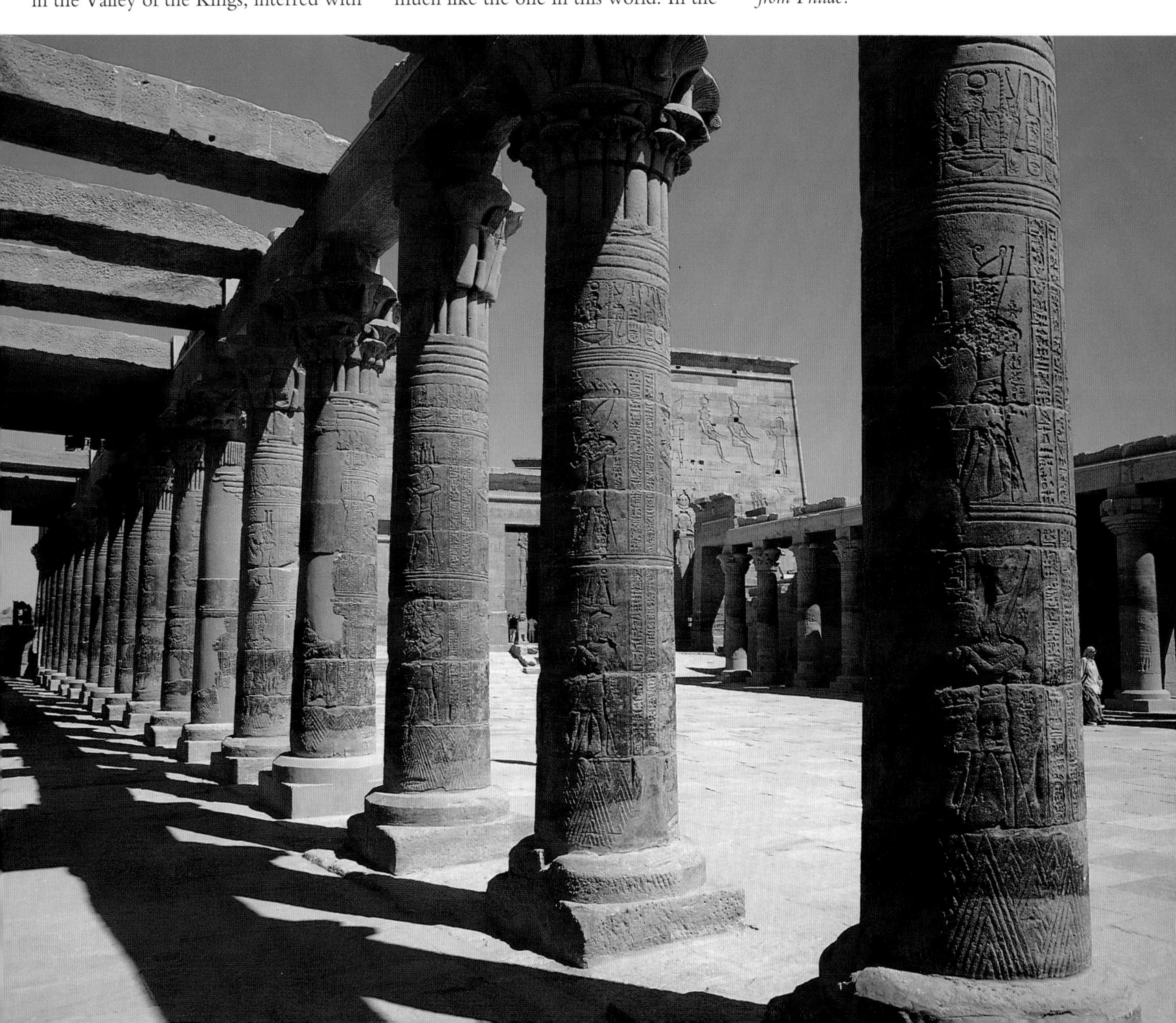

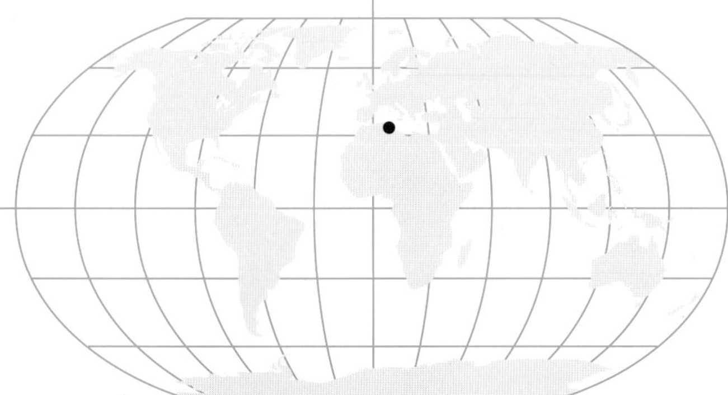

From the 8th Century B.C. Tunisia

CARTHAGE

"The rising city, which from far you see,
Is Carthage, and a Tyrian colony.
Phoenician Dido rules the growing state,
Who fled from Tyre, to shun her brother's hate."
from The Aeneid, *translated by* JOHN DRYDEN

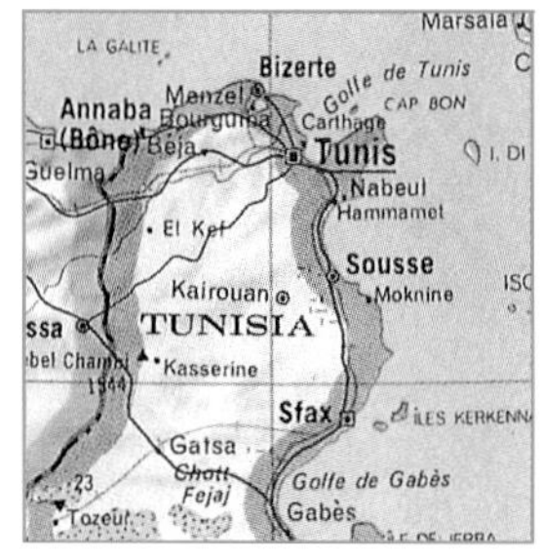

Tunis has an international airport a short distance from the city center and can also be reached by ferry from Sicily. Carthage is, in effect, a suburb of the city, conveniently reached by the T.G.M. urban railroad. The principal sites are spread over about 4 miles (6 km) and, again, the T.G.M. is a useful link between them.

DIDO was the sister of the king of Tyre, the ancient capital of Phoenicia. When the king murdered her husband for his money, Dido gathered a band of supporters and set sail in search of a new kingdom. On the coast of North Africa she built a magnificent city, and it was here that the Trojan prince Aeneas arrived with his fleet during his long search for a site on which to found Rome. Dido's city was Carthage (the word is derived from the Phoenician for "new city"), and the story of her love for Aeneas and her suicide when he left her, poignantly told by the Roman poet Virgil in his epic poem *The Aeneid*, inspired many later writers, artists, and composers.

If Carthage is a prominent feature in European artistic tradition, it is less prominent on the ground. In the middle of the 2nd century B.C., the Roman senate resounded with the words of Cato the Elder, who repeatedly declared that Carthage must be destroyed (*delenda est Karthago*). Carthage, one-time ally, then rival and enemy of Rome, was destroyed in 146 B.C.

It is almost impossible to separate legend from fact. Despite much archaeological work, clues remain elusive. Even the date of the city's founding is uncertain. Literary evidence suggests a time at the end of the 9th century B.C., but archaeological remains indicate no occupation before the middle of the 8th century. The oldest finds are sinister ones. An area known as the Topheth, apparently a sanctuary of the goddess Tanit, produced evidence of child sacrifice on a large scale. In moonlit ceremonies, children of two or three years old were sacrificed to the god Baal Hammon. There seems to have been a tradition of sacrificing members of prominent and ruling families, who were sent to the next world in tombs equipped with goods for the afterlife. The story of Dido's death may be

Hannibal and the Punic Wars

HANNIBAL, the young Carthaginian general who led an army of 38,000 foot soldiers, 8,000 cavalry, and 37 elephants over the Alps to take Italy totally by surprise, has captured the imagination of generations. Unlike Dido, whose story is a mixture of a little fact with a great deal of legend and poetic invention, Hannibal is entirely for real. The business of maneuvering elephants over the Alps may sound like adventurous fantasy, but it happened and an actual route has been traced.

The expedition took place in 218 B.C. Between 264 and 241 B.C. the Romans and the Carthaginians had fought the First Punic War – the inevitable consequence of increasing

Above: remains of the Roman baths at Carthage, among the ruins of century after century.

Facing page: ruined pillars lie peacefully beside the blue Mediterranean. It was from the sea that Carthage was founded by the Phoenicians and by sea that the city built up her trading greatness.

connected with a primitive idea that the death of a king or queen could benefit the country.

During the 6th century B.C. Carthage grew increasingly powerful, built up a fleet, and acquired a number of colonies. Signs of her naval power can be seen in two man-made harbors near the Topheth, and it is these that many visitors find particularly memorable. One was a circular naval harbor, and the island at the center of this had dry-dock space for many vessels. A figure of 220 is quoted by the Greek historian Appian, and much of his description of the harbor area has been confirmed by archaeologists. The naval harbor was connected to a large merchant harbor, whose silted-up entrance has been traced.

The center of the city appears to have been on the Byrsa Hill (the name means "ox hide" and is linked with the legend that Dido originally obtained as much land as could be enclosed by a hide), and there is now an archaeological museum here. Excavations on the side of the hill have revealed some houses and shops belonging to the late 3rd or early 2nd century B.C. But most of the buildings whose remains can be seen today – an amphitheater, for example, and the ground plans of the Antonine Baths and a number of villas – bear the stamp of her triumphant rival, the irresistible power of Rome.

rivalry between the two powers. In the end Carthage was forced to surrender her hold on Sicily and made to pay a huge indemnity. In 218 Hannibal siezed the initiative, overran Etruria, and in 216 defeated the Roman army at the battle of Cannae. Hannibal remained in Italy, undefeated for a number of years, but the Second Punic War ended when Rome invaded Carthage and Hannibal returned to suffer defeat at the battle of Zama in 202. In 149 Rome declared war again, Carthage was besieged, and, in 146, was reduced to ruins in a fire said to have raged for 10 days.

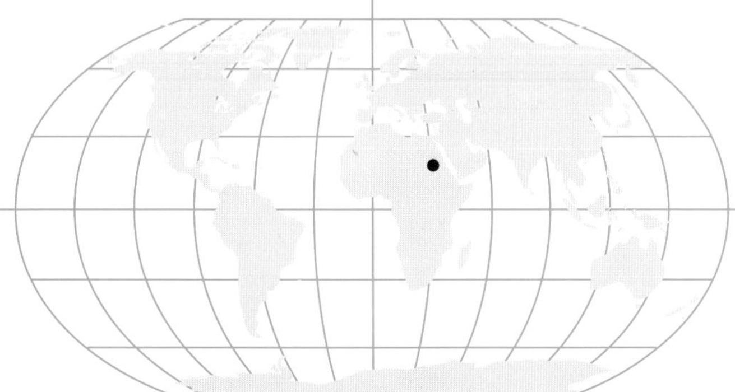

From the 6th Century B.C. Sudan

MEROE

In an ancient African state, kings and queens shared power at the crossroads of several cultures.

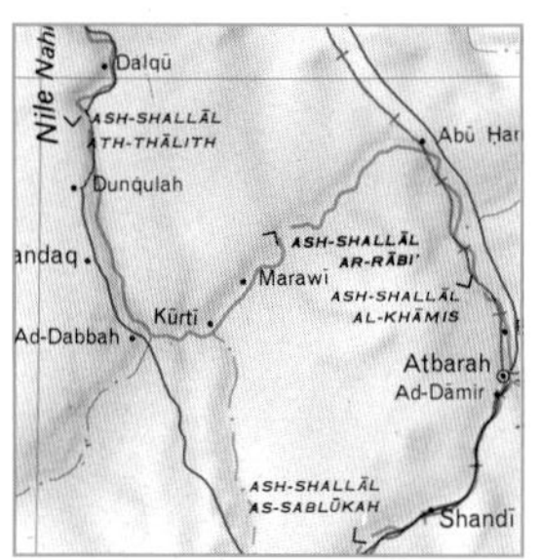

The nearest international airport is at Khartoum, and from here there are trains and buses to the town of Shendi. From Shendi it is a short drive by bus or taxi to Meroe, which is in the vicinity of the small town of Kaboshia.

Right: the influence of ancient Egypt was strong at Meroe, whose dead kings and queens were laid to rest beneath pyramids.

Facing page, above: remains of temple walls amid the desert sands. Lying to the west of the Nile, Meroe was the capital of one of several powerful empires that developed in the interior of Africa.

Facing page, below: in the 1820s an Italian explorer avidly searching for treasure lopped the tops off many of the Meroe pyramids.

THE Greek historian Herodotus, writing in the 5th century B.C., described the remote land of Ethiopia, where there was said to be a shrine called the Table of the Sun. Every night, officials dutifully placed boiled meat on this table, which stood in a field near the town of Meroe. Every day, anyone who wanted to take the meat was allowed to do so, and the king of Meroe boasted that his citizens lived for 120 years, all because of their diet of meat and milk.

The claims for the powers of this diet have not been proved, but Meroe was the capital of a powerful African state, which flourished from perhaps the 6th century B.C. to the 2nd century A.D. and whose influence extended along the Nile for hundreds of miles. A building excavated near the center has even been called the Temple of the Sun, partly because of Herodotus' description and partly because of the discovery of a block of stone with an image of the sun on it. The building also has a sanctuary supported on a platform whose walls are decorated with reliefs of conquered nations.

Other Greek and Roman writers talked of the Ethiopians of Meroe in enough detail for the European explorer James Bruce to guess that the ruins that he glimpsed in the Nile Valley 100 miles (161 km) north of Khartoum in 1772 were those of the place he had read about in classical literature. When archaeologists finally came to study the site at

the beginning of the 20th century, they discovered many tombs, religious buildings, a royal enclosure, pottery, jewelry, and fine metalware, but much is still unexplored and many mysteries remain. One of them is the Meroite language, which has so far defeated attempts to understand it.

Meroe seems to have been a new capital that grew up in a region once subject to Egypt. As the people became more powerful, they in their turn dominated their northern neighbors, but considerable Egyptian influence survived in their art and architecture. Egyptian religion, too, remained important, and there are temples here to Apis, Amun, and Isis. The shape of the temples is distinctly Egyptian, with massive, wedge-shaped masonry and two-dimensional carvings. The kings and queens of Meroe were buried beneath pyramids of dressed sandstone or brick, which were grouped together in cemeteries. Occasionally, Roman and Egyptian styles can be seen in the same building, and Middle Eastern influences can also be detected. One building appears to be a direct copy of a Roman bath complex.

Clearly, the Meroites were people who borrowed much from other cultures and for whom an end to Egyptian domination did not result in a rejection of all that Egypt stood for. Their art suggests that elephants and lions were important to them. Their wealth can be attributed to local deposits of iron ore, and they imported bronze, glass, and even silverware. Although they were ruled by kings, their queens, too, were important figures of authority. We cannot read their writing and can only guess at their way of life.

The Lion God

ALTHOUGH the people of Meroe worshipped a number of Egyptian gods, the lion god Apedemek appears to have been exclusively theirs. A warrior god, he appears in temple reliefs in the company of lions; an Egyptian inscription describes him as one who acts as a companion for both men and women, and who is able to protect and nourish his people. He was worshipped in a temple at Meroe itself, and he also appears in a temple at Naqa, another site where there was once a considerable town. In the latter temple, members of a ruling family are portrayed paying homage to the god.

A Bronze Head Discovered

THE link between the sun temple at Meroe and Herodotus' Table of the Sun may be fanciful, but another discovery at Meroe does seem to be related to an event described by a classical writer. The geographer Strabo tells how the usually unwarlike Ethiopians crossed the frontier into the Roman province of Egypt in 23 B.C., taking advantage of the absence of the majority of the Roman soldiers, who were on a campaign. The Ethiopians attacked three cities, pulling down statues of Augustus Caesar as they went. A fine bronze head of Augustus was found at Meroe, apparently buried with some care, and it is tempting to think that this belonged to one of the statues Strabo referred to.

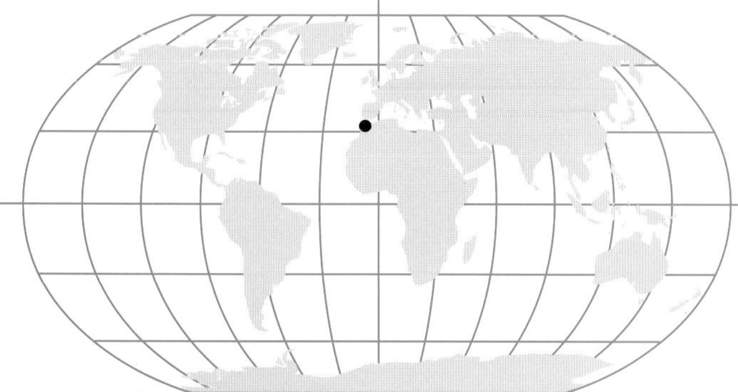

From the 9th Century A.D. Morocco

FEZ MEDINA

A medieval city is still alive and thriving in the 20th century.

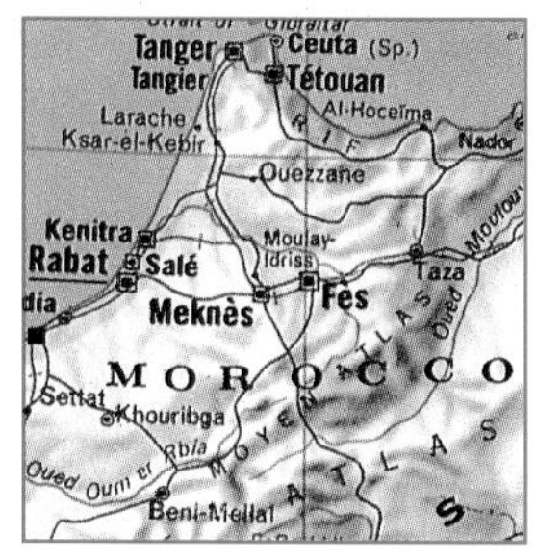

Fez has its own airport with limited international traffic. There are also airports at Tangier, Casablanca (the nearest), Marrakesh, and Agadir, and ferries to Tangier from southern France and Spain. Trains run to Fez from Casablanca and Tangier; buses are available from these cities and from Marrakesh. The Medina is on the eastern side of the city, and there are good bus and taxi services.

Volubilis

FEZ was founded by a descendant of Muhammad called Moulay Idriss, who chose to create his own new city rather than expand the existing Moroccan metropolis at Volubilis. This was originally a Roman city, and the ruins that can be seen today give a good idea of Roman civilization in Africa during the 3rd century A.D. The remains of a basilica, a capitoline temple (dedicated to three deities – Jupiter, Juno, and Minerva), and a forum are at the heart of the site, and there is also a triumphal arch,

Right: a general view of the old medieval city.

Facing page, above: the central courtyard of the Es Sahrij lodging house for students. As a result of a trick of the light, whichever end of the pool you stand at appears to be deeper than the other end. The building dates from the early 14th century.

Facing page, below: the grand triumphal arch was erected at Volubilis in honor of Emperor Caracalla in A.D. 217.

FEZ is a large, modern city with over half a million inhabitants, where it is possible to leave behind the cars, wide streets, and high-rise buildings of the 20th century and enter a medieval metropolis. Medina was the city to which the Prophet Muhammad escaped when he came under threat in Mecca, and Medina has since come to mean the old quarter of any Islamic city. The Medina at Fez is the old city (Fez el Bali) established in the 9th century, where narrow, winding streets, fountains in elegant courtyards, traditional houses, and the noise and bustle of the bazaar combine to offer a window into a different world. Many of the goods on sale may be modern and much may be aimed specifically at tourists, but the atmosphere and the scale of the old city survive.

Fez el Bali was divided into almost 200 different districts, each one a community with its own mosque, water supply, *hammam* (Turkish bath), and bakery. The city is the home of one of the oldest universities in the world and was regarded as a key center for academic debate during the Middle Ages. With nearly 800 mosques (usually with schools attached), thousands of shops, and enough houses for a population of around 125,000, Fez had become, by the 13th century, one of the world's most important cities. To explore it in detail today would take weeks.

The principal mosque, the Karaouyine, was founded in the 9th century and remodeled in the 13th. With room to accommodate 20,000 people, it is the largest mosque in North Africa, and connected with it are the ancient university of Fez and an outstanding library. As so often in Islamic culture, the external appearance is not considered important, and the clutter of buildings around it obscures the outlines of the mosque. Fine artistry, elaborate calligraphy, and ornate tilework exist in abundance inside.

As well as a university, Fez has a large number of *medressahs* (Koran schools). They usually consist of three rooms – school, prayer hall, and library – arranged around a courtyard

with a central fountain. The Bou Inania Medressah is particularly impressive, with decoration that manages to be lavish without being overpowering and that has similarities to the Moorish architecture of Spain. A curious arrangement of windows, wooden blocks, and brass bowls here has been described as a water clock dating from the 13th century, but no one has been able to say how it works. The brass bowls may have been shaped by distant ancestors of the men who can be seen today beating various metals into shape in the Place Seffarine. Dyeing and tanning are two other traditional activities, unchanged for hundreds of years, that can be seen at Fez. At the dyers' *souk* (marketplace) by the river, a watermill is used to crush the seeds that provide vegetable dyes. Further downriver, tanners are hard at work – and can be watched by anyone able to withstand the smell of it.

the remains of some public baths, and a number of houses. Perhaps the chief attraction is the rich variety of mosaics. The House of Orpheus, named after the mosaic found in the dining room, shows Orpheus with his lyre charming a procession of animals and birds. The subject was a popular one with mosaic artists throughout the Roman Empire, and this is a particularly fine example. Other houses contain mosaics showing Bacchus, the god of wine, Actaeon being turned into a stag as punishment for having glimpsed the goddess Diana bathing, and Hercules performing his labors. This region supplied Rome with large quantities of olive oil, and ancient oil presses can still be seen at Volubilis.

Museums

SOME of the treasures found at Volubilis are housed in the Museum of Antiquities at Rabat. Among the exhibits is a bust of Juba, king of this region in the first century B.C., and a lifelike bronze statue of a dog.

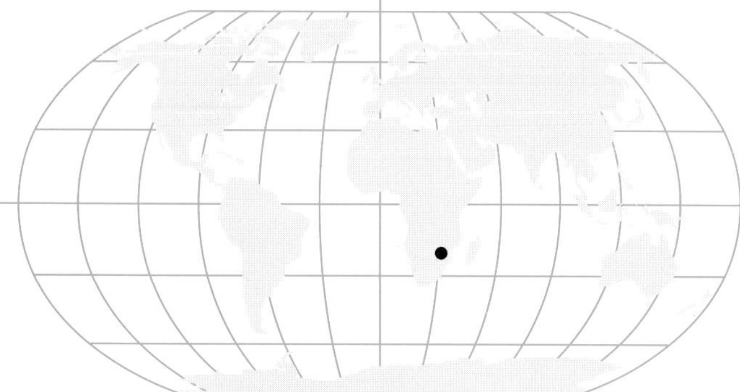

From the 12th Century Zimbabwe

GREAT ZIMBABWE

Magnificent and mysterious stone structures, which some have tried to link with the Queen of Sheba, are pure African work.

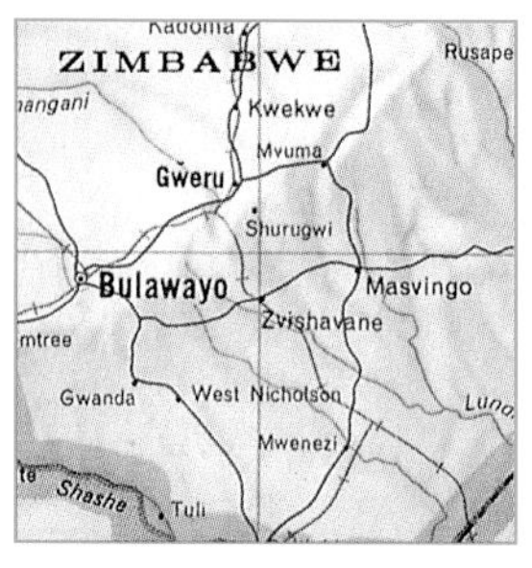

Great Zimbabwe is about 217 miles (350 km) from Harare. From the international airport at Harare, domestic flights go to Masvingo Town. The site is a further 17 miles (28 km) from Masvingo via the Beit Bridge and Morgenster roads. There are also buses from Harare to Masvingo and from Masvingo to Great Zimbabwe.

THE word *zimbabwe* seems to be derived from an expression in the Shona language meaning "venerated houses," and Great Zimbabwe is the site of impressive stone structures built without mortar and without the use of arches or domes. Much about the place remains a mystery, with archaeological work having been hampered by some 19th-century treasure hunters who, under the company name of Rhodesian Ancient Ruins Ltd., indulged in what was virtually licensed plunder of historic sites.

There are three sets of buildings at Great Zimbabwe: an early acropolis or hill fortress, an elliptical enclosure named the Temple, formed by a huge stone wall, and a variety of ruins in a river valley between these two major sites. The ruins stand in a healthy, fertile area with above-average rainfall, something that is likely to have contributed to the growth and prosperity of the people.

The early explorers of Great Zimbabwe persisted in the belief that people other than native Africans must have been responsible for it. Much valuable material was cleared away in the attempt to find some early non-African layer of occupation, but Great Zimbabwe is now known to be an entirely African creation. The earliest levels have produced pottery and other artifacts very similar to those of present-day Bantu people. The acropolis site is thought to have been developed during the 12th or 13th century A.D., and, perhaps as a result of increasing wealth and security, the people built the elliptical structure slightly later. The reason for Great Zimbabwe's growing importance is not known, but it was clearly a thriving place until the 15th century, importing precious goods on a grander scale than any other known settlement in the region.

The remarkable thing about Great Zimbabwe is the quality of the stonework, particularly the northeastern part of the elliptical Temple wall. The wall is over 30 feet (9.1 m) high in places and 16 feet (4.9 m) thick at the base, with intricate zigzag patterns

Right: an entrance to the elliptical enclosure known as the Temple, round which is a massive stone wall, skillfully constructed without mortar. Great Zimbabwe was created by a people speaking the Shona language, whose prosperity may have depended primarily on their huge herds of cattle.

Facing page: part of the zigzag patterns that run along the top of the Temple wall.

running along the top for about a quarter of the 800-foot (244-m) circumference. Skilled masons dressed the granite blocks and laid them in regular courses around a rubble core, and this wall, like those inside the enclosure, is always curved rather than straight. The function of the inner walls and passageways remains obscure, but the structure does not seem to have had a roof. Equally mysterious is the role of a solid stone conical tower on which the zigzag stone pattern reappears.

The acropolis stands on the edge of a 90-foot (27-m) precipice and was approached by steps cut between boulders and the cliff face and wide enough for only one person. This site, too, was protected by a wall with a walkway 13 feet (4 m) wide along the top, on which monoliths were placed at intervals. For Theodore Bent, an early explorer of Great Zimbabwe, the acropolis was notable for its tortuous passages and overfortification. A hundred years after he gazed at this, "the most mysterious and complex structure that it has ever been my fate to look upon," Great Zimbabwe is still a striking yet fundamentally enigmatic place. The great city with its awesome walls – the largest stone monument in Africa after the pyramids – sparked off lively speculation about a lost white civilization deep in Africa, and inspired Rider Haggard's *She*.

Vastness and Power

In 1891 Theodore Bent, his wife, and Robert Swan left England on an archaeological expedition to Africa sponsored by the Royal Geographical Society, the British Chartered Company of South Africa, and the British Association for the Advancement of Science. They spent two months working at Great Zimbabwe, where they employed 30 local laborers (whose reward was one blanket per month) to clear the overgrown ruins. Bent's account of his expedition, *The Ruined Cities of Mashonaland*, published in 1892, gives a colorful idea of the attitudes and methods of work at the time.

Bent records that "serious doubts as to the advisability of a lady undertaking such a journey were frequently brought before us at the outset." The doubters were proved wrong. Mrs. Bent, who had experience of travel in other lands, proved to be the only one of the party who escaped fever. Her husband proudly reports that she did not have a day's illness in a whole year in Africa, and that she took a good many photographs under circumstances of exceptional difficulty.

Although Bent's methods of archaeology have received severe criticism, and the efforts of his cartographer and surveyor, Swan, to read some astronomical significance into the design of Great Zimbabwe are now said to have been based on inaccurate measurements, *The Ruined Cities of Mashonaland* is a compelling account of an early archaeological expedition. Subsequent work has been much more scientific, but it has done nothing to invalidate Bent's acknowledgment of "the vastness and power of this ancient race, their great constructive ingenuity and strategic skill."

About 1200 Ethiopia

LALIBELA ROCK CHURCHES

"They are among the few renowned 'wonders of the world' which, when seen at last, gave me a shock of joy."
– DERVLA MURPHY, In Ethiopia With a Mule

Flights to the airstrip at Lalibela from Addis Ababa and Asmara. The tracks to the town are suitable only for four-wheel-drive vehicles. The political situation in Ethiopia is uncertain at the time of writing, and prospective visitors should check the feasibility of travel.

Right: the churches were hacked out of the rock with the most heroic labor to create a holy city among the mountains.

Facing page, left: the church of St. George was first cut out of the mountain as a block and was then shaped into a Greek cross, before the interior was hollowed out. The top is level with the ground.

Facing page, right: the interior of Bet Mariam, the church of the Virgin Mary, is elaborately decorated.

THE 11 rock churches of Lalibela, carved from the living granite, have been an object of fascinated interest to the outside world since the 16th century, when a Portuguese priest named Francisco Alvarez wrote a description of them. He ended it by saying that he doubted if anyone would believe him.

The churches were made by cutting deep trenches all around a big block of stone until it was completely isolated from the mountain. Then, starting at the top and working downwards, the mass of inert rock was painstakingly chiseled to form a church complete with domes, windows, porches, and doorways. The inside was hollowed out in the same way, leaving pillars and arches rising from the floor to the ceiling.

For centuries the population of Lalibela consisted largely of priests and monks, who tended the churches and offered hospitality to the visiting pilgrims. The town is high in the Lasta Mountains of central Ethiopia, with the solid bulk of Abuna Josef rising 13,747 feet

(4,107 m) above it. Originally called Roha, the town was renamed in honor of the founder of the churches, a king of the Zagwe dynasty, which ruled here from 1173 to 1270. According to tradition, a swarm of bees immediately surrounded him when he was born, and his mother named him Lalibela, meaning "the bees acknowledge his sovereignty."

Lalibela grew up an enthusiastic Christian. He dreamed dreams and saw visions, in one of which he traveled to Jerusalem. He determined to build a holy city of his own at his mountain fastness. Ten churches were built on either side of the appropriately named River Jordan. Skilled masons were brought from Jerusalem and Alexandria, assisted by a local work force and by angels sent from God, who worked all night. After Lalibela's death in 1212, his widow built the eleventh church in his memory.

Given the laborious difficulty of constructing them, some of the churches are surprisingly large. The biggest of them, the Church of the Savior (Bet Medhane Alem), is approximately 110 feet (33.5m) long, 77 feet (23.5 m) wide, and 35 feet (10.6 m) high. The most revered of them is the Church of the Virgin Mary (Bet Mariam), whose lower windows are shaped into Latin and Greek crosses, swastikas, and looped crosses. Inside, the central pillar is kept wrapped in cloth. In one of Lalibela's visions, Jesus appeared and touched this pillar, and both the past and the future are inscribed on it: so it must be veiled, for mortals are not strong enough to bear the truth.

This church stands in a large courtyard, also hewn with Herculean effort out of the mountain. The Church of the Cross (Bet Maskal) was then cut into the north wall of the courtyard. Crosses are carved in its floor, pillars, and walls. On the opposite side of the courtyard is the Church of the Virgin (Bet Danaghel), dedicated to virgin martyrs.

Other churches are connected by a maze of tunnels through the rock. The Church of St. George (Bet Giorgis), the patron saint of Ethiopia as well as of England, was cut in the shape of an equal-armed Greek cross. It stands in a deep pit and can only be reached through a tunnel. Like its sister churches, it is a tribute to the heroic determination of its builders.

Solomon and Sheba

CUT off among their towering mountains from the world outside, the Ethiopians preserved for many centuries a firm belief in their uniqueness and superiority as a nation, and for them the Ethiopian Orthodox Church was the only true vessel of God on earth. Basic to their national identity was the traditional belief that the Ethiopian royal house was descended from King Solomon and the Queen of Sheba.

According to the Ethiopian story, the beautiful queen, whose name was Makeda, heard of Solomon's unparalleled wisdom and resolved to visit him. With her retinue and magnificent gifts laden on 797 camels and countless mules and asses, she made the journey from Ethiopia to Jerusalem, where Solomon entertained her royally and persuaded her to sleep with him. Their son was Menelik, founder of the royal line of Ethiopian emperors, whose original citadel was at Axum. It is said that Menelik took from Jerusalem's Temple the Ark of the Covenant, which has ever since been kept secretly in St. Mary's Church in Axum. One story holds that two Italian soldiers penetrated to its hiding place, but were killed by monks.

There was, in fact, a strong Jewish influence on Ethiopia in early times, and the old ecclesiastical language of the country was a Semitic language related to Hebrew and Arabic. The Ethiopian Orthodox Church, which traces its history back to Syrian missionaries in Axum in the 4th century, values the Old Testament equally with the New. Haile Selassie, the emperor forced from power in 1974, proudly bore the title "Lion of Judah" as head of the chosen people of Ethiopia.

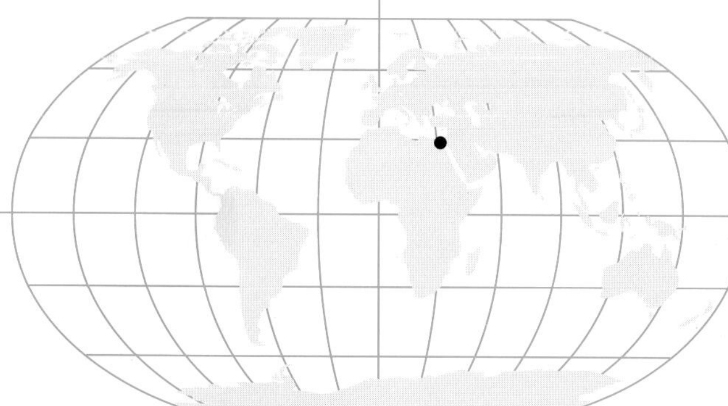

1869 Egypt

SUEZ CANAL

An ancient idea brought to life in the 19th century, but not without struggle.

THE Suez Canal was opened, amid great festivities, in November 1869, but the idea of a link between the Red Sea and the Mediterranean could hardly be described as a new one. In the 7th century B.C. the Egyptian king Necho finally gave up his attempt to build such a waterway, but not before 120,000 slaves were said to have died in the attempt. In 522

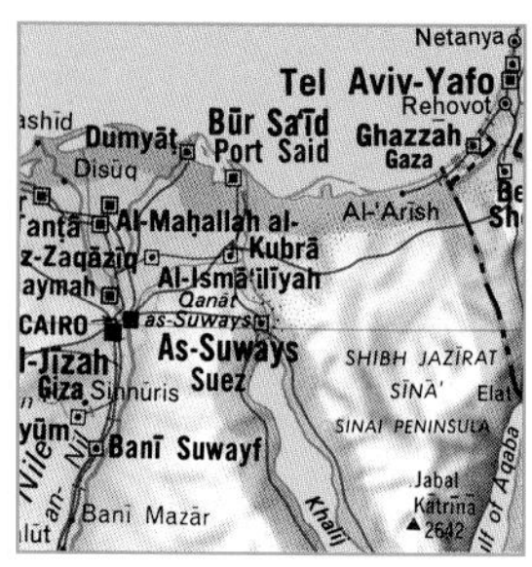

The best way to see the canal is to travel along it by boat. If this is not possible, the town of Ismailia, a short ride by train or taxi from Cairo, is a good vantage point. There are also trips for tourists from Port Said.

The Opening Ceremony

DE Lesseps was a good publicist and a good showman. After 10 years' work on the actual construction of the canal, as well as five years of preparation before construction could begin, he organized a suitably spectacular opening

Right: scene on the canal, running arrow-straight through the desert. Many hundreds of lives were lost in the building of it. Although the British government was initially hostile, it later bought the Pasha of Egypt's holding, giving Britain the lion's share.

Facing page: the thriving town of Port Said is at the northern end of the canal.

B.C., after the Persians had conquered Egypt, their king Darius revived the project and set up an inscription announcing that he had completed the canal. The Greek historian Herodotus, writing in the 5th century B.C., says that this did not follow the most direct route between the seas, that it took a ship four days to travel along it, and that it was wide enough for two triremes to be rowed side by side.

Darius' canal appears to have run eastward from the River Nile before joining one of the lakes on the route of the modern waterway. Improved in Roman times, it eventually silted up and was abandoned. Later generations could not match the enterprise of their ancient ancestors in replacing it – plans by the Venetian empire, by Louis XIV, and by Napoleon came to nothing.

Napoleon's engineer warned of potential disaster because the Mediterranean and the Red Sea differed in height by over 30 feet (9.1 m). Even when this was dismissed as a fallacy, it took the persistence and charm of a very determined man to see the canal through to completion.

Ferdinand de Lesseps, a French diplomat, approached the viceroy Muhammad Said Pasha in 1854 (Egypt at the time was part of the Ottoman Empire) and obtained the right to begin work on a canal that would follow a direct route north from Suez, through the Bitter Lakes, and on to the Mediterranean. He won the support of the viceroy and of a number of French shareholders who had invested in his Suez Canal Company. But the British, who had so much to gain from the creation of a faster route to India, bought no shares. Although the canal would shorten the distance between London and Bombay by 4,563 miles (7,343 km), the government did its utmost to frustrate the project, condemning it as "physically impracticable and far too costly to earn any return."

Between the ceremony marking the beginning of work in 1859 and the completion 10 years later, de Lesseps presided over construction that was difficult at times, but never impossible. At first he used forced labor; later, the work became more highly mechanized and conditions improved sufficiently to attract Europeans to the job. To provide essential drinking water, a special freshwater canal was built to serve the work force of some 25,000 men. At the Mediterranean end of the route, Port Said was created out of nothing on what was virtually reclaimed land, and the canal was driven from north to south until the completion of the freshwater canal in 1863 made it possible for separate work camps to be set up all along the route. The completed canal was 100 miles (161 km) long, 50 feet (15.2 m) deep, and 450 feet (137 m) wide at the top, with passing bays every 6 miles (10 km).

ceremony at which 500 cooks and 1,000 servants catered for 6,000 guests. The composer Giuseppe Verdi was invited to write an Egyptian opera to inaugurate the canal and the new Cairo opera house, but he declined (although *Aida* was staged at Cairo two years later). Dozens of ships, bedecked with flags, arrived at Port Said, and a large flotilla sailed along the canal with the French empress Eugénie, as guest of honor, in the leading vessel. Many of the crowned heads of Europe and beyond came to be part of the fun, and the travel agent Thomas Cook even organized an excursion for tourists. Amid fireworks, acrobats, music, and dancing – as well as some apprehension and last-minute blasting to remove an obstruction – the canal was opened for business.

Thomas Waghorn

De Lesseps acknowledged the contribution of Thomas Waghorn, a British lieutenant in the Indian Army, by having a bust made to commemorate him. Waghorn had spent years arguing for the establishment of an overland mail route between the Mediterranean and the Red Sea, and proved that letters could travel much more swiftly between India and Britain if they were transferred overland from one ship to another. He was resolutely ignored, and British mail continued to be routed around Africa's Cape of Good Hope, even after the canal was opened. The shipping line P & O, however, showing better business sense, regularly transferred passengers between the seas by a combination of boat and camel, and later by train, before it could make use of the canal.

1971 Egypt

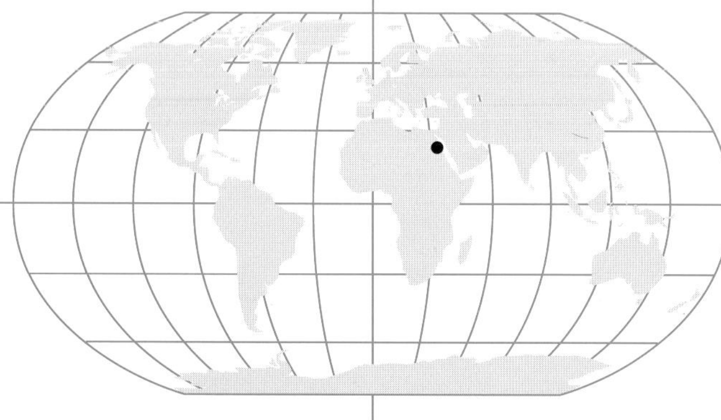

ASWAN HIGH DAM

The dam has brought the Nile flood fully under control for the first time in Egypt's history.

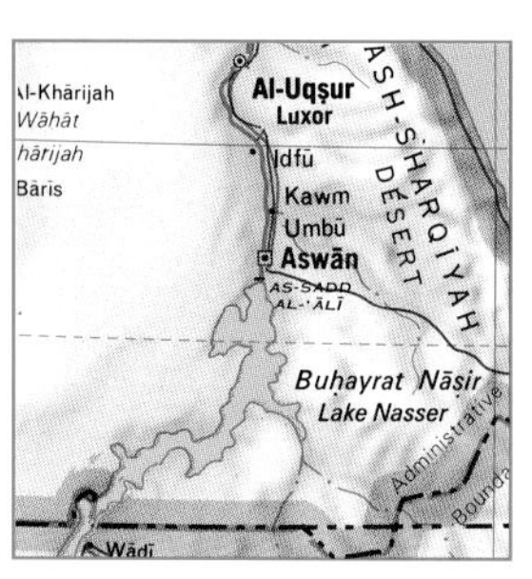

Aswan, on the east bank of the Nile River, is some 600 miles (966 km) south of Cairo by road. Flights and trains from Cairo. Nile cruises touch at Aswan. The High Dam is about 8 miles (13 km) upstream (south) of Aswan.

On January 15, 1971, the new dam across the Nile south of Aswan was formally opened by President Anwar Sadat of Egypt. Work had begun on it 11 years before, in President Gamal Abdel Nasser's time. Standing 364 feet (111 m) high, the dam measures $2^1/_4$ miles (3.6 km) across the top. At the base it is some 3,200 feet (975 m) thick, narrowing to 130 feet (40 m) at the top. It contains enough stone, clay, sand, and concrete to build the Great Pyramid 17 times over.

A four-lane road runs across the dam. There is a triumphal arch and, at the western end of the dam, a monument with four tall, pointed white monoliths grouped in a circle to form a stylized lotus blossom. A canal on the eastern side of the dam drives the turbines of a hydroelectric power station. The dam created a gigantic reservoir, Lake Nasser; one of the biggest artificial lakes in the world, it has an area of 2,025 square miles (5,244 sq km). Stretching south across Nubia and into the Sudan, it is 317 miles (510 km) long.

The Aswan High Dam (*Sadd el-Ali* in Arabic) brought the Nile fully under control for the first time, regulating after untold centuries the annual flooding of the river, on which the life and prosperity of Egypt depended from time immemorial, but which was always erratic. As a result of the dam, there has been a substantial increase in the quantity of land cultivated in Egypt, but there have also been problems to do with the water table and the weather. The dam was designed in Germany, but built with the assistance of the Soviet Union. It was completed at the cost of no fewer than 451 lives.

Four miles (6 km) or so to the north, downstream, is the old Aswan Dam, which was originally completed in 1902. The biggest dam in the world in its day, it is called in Arabic simply *el-Sadd* ("the Dam").

The building of the High Dam destroyed the homes of 60,000 people in Nubia and the Sudan, who had to be moved. Numerous ancient monuments disappeared under water, though some of the most important were saved by an unprecedented international rescue effort marshalled by UNESCO. The beautiful island of Philae, for instance, has vanished forever, but its temples were cut into numbered pieces and

Right: the High Dam, with the hydroelectric power station. In the background is the lotus-shaped monument. Though it brought the expected benefits, the dam also created serious difficulties, including altering the pattern of the weather in southern Egypt, where the rainfall has become much greater.

Facing page: the colossal figures of Pharaoh Ramses II at Abu Simbel, which had to be moved to escape inundation by Lake Nasser.

reassembled like a jigsaw puzzle on a higher island nearby. The principal one is the temple of Isis, dating from the late centuries B.C. and the early centuries A.D., and there are also buildings from the Roman period. Three other temples were moved to New Kalabsha, near the western end of the High Dam. The most spectacular part of the whole operation was the saving of the famous rock temples of Abu Simbel, which lie 175 miles (282 km) south of Aswan.

Aswan itself is a winter resort town whose palm trees are said to produce the tastiest dates in Egypt. Points of interest include the mausoleum of the third Aga Khan, who died in 1957, the ruins of a Coptic monastery, rock tombs and an old Muslim cemetery, ancient remains on the Nile island of Elephantine, and the granite quarries from which stone was hewn centuries ago for the temples and palaces of the pharaohs.

Gods in the Mountain

The rock temples of Abu Simbel, near the border between Egypt and the Sudan, would have vanished under the waters of Lake Nasser had it not been for a spectacular UNESCO-organized rescue operation. The two temples, built for Pharaoh Ramses II in about 1260 B.C., were cut into a mountain. The façade of the larger one was guarded by four stupendous statues of the pharaoh himself, 66 feet (20 m) high and carved out of the rock of the mountainside.

Under the original plan, it was suggested that a huge glass shield should be built around the whole monument to protect it from the waters of the dam, and that visitors be lowered down to it in glass containers. In the end, however, the temples and statues were cut bodily out of the mountain, sawn up into blocks of manageable weight, and then reassembled at a new site nearby.

The larger of the temples was dedicated to a constellation of gods, including Amun-Re of Thebes and the pharaoh himself. It was oriented in such a way that on two days of the year the rays of the rising sun penetrated deep into the temple to shine on the statues of the gods inside the mountain. The façade behind the seated figures of Ramses II is 108 feet (33 m) high. The huge statues are realistic portraits of the pharoah, although one of them is lacking its head, which an earthquake destroyed. Smaller figures represent some of the pharaoh's children and his sister-wife, Nefertari.

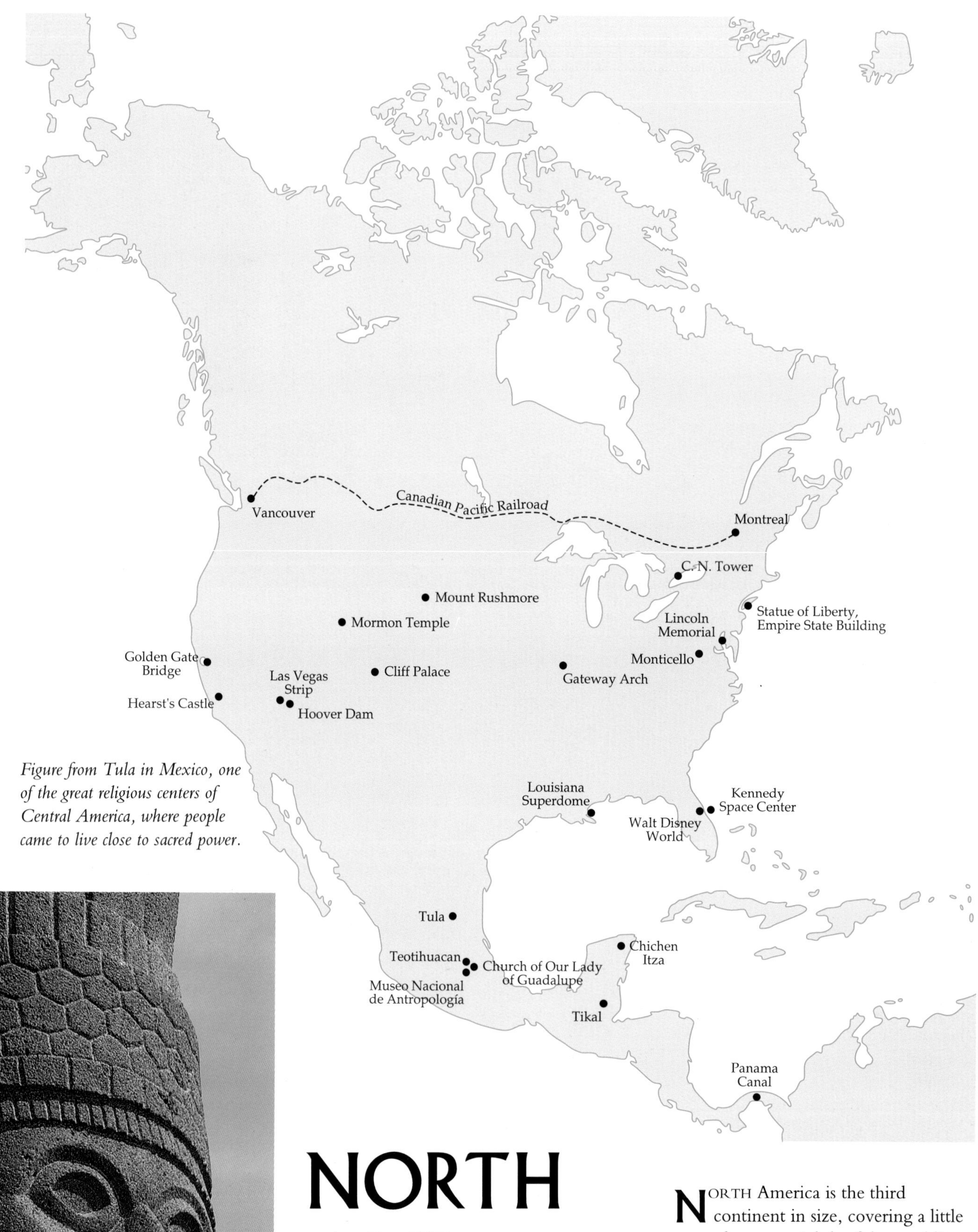

Figure from Tula in Mexico, one of the great religious centers of Central America, where people came to live close to sacred power.

NORTH AND CENTRAL AMERICA

NORTH America is the third continent in size, covering a little more than one-eighth of the world's land surface. Its first human inhabitants arrived from Siberia 20,000 years ago or more, traveling on foot across the Bering Strait, which at that time was dry land, moving into Alaska and on south. In time, farming was invented and agricultural villages developed. In what is now called Mexico, villages grew into towns, city-states, kingdoms, and empires. The complicated jigsaw puzzle of their history and mutual relationships is very far from complete, and the dates are mostly vague.

Isolated from the Old World, the early Americans independently discovered how to grow crops, how to make pottery, how to work copper and gold, and how to construct massive pyramids. They did not discover iron, the plough, glass, or gunpowder. They did invent the wheel, but they never used it for practical purposes.

APPETITE FOR BLOOD

In Guatemala, eastern Mexico, and the Yucatán from about the 4th century A.D. to the 10th, the Maya civilization reached its apogee. The Maya had virtually no metals and only the simplest kind of agriculture, but they produced astronomers, mathematicians, and artists of high quality. They could predict eclipses, and they understood the concept of zero. Tikal, in the jungles of present-day Guatemala, was perhaps the largest of the Maya cities, where people came to live around a major religious center.

Further west, the city of Teotihuacán, with its two great pyramids of the sun and the moon, was larger than imperial Rome. Its history ran its course, and in the 11th and 12th centuries the dominant people in Mexico were the Toltecs, with their capital at Tula. Ball courts sacred to the Toltecs have been discovered, where a game played with a rubber ball was played to the death – the losers being beheaded, presumably as an offering to the gods. The disturbing Mesoamerican appetite for human sacrifice was shown at Chichén Itźa, where in times of drought children were thrown alive into a well to appease the gods and bring rain.

The appetite rose to a frenzy among the Aztecs, who believed that the sun and the earth needed to be nourished with human blood. By 1450 they had built up an empire controlling almost all modern Mexico from their capital at Tenochtitlán (now Mexico City), and on the eve of the Spanish Conquest, Aztec priests were ripping the pulsing hearts out of 50,000 victims a year. The Aztecs made war to capture prisoners for sacrifice and to enslave the peasantry, from whom they exacted a heavy tribute.

Resentment of Aztec oppression gained allies for Hernán Cortés in Mexico and helped him to conquer the Aztec empire with remarkable speed. Other factors were superior technology – steel weapons – and horses. By 1521 he was master of Mexico, and Spain ruled Mesoamerica for the next 300 years. The indigenous civilizations were destroyed and the population converted to Christianity, but it was a Christianity with many pre-Christian elements mingled in it. When a new Mexican national identity developed in revolt against Spain, the rebels carried on their banners the image of the Virgin Mary, in the form of Our Lady of Guadalupe, Mexico's patron saint.

VAULTING AMBITIONS

North of Mexico, the indigenous cultures exercised no such influence on the incoming Europeans. In the 18th century the French fought the British for mastery, and the British won. Although the 13 colonies threw off the yoke of British rule, the influence of the English language, English law, and English traditions remained paramount.

In the 19th century, the drive to settle the West – symbolized today by the Gateway Arch in St. Louis – inspired two of the great engineering achievements of all time, the Panama Canal and the Canadian Pacific Railroad. The first one was 40 miles (64 km) long and the other more like 3,000 miles (4,828 km), but they both brought the east and west coasts of North America closer together.

Immigrants poured into both the United States and Canada as lands of opportunity. Millions were greeted by the Statue of Liberty holding aloft Freedom's torch at the entrance to New York's harbor. North American architects and engineers invented the skyscraper and built the Empire State Building in New York City and the C.N. Tower in Toronto, among many others that could be seen as symbols of the vaulting ambitions of the New World. The vast resources of an industrialized North America erected the beautiful Golden Gate Bridge across the entrance to San Francisco Bay and the Hoover Dam across the Colorado River, and created such palaces of entertainment as Disneyland and the glittering hotels of the Las Vegas Strip. From the John F. Kennedy Space Center in Florida, titanic rockets hurtled skywards, continuing the human quest for dominion over the universe.

Having subdued the earth, the human race set out to conquer space: the Kennedy Space Center in Florida.

From the 4th Century A.D. Guatemala

TIKAL

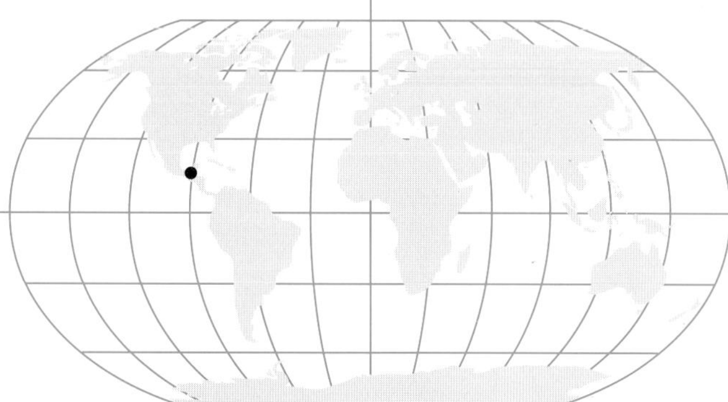

Majestic Maya ruins in a jungle setting.

Guatemala City has an international airport, and domestic flights connect to the town of Flores. The site is about one hour from Flores by road, and buses are available. Tikal can also be reached by road from the neighboring country of Belize.

The Conquest of the Yucatán

TIKAL lies on the Yucatán Peninsula in a region discovered in 1517 by a Spaniard, Francisco Hernandez de Cordoba, and gradually conquered by Spain over the next 30 years. The conquerors saw themselves as exercising a sort of divine right: the pope had declared that the king of Castile was entitled to all the territory west of a demarcation line he had drawn on a map. In return for this gift, the king was obliged to convert the native people to Christianity. If the pope, who exercised God's authority on earth, said that the inhabitants of the Yucatán were

Right: the Great Plaza at Tikal is a huge square surrounded by temples and an acropolis. The city was a product of the Classic Maya civilization, and the remains represent 500 years of building activity on the site.

Facing page: Pyramid I at Tikal. The pyramids here were both temples of the gods and the tombs of Maya rulers.

THE Maya people, ancestors of the present-day Maya Indians, belonged to a civilization that inhabited a wide area of highland and lowland Mesoamerica. Their culture, dominated by religious ceremony, was presided over by ruler-priests. The highly elaborate Maya calendar, the Long Count, involved a cycle of 52 years, and attempts to reconcile this with the European system have produced conflicting results. But radiocarbon dating supports the view that the Classic Maya period, when the civilization reached its peak, was between the 4th and 10th centuries A.D. Tikal, in the northern lowland area of Maya territory, was perhaps the largest center of Classic Maya civilization.

At the heart of Tikal, there was a huge square bordered by pyramid temples on the west and east sides and an acropolis on the north. Beyond this complex there were some 3,000 buildings within an area of 6 square miles (16 sq km) and a population calculated at between 10,000 and 45,000. The acropolis shows signs of having been occupied

continuously for 11 centuries, and the 16 temples to be seen there now stand on the buried remains of countless earlier buildings, including some elaborate painted tombs.

The central ceremonial area covered about 1 square mile (2.5 sq km), and the buildings here were linked by causeways to further squares and their associated structures. So-called "palaces" abound – single-story complexes and rooms, plastered, decorated, and, like almost every Maya building, standing on a platform. The elevation of the central religious buildings clearly enhanced the awe in which they were held, and also served the practical purpose of enabling large numbers of people to have an unobstructed view of any ceremonies taking place. But even relatively modest houses far from the center were built on mud platforms, presumably as a safeguard against floods during the rainy season.

Glimpses of Maya rulers and their religious ceremonies can be seen in stone sculpture as well as in fine carvings on sapodilla wood. This woodwork was used for decorative beams in some of the palaces and for ornate lintels over the doorways of the pyramid temples. Tikal has six steep pyramids, with chambers at the top approached by steps and crowned with elaborate "roof combs"; the largest, known simply as Pyramid IV, is 228 feet (70 m) high. The pyramids served as tombs for wealthy and important people, who were buried with sumptuous grave goods as well as food to sustain them on their journey to the next world. Stone stelae in front of palaces and temples were often sculpted with a favorite theme, that of a ruler or warrior trampling an enemy underfoot.

The word *city* is perhaps not the best description of Tikal; rather, it was an important ceremonial center on whose outskirts large numbers of people chose to live. Although the majority of people did not live in any great splendor, the Maya devoted tremendous energy to the construction of their tombs and temples. In honoring their gods, their elite, and their dead, they created monuments that are still overwhelming and awe-inspiring today.

subjects of the king of Castile, then any resistance shown by those inhabitants could be regarded as rebellion or treachery.

In 1526 one Francisco de Montejo was authorized to lead an expedition to the Yucatán, with certain conditions for the conduct of this expedition laid out in a formal document known as a *requerimiento*. It was stated that the aim of the king of Castile was to win the natives of the New World to allegiance and to the True Faith by means of understanding and good treatment. These intentions were to be explained clearly to the natives through an interpreter. If they failed to comply, the consequences would be serious: the Spaniards would make war against the land and subject the people to the yoke and the authority of the Crown and of the Church. There followed years of guerrilla warfare, and resistance to the *conquistadores* continued long after they had imposed their rule on the Yucatán.

5th Century Mexico

TEOTIHUACÁN

An ancient and mysterious planned city as big as imperial Rome.

Mexico City has an international airport. By bus, the journey from the capital takes an hour (frequent services from the Central de Autobuses del Norte). In addition, there are many organized tours.

Esperanza Culture

ESPERANZA culture is the term used to describe an amalgam of Teotihuacán and Maya culture that can be seen at Kaminaljuyu, near the center of modern Guatemala City. Once an important Maya center, it was apparently conquered by people from Teotihuacán at the start of the 5th century A.D. The victors built a planned city – an imitation of Teotihuacán – in the local clay (the area lacked suitable stone). But rather than wipe out Maya culture, the new inhabitants appear to have absorbed some aspects of it and to have furnished their tombs with Maya-style pottery. Elsewhere in the Maya region, Teotihuacán seems to have influenced art and architecture, and there are examples of Maya and Teotihuacán deities appearing together on ceramic ware. Tombs discovered at Kaminaljuyu have contained many examples of precious grave goods, including large amounts of jade. Again, there is evidence of human sacrifice.

Right: the Pyramid of the Sun is one of the city's two great pyramid temples.

Facing page: the city was laid out on a strict grid and aligned north-south.

TEOTIHUACÁN is an Aztec name meaning "place of the gods," but this remarkable site has its origins in a much older civilization. The early settlement, which dates back to the first century B.C. became the largest city in Mesoamerica by A.D. 500. Covering an area of over 8 square miles (21 sq km) and with a population estimated at 50,000 to 100,000 people (some even say 200,000), it was larger than imperial Rome and was thriving at the same time.

This was a sophisticated city of wide streets, monumental religious buildings, artisans' quarters, and numerous private houses. But archaeological investigation has revealed little factual evidence about the daily life and customs of the people. As builders, they created a highly distinctive city that dominated a large empire and influenced the development of the neighboring Maya peoples. Teotihuacán was planned on a grid system so strict that a river was diverted into a channel rather than allowed to interrupt the network of parallel streets. The main axis, which runs north-south, is a vast avenue 130 feet (40 m) wide and about $1^1/_2$ miles (2.3 km) long, known as the Street of the Dead (another Aztec name). Lined with temples and shrines, it is dominated by two pyramids: the Pyramid of the Moon – actually several interlocking pyramids with an overall height of 150 feet (46 m) – at the north end, and the Pyramid of the Sun standing further south. (The sun and the moon, according to legend, were born in Teotihuacán.)

At the heart of the city there are two monumental public places of assembly, called the Citadel and the Great Compound. The Citadel is a platform 400 yards (365 m) square approached by a grand stairway. On this platform stands another pyramid, the Temple of Quetzalcoatl (the Feathered Serpent, a major god), which originally rose to a height of about 70 feet (21 m) in tiers of richly carved sculpture. Stone serpents, their heads projecting menacingly out of the tiers, look alarming even today; how much greater an impression they must have made when their shining obsidian eyes were still in place and the whole structure was covered in stucco and paint. The Great Compound, which seems to have had an administrative function rather than a religious one, has two large platforms on which a number of buildings once stood.

Much of Teotihuacán remains unexplored.

Some parts suffered at the hands of early archaeologists; the Pyramid of the Sun, in particular, was badly excavated at the beginning of the 20th century and inaccurately reconstructed. With its 248 steps to the top, it is now thought to have been 240 feet (73 m) high, to have contained over a million cubic yards (764,560 cu m) of material (stone over an earth-and-rubble core), and to have had a flat top on which there was a temple.

This highly developed civilization worshipped a rain god and revered the jaguar. Local supplies of obsidian were an important element in a chiefly agricultural economy, while a type of pottery known as "thin orange" was exported widely. Mural paintings of high quality suggest that these were people with confident artistic skills; evidence of human sacrifice during the years of decline points to a less appealing side of their culture. No one knows precisely how Teotihuacán came to an end, but it is certain that the end was violent and that the 8th century saw the city thoroughly sacked and burned.

Pyramid Power

EXTRAVAGANT claims have been made for the mystical power of pyramids. It is said, for example, that organic material, placed beneath the apex, can be preserved and that, placed similarly, razor blades can be sharpened and a person's mind stimulated. Some believe that ancient cultures had an understanding of cosmic energies that we lack today, and that there is a special significance in the way monuments were aligned in relation to the sun, the moon, and the stars. Certainly the orientation of the grid plan at Teotihuacán is very precise. One of the more bizarre theories holds that the Street of the Dead was an ancient runway for extraterrestrial visitors. Although such explanations find few supporters, it does seem likely that the people of Teotihuacán were aware of the movements of the celestial bodies and attached importance to them.

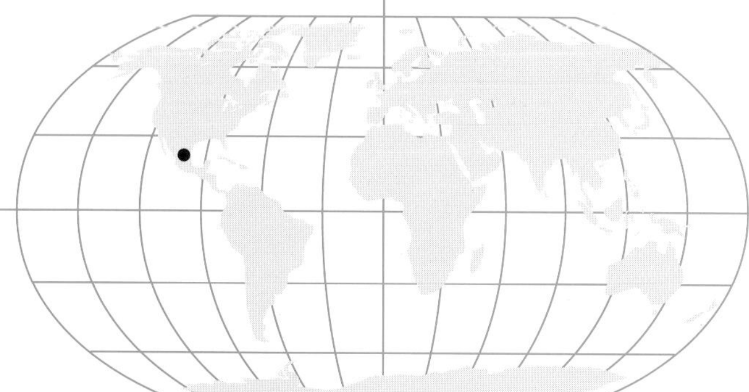

10th Century Mexico

TULA

Home of the warlike Toltec people and their god, the Feathered Serpent.

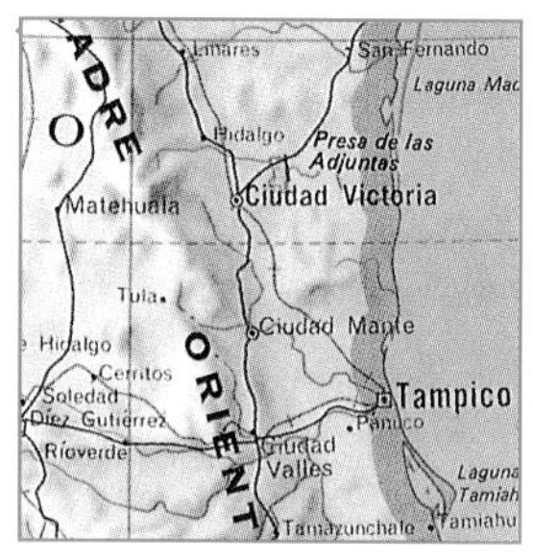

Tula is 50 miles (80 km) from Mexico City, which has an international airport. There is a very frequent bus service from Mexico City's Central de Autobuses del Norte; the journey takes about 90 minutes. Some trains between Mexico City and Querétaro stop close to the site, which is a fair walk from the modern town center.

THE Toltecs were a nomadic people who, in the 8th century A.D., may have been behind the destruction of the civilization based at Teotihuacán. Their own capital was established at Tula, but this in turn was destroyed by enemies, and for a long time its location was in doubt. The Toltecs held sway over Mexico for only about 200 years – from

Right: remains of the pyramid of the snake god Quetzalcoatl, worshipped here as the morning star. On top of the pyramid are the figures known as Atlantes, which originally supported part of the roof.

Facing page: closer views of the Atlantes, grim warrior figures that represent the god, each with his feathered headdress.

the mid-10th to the mid-12th century A.D. – but their legendary skills and achievements survived them, and it has become very difficult to separate myth from fact.

The god Quetzalcoatl – the Feathered Serpent – seems to have been of supreme importance at Tula, and the Toltec rulers sometimes identified themselves with him. His image recurs again and again in the art and architecture of this Toltec capital, snaking up columns and staring out from pyramid walls. One striking feature of Tula is the Serpent Wall, 130 feet (40 m) long and decorated with snakes swallowing skeletons. At the center of the site (where some monuments have been restored, and much excavation remains to be done) stands a pyramid supporting a temple of Quetzalcoatl, who was honored here as a god associated with the morning star.

On top of the pyramid, at the approach to the temple, there are two columns known as the Atlantes. (The name is taken from classical art and is generally used to describe a human figure supporting part of a building.) At Tula the Atlantes are in the form of Quetzalcoatl as the morning star. Standing 15 feet (4.6 m) tall, wearing feathered headdresses and carrying spears, they originally supported part of the temple roof, but this no longer survives. Much of the temple sculpture has also disappeared, but some favorite motifs, like the jaguar, can still be seen. In front of the temple there was once a large, covered assembly space, and some of its supporting columns are still in position. Such colonnades are a distinctive feature of Toltec architecture and one of several Toltec hallmarks that reappear at the Chichén Itzá site in the Mexican state of Yucatán.

Ball courts are another element of Toltec design. In common with other Mesoamerican peoples, they played a game with a rubber ball in a rectangular, high-walled court, and the activity may well have had some religious significance. The remains of two ball courts can be seen at Tula, and one bears a striking resemblance to a ball court at Chichén Itzá.

All the evidence provided by Toltec art suggests that theirs was a warlike race that believed in the power of human sacrifice to placate the gods. A ruler known as Topiltzin Quetzalcoatl apparently tried to reform the Toltecs and end the practice of human sacrifice; he also introduced another race, known as the Nonoalca, to Tula. Whether the city was destroyed as a result of civil war between rival factions, or whether it was attacked by outsiders, is not clear, but Tula did suffer sudden destruction in which the Serpent Wall was knocked down and a large building at the center was burned. Much still lies buried, awaiting the investigation that could reveal more about the city, its people, and their fate.

Quetzalcoatl and Cortés

ACCORDING to one story – part history, part legend – the god Quetzalcoatl, or a ruler-god of the same name, disappeared from view after teaching his philosophy to some disciples, and promised that he would return from the direction of the sunrise on a specific date. The date he announced was very close to that on which the Spanish conqueror of Mexico, Hernán Cortés, arrived from the east. The Aztec emperor, Moctezuma II, fearful that he might be launching an attack on a god, is said to have hesitated before fighting. Similarly apprehensive, the Aztec people were uncertain whether to resist the new arrival or welcome him with the respect due to a god.

Toltec Art and Influence

TOLTEC art, dismissed by some as crude, is full of representations of warriors who seem to have won a considerable empire, with power over at least 20 towns and apparently spreading as far as Chichén Itzá on the Yucatán Peninsula. In addition to portraying warriors wielding weapons, Toltec artists often depicted eagles eating what could be a human heart, large feline animals wearing bells on collars, and hybrid creatures that were part serpent, part bird, part jaguar. Circular temples are associated with the wind god, Ehécatl Quetzalcoatl, and curious reclining stone figures, called chac-mools, are another distinctive motif. Each figure supports a plate on its stomach, the purpose apparently being to hold sacrificial offerings.

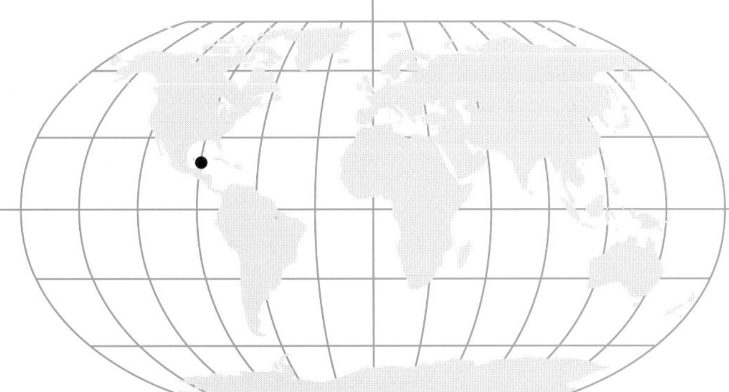

10th Century Mexico

CHICHÉN ITZÁ

One of the most dramatic and sinister places in the New World, where Maya and Toltec cultures meet.

The site is 75 miles (121 km) east of Mérida, and the road known as Route 180 passes close to the ruins. Mérida, the capital of Yucatán, has an airport with connections to some cities in the U.S.A. There are trains from Mérida to Valladolid 25 miles (40 km) from Chichén Itzá, and buses from Mérida to Valladolid pass close to the site.

Human Sacrifice and the Sacred Cenote

THERE are many reminders of the practice of human sacrifice at Chichén Itzá. Near the large ball court, with its images of decapitation on the walls, are three platforms, the Platform of Venus (the morning star associated with Quetzalcoatl), the Platform of the Eagle and Jaguar, and the Skull Rack covered with carvings showing human skulls on stakes. The last of these plainly had some gruesome use, perhaps the display of victims' skulls, and the other two may well have been used as places of ritual sometimes involving sacrifice. The sacred cenote, or well of sacrifice, is approached along a 900-foot (274-m) causeway. This natural well, which is 75 feet (23 m) deep, supplied fresh water and was

Right: a chac-mool figure. Each of these strange Toltec sculptures had a plate on its stomach, apparently to hold offerings to the god.

Facing page: the great temple that represents the year.

CHICHÉN Itzá was an important Maya site until the 10th century A.D. At some later point, as Maya civilization went into decline, Toltec warriors appear to have seized control and turned Chichén Itzá into a bigger and better version of their own capital, Tula. The extensive remains to be seen at Chichén Itzá today are neither purely Maya nor purely Toltec, but an intriguing fusion of the ideas and motifs of both cultures.

This seems to have been a new capital for the ruler-god Topiltzin Quetzalcoatl, known here by the Maya name Kukulcan, and the building that dominates the whole place is a pyramid temple dedicated to him, called El Castillo (The Castle). The pyramid, with nine tiers and 91 steps up each of the four sides, was built on top of an earlier pyramid, which it completely encloses.

The dimensions and the design of El Castillo are fascinating. The days and months of the year are represented by the number of steps and terraces, and 52 sculpted panels symbolize the Maya 52-year cycle. The careful alignment of the building, whose stairways face exactly north, south, east, and west, creates an extraordinary effect at the spring and autumn equinoxes: the shadows cast by the angle of the sun suggest that the serpent god, whose head and tail are carved at the bottom and the top of the main staircase, has come to life and is snaking his way out of the temple.

Chichén Itzá has perhaps the finest ball court in Mesoamerica. It is vast, with two parallel walls 272 feet (83 m) long and 27 feet (8.2 m) high set 90 feet (27 m) apart. Temples stand at each end of the court, but the exact religious significance of the game is not known. Bas-relief panels on the side walls showing decapitated players suggest that these were

contests fought to the death. One account of the game, dating from later, Aztec times, says that the winner was the player who got the ball through one of the stone rings high up on each side wall. He is said to have been rewarded with the clothes of the spectators.

The Temple of the Warriors at Chichén Itzá is approached through a colonnade, and countless such pillars, carved to represent Toltec warriors, once supported a roof. This style of colonnade can also be seen at Tula (the use of columns to form courtyards and to divide internal space seems to have been a Toltec idea). The temple is decorated with carvings and frescoes, and the familiar jaguar and eagle motifs of Toltec art can both be seen. Chichén Itzá also has a Temple of the Jaguars, with one of these animals carved in stone guarding the approach.

The area known as Old Chichén is somewhat overgrown and neglected, but it contains some equally interesting buildings that show fewer signs of Toltec influence. Here there is an observatory – a tower supported on a double platform – and a pyramid in which a number of tombs were found. A building named the Nunnery is actually a large complex of rooms with some good surviving sculpture. The so-called Church, unconnected with Christianity, has a façade covered with Maya masks and other mythological creatures.

Chichén Itzá's supremacy was short-lived. The site seems to have been abandoned sometime around 1224, following an attack by the rulers of Mayapan, another city of great power on the Yucatán Peninsula.

treated as a place of pilgrimage. In times of drought, living victims were thrown into the well in an attempt to provoke the rain god into action, and offerings of precious metals, jade, and sacred images have been retrieved from the depths. Many of the victims appear to have been young children – or at least these were the ones who failed to survive. Victims who managed to stay afloat for the required number of hours were retrieved and treated with respect, for they were considered to have spoken with the gods. Much of the material found in the well is estimated to be of a later date than the Toltec era, however, and it seems likely that the cenote continued to be regarded as a holy place for many years.

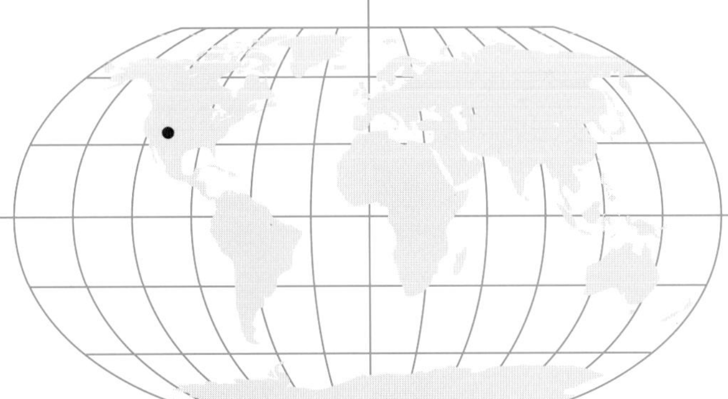

From 1073 U.S.A.

CLIFF PALACE

America's earliest high-rise apartment blocks were built by "the ancient ones."

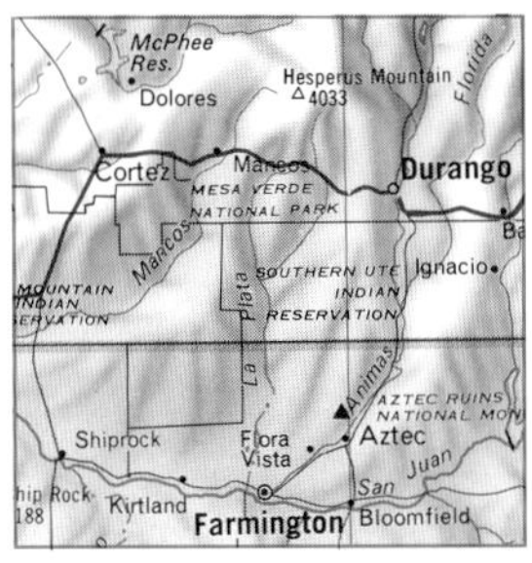

Mesa Verde National Park, close to the southwestern corner of Colorado, lies 21 miles (34 km) south of Route 160 between Cortez and Durango, which has an airport. Turn off 10 miles (16 km) east of Cortez. Buses from all the principal towns in the area. Visitor center and guided tours.

Not He or She

THE Pueblo Indians – the Hopi, Zuni, Keres, Tiwi, and Tewa peoples – are now restricted to a small number of villages in New Mexico and Arizona. Descended from "the ancient ones" who built Cliff Palace, they had developed an impressive civilization by the time the Spaniards appeared in the 16th century in what is now the southwestern United States. They had a strong influence on other Indians of the Southwest, notably the Navajo.

Traditional Pueblo society is unusual in tracing its descent through the female line. Men do the work in the fields,

Right: when rediscovered in the 19th century, Cliff Palace in Colorado looked startlingly like a lost medieval walled city of the Old World.

Facing page, above: a view from a different angle shows the settlement tucked in against the cliff for protection against attack.

Facing page, below: another of the Colorado cliff dwellings, built in under the rock.

One day in 1888 two Colorado cowboys, named Richard Wetherill and Charles Mason, came to the rim of a canyon and gazed in astonished awe at what appeared to be ruined stone castles and towers tucked against the face of a massive cliff. It was as if a crusader army or Moorish warlord had built a walled city in the middle of North America, and then abandoned it.

This and similar discoveries in the area sparked off excited speculation about a mysterious people who had built their towns and citadels there long ago and abruptly vanished off the face of the earth. Gradually it became clear that the vanished people were not a mysterious race, but the prehistoric ancestors of the Pueblo Indians of the southwestern United States. These Native American people were given the name Pueblo ("village") by the Spaniards as they explored northwards from Mexico in the 16th century.

What name the prehistoric Indians gave themselves, no one knows. They had no alphabet and left no written records, and they built their remarkable constructions without benefit of metal tools or modern machinery. They are referred to today as the Anasazi, "the ancient ones," which is what the modern Navajo call them. Their buildings have been described as the first high-rise apartment blocks in America. Cliff Palace, which Wetherill and Mason saw that day in 1888, is the largest of them and the best-known example in Mesa Verde National Park, established in 1906 on the initiative of President Theodore Roosevelt.

Cliff Palace was built between 1073 and 1273, and at its peak would have housed about 400 people living at close quarters in a village arranged vertically rather than horizontally. It had more than 200 rooms for living in, plus storage rooms and *kivas* (special rooms set aside for ceremonies). The rooms were decorated with wall paintings featuring geometric designs and patterns. At the front of the building, an open terrace was used for the community's everyday work, such as making pottery and grinding corn.

Close to Cliff Palace along Chapin Mesa are two more of these complexes – Spruce Tree House, which is tucked under the overhang of a ponderous cliff, and Balcony House. Spruce Tree House, rising to three stories, is 216 feet (66 m) long and 89 feet (27 m) wide. It contains more than 100 rooms, which are rectangular, round, or triangular, to fit into the space under the overhang.

Presumably these inaccessible fortress villages were built for defense. The people who lived in them were farmers, with crops of corn, squash, and beans. They made baskets, cloth, and pottery, and they had domesticated the wild turkey for its meat and its feathers. They

built small dams to trap rainwater for their fields. Earlier, they had lived in pit houses, dug down into the ground; but after they had built their apartment blocks, they used the older houses as underground rooms for religious ceremonies. Somewhere about 1300, perhaps struck by a long drought, they abandoned their homes. A museum in the park has displays of Anasazi life, with necklaces, bracelets made of dog hair, and decorated seashells brought from the Pacific coast.

which is the exception to the rule among Native American groups, and newly married young couples move in with her mother rather than his. Women have a more important and honored position than usual.

Life in the villages is intricately bound up with religious beliefs and ceremonies. One story tells of a Pueblo Indian who, asked by a visitor what his religion was, replied simply, "Life." Pueblo traditional religion is a fascinating mixture of the simple and the sophisticated. The Zuni, for instance, recognize a high god in the sky whose name is Awonawilona. With no personal characteristics, this being is neither masculine nor feminine (or is equally masculine and feminine) and cannot be adequately called either "he" or "she." Perhaps such profundity goes back centuries to the wisdom of "the ancient ones."

From 1531 Mexico

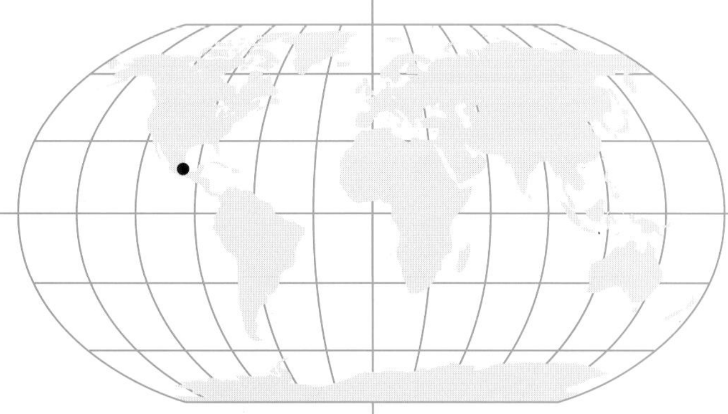

CHURCH OF OUR LADY OF GUADALUPE

The most venerated shrine in all Mexico stands where the Virgin appeared to a poor peasant.

The church is in the district called La Villa de Guadalupe in the northeastern suburbs of Mexico City, $2\frac{1}{2}$ miles (4 km) from the center of the city. The Paseo de la Reforma, built in the 1860s for Emperor Maximilian, leads towards it. Buses or metro train to La Villa. Visitors often combine the trip with a visit to Teotihuacán.

Right: the Old Church of the Virgin of Guadalupe, with its four towers and golden dome, was rebuilt many times over the centuries as the shrine's importance grew. A new, much bigger church has recently replaced it.

Facing page, above and below: the new church, too modernistic in style for many people's taste, has a huge floral entrance. According to the legend, the Virgin miraculously made flowers spring up on the barren hill here.

Facing page, far right: the high altar of the ornate Old Church.

On December 11 and 12 every year, the eve and day of the feast of the Virgin of Guadalupe are celebrated with processions and folk dances all over Mexico. The excitement is particularly intense at the shrine on the outskirts of Mexico City, where thousands of pilgrims come to pay her homage, making the last stage of the journey on their knees.

The shrine is at the spot where the Virgin appeared to an Indian peasant named Juan Diego in 1531. The first church here, a humble adobe building, proved a powerful magnet to pilgrims. Rebuilt and enlarged over subsequent centuries, most recently in 1895, the church has four towers and a dome 130 feet (40 m) high. Inside, massive Corinthian pillars support the roof, and it is said that the vast amount of silver for the altar rail, candelabra, vessels, and other adornments amounts to 56 U.S. tons (62 metric tons). Until the 1970s there was a golden reliquary, set on the high altar of marble and bronze, containing Juan Diego's cloak, miraculously imprinted with the Virgin's image, and behind it a statue of Juan Diego devoutly

kneeling. On feast days a jewel-studded crown was set over the head of the Virgin's image.

Devotion to Our Lady of Guadalupe, far from dying away over the centuries, has grown because she is closely identified with Mexican nationalism. So overwhelming did the number of pilgrims become that in 1976 it was decided to build a new and much bigger church at the site. (The architect, Pedro Ramirez Vasquez, also designed Mexico City's controversial Museum of Anthropology.) The new church, constructed of steel, wood, and plastic, has not pleased traditionalists. The miraculous cloak has been transferred to its own altar in the new church, and pilgrims are carried past it on a moving walkway.

The old church was closed in December 1988. Now it serves as a museum containing religious pictures, sculptures, and many gifts brought to the shrine as thank-offerings by pilgrims and those seeking healing. Nearby, a small chapel stands close to the well that sprang up where the Virgin appeared. Steps lead up to another chapel on top of the hill where Juan Diego gathered the flowers that miraculously bloomed at the Virgin's command.

The Virgin's appearance occurred 10 years after the Spanish conquest of Mexico. Juan Diego was a converted Aztec peasant, whose original Aztec name meant "eagle-that-talks." When he saw the Virgin on the hill, she told him to ask the bishop to build her a church at that spot. Juan Diego politely suggested that she send a Spaniard instead, but the Virgin replied that she was acting out of love and compassion for Juan and his people, the conquered Indians. The bishop at first demurred, asking for a sign. The Virgin then made the flowers spring up on the barren hilltop, and Juan Diego carried them to the bishop in his cloak. When he opened it, the now-famous image of the Virgin was imprinted on it. The bishop was convinced, and the church was promptly built.

Our Lady of Mexico

It is significant that the hill on which the Virgin appeared to Juan Diego was previously sacred to the Aztec mother goddess, Tonantzin. Spanish priests later complained that the Indians coming to venerate the Virgin at the shrine persistently called her Tonantzin.

According to Juan Diego, the Virgin had described herself as "a loving mother to you and to those like you." Whatever the truth of the original events, the story was widely believed by "those like" Juan Diego, the conquered Indians who were bewildered by the destruction of their way of life and the new religion that was being thrust upon them. They welcomed the event because it reconciled the alien religion with the Aztec religious tradition, and they could identify the Christian Mother of God with the Aztec mother goddess.

The church built there soon became the most venerated site in all Mexico. Miracles without number have been attributed to the Virgin of Guadalupe, who is often called La Indita, "the little Indian." Deep veins of native, pre-Christian belief persisted in Mexican Christianity, and Mary became closely identified with Mexican nationalism and the cause of independence from Spain.

When rebellion broke out in 1810, the insurgents' standard bore the image of the Virgin of Guadalupe. The new Republic of Mexico, established in 1823, adopted her colors of blue and white. The first president took her name, Guadalupe Victoria, as a sign of Mexican identity and patriotic zeal.

THE NEW WORLD

The Americas were discovered by Italian sea captains in earnest search of the riches of the fabulous Orient.

The Golden Man of Calima is now in the Gold Museum at Bogotá in Colombia.

CHRISTOPHER Columbus's voyages of discovery were part of the expansion of the Old World that eventually took European settlers and European ways of life all over the globe. He and other early European explorers were trying to reach Asia and the fabled wealth of Cathay by sailing west. Having greatly underestimated the circumference of the globe, they triumphantly assumed, upon landing far across the Atlantic, that Asia was what they had found. It took some time for the truth to sink in.

Columbus set off from Spain with his three little cockleshell ships in the summer of 1492 and made landfalls in the Bahamas, Cuba, and the island of Hispaniola (now Santo Domingo). There he left a few men to make a settlement from which trade relations would be opened with China, which was obviously close to hand. In three subsequent voyages, Columbus discovered more of Cuba, which he decided was China, touched the South American mainland coast, which he took to be the shore of the earthly paradise, and finally explored some of the Central American coast.

When he died in 1506, he was still sure he had reached Asia. He had discovered the New World, but without realizing it.

AMERICA UNVEILED

By this time another Italian sea dog, John Cabot, in the service of King Henry VII of England, had crossed the Atlantic in 1497 to reach Newfoundland, which he thought was the northeastern tip of Asia. In 1499 a Florentine named Amerigo Vespucci set out from Spain on a voyage that took him to the mouth of the Amazon. He too thought it was Asia, but within a few years revised his opinion and claimed to have found a new world. A German writer gave it his name as a compliment.

All was still far from clear, however, and the new land across the sea continued to attract explorers who were hoping to find huge riches and fabulous marvels. In 1509 the Spanish adventurer Juan Ponce de León conquered Puerto Rico and then set off with an expedition to find the mythical Fountain of Eternal Youth. He actually found Florida.

In 1511 a Spanish force under Diego Velasquez conquered Cuba. With them was a soldier of fortune and dedicated womanizer named Hernán Cortés, still only in his 20s. Velasquez sent Hernandez de Cordoba to explore the Yucatán, and word of the great Maya cities began to filter back. In 1519, with a paltry 600 men at his back, Cortés led an expedition to Mexico. Their 16 horses struck awe into the native population, who had never seen such creatures before. Cortés was fortunate to acquire an Indian princess as his mistress, interpreter, and adviser. He gained allies among subject peoples resentful of Aztec oppression. In less than three years he conquered the Aztec empire, to rule a territory from the Caribbean to the Pacific for Spain.

AMAZONS AND GOLD

From northern Europe expeditions set out to find a route to Asia that would avoid Spain's jealously guarded preserves. Giovanni da Verrazano, a Florentine in the service of the French government, sailed along much of the east coast of North America in 1524. He was the first European to set eyes on New York Bay. In the 1530s the French explorer Jacques Cartier discovered and named the Bay of St. Lawrence. Local Huron Indians told him he had found "Canada," which in their language simply meant a village, but he mistook it for the name of the whole area. He penetrated as far as a Huron village where Montreal stands today.

Immigrants had meanwhile poured into New Spain (later to be called Mexico, after the Aztec god). The authorities sent parties to explore to the north, still in search of treasures. In 1540 Francisco Vásquez de Coronado set out to find and seize the rumored wealth of the Seven Cities of Cibola, somewhere to the north of Mexico. He failed to find them, but one of his party discovered the Grand Canyon. Two years after Coronado left, an expedition under João Rodrigues Cabrilho sailed north up the Pacific coast. The island of California was rumored to lie somewhere in that direction, peopled by black Amazons and ruled by a queen, with not a man among them. Their weapons were made of gold, as were the harnesses of their wild steeds. Cabrilho explored most of the California coast without finding either Amazons or gold (though ironically there was plenty waiting inland at Sutter's Mill, that would later spark the Californian gold rush of 1849). His ships may have put into San Francisco Bay. Sir Francis Drake sailed into this huge harbor in 1579 and claimed the area for Good Queen Bess, calling it New Albion.

These first blind probings in quest of gold and wonders opened the way to the discovery and settlement of the new continents, as the civilization of Europe found a whole fresh and revitalizing arena in the Americas.

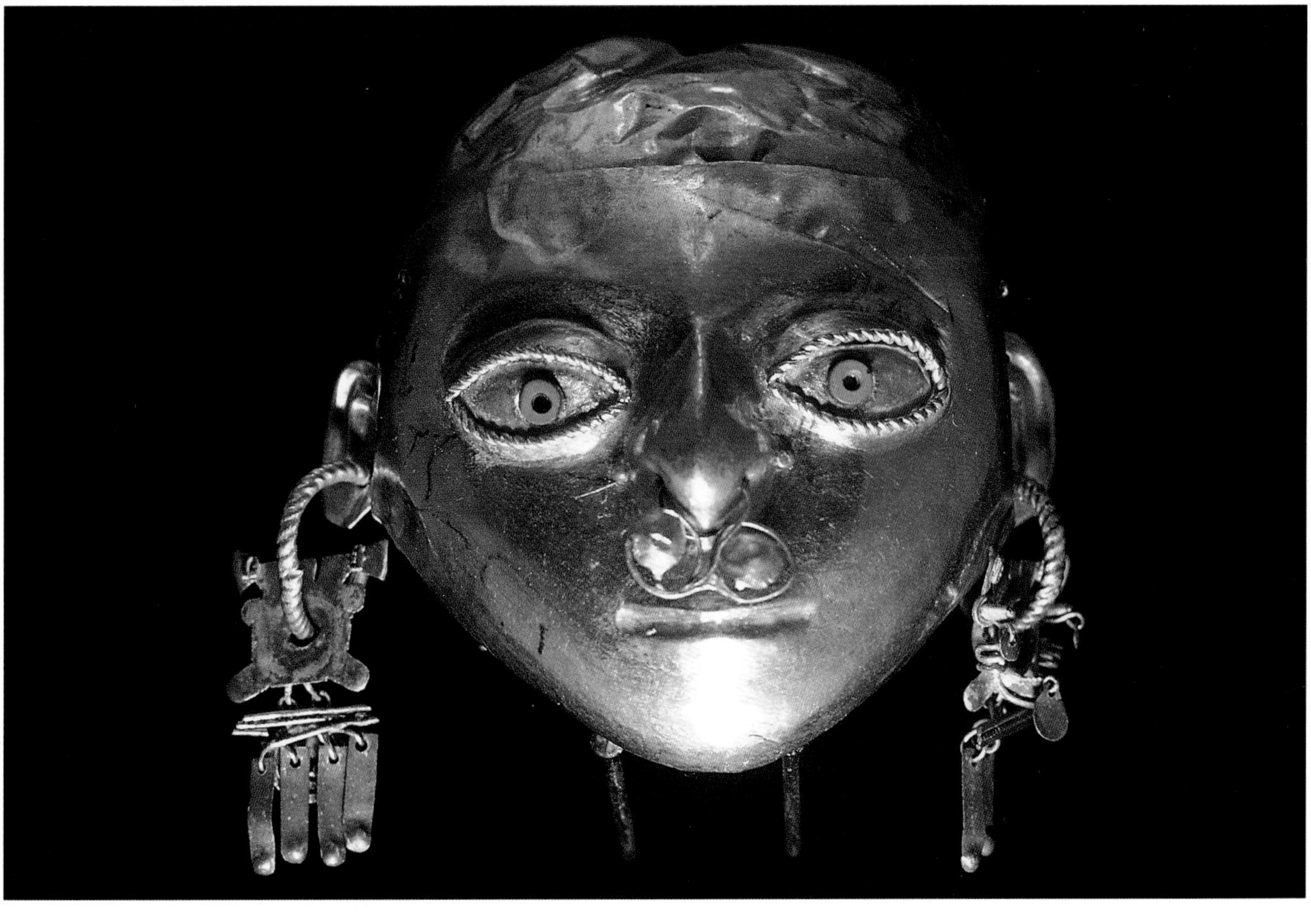

The lure of gold drew adventurers from Europe to the new continent.
Top: fabulous offerings of gold were thrown into Lake Guatavita in Colombia as offerings to the gods.
Above: this gold mask has moving silver eyeballs suspended on tiny wires.
Below: gold mask with jewelled eyes.

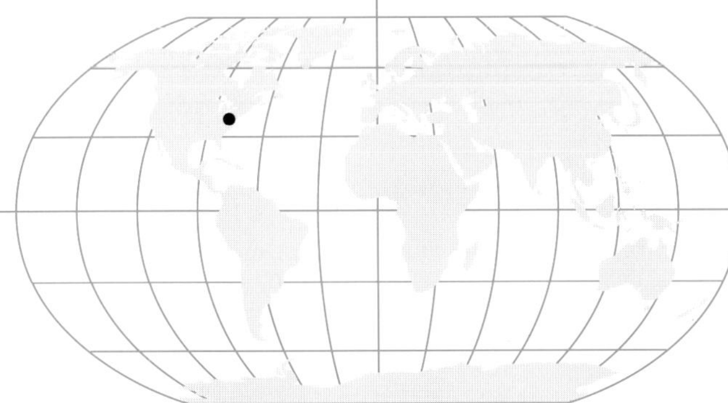

From 1770 United States

MONTICELLO

The home of an architect, gardener, writer, and amateur scientist who also happened to be the third president of the United States.

THOMAS Jefferson (1743-1826) was the third president of the United States and one of the key figures involved in America's Declaration of Independence. An accomplished lawyer, he was the son of a successful farmer from whom he inherited a large estate. He loved music and plants and enjoyed conducting scientific experiments. He had a reputation as a philosopher and theologian and as an amateur inventor. His home at Monticello, in his native

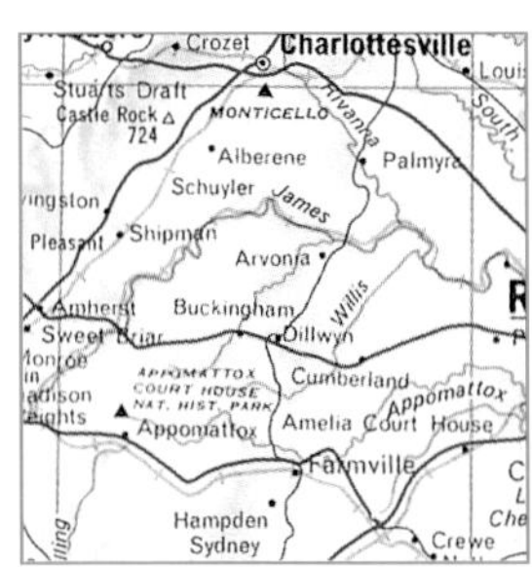

Monticello is on Route 53 3 miles (5 km) southeast of Charlottesville, Virginia. The international airport at Richmond is just one of several from which domestic flights are available to Charlottesville. Charlottesville also has an Amtrak rail station, but services are subject to change.

The Declaration of Independence

JEFFERSON'S first draft of the Declaration stated: "We hold these truths to be sacred and undeniable; that all men are created equal and independent, that from that equal creation they derive rights inherent and inalienable, among which are the preservation of life, and liberty, and the pursuit of happiness." This was altered in the final draft to: "We hold these truths to be self-evident, that all men are created equal, that they are endowed by their creator with certain inalienable rights, that among these are life, liberty, and the pursuit of happiness."

Right: very much Mr. Jefferson's own creation, with its pleasing classical style, the house was designed to look smaller than it really is, and its three stories are neatly disguised as a single floor.

Facing page: Mr. Jefferson died in the house in 1826 and his grave is on the grounds.

state of Virginia, is a memorial to a character of great versatility, not least because he designed the house and the gardens himself, installed gadgets such as dumbwaiters and a revolving service hatch, and took an interest in every aspect of decoration and furniture.

Monticello stands high on a hill with fine views across the surrounding country to the place of Jefferson's birth at Shadwell, and to the University of Virginia, which he founded and helped to design. The house as it appears today is Jefferson's own imaginative reworking of the Palladian style of architecture, with a pedimented portico, 21 rooms, and a shallow dome – the first to be built on an American house. Dating from 1796-1808, this villa is a complete remodeling of an earlier house on the site. Jefferson had designed the first house too, but after five years as a diplomat at the French court, he returned full of new ideas. He described "putting up and pulling down" as one of his "favorite amusements."

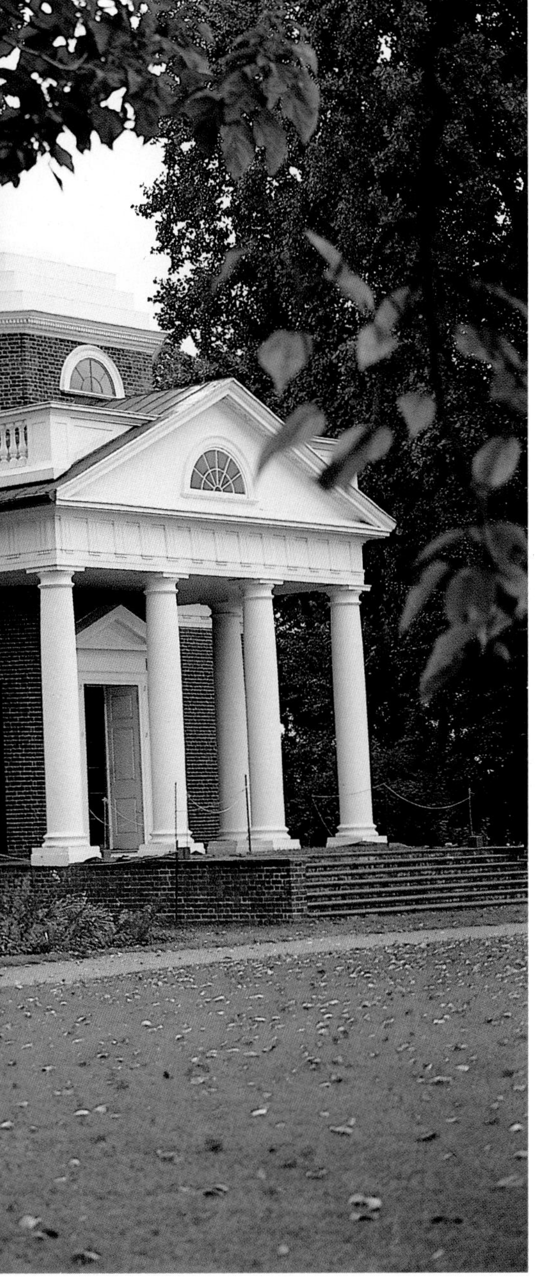

Monticello is the property of the Thomas Jefferson Memorial Foundation, formed in 1923 to purchase, preserve, and maintain the house. It is a place of distinctive character and atmosphere, and the custodians' custom of always referring to "Mr. Jefferson" helps to suggest that the owner himself might very well be waiting in one of the other rooms.

Every attempt has been made to recreate the interior as it was in Jefferson's time, and most of the objects and furniture belonged to the family. One of the particularly evocative rooms is Jefferson's "cabinet" or study, furnished with a revolving chair, a table with a revolving top, a telescope in one of the windows, and two globes – terrestrial and celestial – at the doorway. The library was large enough to hold nearly 7,000 volumes – a valuable collection that Jefferson sold to the federal government in 1815 and which became the core of the Library of Congress collection.

Jefferson carried out much research into the growth and propagation of plants and took great care over the gardens at Monticello. This aspect of his life is well documented in his detailed *Garden Book*, which was used by the Garden Club of Virginia when its members began to restore the grounds in 1939. The many trees, the grove that offers a shady woodland walk, the vegetable garden where over 250 varieties of vegetables and herbs were grown, and the flower garden – all contribute to the splendor of Monticello today. The recently established Thomas Jefferson Center for Historic Plants is a fitting commemoration of a man who wrote, "No occupation is so delightful to me as the culture of the earth, and no culture comparable to that of the garden."

Jefferson as Architect

JEFFERSON'S work as an architect was not limited to the design of his own house. With the assistance of Benjamin Latrobe (responsible for the White House porticoes) and William Thornton (an English architect who made the first plans for the United States Capitol in Washington, later modified by Latrobe), he designed the beautiful buildings of the University of Virginia at Charlottesville. The campus plan adopted here, which was imitated by other universities in America, clearly demonstrates Jefferson's love of plants and gardens. The university library was modeled on the Pantheon in Rome, and many of the other buildings were inspired by Greek and Roman architecture. A Roman building, the Maison Carrée at Nîmes, is said to have been Jefferson's model for the State Capitol at Richmond, Virginia. Constructed between 1789 and 1798, this is thought to be the first neoclassical building in the United States.

1853-1893 U.S.A.

MORMON TEMPLE

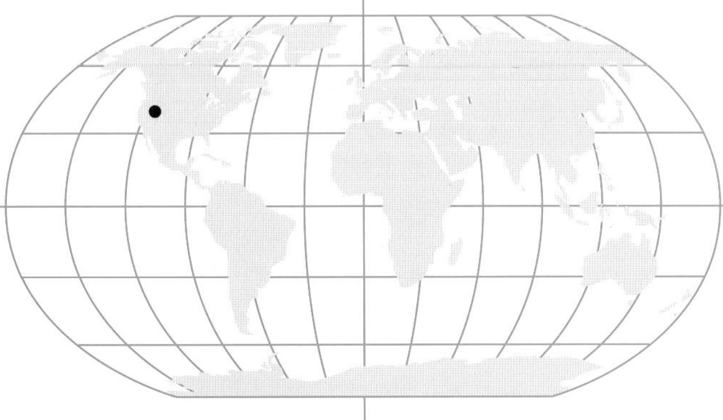

"And the desert shall rejoice, and blossom as the rose."
– Isaiah, chapter 35, verse 1.

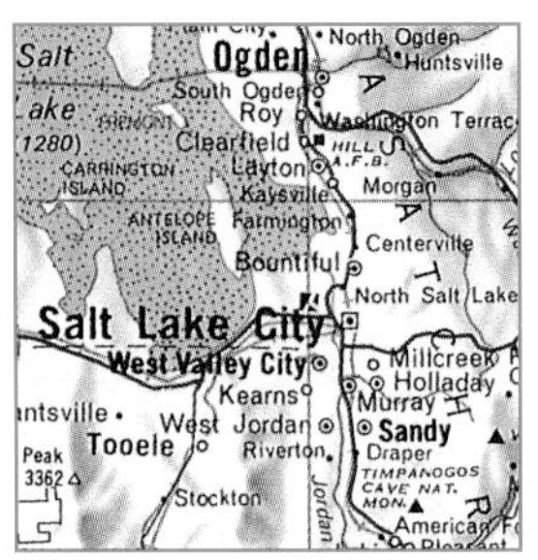

Salt Lake City is at the intersection of Routes 15 and 80, and has its own airport. Train connections with Chicago, Las Vegas, Los Angeles, and Seattle. Numerous long-distance bus connections. The Temple and the Tabernacle are in the middle of the city, with two visitor centers.

City of Zion

The fact that work started on the heavy task of building the Temple within six years of the first Mormons reaching the empty site of the future Salt Lake City says much for the settlers' industry and resourcefulness and for Brigham Young's genius for leadership. The Mormons' founder, Joseph Smith, was murdered by an Illinois mob in 1833. Brigham Young, his successor, looked west for a place that no one else wanted, where the Latter Day Saints, safe from persecution, could build in the wilderness a true Christian community. In 1847 he led a group of pioneers to Utah. They were followed by thousands of Mormon families, many of whom walked 1,300 miles (2,092 km) across the prairies pulling their children and all their possessions in handcarts.

Right: the Temple was designed by the Mormon architect Truman O. Angell, brother of Brigham Young's senior wife.

Facing page: atop one of the pinnacles is the golden figure of the Angel Moroni, carved by the Utah sculptor Cyrus Dallin.

From the first digging of the foundations in 1853, it took exactly 40 years to the day – the figure has a satisfactorily biblical ring to it – to build the Temple of the Church of Jesus Christ of Latter Day Saints. In a restrained Gothic style with few frills and six tall spires, it was built of granite quarried 20 miles (32 km) away and hauled laboriously to the site in ox carts. The architect, Truman O. Angell, was the brother-in-law of Brigham Young, the redoubtable Mormon leader.

With walls 16 feet (4.9 m) thick at the base, the Temple measures 186½ feet (57 m) long by 118 feet (36 m) wide, and the two highest spires soar to 210 feet (64 m). On one of them is a statue of the Angel Moroni, who revealed to Joseph Smith, the Mormons' founder, the golden tablets on which the Book of Mormon was inscribed. Cast in copper and covered with gold leaf, the angel stands 12½ feet (3.8 m) tall and is raising his golden trumpet to his lips to signal the Second Coming of Christ.

The Temple is open only to Mormons, but there is much to interest the visitor in Temple Square and its vicinity, especially the Tabernacle, with its huge turtle-shaped roof. Covering an auditorium 250 feet (76 m) long by 150 feet (46 m) wide with no visible means of support, it is said to have been designed by Brigham Young himself to provide a meeting hall that could hold 7,000 people without anyone's view being blocked by pillars. A

dome-shaped lattice of timbers was erected over the hall, supported on stone pillars at the sides and fastened together with wooden pegs and lengths of rawhide. The organ pipes appeared to be of metal, the balcony of marble, and the benches of oak, but all were in fact made of pinewood skillfully painted to look like the real thing in each case. The Tabernacle turned out to have extraordinary acoustics (you can literally hear a pin drop in it), and its magnificent organ, now swelled to some 12,000 pipes and six keyboards, is one of the finest in existence. The hall resounds with organ recitals every day and, on Sunday mornings, with the famous Mormon Tabernacle Choir, more than 300 strong.

Also in the square is the Assembly Hall, a smaller, granite building used for services. In front of it is the Seagull Monument, which commemorates the birds that appeared in the nick of time to save the first Mormon settlers' vital crop from being devoured by swarms of crickets; in this event the settlers saw the hand of God. The story is told in bronze reliefs on the base, while two seagulls are alighting gracefully on the top. The monument dates from 1913, and the sculptor was Brigham Young's grandson, Mahonri Young.

The nearby Museum of Church History and Art, opened in 1984, has a collection of more than 60,000 items related to Mormon life and history as well as works by Mormon artists. The Family History Library, the largest of its kind in the world, contains the immense genealogical collection of the Mormon Church, available to Mormons and non-Mormons alike. From the Brigham Young Monument, Cyrus Dallin's 25-foot (7.6-m) bronze statue of the great leader contemplates the fruits of his life's work.

Salt Lake City was laid out on a square grid oriented to the cardinal points of the compass, with streets 132 feet (40 m) wide, following the plan that Joseph Smith had prepared for the City of Zion. Brigham Young called the Mormon kingdom Deseret, a name from the Book of Mormon meaning "land of honeybees." Though the Mormon practice of polygamy aroused fierce hostility in the East, Congress recognized Utah as a territory and Brigham Young as its governor. (It became a state in 1896.) Beehive House, where Brigham Young lived with his senior wife, Mary Ann Angell, can be visited in Salt Lake City today. So can Lion House, which he provided for some of his 16 wives and 44 children. Both were designed by Truman O. Angell. Young himself died in 1877.

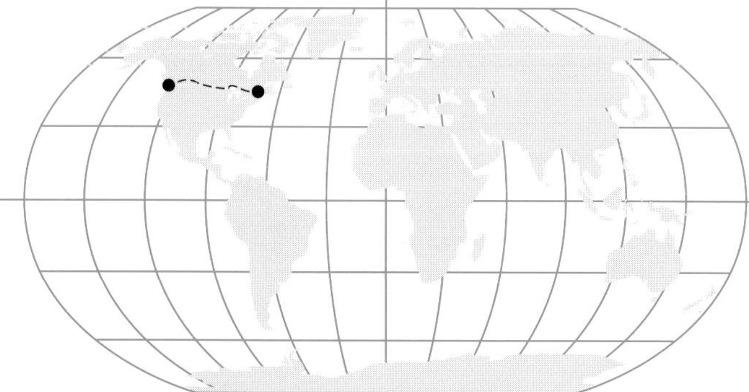

1885 Canada

CANADIAN PACIFIC RAILROAD

In the early days, passengers liked to ride on the cowcatcher as the engine lumbered through the Rocky Mountains.

THE single track between Montreal and Vancouver, 2,918 miles (4,696 km) long, was one of the most heroic feats of engineering history – described at the time as "an act of insane recklessness" – and a vital factor in the development of modern Canada. The story began in 1867, when the country's eastern provinces formed the Canadian Confederation. To the west of them lay a vast emptiness of prairies and mountains. Beyond, on the Pacific coast, was British Columbia, uncertain whether or not to link up with the United States. In 1871 British Columbia joined the Confederation, on condition that a trans-continental railroad be built within 10 years.

In the event, work began in 1881. A formidable American of Dutch descent, William Van Horne, was put in charge. He had begun his career as a humble telegraph operator with the Illinois Central Railroad, and he ended up with a richly deserved knighthood.

The line across the prairies was built rapidly in 15 months. From the supply base in Winnipeg, construction trains moved west with clockwork regularity, each one carrying exactly the quantity of material needed for 1 mile (1.6 km) of track: rails and ties, telegraph poles, bridging material where required. Indians came to watch, squatting gravely on their haunches and admiring the "fire wagons," the engines that heralded the end of their way of life.

Getting the track through the Rocky Mountains was another matter altogether. Beyond the little settlement at Calgary, the line moved swiftly along the Bow River – on one stretch a length of 600 feet (183 m) was laid in a record time of 4¾ minutes – but then an army of 12,000 men was needed to drive over Kicking Horse Pass, 5,340 feet (1,628 m) up among the towering peaks, and down a dizzying descent on the other side, crossing and recrossing the sinuous Kicking Horse River.

The original plan was to follow the Columbia River, but a surveyor named A.B. Rogers discovered a pass (now named after him) through the Selkirk Mountains, which saved 150 miles (241 km). Because of avalanches the line had to be protected with miles of snowsheds, and later a tunnel was driven through the worst section. The highest bridge in North America was built over Stoney Creek, on wooden towers 200 feet (61 m) tall.

Beyond Shuswap Lake the track threaded through the Coast Mountains by way of the wild and almost impassable Fraser Canyon, which Van Horne described as "one of the worst places in the world." It was intended to end at Port Moody on Burrard Inlet, but Van Horne pushed it on down the inlet to the site of what is now Vancouver. Van Horne chose

Trains used to run between Montreal in Quebec Province and Vancouver, British Columbia, but the service was discontinued in 1990. The Canadian Railway Museum at St. Constant, in the southern suburbs of Montreal, has a tremendous collection, including C.P.R. locomotives and the private railroad car used by Sir William Van Horne when the line was being built.

All Aboard for the Pacific

THE last spike of the Canadian Pacific Railroad was driven in a simple ceremony amid the mountains at Eagle Pass on November 7, 1885, at a spot that William Van Horne named Craigellachie. In his book *The Impossible Railway*, Pierre Berton describes how the line's directors arrived at the scene, drawn by locomotive number 148, with its diamond-shaped smokestack and gleaming brass boiler. It was a dull day, the mountains shrouded in clouds, the cedars and firs dripping with wet snow. The oldest of the directors, Donald A. Smith, drove the final spike in total silence, followed by a tremendous cheer as it went home, and the shrill whistling

Above: a train leaves Banff, with the Rocky Mountain peaks towering in the background.

Facing page: the railroad runs beside the Bow River, through some of the most difficult and breathtakingly beautiful scenery in North America.

the name. The city, which owes its existence to the railroad, became the leading port on the whole west coast of North America.

The railroad opened up all of central and western Canada to settlers, who came swarming in by the thousands. Winnipeg waxed fat on its railroad yards and the tide of immigrants pouring through to the prairies. Regina was created by the railroad and was named in honor of Queen Victoria when the first train arrived in 1882. Banff, the first major Rocky Mountain tourist resort, was named by the C.P.R.'s president, a Scotsman from Banffshire. After more than a hundred years, the transcontinental service that began so heroically was ended in 1990.

of the locomotive. Everyone turned to Van Horne, demanding a speech. The great man was not given to oratory. He said simply, "All I can say is that the work has been done well in every way." There was a rush to seize souvenirs, and the whistle sounded again as a voice cried, "All aboard for the Pacific!"

1886 U.S.A.

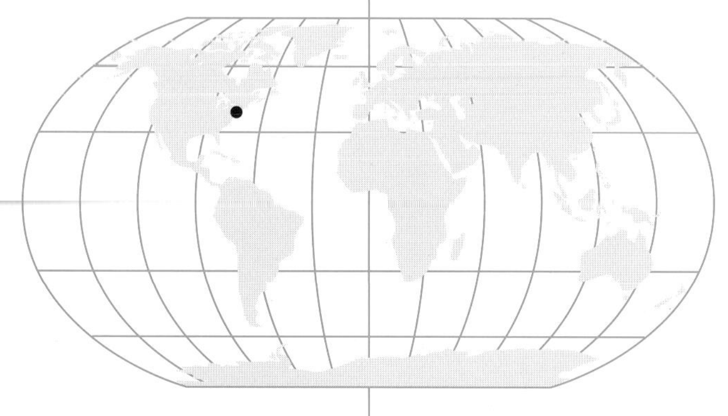

STATUE OF LIBERTY

"Give me your tired, your poor,
Your huddled masses yearning to breathe free . . ."
– Emma Lazarus, "The New Colossus"

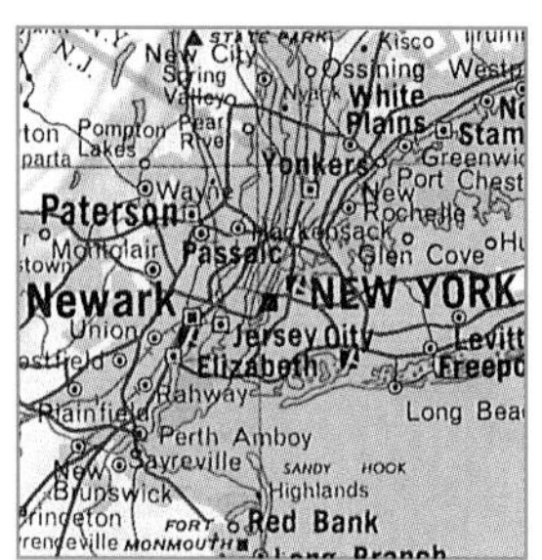

Regular ferries run to the Statue of Liberty from the Battery, at the southern tip of Manhattan Island. The trip offers excellent views of the harbor, New York City, and the statue itself. Separate ferries run to Ellis Island.

Right: Liberty lifts her lamp beside "the golden door," the entrance to New York Harbor, and so the gateway to a new life in the New World, free of the restrictions and poverty of the Old.

Facing page, left and right: the observation deck in the figure's crown commands views that are spectacular in the extreme. The figure was shipped across the Atlantic in pieces, in crates, and assembled on what is now Liberty Island.

The best-known statue in North America, and perhaps in the world, was dedicated by President Grover Cleveland on October 28, 1886, to the roar of a 21-gun salute, the blasts of ships' foghorns, and a din of fireworks. Ever since, passengers on ships entering New York Harbor have seen the towering figure holding aloft Liberty's torch. For many thousands of immigrants, the statue promised freedom from oppression and poverty in the Old World, and it has become a symbol of the United States of America.

The statue was constructed in Paris, where it was formally presented to the American ambassador on July 4, 1884, as a gift from the French people to the American people. It was then taken to pieces and shipped in crates to New York, to be reassembled on the massive pedestal built for it at American expense on Bedloe's Island (now Liberty Island).

The pedestal, designed by the American architect Richard Morris Hunt, stands 154 feet (47 m) high; the statue itself is 151 feet (46 m) tall, so the tip of the torch is 305 feet (93 m) above ground. The statue weights 252 U.S. tons (229 metric tons), with a 35-foot (10.6-m) waist and a mouth 3 feet (91 cm) wide. The right arm, holding the torch, is 42 feet (12.8 m) long, and the index finger alone is 8 feet (2.4 m) long. The figure has the broken shackles of tyranny at her feet. In her left hand she holds a tablet representing the Declaration of Independence. Her crown of seven rays stands for freedom spreading across the seven seas to the seven continents. A spiral staircase inside the statue enables visitors to reach the crown, a climb equivalent to walking up a 12-story building.

The statue had its origins in French politics. In 1865, with Emperor Napoleon III on the throne, an academic named Edouard de Laboulaye and his circle hoped for an end to the monarchy and the establishment of a new French Republic. They hatched the idea of the Statue of Liberty to express approval of the great republic across the Atlantic and to stimulate the notion of sympathy between the peoples of France and the United States. A young sculptor from Alsace, Frédéric-Auguste Bartholdi, was encouraged by Laboulaye to consider the project.

Bartholdi had hoped to build a lighthouse for the Suez Canal in the form of a colossal female figure holding a torch aloft to symbolize the light of progress coming to Asia. He took up the new project with enthusiasm. His Liberty figure was influenced by a famous painting by Delacroix, *Liberty Guiding the People*, and her face reflects the stern features of his own mother.

The huge size of the statue and its exposure to wind and weather posed severe technical problems for Bartholdi and his engineer, the brilliant Alexandre-Gustave Eiffel, creator of the Eiffel Tower. Eiffel built an ingenious iron framework supported by a central pylon. Onto this flexible interior skeleton was attached the statue's visible outer layer, which is only $^{3}/_{32}$ of an inch (2.4 mm) thick. Starting with a small model of the statue 4 feet (1.2 m) tall, Bartholdi then made three more, each bigger than the last, until the full magnificent size was reached.

The Golden Door

THE Statue of Liberty's pedestal contains a museum dedicated to the story of immigration to America. Opened in 1972, it begins with the prehistoric ancestors of the American Indians, who crossed into the unexplored continent from Asia, to the mass immigrations of modern times. Audiovisual displays, models, photographs, drawings, costumes, and artifacts provide material on every incoming group, including the West Africans shipped to the New World as slaves and the massive Irish, Italian, and Jewish immigrations of the 19th century.

The Statue of Liberty inspired Emma Lazarus's well-known poem "The New Colossus," with its references to the "huddled masses" and "wretched refuse" of the Old World coming to be welcomed by Liberty's lamp, lifted "beside the golden door." From 1892 onwards, the huddled masses actually arrived at Ellis Island, near Liberty Island, where boatloads of Germans and Irish, Italians, Slavs, and Jews were processed in a babble of languages and an intense atmosphere of nervous apprehension mingled with hope and excitement. An average of 2,000 new arrivals a day passed through the great hall in the early 1900s; in its peak year of 1907, Ellis Island handled more than a million people. The immigration station closed in 1954, and the complex is being restored as a national monument. There are guided tours for visitors.

1914 Panama

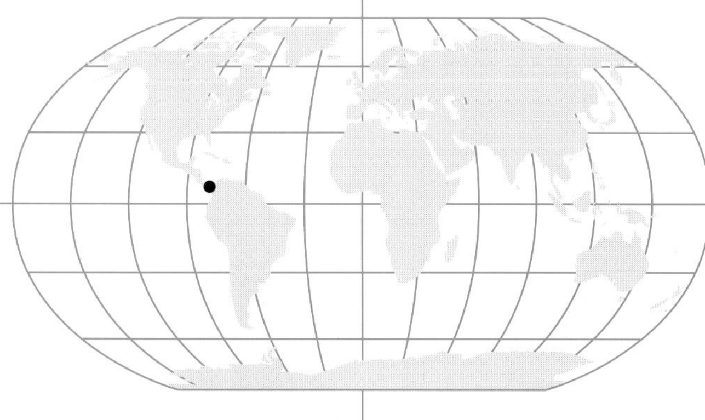

PANAMA CANAL

Workers employed on the first attempt to build the canal brought their coffins with them.

Panama City has an international airport. The Pacific terminus of the canal can be reached by bus to the Miraflores Locks. Nearby are the control room and a viewing area for visitors.

THE first ocean steamer passed through the Panama Canal on August 3, 1914, bringing to fulfillment years of arduous labor to hack a passage from the Atlantic to the Pacific across the Isthmus of Panama. From one shoreline to the other, the canal runs $40\frac{1}{4}$ miles (64.8 km). From deep water in one ocean to deep water in the other, the distance is $50\frac{3}{4}$ miles (81.7 km).

Contrary to the general impression, the canal does not run from east to west. The geography of the Isthmus of Panama is such that the waterway's overall direction from the Atlantic to the Pacific is southeast. Panama City, at the Pacific end, lies southeast of Colón at the Atlantic end. (It is possible to see the sun rise above the Pacific from some places in Panama.)

Building the canal involved construction not only of the waterway itself but also of substantial ports and their installations at each end, huge breakwaters, dams, locks, and artificial lakes. The railroad between Colón and Panama City had to be largely rebuilt as well.

One of the breakwaters at the Atlantic end in Limón Bay is $2\frac{1}{4}$ miles (3.5 km) long and 15 feet (4.6 m) wide at the top. Ships run due south from here to the three Gatún Locks, which raise them 85 feet (26 m) to the man-made Lake Gatún. A cut 500 feet (152 m) wide leads out of the lake to more locks, where there are drops of 31 feet (9.5 m) and 54 feet (16.5 m) down to sea level again before vessels arrive at the Pacific terminus on the Gulf of Panama, protected by a breakwater $3\frac{1}{2}$ miles (5.2 km) long.

The locks were all built in duplicate, 1,000 feet (305 m) long and 110 feet (34 m) wide, to allow ships to pass each other in opposite directions. Giant steel lock gates were installed, 7 feet (2.1 m) thick and up to 82 feet (25 m) high, weighing from 437 to 806 U.S. tons (396 to 732 metric tons). Ships are hauled slowly through the locks by locomotives – usually six to a ship – which crawl along the lock walls.

The first attempt to build the canal failed dismally. Ferdinand de Lesseps, the creator of the Suez Canal, formed a company that began work in 1880 to cut a waterway 30 feet (9.1 m) deep and 72 feet (22 m) wide, going from ocean to ocean at sea level all the way. The difficulties proved insuperable, and de Lesseps's work force dropped like flies with yellow fever

A Path Across Darien

THE first explorer to set foot in Panama was a Spaniard, Rodrigo de Bastidas, who landed in 1501. With him was Vasco Núñez de Balboa, who stayed on with a party of settlers

Right: a tanker runs through the canal, crossing the narrow land barrier between the Atlantic and Pacific oceans.

Facing page: a ship is entering one of the Gatún Locks, where vessels from the Atlantic end of the canal are raised to the level of the man-made Lake Gatun. Millions of cubic yards of concrete went into building the huge locks.

and malaria. The project became so notorious a death trap that some construction workers brought their coffins with them from France. It is said that the death toll had reached 20,000 when the company went bankrupt and work was abandoned in 1889.

In 1903 Panama and the United States signed a treaty that granted the American government the right to build the canal, but first the threat of disease was dealt with. William Crawford Gorgas, an American army surgeon, descended on the area, and in two years he eliminated yellow fever entirely and put malaria firmly in its place. Construction work on the canal began in 1907 with Colonel G.W. Goethals, U.S. Army, as chief engineer. The canal was built with high hopes of encouraging not only commerce but peaceful communication between nations. Ironically, its opening to the world's ships coincided with the outbreak of one of the most destructive wars in world history.

and who, on September 25, 1513, was the first European, "silent upon a peak in Darien," to gaze upon the Pacific. The possibility of cutting a canal across Central America was raised as early as 1550, in a book by a Portuguese navigator, Antonio Galvao. He suggested the Isthmus of Darien, 30 miles (48 km) wide at the point where Central America and South America join, as one likely site.

The Spanish government, however, proved averse to a canal that might threaten its monopoly position in Central America. Spanish silver and gold were shipped up the Pacific coast from Peru to the south coast of Panama and then carried on mules across the isthmus to Colón. The Cruces Mule Trail drew pirates like bees to a honeypot. In 1671, for instance, the English buccaneer Henry Morgan swooped, burned Panama City, and carried off 200 muleloads of loot. On the whole, though, the Spaniards got their treasure safely through, and a Scottish attempt to settle a colony in Darien in the 1690s failed.

The Spanish government made various surveys for a canal in the 1770s, but nothing came of them. After gold was discovered in California in 1849 and prospectors swarmed west, a railroad was built with great difficulty between Colón and Panama City. When it opened in 1855, the overseas trade of the Central American countries shifted from ports on the Caribbean side to those on the Pacific coast. Trains followed much the same route that in a few decades would be taken by ships.

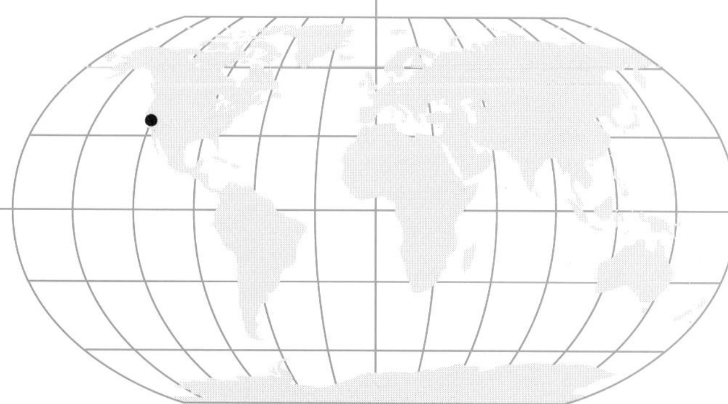

From 1919 U.S.A.

HEARST'S CASTLE

The Old World yielded its treasures to adorn William Randolph Hearst's palace above the Pacific.

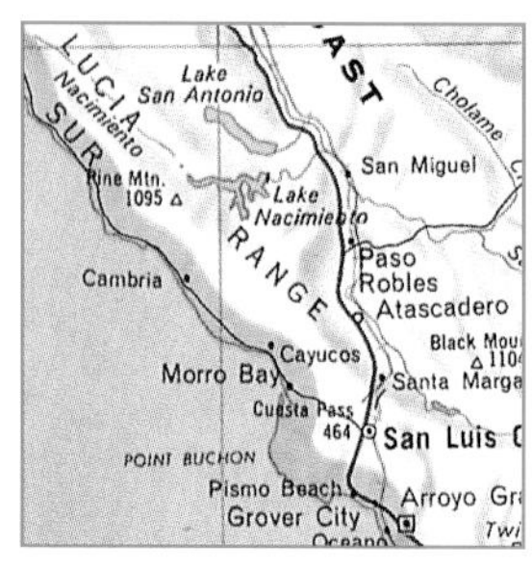

The Hearst-San Simeon State Historical Monument, as it is officially known, is 30 miles (48 km) north of Morro Bay, off California State Highway 1, roughly halfway between Los Angeles and San Francisco. Guided tours explore the house and gardens.

HEARST'S Castle – or simply San Simeon, as it is often called – is an extraordinary and sometimes captivatingly beautiful mansion of gigantic splendor, created at almost unimaginable expense by one determined man, who ransacked Europe to furnish and adorn it. Anything he could not buy, he had copied. He himself liked to call the place simply "the ranch," but the money and love he readily lavished on it belie the casual term. Those who have not been there probably draw their mental picture of it from Orson Welles's film *Citizen Kane*, whose central character was based foursquare on William Randolph Hearst.

The Missions

BURIED in front of the altar of the mission church in Carmel is Father Junipero Serra, a Franciscan friar born in Majorca. Diminutive (he stood only 5 feet 2 inches [1.57 m]) yet fiercely energetic, he was the leading figure in missionary work to convert the local Indians to Christianity between 1769 and his death in 1784. After building his first mission in San Diego, he and his followers constructed others further north, until eventually there was a chain of 21 of them in California. With their cool beige and terra-cotta Spanish-style architecture, they are evocative reminders of a vanished age, when the friars busily instructed their charges in farming and cattle-raising as well as Christianity. Unfortunately, the missions decimated the native population, which fell victim to European diseases.

Right: the beautiful outdoor pool, with the California hills beyond, where Hearst planted more than 6,000 trees.

Facing page, above: the grand dining hall.

Facing page, below: the delectable California coast.

It is entirely typical of San Simeon that it should boast not one, but two mammoth swimming pools. The indoor one is a Roman bath, brought over from Europe and reconstructed. The ravishing outdoor one, which holds 345,000 U.S. gallons/276,000 imperial gallons (1.3 million liters) of water, has a Greek temple front at one side of it, with classical statues and colonnades, and a delectable view over the hills.

The house stands high above the California coast, looking out over the Pacific and the diminutive harbor to which crates of art objects, furniture, entire rooms, entire buildings were brought at Hearst's command. He inherited the land here, and a fortune, from his father, the mining magnate George Hearst, who died in 1891. William Randolph was to multiply the fortune many times over in the newspaper business as one of the founding fathers of sensationalist "yellow journalism." He began work at San Simeon in 1919, after his mother died, and hired the architect Julia Morgan to help him realize his dreams.

Hearst's agents abroad scoured the world for priceless antiques, medieval tapestries, tiles, Chinese jade, and porcelain. It is said that he had a complete monastery shipped from Spain, stone by stone, and left it in packing cases for several years because he could not quite decide what to do with it. The house contained the world's largest collection of Greek vases in private hands. Sometimes whole rooms were designed around an object that Hearst particularly liked. Some rooms were built, knocked down, and rebuilt as he changed his mind.

The result is strikingly impressive. Italian, French, Spanish, and Moorish architectural styles are blended together and objects from completely different periods and styles mixed into a whole unified by Hearst's own taste. His main dining room was set up to look like a medieval baron's hall of colossal proportions, hung with banners from Siena; the refectory table is so long that you feel you might need binoculars to see the far end. Along it at intervals are clusters of sauce bottles.

Hearst and his mistress, the delightful film actress Marion Davies, entertained here in a style as lavish as the castle itself. All the great names of Hollywood's golden age came to stay, from Charlie Chaplin, Mary Pickford, and Rudolf Valentino to Gary Cooper, Clark Gable, and Cary Grant. To the alarm of nervous guests, the grounds were roamed by Hearst's private menagerie of yaks, bears, monkeys, and kangaroos, shipped from far-flung climes. The house was still not complete when Hearst died in 1951. Clearly, he could never have contemplated finishing it.

Big Sur

RUNNING north along the Pacific shore, the coast road provides dramatic views of rugged cliffs, beaches, rocky coves, and thundering breakers. Literary and artistic people, and many interested in New Age ideas, have been attracted to the Big Sur area. The giant redwood trees grow here, and inland are the mountains of Los Padres National Forest. The Spaniards called this El Gran Pais del Sur, "the big country to the south" of their settlement at Monterey. Jack Kerouac wrote about Big Sur, Henry Miller lived here for 17 years, and before that the poet Robinson Jeffers loved this area. Beyond Big Sur, the town of Carmel, which hit international headlines when actor/director Clint Eastwood was elected mayor, has numerous galleries and craft shops, and considerable old-world charm. Mission San Carlos Borromeo de Carmelo, built here in 1777, is one of the most attractive in California.

1922 U.S.A.

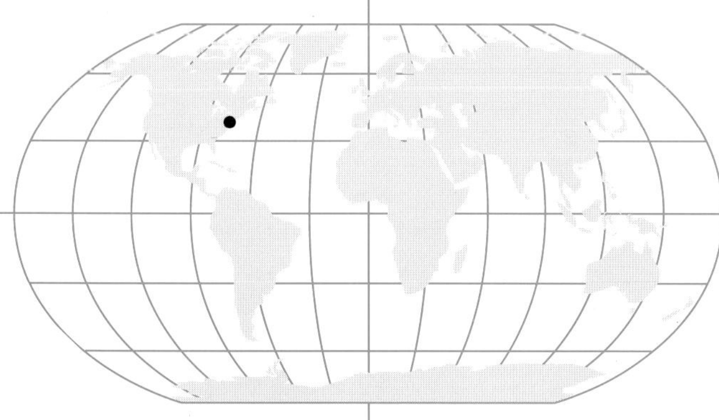

LINCOLN MEMORIAL

"With malice toward none; with charity for all, . . . let us strive on to finish the work we are in; to bind up the nation's wounds." – Abraham Lincoln, Second Inaugural Address (March 4, 1865).

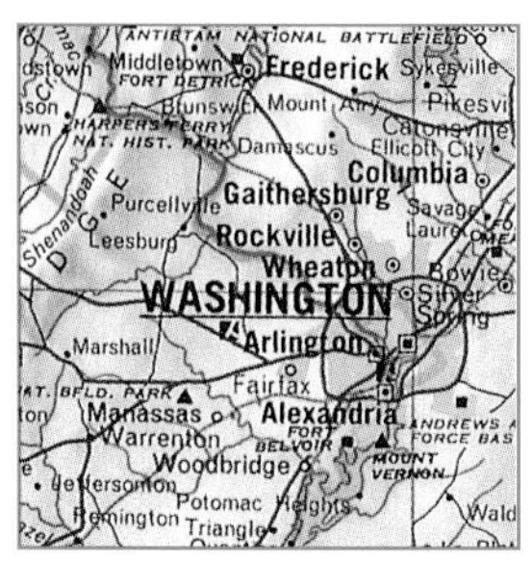

The Lincoln Memorial, one of the most visited sites in Washington D.C., is in Potomac Park at the foot of 23rd Street N.W., within walking distance of the White House and the Capitol. Nearest metro station: Foggy Bottom.

Of all the great presidents of the United States of America, perhaps the one whose memory has been held in the most enduring affection and admiration in the world at large is Abraham Lincoln. His monument in Washington D.C. is a dignified, restrained, and moving tribute to the man and to the virtues of tolerance, honesty, and constancy that it was intended to honor.

Within two years of his death in 1865, there were proposals for a memorial in Washington, but it was not until 1915 that the foundation stone was laid. The memorial was dedicated on May 30, 1922. The designer was the architect Henry Bacon, something of a specialist in monuments, who also designed the one to Lincoln in the city of Lincoln, Nebraska.

The memorial is a classical Greek temple in form, in the manner of the Parthenon. The rectangular building is flanked by 38 tremendous Doric columns of white Colorado marble, 44 feet (13.4 m) high with a diameter of 7 feet 5 inches (2.26 m) at the base: two to mark the entrance and the remaining 36 standing for the 36 states of the Union at the time of Lincoln's death. On the parapet above, 48 festoons represent the 48 states of the Union when the memorial was dedicated. The colonnade is 188 feet (57 m) long by 118 feet (36 m) wide.

Inside, in a chamber 60 feet (28 m) high, is a colossal statue of the president by Daniel Chester French, 19 feet (5.8 m) high and the same distance wide. Showing him seated in a massive chair, in a mood of contemplation that viewers can interpret in their own ways, the

The Last Act

On the evening of April 14, 1865, five days after the surrender of the Confederate Army under General Robert E. Lee at Appomattox Court House, President Lincoln and his wife attended Ford's Theater in Washington to see a comedy called *Our American Cousin*. At 10:15 p.m. a deranged actor named John Wilkes Booth fired a pistol at the president, mortally wounding him. Mr. Lincoln was carried to the house across the street, where he remained unconscious in one of the bedrooms. Mrs. Lincoln, who was in an hysterical state, waited in intense anxiety in the parlor as members of the

Above: looking like a classical Greek temple, the memorial is symbolically related to the number of states of the Union, in President Lincoln's time and when it was dedicated.

Facing page: the magnificent statue of the seated Lincoln by America's most admired sculptor of the day, Daniel French, who was 72 when the memorial was dedicated.

statue appears to be carved from one immense block of Georgia marble. In fact, it is made of 28 pieces, so smoothly fitted together that the joints are not visible.

French was one of the most popular and successful sculptors of his day. He got his start as a boy when his ability to carve comical figures out of turnips impressed his stepmother. He made his name at 24 with his statue of "The Minute Man" in his home town of Concord, Massachusetts, and created a colossal figure of "The Republic" for the World's Columbian Exposition of 1893 in Chicago.

Beyond the President's head is an inscription: "In this temple, as in the hearts of the people for whom he saved the Union, the memory of Abraham Lincoln is enshrined forever." Also cut in the walls are the words of two of his great speeches, the Gettysburg Address of 1863 and the Second Inaugural Address of 1865. There are murals by Jules Guerin on the themes of the reconciliation of North and South, and the freeing of the slaves.

The monument is floodlit at night, to spectacular effect, and a wreath is placed every year on February 12, Lincoln's birthday. There are guided tours of the caves deep underneath the building, with their stalagmites and stalactites. Close to the Potomac River, the memorial is aligned with the Capitol and the Washington Monument, toward which stretches the beautiful Reflecting Pool. To the west, crossing the Potomac, is the Arlington Memorial Bridge, itself a symbol of the reconciling of North and South on which President Lincoln set his heart.

Cabinet gathered at the house. At 7:22 in the morning, Edwin M. Stanton, Secretary of War, emerged from the bedroom to announce the president's death, with the words: "Now he belongs to the ages." Mr. Lincoln was 56.

Ford's Theater closed down after the assassination, but has reopened, restored exactly to its appearance on the fatal evening. It contains a museum of Lincoln relics and objects, including letters and books, White House china, the clothes the President was wearing that night, the pistol with which he was assassinated, and the diary kept by John Wilkes Booth. The house across the street, in which Mr. Lincoln died, has also been restored and is open to the public.

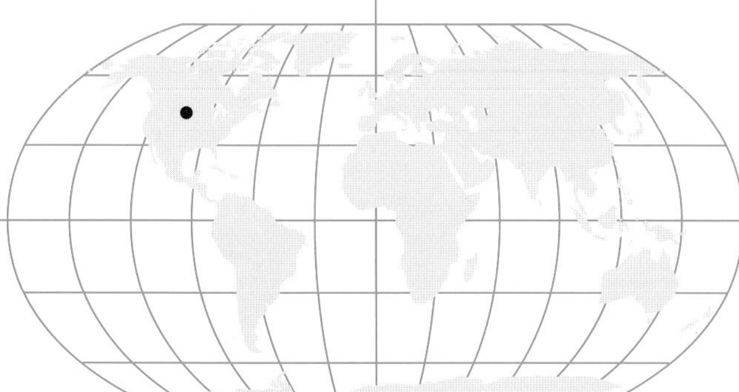

From 1927 U.S.A.

MOUNT RUSHMORE

With dynamite and jackhammer, Gutzon Borglum created a remarkable "shrine to democracy" in the Black Hills.

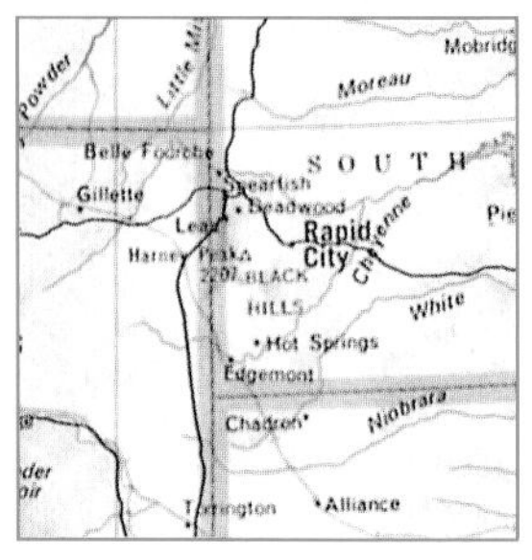

Mount Rushmore is on Route 244, 3 miles (5 km) south of Keystone, South Dakota. There is a visitor center on site and Borglum's studio can be seen. Helicopter trips provide by far the best view of the monument. The nearest main town is Rapid City, which has an airport (flights to New York City and London). Bus connections with Minneapolis, Cheyenne, and Omaha.

CARVED in the granite of Mount Rushmore in the Black Hills, four huge faces of American presidents, 60 feet (18 m) high, gaze out upon the world: George Washington, Thomas Jefferson, Theodore Roosevelt, and Abraham Lincoln. It is said that the sculptor, Gutzon Borglum, particularly wanted to include Theodore Roosevelt because his eyeglasses posed a special challenge to Borglum's skill.

Those who have seen Alfred Hitchcock's 1959 movie *North by Northwest* will remember Cary Grant and Eva Marie Saint scrambling giddily over the faces, with their ears and noses of awesomely gigantic proportions. The idea of the monument was conceived originally by a local historian and publicist named Doane Robinson as a spectacular project to draw tourists to the beautiful Black Hills. In 1924 he interested Gutzon Borglum and it was decided to create a "shrine to democracy" with the colossal carvings of the presidents. Borglum intended them to be shown down to waist level and, as the project was never finished, it has been remarked that it was just as well that he began with the heads.

Borglum was 60 when work began at Mount Rushmore in 1927, and it preoccupied him for the rest of his life. A short, bald man, intensely energetic, patriotic, and outspoken – and extremely difficult to work with – he made a lively impression on the media and gained far more public recognition than an artist normally commands. He designed the monument and directed the sizeable work force of local laborers and miners, who blasted the great heads out of the mountain face with dynamite and shaped them with hammer and chisel, while dangling on swaying platforms.

Borglum had ideas as grandiose as his name, which in full was John Gutzon de la Mothe Borglum (he had a younger brother, also a monumental sculptor, who was christened Solon Hannibal Borglum). He was born in 1867 near Bear Creek, Idaho, of parents who were Mormon immigrants from Denmark. His father worked as a woodcarver and was later in homeopathic practice in Nebraska. Gutzon Borglum was sent to a Roman Catholic boarding school in Xavier, Kansas, where his skill in drawing impressed his Jesuit teachers.

Right: the Mount Rushmore project was never completed, but all four heads were successfully finished and the last of them, that of Theodore Roosevelt, was formally dedicated in 1939. The lion's share of the cost was met by the U.S. taxpayer.

Facing page: seen from a distance, the huge heads gaze stonily from the mountain.

He studied art in Paris, where he met and admired the great sculptor Auguste Rodin, before returning to the United States. In 1915 he was invited to carve a giant head of Robert E. Lee at Stone Mountain, near Atlanta, Georgia. He succeeded in transforming this project into something altogether bigger – a parade a quarter of a mile (1/2 km) long of Confederate infantry and cavalry to be carved out of the mountain, with heroic figures of Lee, Stonewall Jackson, and Jefferson Davis on horseback. Borglum and the committee could not come to terms, however, and the project fell through.

At Mount Rushmore, Borglum quarreled fiercely with the National Park Service, and the work was constantly interrupted by shortage of money and bad weather. All the same, Washington's head was formally unveiled in 1930, Jefferson's in 1936, Lincoln's in 1937, and Roosevelt's in 1939. Borglum was 73 when he died in 1941, his great work still unfinished. His son, Lincoln Borglum, worked on it for a while until funds finally ran out. The monument had cost almost $1 million.

Indian Shrine

Not far from Mount Rushmore, another enormous figure is being carved in the living rock of a mountain. Designed by the late Korczak Ziolkowski, it is to depict the great American Indian leader Crazy Horse, bare-chested and on horseback, in a carving 563 feet (172 m) high and 641 feet (195 m) long. The sculptor was asked to create the monument in 1939 by Sioux chiefs, who wanted to show that "the red men had great heroes too." Ziolkowski worked on it until his death in 1982 and left detailed instructions for the completion of the project.

The Black Hills were sacred territory to the Sioux, and the United States government confirmed this in a treaty of 1868 for "as long as rivers run and grass grows and trees bear leaves." This proved not to be as long as expected, because in 1874 gold was discovered in the hills at French Creek. Prospectors swarmed in, and the Indians went to war. They won a famous victory at the Battle of the Little Bighorn, where General George Armstrong Custer and his force of cavalry were wiped out to the last man. Inevitably, however, the Indians, led by Sitting Bull, Crazy Horse, and other chiefs, lost the war and white settlers took over the Black Hills. It is perhaps ironic that the Crazy Horse Memorial is being fashioned just a few miles north of the town of Custer.

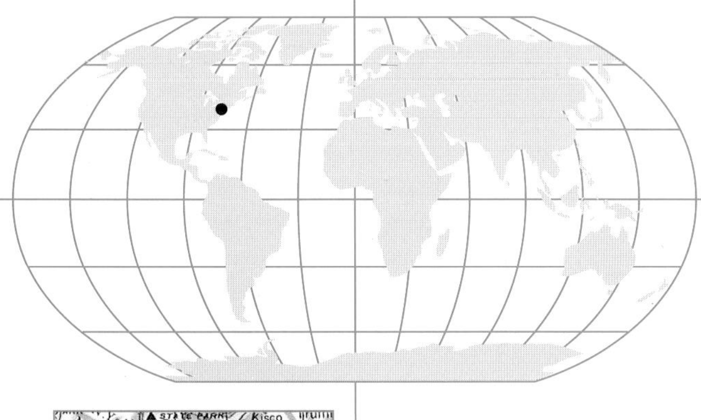

1931 United States

EMPIRE STATE BUILDING

The race up the 1,860 steps to the top every year takes the winner about 20 minutes.

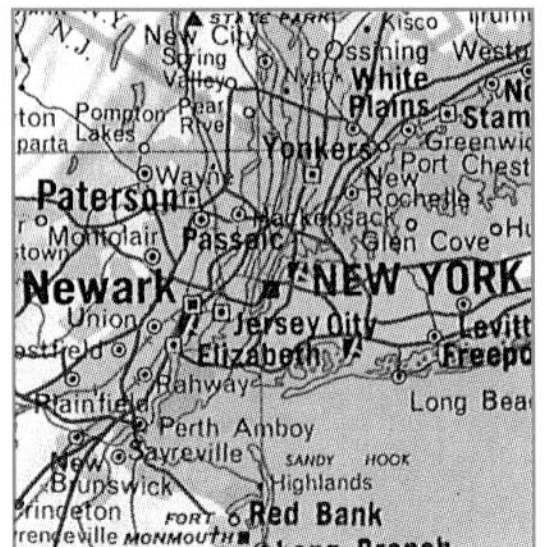

The Empire State Building, at 350 Fifth Avenue, New York, is between 33rd and 34th Streets, with the nearest subway station at 34th Street. Fifth Avenue is the city's principal north-south street, famous for its smart shops and hotels.

Above: the building is depicted inside its own spacious, marble-lined lobby as the Eighth Wonder of the World, an appropriate companion for the classical group of seven.

Facing page, left and right: simple and elegantly proportioned, with its rising floors adroitly stepped back, the great skyscraper is a reproach to some of the glass boxes that followed it.

RANKING with the Great Pyramid and the Taj Mahal among the best-known buildings of the world, this towering edifice is still a potent symbol of the excitement, glamour, and sheer exuberant excessiveness of New York City. For more than 40 years it lodged itself firmly in everyone's mind as the world's tallest building, and although it has been overtaken by younger rivals, it is still for many people the skyscraper of skyscrapers.

The building's statistics are appropriately awesome. Its 102 stories rise to a height of 1,250 feet (381 m); the television tower on top makes the total height 1,472 feet (449 m). It was originally planned to moor airships to the top of it, but the idea was abandoned. The building occupies a site of some 2 acres (0.8 hectares) on Fifth Avenue. Although it weighs a mammoth 365,000 U.S. tons (331,000 metric tons), the foundations are only two stories deep, but it is held upright by steel beams weighing 60,000 U.S. tons (54,400 metric tons). There are 10 million bricks in it, and the electrical wiring runs for $2\frac{1}{2}$ million feet, about 430 miles (692 km). There are 5 acres (2 hectares) of windows, and cleaning them is a full-time occupation. The staircase from the ground floor to the top has 1,860 steps, and once a year there's a race up them (winning time is about 20 minutes). There is office space for 15,000 people in the building, and the serried ranks of elevators can move 10,000 people an hour.

With so many other tall office blocks all around it, it is difficult to get a good view of the great building at ground level. It is in a simple and elegant Art Deco style. The gray stone façade has strips of stainless steel running up it, and the higher stories are neatly set back. Inside, the marble-lined lobby is 90 feet (30 m) long and rises three stories, with panels depicting the seven classical wonders of the world, plus an eighth: the Empire State Building itself. The Guinness World Record Exhibit Hall has displays on records and record holders. Elevators rise swiftly to observation decks on the 86th and 102nd floors. The views are immense, and the spectacle of the city at night particularly awesome.

Named in compliment to the state of New York (nicknamed the Empire State) and designed by Shreve, Harmon, and Lamb, the building cost $41 million (well below estimate) and was erected at a speed that has never been surpassed. It rose at the rate of $4\frac{1}{2}$ floors a week, and in one hectic period $14\frac{1}{2}$ stories were added in 10 days. It was formally opened on May 1, 1931, but with the United States in the grip of the Depression, the space proved hard to rent and the project was sardonically known as the Empty State Building. It took 10 years before it was fully occupied.

The first suicide happened in 1933. In that year the classic movie *King Kong* planted the building's image firmly in audiences' minds by showing the monster ape clinging to it while beating off attacking airplanes. In a fog in 1945 a plane crashed into the 79th floor, causing 14 deaths and $1 million worth of damage.

High Society

THE Fifth Avenue block on which the Empire State Building stands today was a hub of polite society in the 1860s, as carriages and callers arrived at the elegant mansions of two of the wealthy Astor dynasty. John Jacob Astor III and William Backhouse Astor Jr. had built themselves houses next door to each other, and Vanderbilts, Morgans, and other rich and fashionable families were drawn to the area and built themselves mansions there. The formidable Mrs. William Backhouse Astor reigned as queen of the New York smart set, but in time quarreled with her nephew, William Waldorf Astor, who decided to annoy her by pulling down his house, which was next to hers, and building the Waldorf Hotel in its place. The strategy was so successful that she moved further uptown. Her son, John Jacob Astor IV, then followed his cousin's suit, tore down his mother's house, and built the Astoria Hotel. The two hotels joined forces in the 1890s as the Waldorf-Astoria, the most select hotel in town until it was demolished in 1929 to make way for the Empire State Building.

THE AMERICAN SKYSCRAPER

Both the word *skyscraper* and the thing itself are American inventions of the 1880s.

Steepling towers of commerce: the Lower Manhattan skyline before 11 September 2001

No city in the world has a more astonishing collection of skyscrapers of all styles than New York, whose principal streets are sunless canyons sunk deep beneath towering buildings that blot out the sky, except for a narrow strip far overhead. The birthplace of the skyscraper, however, was not New York City but Chicago, not much more than a hundred years ago.

The creation of high-rise office and apartment blocks was forced to await the development of the humble elevator. It was no use planning a building six stories tall without a way of raising and lowering occupants up and down it. Goods hoists had been in use for centuries, but they were not safe for people because the ropes sometimes broke. The difficulty was solved by Elisha Gates Otis, who invented a device that held the elevator safely in the shaft if the ropes gave way. He demonstrated it in New York in 1854.

HEADING FOR THE HEIGHTS

The possibility of constructing tall buildings on iron frames had been demonstrated in Europe, notably by the Crystal Palace, a soaring prefabricated splendor of iron and glass erected in London for the Great Exhibition of 1851. The growing need for office space in major American cities powered a demand for taller structures.

In the 1880s a commercial boom in Chicago sharpened this demand, and a leading local architect, William Le Baron Jenney, designed the Home Insurance Company Building, 10 stories high. For the first time the steel frame supported not only the floors, but also the outside walls. The way was opened for still taller.buildings, and the next 10 years saw the erection of more than 20 buildings in Chicago of 12 stories or more.

Working briefly in Jenney's office before setting up independently was the morning star of skyscraper evolution, Louis Sullivan. The son of an immigrant Irish dance teacher in Boston, he moved to Chicago in 1873. In 1889 he and his partner, Dankmar Adler, completed the Auditorium Building and moved themselves into its 16th floor to occupy what was then the highest office suite in Chicago. (Frank Lloyd Wright worked there as a young apprentice.) Sullivan went on to design the impressive 10-

story Wainwright Building of 1891 in St. Louis, with the vertical lines deliberately stressed and a projecting cornice above an elaborate frieze at the top. He also did the 16-story Guaranty Building in Buffalo. But Sullivan was a difficult man; his business declined and he was reduced to poverty by the time of his death in 1924.

In New York City in the early 1900s, a rapid increase of population and rising land prices stimulated a demand for high-rise buildings there. Architects built them higher and higher, in styles derived from the architecture of the past. The triangular 21-story Flatiron Building of 1902, one of the first in the city, is in a Renaissance idiom. The Metropolitan Life Insurance Building of 1909, 700 feet (213 m) high, was modeled on St. Mark's in Venice. The Woolworth Building of 1913 – at 52 stories the tallest in the world at the time – looks like a Gothic cathedral, with pinnacles and a spire.

MAGIC IN THE AIR

There was a certain magic in the idea of "the tallest building in the world," as well as a strong element of competitiveness. The delightful Art Deco-style Chrysler Building, whose architect was William Van Alen, was built in 1930. Van Alen's former partner, H. Craig Severance, had been commissioned to design the world's highest building for the Bank of Manhattan on Wall Street. Which he did, but the record held for only a few minutes. The crafty Van Alen had hidden the elegant spire of his skyscraper inside the building, and as soon as Severance's building was finished, he triumphantly poked the spire up through the roof to surpass Severance at 1,040 feet (317 m). Van Alen in turn was quickly outdone by the Empire State Building.

The tallest building in the world, the Sears Tower in Chicago.

After 1945 leading practitioners of the International Modern Style designed skyscrapers in New York, most notably, perhaps, the crisp, 38-story Seagram Building of 1958 on Park Avenue, by Mies van der Rohe and Philip Johnson. In 1973 the dismal 110-story Sears Tower in Chicago became the world's tallest building at 1,454 feet (443 m); television antennae take it up to 1,707 feet (520 m). It has 16,000 windows and a population of 16,700 people.

A reaction was developing, however, against the detritus of undistinguished glass boxes with which cities everywhere in the world were being littered. In the 1980s architects moved to more graceful and less regimented styles. The cluster of high-rise blocks in downtown Los Angeles is one example, and in 1983, in New York City itself, Philip Johnson and John Burgee built the 40-story AT & T Building on Madison Avenue, with a roofline looking like an 18th-century bookcase. A tyranny as well as a pediment had been broken.

Today's Dallas skyline has an interesting variety of styles and shapes.

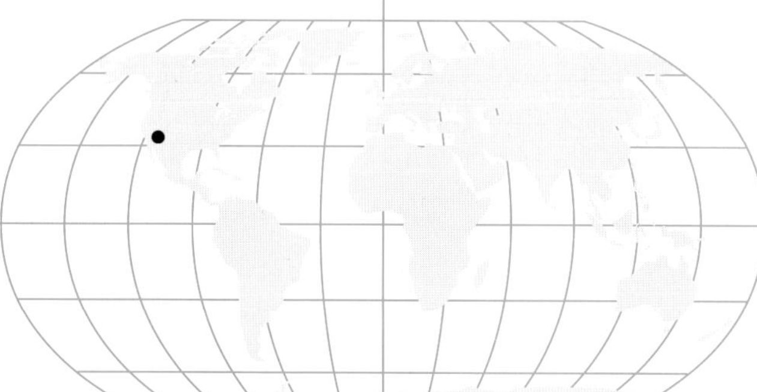

1936 United States

HOOVER DAM

A gigantic concrete dam tamed the wild Colorado River.

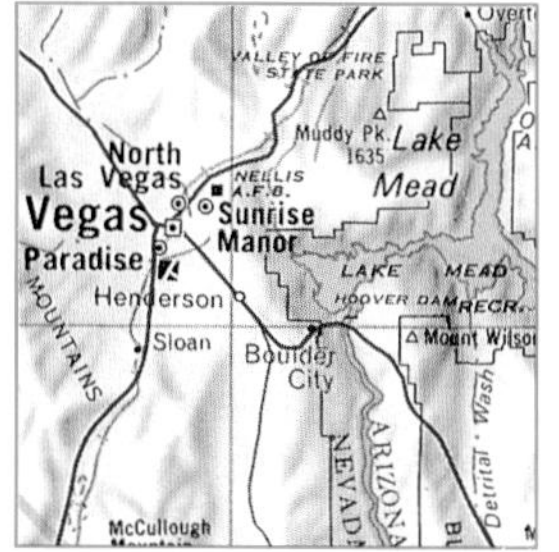

The Hoover Dam is on Route 93, 11 miles east of Boulder City, Nevada, and some 35 miles southeast of Las Vegas. Guided tours of the dam from the Visitor Center. Numerous tours from Las Vegas, which has an international airport.

Right: standing the height of a building of 70 stories, the Hoover Dam was the biggest ever built up to that time, and the huge construction of concrete and steel is one of the great engineering achievements of the 20th century.

Facing page, left and right: views of the dam, with Lake Mead behind it. The lake supplies Los Angeles and San Diego with water and sends electricity across three states.

THE mighty Colorado River is 1,450 miles (2,333 km) long, and the area it drains amounts to 1/13th of the United States. From its headwaters in the Rocky Mountains, it flows southwest across the states of Colorado and Utah, and through the Grand Canyon, to form the border between Arizona and Nevada, and then between Arizona and California, before crossing into Mexico and finally reaching the sea in the Gulf of California.

An unpredictable river, it was always flooding. In 1905 it abruptly changed course altogether, creating the 300 square miles (777 sq km) of the Salton Sea and threatening to inundate the entire Imperial Valley in California. To bring the river under control and improve irrigation, and at the same time generate electricity, it was decided to build a vast dam on the river along the Arizona-Nevada border. Congress provided the money in 1928, and construction work began in 1931. As Herbert Hoover was president at the time and had taken a vigorous interest in the project, the dam was named after him. It was completed in 1936, but in formally dedicating it President Roosevelt called it the Boulder Dam, which it remained until 1947, when Congress restored the original name.

The dam, at that time the biggest ever built, is a huge mass of 3¼ million cubic yards (2½ million cu m) of concrete. Nine million U.S. tons (8.2 million metric tons) of rock had to be excavated to build it, and it has as much steel in it as the Empire State Building. It is 660 feet (201 m) thick at the base and stands 726 feet (221 m) high, or about the height of a 70-story skyscraper. It measures 1,244 feet (379 m) along the top and is 45 feet (14 m) thick at that point.

Immediately to the north, the dam created Lake Mead, one of the largest man-made reservoirs in the world. A jagged, irrregular shape, it is 110 miles (177 km) long with a coastline of 822 miles (1,323 km). Run by the National Park Service, it is used for sailing, boating, and other water sports.

North of Lake Mead lies the spectacular 35,000-acre (14,165-hectare) Valley of Fire National Park, so named because the sandstone rocks here are a fiery shade of red, toning down to tangerine and lavender. Wind and weather have carved them into domes, beehives, and other weird shapes, including a particularly dramatic one that looks like the head and trunk of an elephant. On some of the rocks are mysterious carvings and paintings made centuries ago by the Anasazi people, ancestors of today's Pueblo Indians and best known for their remarkable cliff dwellings. Whether the marks are a language or a form of map is not known. Ten thousand or more of these people lived in a "lost city" on the banks of the Muddy River nearby, in an area partly covered by Lake Mead, and there is a museum of Indian artifacts.

Some 4,000 of the Hoover Dam work force lived at Boulder City, a pleasant little suburban-style community specially built for them to segregate them from the fleshpots of Las Vegas. The head of the project is said to have pronounced that Las Vegas was "no place for people to live."

Too Near the Hotel

ON its way to the Hoover Dam, a triumph over nature, the Colorado River passes through a greater wonder still, of its own making. The Grand Canyon is a gigantic chasm, a mile (1.6 km) or more deep and some 277 miles (446 km) long. The deepest and most spectacular stretch is the 56 miles (90 km) from Lake Powell down to Lake Mead, which is in Grand Canyon National Park. The canyon is famous for its layered and intricately sculpted cliffs and peaks, cut by ravines and gulches, and for its colors, which range from a dull red through shades of pink, buff, and green to violet, gray, and brown. Often a light blue haze hangs in the distance.

Europeans did not set eyes on the Grand Canyon in its majesty until 1540, when Indians brought a party of Spaniards from Francisco Coronado's expedition here. Trappers passed through, but the canyon was not properly explored until the 1860s and 1870s. Prospectors staked claims, which turned out to be more valuable for their tourist potential than their mineral ore. The number of visitors grew after a rail spur was built to Grand Canyon Village in 1901. In 1905 the El Tovar Hotel went up. One of the guests complained that the canyon had been built too close to the hotel.

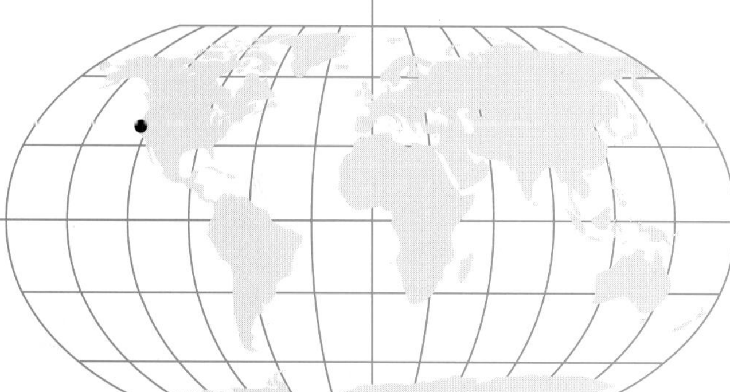

1937 United States

GOLDEN GATE BRIDGE

The graceful, deep-orange symbol of San Francisco is one of the world's longest suspension bridges.

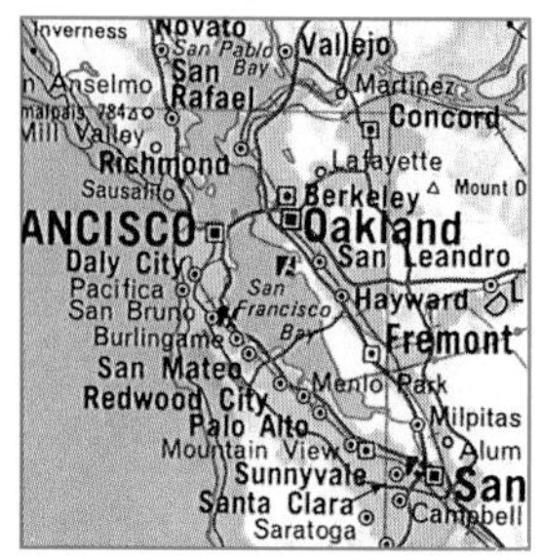

San Francisco, California, has an international airport and is also within easy reach of Oakland International Airport, across the bay. Trains from Chicago and Denver and from San Diego and Seattle stop at Oakland Depot, and there are bus connections from here to the city. The Golden Gate Bridge is at the northernmost point of San Francisco and is part of US Highway 101.

WHEN it opened on May 27, 1937, the Golden Gate Bridge, linking San Francisco with Marin County, finally silenced all those people who had said that this was the bridge that could not be built. It was, however, a bridge that was very difficult to build, and there were many casualties among the workers who labored for four years to complete its 1.7 miles (2.7 km), struggling against high tides, fierce currents, and thick fogs.

Right: the bridge crosses the Golden Gate, the entrance to one of the world's largest and safest natural harbors, a drowned river valley which is almost landlocked and which accounts for San Francisco's history as a major port.

Facing page: the bridge raises its "international orange" towers and cables to the sun. The walk across it is a popular excursion.

The bridge was designed by an engineer, Joseph Strauss, with the assistance of a consultant architect, Irving Morrow, who introduced some Art Deco detailing. For over 20 years it had the longest suspension span in the world – 4,200 feet (1,280 m), between twin towers that rise 746 feet (227 m) above the level of high tide. It was the building of the foundations for the south tower that proved the most hazardous part of the job. The men who did it, working from barges, were tossed by huge tidal swells as they constructed a vast concrete fender in which the bridge caissons could be sunk.

Once the two towers were in place, equally courageous workmen had to clamber along catwalks slung between them in order to position the suspension cables. Each cable was 36½ inches (93 cm) in diameter and composed of 27,572 separate strands of wire. The strength of the bridge is awesome, with each tower

carrying a vertical load of 210 million pounds (95 million kg) from each cable, and each shore anchorage block required to withstand a pull of 63 million pounds (28.5 million kg).

From its earliest days, the Golden Gate Bridge has always been painted a distinctive color known as International Orange. Red or orange is regarded as the traditional color for steel structures, a consequence of the red lead, a classic anticorrosive substance, added to the paint. In the case of the Golden Gate Bridge, the color also helps visibility in the frequent fogs that envelop San Francisco. The discovery that the traditional paint can harm the environment, because of a tendency to decompose in foggy conditions, has resulted in tireless research to devise a harmless paint formula that will preserve the familiar and much-loved orange color. While this work goes on, parts of the bridge have had to be painted gray – a departure from tradition that has not been well received.

The bridge, originally built with funds raised from a $35 million bond issue, has become a key symbol of San Francisco. Despite the noise and pollution generated by the 120,500 cars that cross it every day, the pedestrian path along the bridge is a popular one, and it provides a setting much used by film directors. During the party held to celebrate the 50th anniversary of the bridge in 1987, the whole structure was closed to traffic so that all the party-goers could walk across. As it happened, there were simply too many of them, and the idea had to be abandoned as impractical and possibly even dangerous.

Golden Gate Park

A THOUSAND-acre (405-hectare) park offering a great variety of entertainment, not to mention magnificent horticultural delights, lies south of the Golden Gate Bridge and stretches eastward almost halfway across San Francisco. Work on the park began in 1870. The original designer, William Hammond Hall, was succeeded by a Scotsman, John McLaren, who devoted 56 years to the care and nurture of this unique city park. McLaren, who is estimated to have planted 2 million trees, successfully transformed an unpromising area of shifting sand dunes into mature and thriving gardens. He is reported to have made a number of rules for the administration of the park: no workman was to wear gloves or to smoke during working hours; signs forbidding people to walk on the grass were outlawed; and garden statuary was treated with suspicion and likely to be hidden behind thick shrubs. In 1894 Golden Gate Park was the setting for a highly successful Midwinter International Fair, an event that attracted 2½ million visitors. The park has several museums, a bandstand, numerous lakes, and outstanding displays of trees, shrubs, and flowers. One appealing idea is the Shakespeare Garden, where plants mentioned in the Bard's poems and plays can be seen.

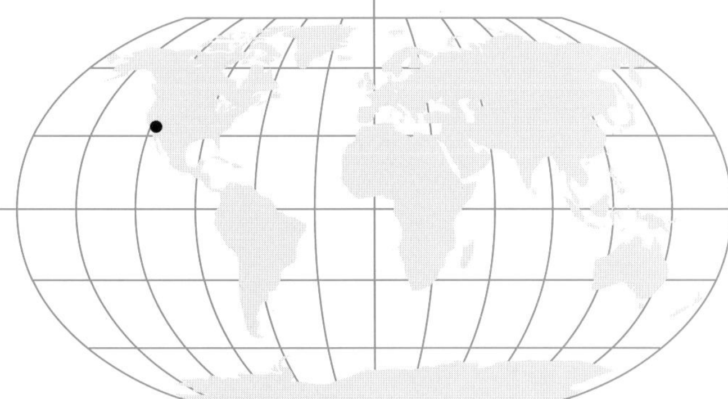

From 1946 United States

LAS VEGAS STRIP

"It will become one of the world's greatest playgrounds."
– *Bugsy Siegel (1946)*

McCarron International Airport is 5 miles (8 km) from downtown Las Vegas, Nevada, (there are slot machines in the terminal for inveterate gamblers). Train and bus connections to all major American cities. Visitor center on the Strip. Numerous guided tours of the city and surroundings.

America's glitziest gambling capital is a gaudy adult playland and a conspicuous example of the type of architecture known as "commercial vernacular." Hotels and casinos raise their fantastic towers and domes above the glittering gulch of the Las Vegas Strip, with shopping malls, hamburger joints, and wedding chapels. Gambling goes on all day and all night. You can win $1 million on the city's slot machines, and untold fortunes at craps or roulette. Not many do, of course, and a gas station on the Strip humanely offers "free aspirin and tender sympathy." The self-styled Entertainment Capital of the World is also famous for shows featuring top singers and comedians, and glamorous showgirls.

Las Vegas boasts the greatest array of "neon sculpture" in the world, as huge signs flash and glow in red and blue and green. Pink and blue lights cascade down the façade of the Sands Hotel to explode in starbursts that could be seen 3 miles (5 km) away when it opened in 1958. Circus Circus proclaims its presence with a sign 125 feet (38 m) high featuring a showgirl and a clown sucking a lollipop. Inside, in a building shaped like a vast tent, there are free circus performances all day and half the night and an old-fashioned midway with carnival stalls and games. And a casino, naturally. The general effect of the Las Vegas Strip at night has been summed up as "Armageddon in neon."

The Strip is a 3½-mile (6-km) stretch of Las Vegas Boulevard South, running from the downtown area to just below Hacienda Avenue. Many of the casinos have taken their cue from Disneyland's success and adopted fantasy themes. Perhaps the most famous of them all is Caesars Palace (no apostrophe – the place belongs to everyone, not just Caesar), which opened originally in 1966. At the front is a triumphal arch whose Corinthian columns support a triangular pediment topped by statues. Attractions inside, besides the casino itself, include Roman gardens, a shopping area dominated by a giant replica of Michelangelo's *David*, a moving walkway that carries you through ancient Rome brought to life by the combined use of holograms and laser effects, and a dance area called Cleopatra's Barge. The guards are dressed as Roman legionaries and

Right and facing page, above: the greatest array of neon art in the world.

Facing page, below: the gateway to Caesars Palace, one of the city's extravagant and palatial fantasies.

Patch of Profit

Las Vegas means "The Meadows," and a Mormon settler in the 1850s described the area as "a nice patch of grass" on the trail between Santa Fe and Los Angeles. It is this grass patch in the middle of the Nevada desert that has been transformed into the premier popular gambling resort in the world.

Indian attacks and the heat (the daytime temperature averages 110°F for much of the year) defeated the Mormons' attempts at farming. Early in this century Las Vegas was a minor railroad town with a few houses, saloons, and a brothel, but in 1931 the state of Nevada legalized gambling. At the same time construction workers poured into the area to start building the Hoover Dam 35 miles (56 km) away. The population swelled and the first gambling joints opened up.

Today's Las Vegas, however,

the waitresses are toga-clad.

The Excalibur – which opened in 1990 as the world's largest hotel, with more than 4,000 rooms, 4,000 staff, seven restaurants, and 100,000 square feet (9,300 sq m) of gambling space – looks like a medieval castle and has a Middle Ages shopping village and an "entertainment dungeon." The fabulous Mirage, opened in 1989 at a cost exceeding $600 million, has acres of palm trees and tropical plants, lagoons, and a 50-foot (15-m) waterfall, and white tigers prowling behind glass. The Aladdin, with a genie's lamp atop the building, pursues an Arabian Nights theme in Moorish style, with harem decor and waitresses dressed like belly dancers. At the Tropicana you can take a swim without having to stop gambling: blackjack is played in the pool, and for any bills that get wet, there is a money-drying machine.

dates essentially from 1946 and the inspiration of Bugsy Siegel, a gangster with a vision, who opened the Flamingo Casino on the Strip on December 26 that year. He was murdered in Los Angeles the following year, but his formula of combining safe gambling with big-name entertainment was a winner, and more casinos opened, discreetly financed with mob money.

In 1966 the wildly eccentric recluse and billionaire Howard Hughes occupied an entire floor of the Desert Inn with his entourage. When the hotel asked him to move out, he retaliated by buying the place. He then expanded his Las Vegas interests and built the Landmark Hotel with its 31-story tower and circular gambling arena. Hughes made Las Vegas investment respectable, and the big hotel chains began to move in to create today's gambling and fantasy mecca.

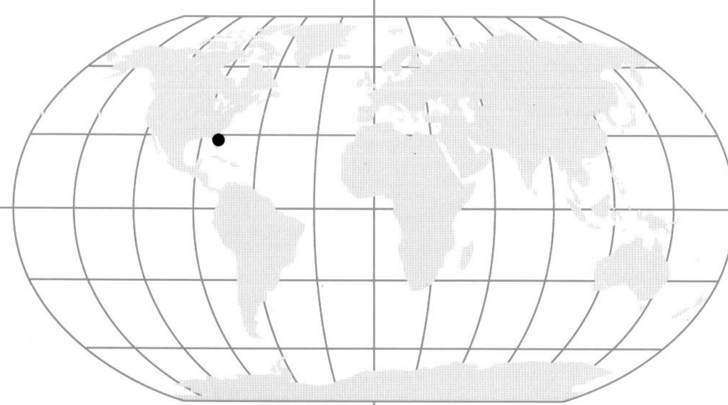

From 1949 United States

KENNEDY SPACE CENTER

The place where astronauts left earth in order to visit the moon, named after the president who decreed that they should go.

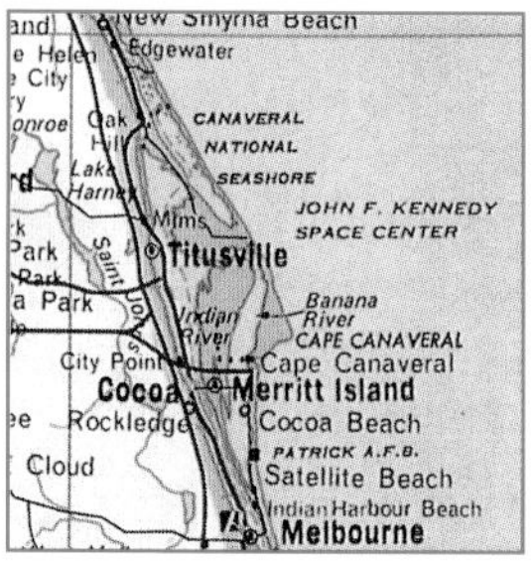

ON May 25, 1961, President John F. Kennedy issued a message to Congress stating that the USA would put a man on the moon before the end of the decade. The announcement came just over a month after the Soviet cosmonaut Yuri Gagarin had completed the first manned space flight around the earth. Throughout the sixties and early seventies, Cape Canaveral in Florida would hold the attention of millions of people

Orlando, Florida, has a major international airport, a Greyhound bus terminal, and an Amtrak station. Spaceport USA and the Kennedy Space Center are about an hour's drive from Orlando heading east toward the coast.

The Importance of Latitude

LAUNCH sites must be chosen in places where any accident or failure of equipment will not be hazardous to large numbers of people. There are also good reasons for choosing a site close to the equator. The velocity of the earth as it revolves is greatest at the equator and diminishes to zero at the two poles. A rocket launched at the equator in the direction in which the earth revolves (i.e., easterly) begins its journey with the additional velocity of the earth at that point, which amounts to a speed of 1,029 m.p.h. (1,656 km/h). This bonus can be taken into account when calculating the rocket power needed.

Right: not the towers of a long-forgotten civilization, but space rockets on display at the Kennedy Space Center.

Facing page, above: rocket at rest.

Facing page, below: the mammoth transporter crawls towards the launch pad.

throughout the world every time a rocket was launched on its way toward the moon. After President Kennedy was assassinated, the fulfillment of his declaration became even more a matter of national honor, and the area from which the space missions were launched was renamed Cape Kennedy. Since 1979, in response to local wishes, the name has become Cape Canaveral again, but the Kennedy Space Center remains a powerful and fitting memorial to the president who was determined to put Americans on the moon.

The Cape Canaveral area of Florida was already the site of a U.S.A.F. base when, in May 1949, it was chosen as a suitable place for a military rocket test range. This was a region of swampland close to the sea and away from major population centers. In 1962, as the moon exploration program gathered momentum, NASA took over 138,000 acres (55,850 hectares) of the Merritt Island area north of Cape Canaveral, and it was here that the Kennedy Space Center was built. The Apollo moon program, whose rockets were launched from Merritt Island, lasted 11 years, from October 1961 to 1972, and during that time there were six successful landings on the moon. Since then the development of the space shuttle, also launched from Merritt Island, has focused world attention on this part of Florida once more.

The Kennedy Space Center is open to visitors. Although much of it has to be viewed from a bus, it is remarkable that it can be viewed at all. As a tourist destination it is called Spaceport USA, and its attractions include a museum – a rather bizarre word for an exhibition of rockets that have traveled thousands of miles beyond the earth's surface and returned again.

The history of space exploration is well described and illustrated, and visitors can see the various launch areas, including that used for the space shuttle. One of the most astonishing parts of the whole complex is the Vehicle Assembly Building, in which all the prelaunch procedures for the Apollo missions were carried out. When these procedures were complete, the rocket was moved from the Assembly Building by a vast crawler transporter, which nudged it at the rate of 2 m.p.h. to the launch pad. The Assembly Building, still used for shuttle missions, occupies almost 8 acres (3 hectares) and stands 525 feet (160 m) high.

Although it is not generally possible to visit the center on launch dates, much of the atmosphere and excitement of the procedure is conveyed in a film that shows the training of a shuttle astronaut and uses scenes of an actual launch, projected on a vast screen, to communicate the experience to an audience.

The Space Shuttle

PUTTING an astronaut on the moon was the greatest goal of the 1960s, and with just a few months to spare, it was achieved in July 1969. After the initial excitement of this first visit to another world, it was perhaps inevitable that interest would die down and the enormous cost of the moon missions would begin to be questioned. Calls for a new type of space research resulted in the space shuttle. Functioning more like an airliner than a moon rocket, the first shuttle was launched in April 1981, journeying into space and returning again to earth. In January 1986 the 25th shuttle mission suffered disaster, with an explosion after takeoff in which all seven astronauts died; millions watching on television witnessed the tragedy. Inquiries led to safety modifications, and the shuttle program continues.

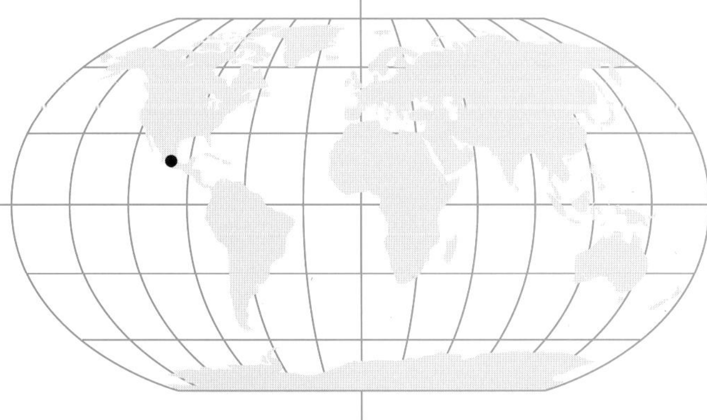

1964 Mexico

MUSEO NACIONAL DE ANTROPOLOGÍA

Thousands of victims were ritually slaughtered on the stone of sacrifice.

The museum is in Chapultepec Park, Mexico City, which is reached along the Paseo de la Reforma (Mexico City's equivalent of Fifth Avenue in New York), laid out originally for Emperor Maximilian. Nearest metro stations, Chapultepec and Auditorio. Buses along Paseo de la Reforma.

Right: the interior courtyard is shielded by a concrete canopy supported by a single pillar.

Facing page, left: one of the Quetzalcoatl figures from Tula. The museum houses the world's finest collection of pre-Columbian material.

Facing page, right: the forbidding figure is the Aztec rain god, Tlaloc. Victims were sacrificed to him in the belief that their falling tears would magically stimulate the fall of rain.

AMONG the countries of Latin America, enthusiasm for modern architectural styles has been most evident in Mexico and Brazil. Mexican architecture has been particularly daring. Le Corbusier exerted a strong influence on young Mexican architects in the 1930s, and a refugee from Spanish Fascism, the engineer and architect Felix Candela, who settled in Mexico in 1939, designed highly adventurous buildings in concrete.

One of the leading architects in Mexico since the Second World War, Pedro Ramirez Vasquez, designed the National Museum of Anthropology (he also built the new, recently completed Church of Our Lady of Guadalupe). The museum, in Chapultepec Park, opened in 1964. It is a two-story modernistic building faced in rough granite, with the museum galleries arranged around a long, rectangular interior courtyard. This is partially shielded from sun and weather by a kind of parasol or canopy; supported like the cap of a mushroom on a single pillar of concrete, it is said to be the largest expanse supported on one pillar in the world.

The museum itself is widely regarded as the finest in Mexico – indeed, one of the finest anywhere – with an unrivaled collection of objects from before the arrival of the Spaniards in the New World, covering some 100,000 square feet (9,300 sq m). The exhibits are so excellently organized that, although there are no explanations in English, the displays are riveting. Multilingual 2-hour tours of the highlights are available.

Probably the highlight of all the highlights is the gruesome sacrificial stone on which Aztec priests ritually slaughtered victims to nourish the gods. The victim was stretched out over the stone, face upwards, and held by five priests by the head, arms, and legs. A sixth priest, in a blood-red robe, sliced open the victim's breast with a knife as sharp as a razor, thrust his hand into the wound, and ripped out the pulsing heart, which he held up to the sun. Thousands met their death on the stone.

Other especially striking objects include the celebrated "calendar stone," which has become a symbol of Aztec civilization. It is a huge block of basalt, weighing more than 27 U.S. tons (24.4 metric tons) which was somehow dragged into the Aztec capital of Tenochtitlán from a quarry outside and then carved with skilled precision in rock so hard that the details are still clear-cut. In the center is the head of the sun god, Tonatiuh, surrounded by concentric circles with signs representing the days of the month and the cardinal points of the compass. Also in the museum are figures and statues of other deities of ancient Mexico, including the Feathered Serpent (Quetzalcoatl), numerous objects recovered from Teotihuacán and from the sacrificial well at Chichén Itzá, gigantic Olmec stone heads, feathered headdresses, and a copy of the painted temples of Bonampak, with pottery, weapons, and jewels. In addition, the museum has displays on present-day native Mexican peoples.

In the 1970s a survey revealed that far fewer Mexican working-class families were visiting the museum than had been hoped. In an interesting development a kind of "museum-mission" was built in the slum area of Tacubaya, and objects from the museum were displayed there in a lively and informal atmosphere that succeeded in attracting local interest.

In the Park

BESIDES the Anthropology Museum, other attractions in Chapultepec Park (Chapultepec means "Grasshopper Hill") include a large zoo where pandas have been bred successfully, attractive gardens and lakes, an amusement park, and several other museums. On the other side of the Paseo de la Reforma is the National Museum of History, which deals with the country's past since the Spanish Conquest. This is in Chapultepec Castle, built in the 1780s, which is where Emperor Maximilian and Empress Carlotta lived during their brief tenure of power in the 1860s. Put on the Mexican throne by an invading French army, Maximilian was executed by firing squad in 1867. The imperial living quarters can be seen, and there are notable collections of clocks, pianos, carriages, vases, and religious art. The nearby Museo del Caracol (Museum of the Snail, so called because of its shape) gives children an introduction to the history of Mexico. Also in the park are the Museum of Modern Art, with work by Diego Rivera and other leading Mexican artists, as well as paintings by Magritte and others, and the Museo Tamayo, which houses the private collection of the modernist painter Rufino Tamayo.

The Aztecs built their capital, Tenochtitlán, here in 1325. According to their traditions, an oracle had pronounced that they should build at the spot where they saw an eagle perching on a cactus and devouring a snake, and they saw the portent at this spot. Cortés and his men destroyed Tenochtitlán in 1521 and built their own capital on the ruins. Today the metropolitan area of Mexico City has a population of over 18 million and is the largest city in the world.

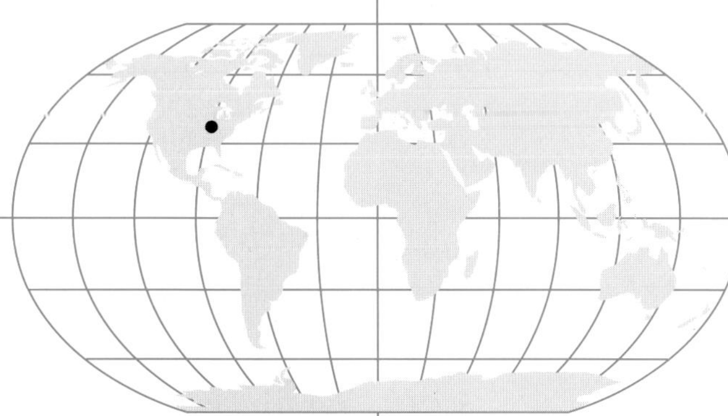

1965 United States

GATEWAY ARCH

The soaring arch captures the excitement of the winning of the West.

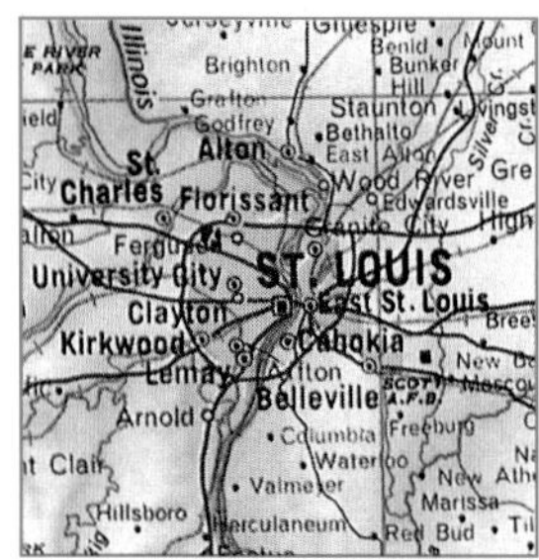

Lambert-St. Louis International Airport is 13 miles (21 km) northwest of St. Louis, Missouri. Rail and bus connections with New York, Chicago, Dallas, Los Angeles, etc. Riverboats to Memphis, New Orleans, Cincinnati, Pittsburgh.

THE Gateway Arch, a towering symbolic doorway in glittering stainless steel, commemorates the role of St. Louis in pioneer days as "the gateway to the West." Standing 630 feet (192 m) high, it has the shape of a rainbow, which has symbolic connotations of hope for the future and reconciliation between God and mankind. In the Bible, when the waters of the Great Flood receded and Noah and his family and the animals stepped safely from the Ark onto dry land to begin the repopulation of the empty earth, God set the rainbow in the sky as a sign that never again would a deluge be sent to destroy life. So the rainbow shape seems admirably suitable for a monument to the thousands of men, women, and children who set out with high hopes from the known, familiar world to populate a land

Riverside

NEAR the Gateway Arch is Eads Bridge, built in 1874 and designed by James R. Eads. Now designated a national historic landmark, it crosses the Mississippi on three bulky iron and steel cantilevered spans. Also close by, moored in the river, is a Second World War minesweeper, the U.S.S. *Inaugural*. One of the few buildings in the area not destroyed to make way for the Memorial is the Basilica of St. Louis, built in the 1830s and the oldest cathedral west of the Mississippi.

Right: seen from across the river, the graceful arch rises like a rainbow of hope for the future. The paddle wheelers on the Mississippi are reminders of the key role of St. Louis as a center of communication, trade, and exploration.

Facing page: the stainless steel arch gleams in the sun.

of wide open spaces in the West.

Designed by American architect Eero Saarinen and completed in 1965, the curving arch conveys a sense of the excitement of the enterprise and of the tremendous achievement that the conquest of the West represents. Elevators inside it rise to portholes high at the peak, which command wonderful views of the city of St. Louis and the Mississippi River.

The arch stands beside the river in the Jefferson National Expansion Memorial, which is on the site where the original village of St. Louis stood. It was founded in 1764 by a French fur trader from New Orleans, who named it after Saint Louis (King Louis IX) of France. It became part of the United States in 1803 and was a focal point of westward exploration and expansion. In 1804, dispatched by President Jefferson, Meriwether Lewis and William Clark set out from nearby St. Charles on a journey into the unknown West that would take them to the Columbia River. Zebulon Pike left from St. Louis on expeditions that discovered the source of the Mississippi and penetrated the Rocky Mountains. In the days of steamboats and, later, with the coming of the railroads, St. Louis was the principal departure point for the mass emigration that won the West. In St. Louis the hopeful pioneers could equip themselves with every necessity from wagons and oxen to rifles, tools, or pots and pans.

The story is told in the Museum of Westward Expansion, which brings together photographs, maps, paintings, and objects from pioneer and Indian life. There is also a film about the building of the Gateway Arch itself.

Also part of the Memorial is the Old Courthouse, with its handsome Greek Revival-style portico of fluted Doric columns, begun in 1839. It was not completed until 1862 and the Renaissance dome was only added after prolonged controversy as to whether it would cause the building to collapse. The courthouse is best known as the scene of the Dred Scott slavery trial, which brought about the Supreme Court ruling that a slave or the descendant of slaves could have no standing in a federal court – a decision that helped provoke the outbreak of civil war in 1861.

Dramatic Gift

The competition to design the monument in St. Louis was won by Eero Saarinen in 1948. He was then in his late 30s. Born in Finland in 1910, as a boy he won a Swedish matchstick design competition. His father, the architect Eliel Saarinen, moved the family to the United States in 1923. The younger Saarinen studied architecture at Yale and joined his father's practice. Both of them entered the St. Louis competition, and there was an embarrassing mix-up when the jury cabled to inform Eliel that he had won, and a few days later had to send a message that it was Eero's design that had taken first place.

Eero Saarinen made his name as a designer of modern furniture (including the "womb chair") as well as in architecture. He had a gift for the dramatic and he did not accept the restraints of the International Modern Style. His buildings include the chapel and Kresge Auditorium at the Massachusetts Institute of Technology and the TWA Terminal at the John F. Kennedy Airport, New York City. He did not live to see the Gateway Arch completed, dying of a brain tumor in 1961 at the age of 51.

1971 United States

WALT DISNEY WORLD

A world of imagination has been brought to life for children of all ages.

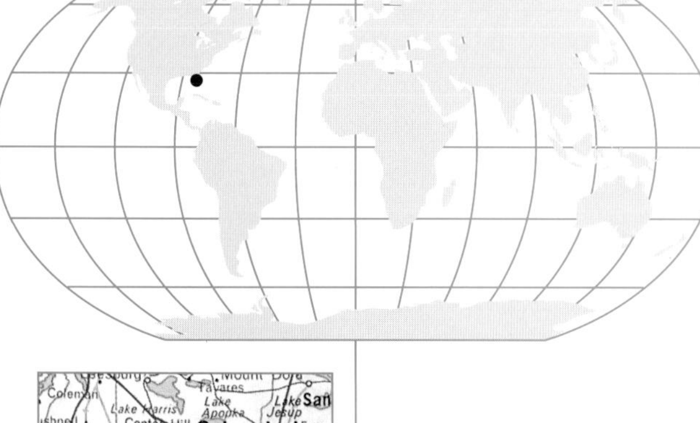

Walt Disney World is 15 miles (24 km) southwest of Orlando, Florida, off Interstate 4 and US 192. Kissimmee rail station has connections to New York and Miami. Bus connections to all major American cities. Orlando has an international airport.

The Time of Your Life

WITH Walt Disney World leading the way, the Orlando area of Florida now bristles with visitor attractions, with new ones being added every year. In 1989 Disney/MGM Studios opened up, with a studio tour for the public, and Universal Studios also has a tour. The huge Sea World opened as the world's largest marine-life theme park, featuring a giant 4,500-pound (2,040-kg) performing killer whale and, later, a baby killer whale, the first ever born in captivity. A particularly fiendish attraction here is called Shark Encounter. A people-mover

Right: the centerpiece of Walt Disney World is Cinderella's Castle, a fairyland stronghold that owes much to Ludwig IV's Bavarian dream castles.

Facing page, left: Spaceship Earth and the monorail at the EPCOT Center, where the future is on show.

Facing page, right: cruising down the river.

Facing page, below: a performing killer whale makes a splash at the huge Sea World aquarium.

THE original Disneyland opened in 1955 at Anaheim, California, on the southern outskirts of Los Angeles. An entertainment complex of a new kind, it combined four fundamental characteristics. The first was a central theme – the "magic kingdom" of Disney cartoons and characters. To this was added a host of effective illusions, using the latest technology, so that visitors felt as if (or almost as if) they were riding in a boat through the jungle, seeing ghosts in a haunted house, or being carried down to the bottom of the sea in a submarine. The third ingredient was exciting fairground rides presented in a delightfully elaborate thematic fashion. The fourth was that Disneyland catered to the family, with a firm emphasis on safety, courtesy, and cleanliness. Aimed not only at children, but at all the young at heart, the mixture proved immensely successful, and the California Disneyland welcomed its 300 millionth paying customer in 1989.

Walt Disney World in Florida opened on October 1, 1971, on a site of 28,000 acres (11,300 hectares), the largest complex of its kind in the world. Costing $400 million to create, it is a bigger and newer version of the California original, with many of the same attractions. Like the California model, the park is divided into areas with names like Fantasyland, Adventureland, Frontierland, and Tomorrowland. Frontierland, for example, is the world of American legend and the Wild West, with a haunted house, paddle wheelers sailing downriver past pioneer scenes, a journey by raft to Tom Sawyer's Island, and a fort guarded by animatronic characters who can be zapped with toy guns. There's also an old-time vaudeville show called the Diamond Horseshoe Revue, a Western hoedown presented by animatronic bears, and the Hall of Presidents, where dignified animated figures from the past speak as large as life.

Rides and attractions are constantly updated and new ones introduced. There's no shortage of gift and souvenir shops, live music, and pleasant places to eat and drink anything from an ice-cream soda to a full meal. You are frequently confronted by a life-size Mickey Mouse or Donald Duck or any of a host of other characters, who parade with a marching band at intervals. You can ride a monorail, a steam train, a fire engine, a horse-drawn trolley car, or a cable car with an aerial view of the complex. The whole place is kept miraculously clean by an unobtrusive army of workers.

At the heart of it all rises Cinderella's Castle, battlemented and turreted, like something from fairyland and owing much to Ludwig of Bavaria's Neuschwanstein. Underneath, unseen by the public, is the maze of passages used by Mickey and friends to pop up suddenly in unexpected places above ground.

The EPCOT Center (short for Experimental Prototype Community of Tomorrow) opened in 1982 with lively displays on the shape of things to come and scenes from countries across the world. Then there is Discovery Island and its lake, with giant Galapagos tortoises and an aviary of exotic birds, and River Country, with a huge pool, water flumes, and a nature trail. There's also a shopping village and numerous hotels. To do the whole complex justice takes four or five days.

carries visitors through a tunnel inside a vast tank in which sharks of alarming size and demeanor are thoughtfully swimming. There's a Penguin Encounter too, with more than 200 penguins and seabirds in a simulated polar environment. Sea World has nine different restaurants and a Polynesian luau most evenings.

Not far away there are alligators at the Central Florida Zoological Park, Reptile World, and Gatorland Zoo, and a look ahead into the 21st century at Xanadu, with a computer-programmed house complete with robot butler. At Circus World there are performing animals, high-wire acts and clowns, and one of the world's most terrifying roller coasters. There's jousting at Medieval Times. And if all this does not suffice, you can find a museum of containers at the international headquarters of Tupperware, a good scientific museum and planetarium at the Orlando Science Center, an Elvis Presley Museum, and a vast collection of seashells at the Beal-Maltbie Shell Museum. Which should be enough for even the most insatiable pleasure seekers.

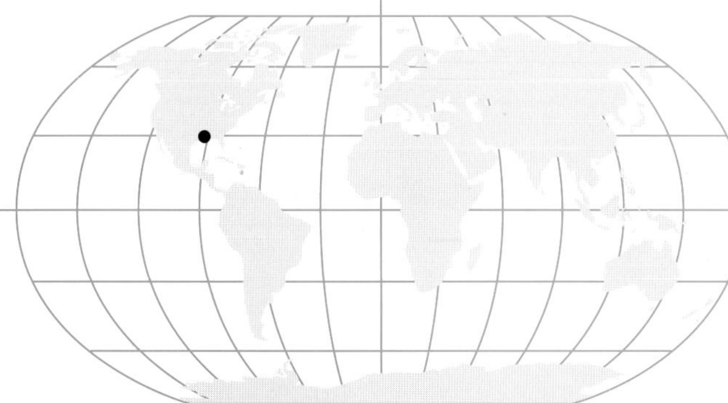

1975 United States

LOUISIANA SUPERDOME

A city of old-world charm sprouted the New World's most up-to-date sports arena.

The Louisiana Superdome is at 1500 Poydras Street, New Orleans. Guided tours for visitors. Moisant International Airport is 15 miles (24 km) west of New Orleans, with connections to all major American cities. Train and bus links with New York, Washington D.C., Chicago, Los Angeles.

THE Superdome opened on August 3, 1975, at a cost exceeding $180 million. The world's largest facility of its type, it has been unkindly likened to an enormous overturned soup bowl or first cousin to a gigantic doorknob, but no one has ever doubted that it does its job. Primarily a stadium for American football, it is the home of the New Orleans Saints. The Sugar Bowl classic is played here on New Year's Day every year, and the Super Bowl was held in the stadium in 1990. It is also home ground to the Tulane University team, whose big game against Louisiana State University, from Baton Rouge, is staged here in odd-numbered years.

This is a multipurpose stadium, however – a "public assembly facility" – and smaller areas are partitioned off as required for concerts,

Right: looking menacingly slit-eyed, like a science fiction monster, the Superdome rises above its parking lot. The building has its own controlled "climate" inside, governed by computer.

Facing page: there could scarcely be more of a contrast than with this charming house, with its lacy ironwork, in the old French Quarter of New Orleans.

Mardi Gras balls, boxing matches and basketball games, trade shows, business conventions, and other events. There are circuses here and ice shows, and in 1988 the Republican Party held its national convention in the Superdome.

The structure took four years to complete and its vital statistics are suitably impressive. The complex covers 52 acres (21 hectares) of ground. The dome itself has a diameter of 680 feet (208 m) and stands 27 stories high, with a roof covering more than 9 acres (3.6 hectares). Inside is a playing arena of titanic dimensions – 160,000 square feet (14,900 sq m) of concrete – which is covered with 15-foot (4.5-m) strips of artificial turf known as Mardi Grass. The seating capacity for football games is 70,000, with parking for 5,000 cars and 250 buses.

There are no windows in the dome, which has a computer-controlled "climate" inside that requires more than 9 U.S. tons (8.2 metric tons) of equipment. Huge video screens provide instant replays, information, and entertainment. There's 4,000 miles of electrical wiring and more than 15,000 lighting fixtures. There are four ballrooms, two restaurants, 32 escalators, a clubhouse, innumerable meeting rooms, and an ample supply of bars and cocktail lounges.

Serious misgivings were expressed at the time about the construction of this enormous project, but it has given a badly needed lift to what was then a run-down district of New Orleans. The city was the biggest in the South in its time, but by 1950, with its population declining, it had dropped into second place behind Houston, and by 1970 it was down to fifth. The building of the Superdome proved to be part of a recovery that has brought the central business area of New Orleans a cluster of towering office skyscrapers and vast luxury hotels. The city has become a major tourist destination and attracts nearly a million visitors a year to business conventions alone.

The combination of up-to-date facilities and old-world charm has proved a powerful draw in New Orleans' case. The city, of course, is best known for its delightful French Quarter, with narrow streets and old houses, as the birthplace of jazz, and for its sensational Mardi Gras festivities every spring.

The French Quarter

NEW Orleans' history began in 1718, when a Frenchman from Canada, the Sieur de Bienville, planted a settlement here on the bank of the Mississippi. Like so many early European adventurers in the New World, he was in search of fabulous treasures of gold rumored to be hidden away somewhere in the vicinity. He never found the gold, but the city flourished. It was laid out with a main square and a grid of streets, protected by ramparts of earth. The square is still there – called Jackson Square today – and in the old quarter behind it, with Bourbon Street as the main artery, the narrow streets are lined by charming old houses with lacy ironwork balconies and secluded courtyards. Some of the best restaurants in the world are to be found here, with jazz bars and a lively nightlife.

Mistick Krewe

ONCE a year in February or early March, the French Quarter explodes in the street parades and spectacular private balls of Mardi Gras. The day itself – literally "Fat Tuesday" – precedes Ash Wednesday, which begins the traditional Christian fast of Lent, but the celebrations start several days before that. More than 50 different "krewes" or societies mount processions through the streets, with revelers in fantastic costumes, decorated floats, kings and queens in crowns, wigs and jeweled tunics, marching bands, and general pageantry. The major societies, such as the Krewe of Rex or Bacchus, mount a parade of 20 floats or more apiece, on a different theme every year. The custom goes back to the 19th century; the oldest and most exclusive of the groups, the Mistick Krewe of Comus, was founded in 1857.

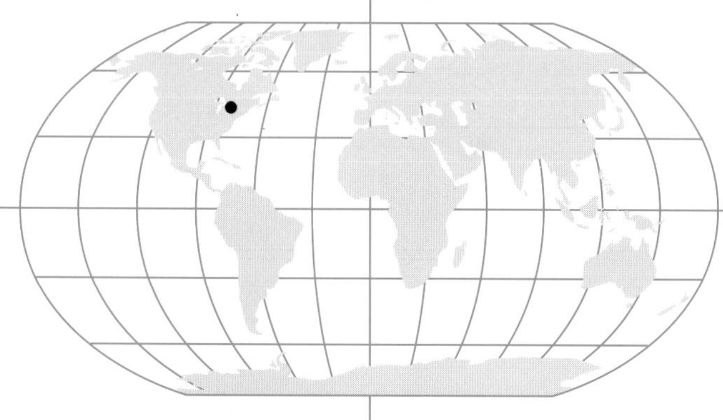

1975 Canada

C.N. TOWER

The successor to the Eiffel Tower and the Empire State Building is the tallest structure in the world.

Toronto has an international airport. The C.N. Tower is visible for miles. It stands on the waterfront of Lake Ontario near the Union Station of the Toronto subway, and can also be reached by bus, streetcar, or car. The tower is open daily, with parking available nearby.

The Tallest Towers

THE Eiffel Tower held the record for the world's tallest building from 1889 until 1931, when the Empire State Building succeeded to the title. Forty years later, in 1971, the Ostankino Tower in Moscow rose to 1,761 feet (537 m), only to be surpassed in 1975 by the C.N. Tower. A century ago a tower of 1,000 feet (305 m) was considered an astonishing achievement. Today a building of 2,000 feet (610 m) appears to be well within the bounds of possibility. One day, perhaps, a new structure will relegate the C.N. Tower to second place.

Right: observation galleries in the Skypod command views of up to a hundred miles in clear conditions. The tower was designed to double as a tourist attraction as well as a communications center.

Facing page, left: seen across the water of Lake Ontario, the tower rises to pierce the sky far above the city's modern high-rise blocks.

Facing page, right: looking up at the dizzying tower.

THE tallest self-supporting structure in the world, the Canadian National Tower measures 1,815 feet 5 inches (553.3 m) to the top of its antenna and took 40 months to build. It has the very practical purpose of acting as a communications center, receiving and transmitting signals at a point well above the mass of Toronto's high-rise buildings, but it is also a world-famous landmark, entertainment center, and tourist attraction.

Before work began on the tower in February 1973, members of the planning team embarked on a fact-finding world tour of inspection of other towers. Theirs was to be the biggest, and it was also to be the very best possible in terms of visitor facilities. Far from keeping the public at bay, it would welcome large numbers of them (the current average is around 1.7 million a year) and offer the opportunity to look out over not just Toronto but distances up to a hundred miles.

Drawing on what they had seen elsewhere, the designers produced a scheme for a fine, needlelike tower equipped with a so-called Skypod – a circular capsule housing indoor and outdoor observation galleries, a nightclub, and a revolving restaurant at a height of 1,150 feet (351 m). If that is not high enough, the world's highest observation gallery, known as the Space Deck, provides even more remarkable views at 1,465 feet (447 m). At this height it is sometimes possible to feel the building swaying slightly, but the visitors are assured that this is as it should be. All very tall structures are designed to cope with turbulence at altitude – they would be dangerous if they did not yield slightly.

As the world's tallest structure, the C.N. Tower called for very careful safety considerations. Although many of the construction problems faced by the designers, engineers, and builders were similar to those tackled in other high-rise buildings, this project was a venture into uncharted territory, and it was essential that the expertise of everyone involved could be relied upon completely. No

individual architect or engineer is credited with the overall design. The C.N. Tower as it stands today evolved over a number of years as a result of teamwork (the initial proposals were for a very different structure – three towers inter-linked by bridges – but this proved impractical).

The story of the tower's construction is well illustrated by a photographic exhibition in the Skypod. It is a tale of scarcely believable statistics involving 53,000 cubic yards (40,522 cu m) of concrete, 80 miles (129 km) of post-tensioned steel, and 5,600 U.S. tons (5,080 metric tons) of reinforcing steel. The total weight of the building is calculated at 145,600 U.S. tons (132,080 metric tons) and the whole thing was built by 1,537 workers. For the foundations alone it was necessary to move over 69,440 U.S. tons (63,000 metric tons) of earth and shale, digging up to 50 feet (15 m) deep.

A magnificent and elegant creation, the C.N. Tower demonstrates that skillful engineering and careful calculation can produce harmonious and appealing buildings.

Psychology and Elevators

FOUR elevators travel up the tower at a speed of 20 feet (6 m) a second; they can transport 1,200 people an hour in one direction. The journey to the Skypod takes 58 seconds, a rate of ascent similar to that experienced at takeoff in a jet plane. The designers of the tower realized that the combination of speed, height, and restricted space could unnerve some visitors while they traveled upwards, so psychologists were called in to offer advice. The result: the design of the elevator cars gives the sense of being in a safe, secure cocoon, and their speed, calculated for maximum comfort, can be reduced during windy conditions. Each elevator has one glass wall giving spectacular views and also, apparently, contributing to passengers' sense of well-being.

SOUTH AMERICA

A reed boat is poled on Lake Titicaca, with the snowy Andes peaks behind.

THE world's fourth largest continent, South America is about 4,600 miles (7,403 km) long, which makes for a remarkable range of climate and landscape. The north coast is on the Spanish Main, of buccaneers and treasure galleons, and the northern part of the continent is crossed by the equator. Thousands of square miles are covered by the dense jungles of the Amazon, while far to the south Tierra del Fuego is close to the icebergs of the Antarctic. At the same time, in the Andes, towering snowcapped peaks rear up within sneezing distance of the equator.

Long ruled by the Spanish and Portuguese, South America today consists almost entirely of independent Spanish- or Portuguese-speaking republics. On the east coast are two of the largest and liveliest cities in the world: Rio de Janeiro and Buenos Aires. The earliest South American civilizations, however, grew up on the other side of the continent, where the Andes Mountains run down parallel to the western coast like a great wall.

TEMPLES AND PATTERNS

The Andes mountain ranges have an average height of some 13,000 feet (3,960 m) and numerous peaks above 20,000 feet (6,096 m). In Peru and Bolivia there are two parallel ranges, and between them is the Altiplano, or high plateau of plains, hills, and valleys. The first city-states and empires rose here and on the coastal plain between the mountains and the sea. Because none of them left written records, their history is wrapped in mystery and dates tend to be vague in the extreme.

The people of Nazca, on the

southern coast of Peru, created what has been called the world's largest work of art in the barren plain nearby. With laborious toil they removed the stones that carpeted the ground to reveal the whitish soil beneath, in such a way as to create lines and patterns on the earth. Some of the straight lines are 5 miles (8 km) or more long, drawn with remarkable accuracy. There are also geometric shapes and pictures of birds and fish, spiders and monkeys. It must have taken years upon years of work to complete this huge display – and no one now knows what it was for.

On the Altiplano, close to Lake Titicaca, the highest lake of substantial size in the world, are the ruins of Tiahuanaco. Here, monumental stone temples and gates, with sunken courts and massive sculptures, remain from the capital of an Andean empire whose history goes back, perhaps, to the 2nd century A.D.

At Chan Chan in Peru are the remains of the capital of the Chimu empire. This metropolis of temples and palaces, gardens and tombs was the largest adobe city on earth when the Spaniards found it and sacked it. Prior to this, in the 15th century, the Chimu people were conquered by the Incas, who, from their capital at Cuzco, built up the largest empire in the Americas, sustained by a professional army, a diligent bureaucracy, and a road system that still inspires awe today. Far more is known about the Incas than their Chimu predecessors, because they were in possession when the Spaniards arrived.

THE IMPACT OF EUROPE

Christopher Columbus touched at the coast of Venezuela in 1498, on his third voyage of discovery, and other explorers followed in his wake. In 1531 Francisco Pizarro sailed south from Panama in search of the gold of El Dorado with 180 men and 27 horses. He landed on the Peruvian coast near the equator. Aided by a civil war among the Incas, which he skillfully exploited, Pizarro conquered the entire empire in a few months. One of his subordinates, Pedro de Valdivia, pressed southward into Chile, giving Spain in the 1540s mastery of the whole western strip of South America from Colombia to Santiago.

Over on the other side of the continent, the Portuguese took control of Brazil in a more peaceful fashion, there being no great empire to plunder and subdue. Sugar plantations were developed and black slaves shipped across from West Africa to work them.

Where the conquerors went, the priests followed soon after to convert the Indians to Christianity. Magnificent buildings like the great baroque Jesuit church of La Compañía in Quito, Ecuador, testify to the wealth and the impact of the Roman Catholic Church on the continent. The opulent Teatro Colón in Buenos Aires, one of the world's grandest opera houses, equally bears witness to the impress of European culture.

The South American countries gained their independence during the 19th century, and since then their politics have been a maelstrom of coups, revolutions, and tyrannies. Since the Second World War there have been severe economic difficulties, but some tremendous feats of engineering, architecture, and organization have been successfully carried through. The city of Brasília was built in three years in a place where there had been nothing but trees, dirt, and jaguars, and the Itaipu Dam project has created the biggest power plant in the world.

At Brasília, a new capital city for Brazil was created out of nothing in three years.

6th Century B.C. Colombia

VALLEY OF THE STATUES

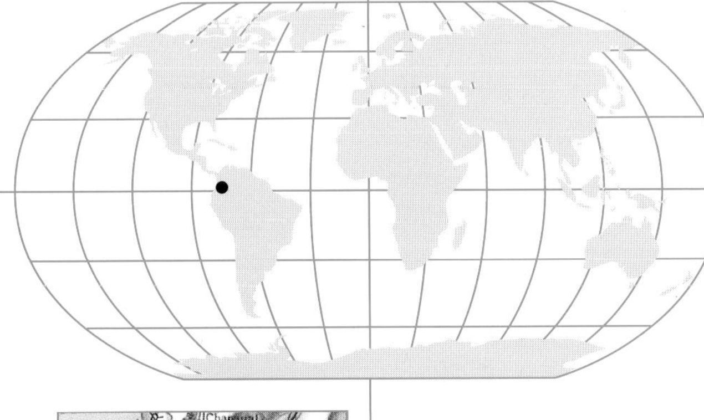

Funereal statues are guarding a lost civilization.

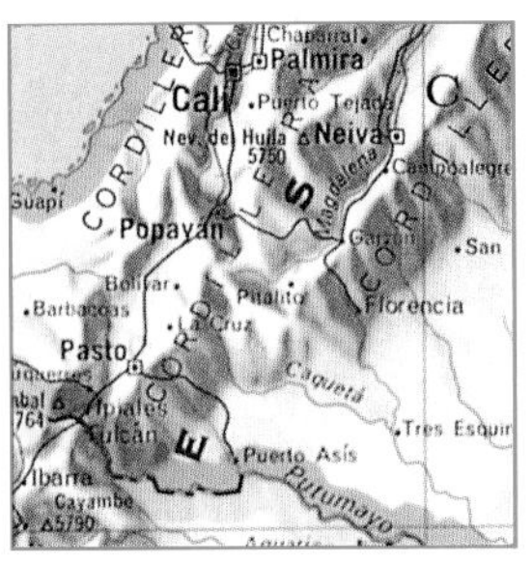

At San Agustín, Colombia. The nearest international airport is at Bogotá, 369 miles (594 km) to the northeast. Internal flights go to Pitalito, 25 miles (40 km) from San Agustín, and to Neiva and Popayán. There is also a bus service from Pitalito (6 hours to Neiva). It is another 6-hour bus ride to San Agustín. From Popayán, the bus journey to San Agustín takes 12 hours.

Puracé National Park

PURACÉ National Park lies 37 miles (60 km) east of Popayán in one of the most dramatic mountain regions of Colombia, with altitudes ranging from 8,200 to 15,750 feet (2,500 to 4,800 m). Covering 320 square miles (830 sq km), it has within its limits the sources of Colombia's three main rivers, the Magdalena, the Cauca, and the Caquetá. In the northern part are several volcanoes, the highest being Puracé (the only active one) at 15,682 feet (4,780 m). There are also waterfalls (the Cascada San Nicolas and Cascada de Bedon) and sulphur springs (the Termales de San Juan).

Above: this figure has a human face and a jaguar's fangs.

Right: little is known about the civilization which left behind these stone statues, with cemeteries and house platforms, high in the Andes Mountains in Colombia.

Facing page: a tomb platform, supported by more of the mysterious stone figures.

AT an altitude of 5,900 feet (1,800 m) in the northern Andes is one of the most important archaeological finds in the South American continent, the Valley of the Statues. So far 500 statues – monumental stone figures of men, animals, and gods – have been discovered, scattered across 20 sites on the densely forested slopes of the canyon formed by the Magdalena River. Amid profuse deep-green vegetation, abundant waterfalls, and hosts of orchids, the crudely carved statues with their implacable expressions seem sternly reticent. They are the mysterious remnants of a lost culture about which virtually nothing is known.

Since they were discovered in the mid-18th century by a Spanish monk, Fray Juan de Santa Gertrudis, archaeologists have even failed to agree on the statues' date of origin. Some estimate the 6th century B.C., while others suggest the stones were erected later, possibly by a civilization suppressed by the Incas just before the Spanish Conquest. Parallels have been drawn with the statues of Easter Island in the Pacific, but most experts relate the culture to that of pre-Columbian Mesoamerican and Andean civilizations.

With many of the statues placed next to underground tombs, it is probable that the valley was a ceremonial center where the dead were buried after elaborate funeral rites. Some of the statues have been identified as sacred animals, such as the jaguar, frog, and eagle. Others are anthropomorphic figures, either realistic or stylized. They vary in height, the largest being 23 feet (7 m) tall.

The sites most easily accessible from San Agustín are found in the Parque Arqueológico, 1½ miles (2.5 km) from the town. The 130 statues in the park are as originally placed, though some have been set up on end and fenced with wire. A further 35 in the Bosque de las Estatuas ("Forest of the Statues") have been rearranged and linked by gravel footpaths. Perhaps the most important ceremonial site, the Fuente de Lavapatas, is also located in the park. This spring was presumably used for ritual ablutions and to worship aquatic deities. In the rocky bed of the stream is a labyrinth of ducts and terraced pools, and chiseled figures of serpents, lizards, and humans. There is also a museum in the park exhibiting pottery and artifacts from the region.

Further afield, north of the Magdalena River, is the site called the Alto de los Idolos, 6 miles (10 km) on foot from San Agustín, on a hill overlooking the town. Here are the statues known as vigilantes, each guarding a burial tomb. A few have been excavated to expose large stone sarcophagi, some covered with a slab carved in the likeness of the occupant. Nearby is Alto de las Piedras, where the tombs are lined with stone slabs painted red, black, and yellow. One of the most famous statues, Doble Yo, which has four figures carved on a single stone, is at this site. The only surviving painted statue is at La Pelota, while the site at La Chaquira is noted for the deities carved into the mountain face.

Tierradentro Archaeological Park

EXTENSIVE archaeological remains from a different but also little-known culture are at Tierradentro Archaeological Park, 130 miles (210 km) from San Agustín. About a hundred underground burial chambers, some as deep as 33 feet (10 m), have been scooped out of the rock. The arched ceilings of the chambers are supported by columns; walls, columns, and ceilings are painted with geometric patterns in black and red on a white background. Some of the chambers also have figures carved in relief on the columns and walls. Buses go to the park from Popayán and San Agustín via La Plata.

1st Century A.D. Peru

THE NAZCA LINES

A network of lines etched in the desert portrays huge animals and birds.

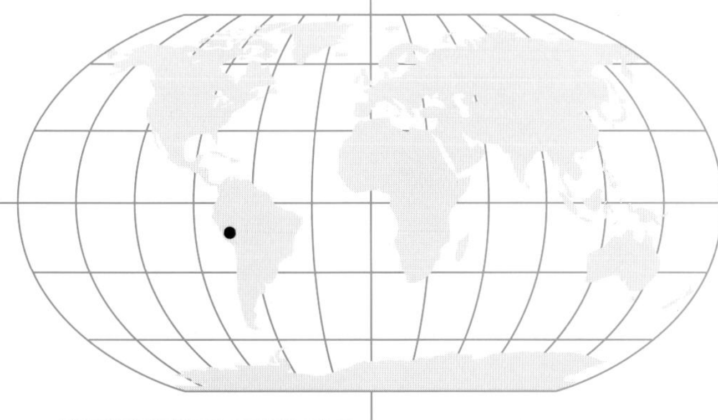

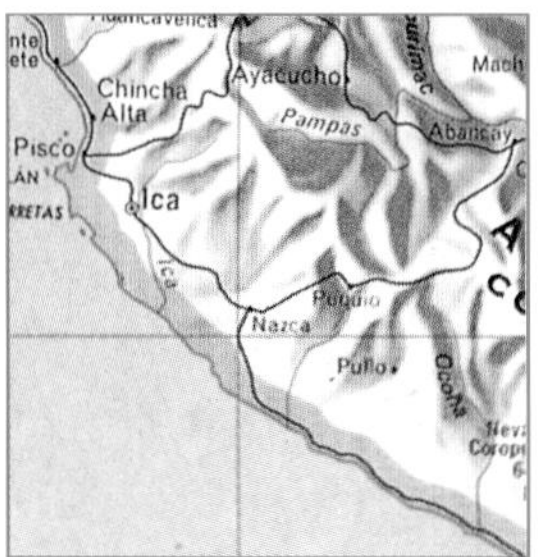

International flights arrive at Lima. Nazca is 280 miles (450 km) south, 6 hours away by bus. From Nazca, there are regular 45-minute flights over the lines, which can only be fully appreciated from the air. Round trips may also be booked from Lima, Pisco, or Ica, but involve a change of plane.

Above: why draw patterns and pictures, like this one of a giant hummingbird, on the floor of the desert where they can only be properly seen and recognised from the sky? All sorts of theories have been advanced, but no generally accepted answer to this question has yet emerged. The Nazca Lines remain an intriguing mystery.

Facing page, left: another of the huge "drawings" depicts a monkey.

Facing page, right: a vividly colored Nazca "stirrup pot."

THE Nazca Lines are large patterns, composed of geometric shapes, straight lines, and figures of birds and animals, etched in the desert of the Pampa Ingenio in the Nazca Valley. On the ground they appear as a network of yellow pathways crisscrossing the deep-red gravel of the desert. Only from the air is the gigantic two-dimensional menagerie identifiable: a spider, for instance, measures 164 feet (50 m); a giant condor has a wingspan of 394 feet (120 m); a lizard is 591 feet (180 m) long; a monkey 328 feet (100 m) tall.

This maze of designs, spread over some 193 square miles (500 sq km) of desert, was created by removing the surface crust of stones to expose the yellowish-white layer beneath. The purpose of the Nazca Lines remains a puzzle, although ever since they were "discovered" in 1926 there has been no shortage of theories of varying plausibility. Alfred Kroeber and Mejia Xesspe, the first to notice the lines, thought they were irrigation channels, although Xesspe later advanced the view that they were similar to Inca *ceques*, or sacred paths. The cairns of stones that mark the "ray centers" (the points at which the lines converge) also indicate a ceremonial purpose.

Paul Kosok, visiting the area in 1941, happened to observe the sun setting beyond the end of one of the lines after the summer solstice, and was led to regard them as "the largest astronomy book in the world." This is the theory elaborated over 30 years by the German scholar Maria Reiche. In her interpretation, the straight lines and spirals represent the motion of the stars and the animal figures the constellations. The study of astronomy, of course, had its practical application in agriculture; the correlation between the motions of stars and the availability of water was significant in an area of erratic supply.

The most farfetched, and best known, of all the theories is the suggestion by Erich von Daniken, in his book *Chariots of the Gods*, that the lines mark entry ports for visitors from outer space. Equally fanciful is the idea that the ancient Nazcas flew in hot-air balloons, a notion faintly supported by the fact that the lines are best seen from the air and what could be burn marks from balloon launches can be seen in many of the figures. And yet another theory, propounded by Georg A. von Breunig, claims the lines are the tracks of running contests. Or it may simply be that the lines are maps, as the archaeologist Josue Lancho has suggested, showing the way to important sites such as underground aqueducts. Less contentious is the date when the lines were made, although the latest estimate by archaeologists, which puts it at around the first century A.D., is considerably earlier than was once thought.

What is indisputable is the fascination exercised by the Nazca Lines on both professional and lay observers. To protect them for the future, visitors are now forbidden to walk or drive on the lines. A viewing tower 12 miles (20 km) north of Nazca gives a slanting view of three of the figures, but it is recommended only for those with a fear of flying. The scale of the markings and the variety of the designs lose all impact when seen from ground level.

The Pyramids of Cahuachi

The Pyramids of Cahuachi are part of an extensive archaeological site in the Nazca Valley. Among workaday constructions of adobe and *quincha* (canes bound together and covered with mud) rise several public or ceremonial buildings, the most prominent of them being the Great Temple. A stepped pyramid 66 feet (20 m) high, it takes advantage of a natural rise in the ground, which is faced and capped with walls made of elongated adobes. Around the base are adobe-walled rooms and plazas, the largest measuring 148 by 246 feet (45 by 75 m). In the early stages of Nazca culture (which lasted from A.D. 100 to 800), the priestly function seems to have been an important one. Little is known of the religious practices; however, it is evident from the portrayal of animals on Nazca pottery and textiles that certain creatures, such as felines, were regarded as sacred.

Also on the site are burial pits from different periods. Some of these, when excavated, were found to contain offerings of food and pottery.

Nazca Pottery

Ceramics from every phase of Nazca culture are exhibited in abundance in many of Peru's museums, most notably the Museo de Arqueología y Etnología de la Universidad Nacional Mayor de San Marcos, in Lima. The early pots are distinguished for the realistic manner in which they depict, in vibrant color, animals and birds (condors, jaguars, llamas, hummingbirds) and plants (maize, chilies, lima beans). Later designs are more abstract, and the pots more angular.

From 3rd Century A.D. Bolivia

TIAHUANACO

An important religious and cultural center whose influence spread far and wide.

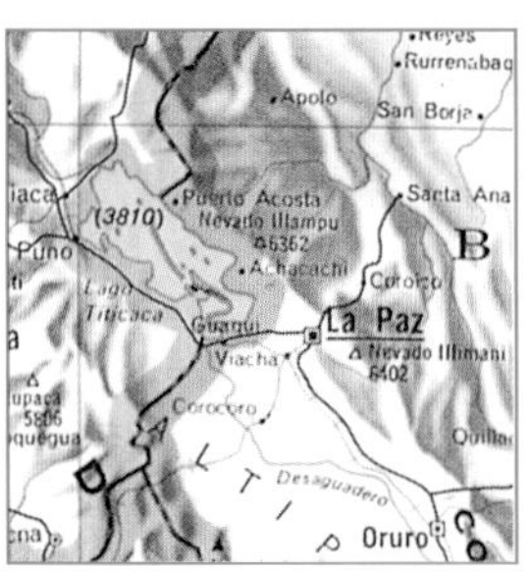

Near Lake Titicaca. This is a remote area and visits require careful planning. Bolivia's international airport is at La Paz. A car or jeep is recommended for the journey to Tiahuanaco and Lake Titicaca, and good maps are essential.

Lake Titicaca and the Tortora Reed

THE surface area of Lake Titicaca is about 3,200 square miles (8,287 sq km) and, at an altitude of 12,500 feet (3,810 m) it is the highest navigable lake in the world. The lake, which is saline, straddles the border between Bolivia and Peru; it is a 13-hour ferry journey from country to country. The tortora reed, a plant that grows in abundance here, has been used for centuries as a building material, not just for huts on land, but also to create whole islands that float on the lake. Some of these islands, first constructed by the Uros

Above: silent, solitary, and enigmatic, a hulking stone figure stands at Tiahuanaco.

Facing page, above: the Gate of the Sun was cut from one block of stone. Above the opening is carved the figure of a god, wearing a necklace of puma heads and holding in each hand a staff topped with the head of an eagle.

Facing page, below: one of the reed islands on the lake.

AMONG the more colorful interpretations of Tiahuanaco are the claims that it was the site of the original Garden of Eden, and that it served as a terrestrial base for ancient astronauts some 12,000 years ago. The conventional version of events, by contrast, sees this ceremonial site near Lake Titicaca as the center of a powerful and religiously minded civilization whose influence was widely felt, both within South and Central America and possibly even as far away as Easter Island.

The date at which this society flourished is not easily established. The period from the 7th to the 11th century A.D. is frequently cited, but there is evidence of occupation here at a much earlier date, and the roots of Tiahuanaco culture appear to reach back at least to the 2nd century A.D. The site has suffered at the hands of later generations. The Spanish viewed it as a pagan shrine and therefore something to be abused, and only a few decades ago some of the characteristic monolithic statues were carted away as a convenient source of stone for the construction of a railroad bed. Fortunately, enough of ancient Tiahuanaco survives to leave no doubt about the great skill of the people who built it.

Tiahuanaco was built at an altitude of 13,000 feet (3,962 m) in an area that lacks the natural resources to support a large population. This fact, plus the existence of buildings of a ceremonial rather than residential nature, suggests that Tiahuanaco was never a city as such, but more of a shrine or pilgrimage center.

As so often in early South and Central American sites, great care was taken over the orientation of the different buildings, and it seems probable that observation and worship of the sun took place here. One of the most impressive monuments is the Gate of the Sun, carved from one block of stone in the form of two massive uprights and a heavy lintel. A figure of a god – perhaps the creator, Viracocha – is sculpted above the opening between the two uprights, and he is surrounded by the reliefs of small figures, all running toward the god. This style of gateway, which appears elsewhere in South America, is thought to have originated here.

The Kalasasaya Platform is a large raised area approached through a sunken court, which seems to have stood at the meeting point of a number of broad avenues. The walls of this platform are faced with large stone blocks, some of which project from the surface in a style that may have inspired the builders of Teotihuacán in Mexico. On the Kalasasaya Platform were found monolithic stone statues with large, staring eyes, and similarities have been seen between these and the stone warriors of Tula, also in Mexico.

Tiahuanaco is the site of at least two stepped pyramids, a semi-subterranean temple and a number of unexcavated buildings. A distinct style of ceramic and textile decoration seems to have originated here; animal imagery, along with abstract designs, was popular.

Indians, are still inhabited.

The tortora reed is also used by the local people in the construction of boats. When the Norwegian explorer and writer Thor Heyerdahl set out to demonstrate that reed boats could have carried people thousands of miles across the oceans in the distant past, he looked to the Indians of Lake Titicaca for advice on boat-building techniques. Heyerdahl's discovery that some of the people of Easter Island – some 2,600 miles (4,200 km) off the coast of Chile – had a knowledge of reed boat building lends support to the theory that there were strong links with South America, and perhaps with Tiahuanaco and Lake Titicaca in particular.

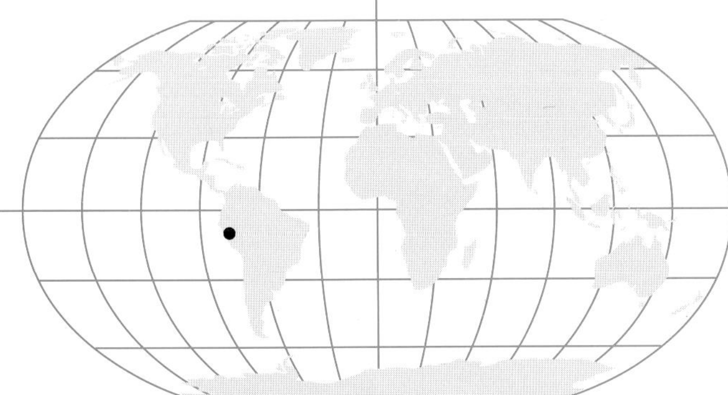

From 12th Century Peru

CHAN CHAN

The world's largest adobe city, where the people made plants out of precious metals and decorated buildings with gold.

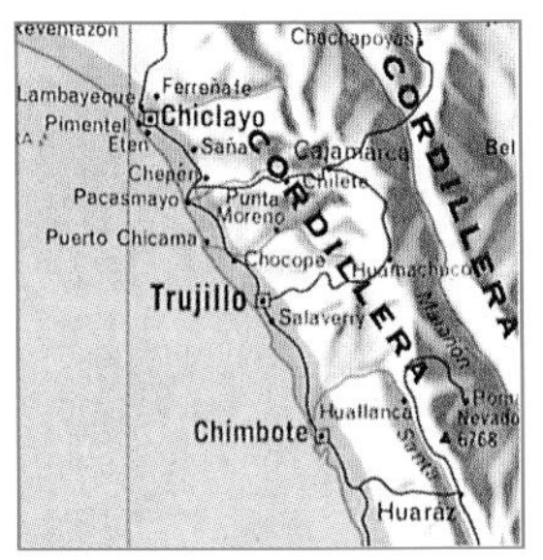

There are extensive remains in a number of different areas. Some are official tourist sites, others are less easily found. Trujillo, the nearest town, has an airport with connections from Lima. The journey by bus from Lima takes about 9 hours. Chan Chan is north of Trujillo, and the Temples of the Sun and Moon lie to the south. Both sites can be easily reached by taxi or local buses.

IN the narrow coastal region of Peru that lies between the Andes and the Pacific Ocean where there is no natural source of stone, the common building material is adobe – brick made from sun-dried mud. The substantial remains of a huge, ancient city constructed of this material can be seen at Chan Chan, once the capital of the wealthy, populous, and powerful Chimu empire.

From Chan Chan, a city covering an area of about 6 square miles (16 sq km), the Chimu appear to have controlled a region stretching for about 600 miles (966 km) along the coast. These people are believed to have risen to prominence in the 12th century, after the decline of the powerful Tiahuanaco civilization. They were accomplished builders and engineers (Chan Chan could not have existed without careful management of scarce water supplies) and highly competent metalworkers. Their basic building units – adobe bricks in a variety of shapes – were modest enough, but there is evidence that some of the more important buildings at Chan Chan were once decorated with beaten gold panels. Examples of brick mosaic designs and ornamental patterns incised in mud plaster can still be seen, but all the precious items at Chan Chan (there is talk of gardens where the plants were made of gold) disappeared long ago.

Stories about the foundation of Chan Chan speak of a man called Naymlap who arrived by sea, established a city, and then departed westward again. The city is also associated with a dragon who created the sun and the moon, and the various strands of myth and legend provide very few clues to the truth. It is clear that the Chimu had a highly developed sense of social organization. The rectangular planning of the different areas at Chan Chan suggest an appreciation of logic and order, and there may be some symbolic significance in the precision with which different buildings are aligned.

The heart of Chan Chan was the temple-citadel of Tschudi, where the council chamber is a particularly fine survival. Here 24 seats were formed in the walls surrounding a rectangular courtyard. This seems to have been a debating chamber, and its unusual acoustic effects make it possible for people sitting in different seats to communicate by whispering rather than shouting (this can still be

Right: remains of one of the temples of the vast city, which may have had a population of between 40,000 and 50,000 inhabitants. The buildings were constructed of bricks of sun-dried mud.

Facing page: a vivid motif of birds and fish adorns a wall at Chan Chan.

experienced today). The council chamber is one of a number of buildings surrounded by a defensive wall. Barracks, a reservoir, residential areas, and platforms used for religious ceremonies can also be seen.

The Tschudi citadel seems to have been one of about 10 separate complexes at Chan Chan, some of which had walls up to 30 feet (9.1 m) high. Huaca Esmeralda (the Emerald Temple) and Huaca Arco Iris (the Rainbow Temple) are just two of the numerous other impressive sites. The Emerald Temple, only discovered in 1923 and seriously damaged by severe rains two years later, is in the form of a pyramid with two temple platforms and a wealth of unusual relief decoration full of images of the sea and fish. The Rainbow Temple (this is just one name for a building also associated with dragons and a serpent-like creature) is another pyramid, surrounded by a high wall and elaborately decorated with images of different creatures.

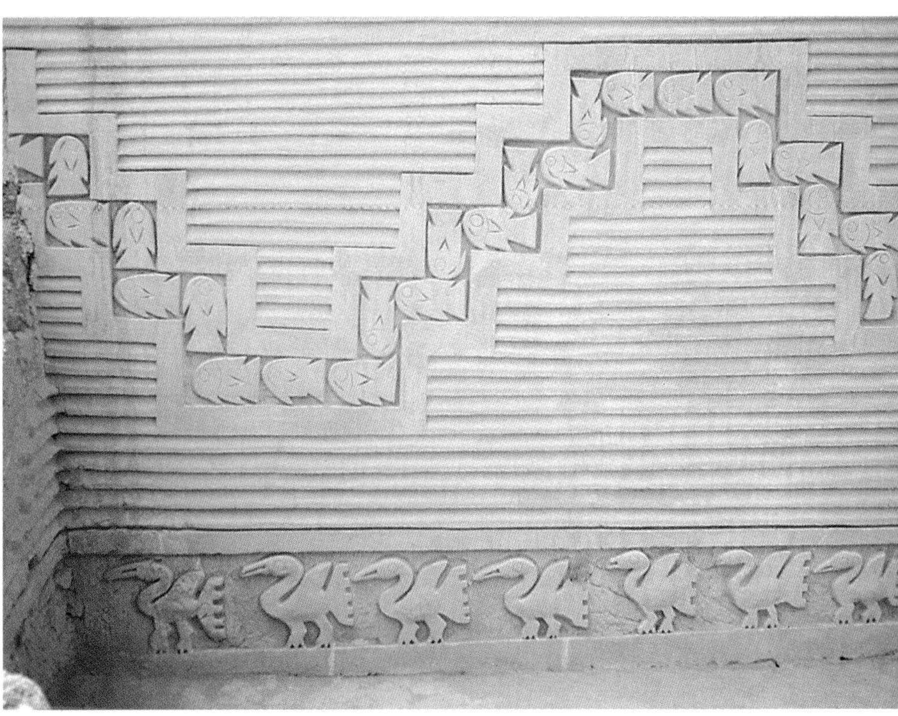

Temples of the Sun and Moon

One legend connects the founding of Chan Chan with the creator of the Sun and Moon, and pyramid temples to both deities are close to the Moche River, not far from Trujillo. The Temple of the Sun seems to have been built by an earlier civilization than the Chimu; it has been attributed to the Mochica people and is said to date from the 6th century A.D., but some authorities think it was built two or three hundred years later. A colossal adobe structure, it has a base that measures 340 feet (140 m) square and stands 75 feet (23 m) high on top of a platform 60 feet (18 m) high.

The Temple of the Moon, a short distance away, seems to have been built about the same time, and archaeologists have suggested that both pyramids were part of a single complex, perhaps connected with a cult of the dead. Evidence of a large graveyard has been found, and there were once a number of ceremonial buildings in addition to the two temples. The Temple of the Moon is noted for its fine frescoes. One of these shows numerous inanimate objects, including pieces of armor and weapons, coming to life and attacking people. This is a motif that can be seen on some Mochica pottery, and it lends support to the idea that these temples do, in fact, belong to the 6th century A.D.

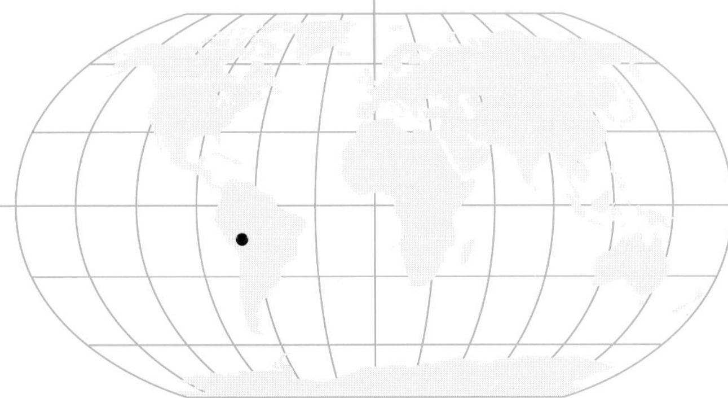

15th Century Bolivia

THE INCA TRAILS

Finely engineered and paved Inca roads provide enjoyable walking today.

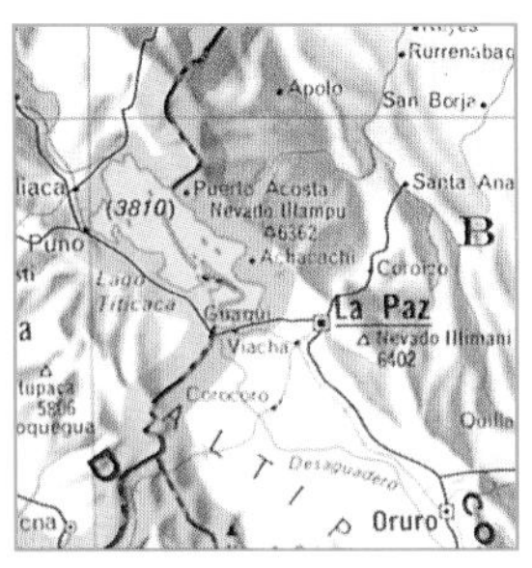

In the Cordillera Real, near La Paz. International flights arrive at La Paz, the highest commercial airport in the world at 13,180 feet (4,018 m). There is supposed to be a bus service linking La Paz with Ventilla, the start of the shorter Takesi (Inca) Trail; more dependable are trucks traveling from Cota Cota on the city's outskirts. For the longer trail, starting at La Cumbre, buses leave from 344 Avenida de las Americas, Villa Fatima, and trucks from further up the street.

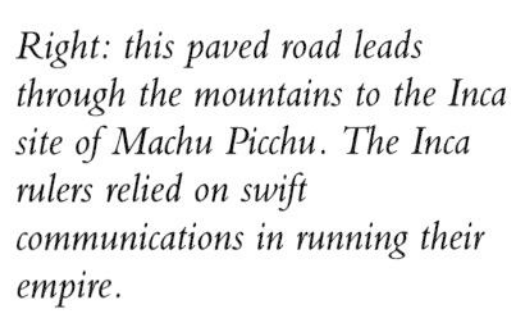

Right: this paved road leads through the mountains to the Inca site of Machu Picchu. The Inca rulers relied on swift communications in running their empire.

Facing page, above: walkers on a precipitous Inca route through the Bolivian Andes. Problems with litter and damage have unfortunately accompanied the recent boom in hiking these trails.

Facing page, below: strings of knotted llama wool were used to convey information and carried by runners in relays along the roads.

The Inca Trail, Cuzco, Peru

THE most well-trodden Inca trail is the one leading to Machu Picchu in Peru from a point outside Cuzco. In the summer months anyone walking it is unlikely to find solitude in the mountains or among the ruins; and even without running into other people, a hiker will surely stumble upon the litter they left behind. A litter explosion has accompanied the hiking boom. In 1980 the South American Explorers Club organized the first of several cleanups in which 880 lb. (400 kg) of unburnable debris was collected. Placing a few litter receptacles along the route is not the solution. The trail, part of the Historical Sanctuary of Machu Picchu, is designated a UNESCO World Heritage Site, and development – anything from bins to public lavatories – is forbidden.

THE Incas, like the Romans, were builders of roads. Like the Romans, too, they preferred to take the most direct route, but unlike them they had to surmount the obstacle of the Andes. This meant their engineers had to perfect techniques that could cope with the often precipitous mountain terrain: where the gradient was steep, they cut steps; where outcrops of rock impeded the shortest route, they bored tunnels. Suspension bridges were cast over gorges. In the uplands, retaining walls were built of stone to keep back the snow; in the desert, adobe walls protected the roads from drifting sand.

Strictly speaking, however, it is incorrect to attribute every mile of paved trail to the Incas, because they inherited roads built by earlier civilizations. Whoever was first responsible for them, many of these roads may still be walked today and their characteristic features admired. The finest preserved stretch of Inca paving, for example, is in Bolivia, on the Takesi or Inca Trail. About half its length of 25 miles (40 km) is made of irregular pieces fitted together like the precursor of a type of present-day paving found in suburban gardens. The climate, though, is not so temperate, and during the two days required to complete the hike, the scenery shifts between extremes, from black, bare granite mountains brooding over the start of the route to the jungle vegetation of the humid Yungas Valley at the end.

From Ventilla the trail rises steeply to the pass at 15,255 feet (4,650 m). In spite of the easeful, shallow steps up the mountainside, this is an arduous and chilly stretch; the reward, however, is magnificent views of snow peaks and the Yungas below. The trail then descends

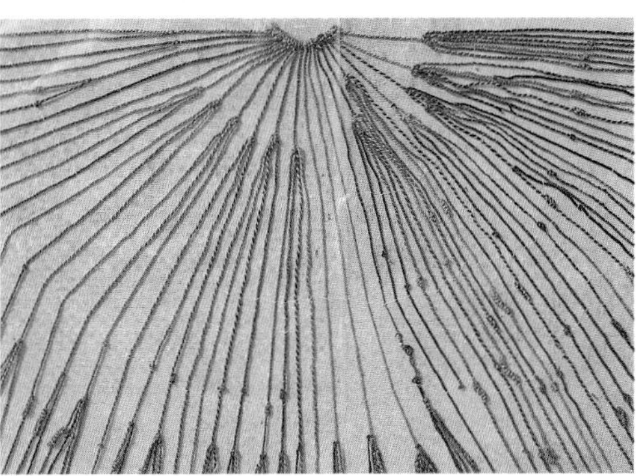

to the village of Takesi, after which encouraging signs of plant life reappear, starting with carpets of moss on the rock. The trail follows the Rio Takesi, then curves around Palli Palli hill to Kakapi and down to the Rio Quimasa Chata. It crosses the Takesi again, the lowest point at 6,890 feet (2,100 m), and finishes at Chojilla.

The longer but less strenuous hike from La Cumbre ("The Summit") at 15,500 feet (4,725 m) to Coroico offers a similar scenic contrast over four days. It too has excellent paving in its first stages. It begins where a statue of Christ helpfully points to a path leading to the highest point at 15,910 feet (4,850 m), marked by a stone cairn. From there it is downhill all the way along a clear trail to the village of Achura. Between here and Choro the paving is especially fine, with low steps often arranged in a fan shape around curves. The path narrows after the treeline is passed and becomes progressively more overgrown as the vegetation becomes more tropical. After the suspension bridge at Choro, the path follows the Rio Huaranilla to Chairo, finishing up among the citrus and banana plantations of Coroico.

The Inca Road Network

GOOD communications were vital in establishing and administering the Inca empire. Altogether about 25,000 miles (40,000 km) of roads – varying in width from 20 inches (50 cm) where there were steps, to 20 feet (6 m) where the land was flat – traversed their territories, from the Amazon in the east to the coastal plain in the west, from what is now Colombia in the north to Argentina in the south.

All roads led to Cuzco, the capital. From there the Sun King sent his messengers (*chasquis*) to the furthest outposts. The *chasquis* ran in relays, covering nearly 200 miles (320 km) a day, exchanging the baton at rest houses (*tambos*) at intervals along the trails. The baton was a knotted llama wool string called a *quipu*. Different colors and thicknesses of wool, and the number of knots, conveyed different messages. Crop yields, for instance, or the supply of gold and silver, or the size of llama herds, or the tally of enemies killed in battle – all could be read by anyone who knew the code. The Incas had no written language, just as they had no horses and no wheeled transport. They went everywhere by llama or on foot.

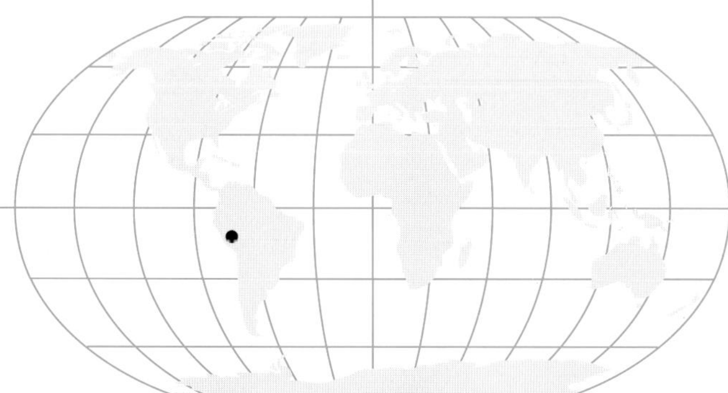

15th Century Peru

MACHU PICCHU

A place of mysterious ritual and sun worship where women greatly outnumbered men.

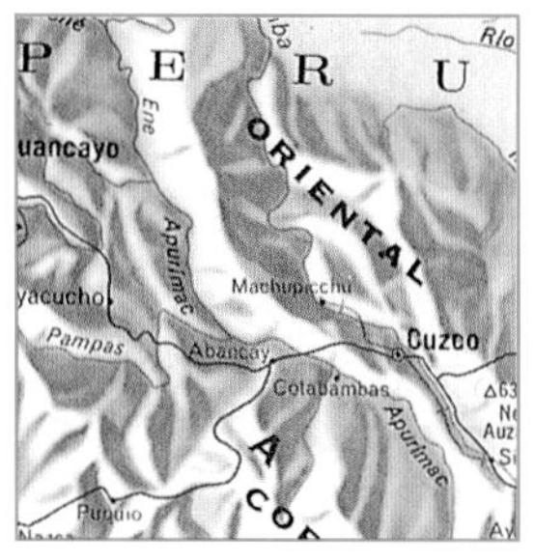

Machu Picchu is about 60 miles (97 km) downriver from the town of Cuzco, to which there are domestic flights from Lima. There are ordinary and tourist train services from Cuzco to Machu Picchu (Puente Ruinas station), where buses generally connect with the trains. The climb up to the site from the station on foot can take as much as 3 hours.

FIFTEEN hundred feet (457 m) above the Urubamba River in the Peruvian Andes, a long-lost ceremonial site perches on the saddle between two mountains. The place is called Machu Picchu – "The Old Peak" – but the name has been borrowed from a nearby mountain and attached to this remarkable settlement only because its own original name is unknown.

When Hiram Bingham, an archaeologist from Yale University, discovered this remote, 5-acre (2-hectare) site in 1911, he believed that he had succeeded in his search for Vilcabamba – the famed last refuge of the Incas, where they survived for 36 years after the Spanish conquerors had driven the emperor from his capital at Cuzco. Bingham was astonished at the scene before him and recorded his first impressions as follows: "I began to realize that this wall with its adjoining semicircular temple... were as fine as the finest stonework in the world. It fairly took my breath away." The magnificence is not in doubt, but the identification of this site with Vilcabamba is now known to have been mistaken. The real name of Machu Picchu, and much else about the place, is matter for speculation.

Machu Picchu appears to have been more an important ceremonial or religious complex than a city. The date of its construction is uncertain, but it probably belongs to the astonishing period of expansion of the Inca empire at the end of the 15th century. According to one estimate, as few as 1,500 people may have lived here. The skeletons discovered here suggest that the female-male ratio was 10:1, and this ratio has been used to support the theory that Machu Picchu was a center of sun worship and a sanctuary for women known as Virgins of the Sun.

Further evidence of the importance of the sun at Machu Picchu is provided by the *Intihuatana* ("Hitching Post of the Sun"). This curiously shaped stone structure seems to have been a complex astronomical device. Nothing else like it survives, but it is thought to have been used to calculate significant dates, such as the solstices. Its name seems to refer to a ceremony in which the sun was said to be tethered to the post at the winter solstice. Solar observation also seems to have taken place at

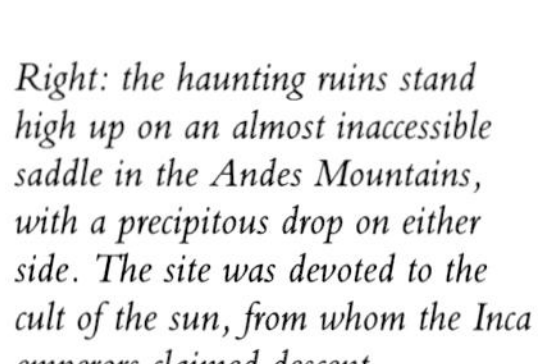

Right: the haunting ruins stand high up on an almost inaccessible saddle in the Andes Mountains, with a precipitous drop on either side. The site was devoted to the cult of the sun, from whom the Inca emperors claimed descent.

Facing page: the Hitching Post of the Sun, where a ritual was performed to tether the sun at the winter solstice each year.

the Tower of the Sun – a building with a horseshoe-shaped plan and a special window oriented to catch the sun's rays at the winter solstice – and at the Temple of the Three Windows, where the alignment of these windows with an upright rectangular stone at the center of the building is clearly deliberate. An Inca sun festival, known as Inti Raymi, is known to have taken place during the summer and winter solstices.

Machu Picchu was a place of gardens and terraces, grandiose ceremonial buildings and palaces. There is evidence of aqueducts, fountains, and bath buildings and the cultivation of maize, potatoes, and other vegetables. The different levels and terraced gardens were connected by hundreds of steps. The site, which remained a secret from the Spanish invaders, was abandoned for unknown reasons. Civil war among the Incas has been suggested, or some defilement of its sanctuary.

Miraculous Masonry

Hiram Bingham commented on the amazing stonework at Machu Picchu, and the skill with which the huge white granite blocks have been laid without the use of mortar is perhaps the most striking thing about the site. Many of the shaped stones are locked together, their edges carefully contoured so that one stone fits into another with perfect precision. The result is a wall with joints of almost imperceptible width, and the buildings constructed in this way have proved exceptionally resilient. When Bingham arrived at Machu Picchu, it had been abandoned for several hundred years; but although the jungle had encroached and much clearance work was necessary, structural damage was surprisingly limited.

Some say that the Incas, who had no iron tools, no beasts of burden, and no knowledge of the wheel, could not possibly have produced masonry of such quality. They were an advanced civilization, but without the practical materials necessary to cut and transport great monoliths they could not have created Machu Picchu. At this point some people start talking about visitors from outer space, or levitation, or psychic powers. A simpler explanation would be to attribute the work to some pre-Inca community. All that is certain is that no one knows how Machu Picchu was built. Whatever the method – it *was* built, and provides a tantalizing glimpse of an enigmatic people.

THE INCA EMPIRE

The time of the Incas is looked upon as a golden age.

Gold mask of the Inca period. Inca wealth in gold was a magnet to the Spaniards.

When Francisco Pizarro and his men landed on the coast of Peru in 1532, they invaded a formidable empire of immense wealth, which controlled the western side of South America for a distance of more than 2,000 miles (3,220 km). Inca authority stretched from modern Ecuador south through Peru and Bolivia into Chile.

This empire, with its capital at Cuzco, had been built up over the previous century by energetic and warlike rulers. It was kept in being by a standing army and a bureaucracy that regulated practically every aspect of human life. Although it had never invented writing or the wheel, the empire developed irrigation systems and mines, and built impressive temples, palaces, and fortresses. Inca architecture was so skillful that earthquakes in 1950 and 1986, which badly damaged buildings of the Spanish Colonial period and later, left Inca constructions placidly untouched.

SON OF THE SUN

At the head of the empire stood the supreme ruler, the Sapa Inca himself, son of the sun, and the sun god's divine viceroy on earth. To keep the royal line pure, his principal wife was his own sister (as with the pharaohs of ancient Egypt). Around him was a court composed of other members of the imperial family, who ran the civil service departments that administered the empire. Tribute was exacted from the peasants, who also provided the conscript labor that built the temples, palaces, and roads (exploitation of the toiling masses was not a Spanish invention). At the same time, the Inca government ran a kind of welfare state for its people, in which surplus grain was stored for distribution when the harvest was poor. Food production is said to have been higher then than in modern times. One-third was left for the peasantry.

A key factor in the smooth running of the empire was the road network, which at its height totaled some 25,000 miles (40,000 km) of paved highways. The coast road alone ran a distance of some 2,250 miles (3,600 km). Forced labor built these highways, which tunneled under hills, crossed swamps on causeways, and leapt over chasms on vine suspension bridges. The Inca armies could move rapidly along these roads to trouble spots anywhere in the empire. The invading Spaniards found them useful too.

Though there was no system of writing, the civil service kept the records essential to any bureaucracy on strings knotted at intervals, called *quipus*. The knots recorded figures in a decimal system. They were also used as aids to memory by official historians, who kept an account of Inca achievements and traditions.

The state religion of the empire was the worship of the sun. Machu Picchu, high on its lonely ridge in the Andes, was one of the ceremonial sites, where the Virgins of the Sun tended the temple. Human beings and animals were sacrificed to the gods.

ANIMAL CITY

The Incas originally established themselves at Cuzco in the 13th century. According to their own later tradition, they were commanded to settle there by the sun god, Inti, because it was the center of the world. They began to attack neighboring villages and take tribute from them. In 1438 the first great Inca leader, Pachacuti, seized the throne from his brother. He and his successor, Topa, built the empire by wars of conquest and established a strong, centralized state. The Inca capital at Cuzco was rebuilt, with the streets forming the shape of a giant animal, whose head was the great citadel of Sacsahuaman.

Pot with the head of a puma. Conquered peoples contributed much to Inca art.

When Pizarro arrived, a war was in progress between rival factions. Exploiting the situation, Pizarro captured Atahualpa, the reigning Sapa Inca, extorted from him a fortune in gold, tried him on charges of treason, incest, and the worship of idols, and had him executed. A new emperor was installed, but the Spaniards were in control. They subsequently quarreled and fought a civil war among themselves, but Spanish dominance was not seriously threatened, and the last Sapa Inca, Tupac Amaru, was caught and executed in 1572. Spanish propaganda diligently spread the message that the Inca rulers had usurped power from earlier local chieftains and that Spain had righteously intervened to depose an illegitimate regime.

The Incas were not forgotten, however. In the 18th century a rebel of mixed Indian and Spanish blood, calling himself Tupac Amaru II and claiming to be the descendant of the Inca emperors, led a revolt against Spain. Thousands of Indians rose in his support, and thousands paid with their lives in the brutal repression that followed. Tupac Amaru II himself was quartered in the main square of Cuzco in 1782. He is now regarded as a forerunner of the modern independence movement. Many South Americans still look back wistfully to the Inca empire as a golden age before the Europeans came.

The fortress of Sacsahuaman dominated Cuzco, which was built in the shape of a giant puma. The zigzag walls were the animal's predatory teeth.

1605 Ecuador

LA COMPAÑÍA CHURCH

This Jesuit church has been described as Quito's answer to the Sistine Chapel.

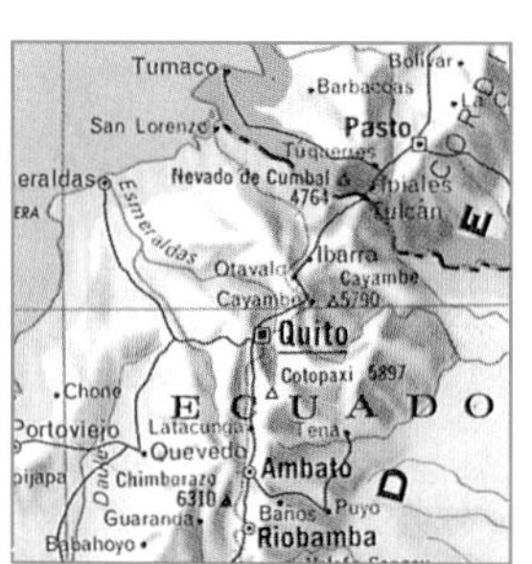

The Church of La Compañía is on Calle Garcia Moreno, close to the Plaza Independencia in the old quarter of the city of Quito. Quito's Mariscal Sucre Airport has connections to Miami, New York, and Los Angeles, and to European cities. An alternative is to fly to Lima, Peru, and continue by bus to Quito.

Beautiful but Dangerous

QUITO was the principal city of the northern part of the Inca empire, and had earlier been the capital of an independent kingdom. It was seized for Spain in 1534, and Francisco Pizarro's brother Gonzalo was appointed governor. It was from Quito in 1541 that Francisco de Orellano set out with an expedition in search of El Dorado. They never found "the golden man," but they did find the Amazon River and, with great

Above: richly decorated and ornate, the splendid exterior expresses the dominating power and wealth of the conquering Europeans who built it.

Facing page, above: tons upon tons of gold were lavished on the interior. The rights and wrongs of the conversion of the South American peoples are still hotly debated.

Facing page, below: the dome is richly tiled in blue (left) and above the high altar is a figure of the Virgin (right).

THE military conquest of the Inca empire was immediately followed by the spiritual conquest, as the native peoples' religious systems were destroyed and they were converted en masse to Christianity. The Indian missions were run by the friars – the Franciscans, Dominicans, and Augustinians – and by the Jesuits. Their earliest churches were simple buildings, and for large congregations Mass was celebrated in the open air. By the 1550s, however, much grander edifices were going up, constructed by Indian labor under the direction of the priests.

Spanish in their architecture, these were fortresses of the faith with walls like bastions, as if to guard the holy mysteries within from assault or contamination by the native Indians outside. At the same time, as the region's wealth in gold and silver was exploited (a whole mountain of silver was discovered at Potosí in Bolivia in 1545), the churches were richly adorned to the greater glory of God.

The baroque Church of La Compañía (the Society of Jesus) in Quito is widely acknowledged to be one of the finest and richest churches in all South America. Building began in 1605, but the church was not completed until far into the 18th century. Its massive exterior under green and gold domes is ornamented with twisting columns and statues in niches. The interior is sumptuously ornate in red and gold, and it is said that 7 U.S. tons (6.4 metric tons) of solid gold went to adorn its altars, walls, and balconies. The main altar, under its handsome cupola, and 10 side altars are thickly plastered with gold leaf. The wooden pulpit and confessionals are elaborately carved. Every inch of the interior is painted and ornamented in glowing colors, and there is a Moorish look to some of the intricate designs.

The church is, in effect, a gallery of the Quito school of art, which is today much admired. The Franciscans founded an art school in the town in 1535. Indian and mestizo (mixed Indian and Spanish) craftsmen learned to produce religious painting and sculpture in

the European manner, but native influence played on it as well, to striking effect. The ceiling paintings in La Compañía Church have been described as Quito's answer to the Sistine Chapel.

A great treasure, a painting of Our Lady of Sorrows framed in gold and emeralds and normally kept in a bank vault, is brought out on special occasions. The church also cherishes

the remains of Quito's saint, Mariana Paredes y Flores, who died in 1645. Of Spanish family, she cared for the poor Indians and subjected herself to fiercely cruel penitential practices. When an epidemic broke out in the city, she offered her life to God to pay for others' sins, and she died soon afterwards. She was canonized in 1950.

The friars also built on a grand scale in Quito. Close to La Compañía is the palatial baroque Church of San Francisco, with more Quito school paintings. The Church of San Domingo is famous for its figure of the Virgin of Mercy on its principal altar. The former convent of San Agustín is now a museum. The old quarter of Quito is tightly packed with churches and monasteries, whose bells compete with each other to sound the hours, in a crystallization of Christianity in South America.

resourcefulness and courage, followed it all the way to the Atlantic.

Quito today is a charming town of Spanish-style houses, squares, and cool fountains, close to both the equator and a towering array of snow-wreathed volcanoes. Rearing its snowy head 15,715 feet (4,790 m) above the town is Pichincha, the "Boiling Mountain," which spits out black smoke. Some 40 miles (64 km) away, set in a national park, is bigger game, Cotopaxi, the highest active volcano in the world at 19,347 feet (5,897 m). The most dangerous and the most beautiful of Ecuador's peaks, it has a gorgeous snowcapped cone, emitting sulphurous yellowish vapor, above a base 12 miles (19 km) in diameter. Llamas and wild horses graze its lower slopes, and a dirt road winds up to a simple lodge at about 15,750 feet (4,800 m). Only suitably equipped mountaineers go higher, but the views from the summit are said to be incomparable. A British pioneer of mountain climbing, Edward Whymper, the conqueror of the Matterhorn, climbed Cotopaxi in 1880 and spent an uncomfortable night on top. In the same year he was the first man known to have scaled the still higher peak of Chimborazo, 20,702 feet (6,310 m).

1908 Argentina

TEATRO COLÓN

Great singers from Enrico Caruso to Luciano Pavarotti have filled this opulent grand opera house with glorious sound.

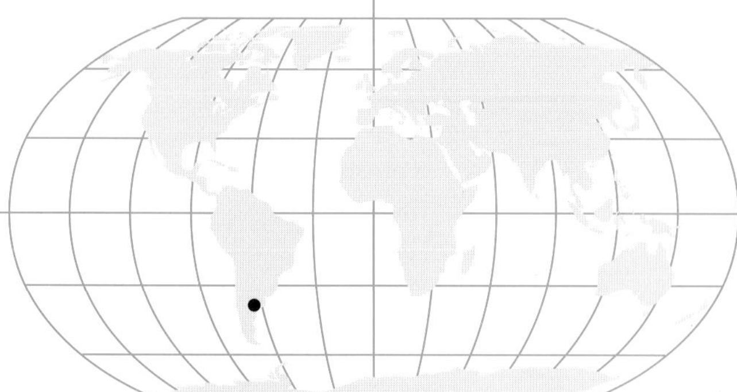

The theater's main entrance is on the Plaza Lavalle, Buenos Aires. Guided tours for visitors. Buenos Aires has two airports and connections with New York, Miami, and major American cities, and with London and the principal European airports. Rail and bus links with other South American capitals. Regular boats from Montevideo in Uruguay.

Right: occupying the bulk of a city block, the opera house in its mixture of European styles is an impressive example of Old World cultural imperialism in the New World.

Facing page: the tall obelisk in the Avenida Nueves de Julio points skyward to celebrate the first founding of the city in 1536.

ONE of the grandest of the world's grand opera houses, with acoustics of almost legendary perfection, the Teatro Colón raises its awesome Renaissance classical bulk above the Avenida Nueves de Julio in Buenos Aires. Filling most of an entire city block, it was begun in 1890, but not finished for 18 years. Political maneuverings and bureaucratic delays hindered progress. The opera house was a by-product of the rapid growth of Buenos Aires in the 19th century. The population rose from 40,000 in the year 1800 to 1,300,000 in 1910, as immigrants came in from Italy and Spain.

Opera has a long and honorable history in Buenos Aires, ever since the first production of Rossini's *Barber of Seville* in 1825, and as the city waxed prosperous in the 19th century, theaters were built in increasing numbers. The plan for an opera house that would put them all almost literally in the shade was the brainchild of an engineer named Francisco Tamburini, but he died in 1892, soon after work had started. He was followed by two architects in succession, Victor Meano and Julio Dormal, and the Teatro Colón formally opened its doors on May 25, 1908, with a performance of Verdi's *Aida*. Meano described the completed building as being essentially Italian Renaissance in style, with the grace, variety, and a certain bizarre quality added from French architecture, allied to a German solidity of detail.

If the exterior is imposingly handsome, the interiors are of a breathtaking splendor, with marble corridors, classical columns, groups of statuary, and acres of gold leaf. The grandest of the great halls is the famed Salon Dorado, or Golden Room, with its gleaming gilt and array of crystal chandeliers. The huge auditorium, resplendent in gold and plush red velvet, can seat an audience of 2,500 people with room for about 1,000 more standing. The stalls alone seat 632 people in such spacious comfort that ladies in full evening dress can walk between the rows without those already seated having to stand up. Tier upon tier, the boxes and balconies rise to the topmost seventh floor, called El Paraíso, or Paradise. Above it all is a dome, from which hangs a colossal 600-light chandelier, surrounded by paintings by the Argentine artist Raul Soldi.

The auditorium, huge as it is, is outmatched in scale by the enormous stage area, recently renovated and so large that a symphony orchestra and a ballet company can both rehearse on it at the same time, separated by a soundproof metal screen that prevents them hearing each other. Besides opera, the theater stages concerts and ballet and is the headquarters of the Buenos Aires Philharmonic Orchestra and the Colón Ballet as well as the opera orchestra and chorus. The theater is self-sufficient and makes its own scenery, costumes, wigs, and props. Beneath the stage are three floors of rehearsal rooms, workrooms for carpenters, tailors, and the rest, and storage rooms for more than 16,000 costumes and 30,000 pairs of shoes.

The roster of great conductors who have appeared here stretches from Toscanini and Richard Strauss to Beecham, Klemperer, Karajan, and Bernstein. The list of opera singers is a "who's who" of greatness: Lily Pons, Chaliapin, Gigli, Lotte Lehman, Lauritz Melchior, Maria Callas, Joan Sutherland, Elizabeth Schwartzkopf, Eva Marton... and in productions of a sumptuousness to match their genius.

Sleepless Paradise

ONLY a couple of blocks from the Teatro Colón is Buenos Aires' answer to the Eiffel Tower, the 230-foot (70 m) obelisk that stands on the spot where the flag of the independent republic of Argentina was first flown. Erected in 1936, it is in the middle of the Plaza de la Republica, through which runs the Avenida Nueves de Julio, 425 feet (130 m) wide and claimed to be the broadest city boulevard in the world. It is named after July 9, 1816, the date on which Argentina declared complete independence from Spain.

The obelisk was built to mark the 400th anniversary of the first attempt to found Buenos Aires, by a party of Spaniards in 1536. They were driven away by hostile Indians in 1541. A second group of Spanish settlers, who arrived in 1580, were more successful. Buenos Aires today, capital of Argentina and home to one out of every three Argentines, is one of the most enjoyable cities in the world and South America's nearest equivalent to Paris, with wide streets and sidewalk cafés, fine restaurants and smart shops, excellent theaters and art galleries, a wealth of churches and museums. The nightlife is lively and lasts all night long, and the city has been described as a paradise for insomniacs. One particularly remarkable sight is the Recoleta cemetery, where Eva Perón is buried, a city of the dead full of extravagant tombs and mausoleums in a rich mixture of styles, from Moorish and Byzantine to classical and baroque.

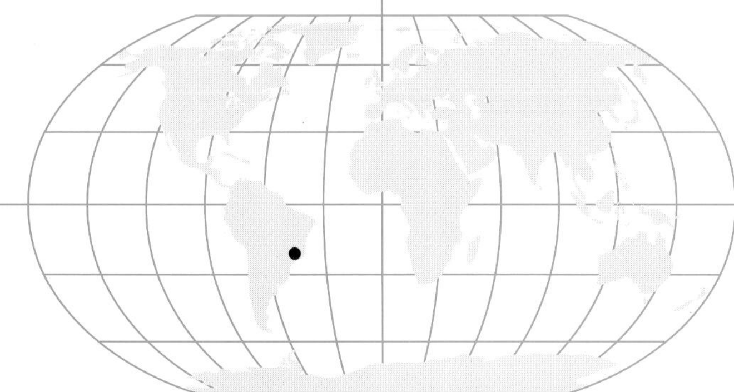

1931 Brazil

STATUE OF CHRIST THE REDEEMER

A huge statue of Jesus Christ surveys the panorama of a teeming city.

"GOD made the world in six days; the seventh he devoted to Rio." So Brazilians explain the almost miraculous beauty of the setting of the city that, until the establishment of Brasília in 1960, was their capital. Surrounded by mountains rising out of a tropical blue sea, bordered by palm-fringed beaches of white sand, Rio is endowed with all the features of an imagined paradise. But what most strikingly identifies it is a man-made landmark, the statue of Christ the Redeemer (Crito Redentor). Standing 100 feet (30 m) high, on a pedestal of 22 feet (7 m), it overlooks the city from the top of the 2,428-foot (740-m) granite mountain called Corcovado, or "Hunchback," because of its shape.

The idea for the statue was first broached in 1921, when Brazil celebrated the 100th anniversary of its independence. A popular magazine proposed a competition to choose a national monument. Hector da Silva Costa emerged the winner with a plan for a giant statue of Christ, his arms outstretched "to embrace the city" in a pose suggesting both compassion and a sense of accomplishment. Da Silva Costa's idea met with enthusiasm (in contrast with an earlier scheme to erect a statue of Columbus on Sugar Loaf Mountain), and funds for the project were raised privately by means of collections in churches throughout Brazil. Within 10 years, the massive figure was in position.

Designers, engineers, and sculptors met first in Paris to deliberate on the considerable problems of mounting a statue on top of a granite peak exposed to the elements at over 2,400 feet (732 m) above the sea level. The French sculptor Paul Landowski began modeling the head and hands, while work on the body and arms was consigned to the engineers and architects. The size of the task is reflected in the statue's gigantic dimensions: the head weighs 39 U.S. tons (35.6 metric tons) and stands 12 feet (3.7 m) high, each hand weighs 10 U.S. tons (9.1 metric tons), and the distance from fingertip to fingertip measures 75 feet (23 m).

The statue was brought from Paris and faced in soapstone before being winched up

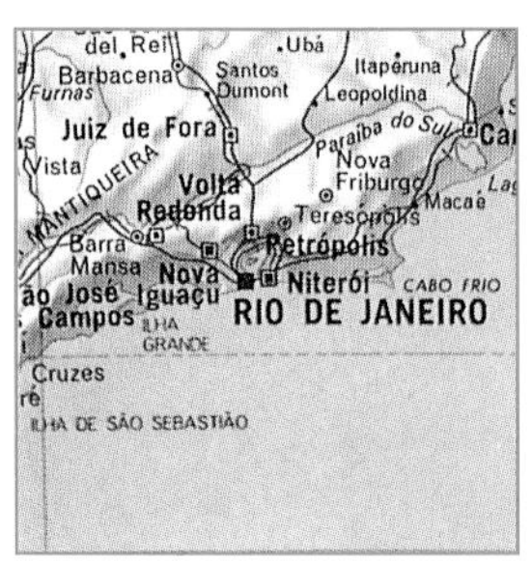

Rio de Janeiro's international airport is on Governador Island, 26 miles (16 km) outside the city. Shuttle flights from São Paulo arrive at the more central Santos Dumont Airport. The peak of Corcovado on which the statue stands is reached by rail from Rua Cosme Velho station or by road from the Laranjeiras district. A climb of 220 steps leads to the base of the statue.

Pico da Tijuca

A THIRD viewing platform over the city is Pico da Tijuca, a peak cloaked in the lush tropical vegetation of the Tijuca Forest. On the way to the summit at 3,320 feet (1,012 m), a two- to three-hour walk, is the Emperor's Table (Mesa do Imperador), a mammoth concrete picnic table where the emperor and his retinue used to dine. It now furnishes a good view of Rio's south side.

Right: with arms spread wide on the mountain peak to embrace the teeming city below, the statue was intended to express both divine compassion and a sense of achievement at the centenary of Brazilian independence.

Facing page, above: the statue was built in Paris and had to be winched into position.

Facing page, below: the tall peak of Sugar Loaf Mountain rises above the bay.

Corcovado. It was inaugurated on October 12, 1931, by Guglielmo Marconi, who designed the floodlighting. The switch was thrown from his yacht, moored not in Rio's harbor but thousands of miles away in Genoa, Italy. The ceremony was repeated in 1965 by Pope Paul VI, when new lighting was installed, and again on October 12, 1981, when Pope John Paul II marked the statue's 50th anniversary of watching over the city.

A rail link, built by Francisco Passos and Teixeira Soares in 1885, stops 130 feet (40 m) below Corcovado's summit. From the station 220 steps lead to the base of the statue and its balcony overlooking the city. The panorama embraces Copacabana and Ipanema beaches to the right, Maracana Stadium (the largest in the world) and the international airport on the left, and in front the distinctive outline of Sugar Loaf Mountain.

Sugar Loaf Mountain

An alternative view of Rio de Janeiro's spectacular setting is afforded from the top of Sugar Loaf Mountain (Pão de Açucar) at the entrance to Guanabara Bay. It is usually assumed that the name Pão de Açucar describes the mountain's pointed shape, which can be likened to a cone of raw sugar, but it is more probably derived from *pau-nh-acuqua*, the phrase in the language of the Tupi Indians meaning "high hill." The first recorded ascent was by Henrietta Carstairs, a British nanny, who planted the Union Jack on the pinnacle in 1817. Brazilian expeditions followed, and in 1913 a two-stage cable car was completed, linking Praia Vermelha with Morro da Urca and the summit. In 1972 a new, Italian cable car was installed, increasing capacity from 112 passengers per hour to 1,360. The safety record remains unblemished. At 1,300 feet (396 m) – almost half the height of Corcovado – Pão de Açucar gives a less panoramic view than its rival but offers more diverse attractions: at Morro da Urca there is a restaurant, a children's playground, and an amphitheater offering nightly samba shows.

1960 Brazil

BRASÍLIA

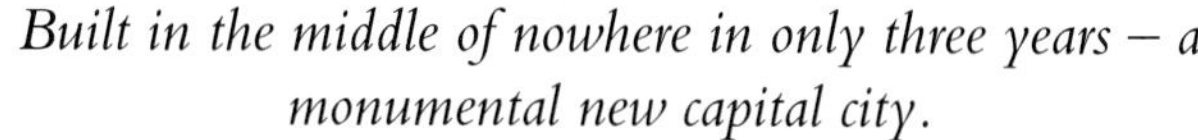
Built in the middle of nowhere in only three years – a monumental new capital city.

Brasília has its own international airport. There are domestic flights from Rio de Janeiro (about 90 minutes) and also a train service from São Paulo (about 24 hours). The city is served by long-distance buses from many places in Brazil.

Traffic Without Jams

LE Corbusier's theories about town planning were first voiced in the 1920s, when he realized that traffic congestion was a growing problem threatening every city that did not take steps to deal with it. In a new city, he believed, pedestrians should be separated from busy highways and the quality of life thus improved. These ideas were put into practice in Brasília, with separate road systems for pedestrians, for private cars, and for commercial vehicles. Traffic jams are said to be inconceivable.

Above: the spectacular interior of the cathedral, likened to an immense crown of thorns. It was designed by the Brazilian architect Oscar Niemeyer, who had earlier worked on the UN headquarters in New York City.

Right: modern art in the modern city. The Warriors statue has the Palacio de Planalto in the background.

Facing page: the tall Congress building, with its twin 28-story towers.

THE idea of a new capital for Brazil was first suggested in the 19th century, and was written into the constitution when the country became a republic in 1898. In this vast land where a majority of the people and the wealth was concentrated in a narrow coastal region around Rio de Janeiro, a new capital inland would be a means of opening up the interior. Nothing came of the proposal until 1956, when Juscelino Kubitschek was elected president after a campaign in which the promise of a new capital had been a major theme.

Kubitschek lost no time. He announced that Brazil would advance by 50 years in five years, and Brasília was duly created out of nothing in the middle of wilderness in a mere three years. The city was formally inaugurated on April 21, 1960. Today some people consider it one of the world's most beautiful cities, a place of magnificent open spaces, gardens, and highways where major buildings stand like stunning works of art. Others would claim that this is one of the least appealing places to live and work, lacking human scale and warmth. It is probably still too early to judge. A planned city, only 30 years old, can hardly compare with an ancient metropolis shaped by centuries of development and rich in the building styles of different eras, but it can and should offer a less stressful way of life in attractive surroundings.

The overall plan, which has been compared to the shape of an airplane or a bow and arrow, was the work of Lucio Costa and was chosen as the result of an international competition. There are two main thoroughfares: the curving Highway Axis running through the commercial and residential centers and, crossing this, the Monumental Axis is lined by the major public buildings designed by Oscar Niemeyer.

Creating Brasília was a daunting task, with no roads to the site and no building supplies nearby. Everything had to be flown in to the new site, where an army of thousands of laborers from all over the country worked around the clock. These workers also built another city – the shantytown known as Freetown, where they lived and where the population soon rose to 100,000.

Work began with the excavation of the huge Lake Paranoa, 50 miles (80 km) long and 3 miles (5 km) wide, which was to become a popular place for recreation and water sports within easy reach of the city. Tremendous care was lavished on the government and public buildings. The Plaza of the Three Powers was designed to be the center of government, with the president's palace, the National Congress, and the Federal Supreme Court grouped around a large square. The Congress building has two identical 28-story towers, and below these stand two low buildings – the Senate chamber and the House of Deputies. The Senate has a smooth dome over it; a similar dome, but inverted like a huge bowl, tops the House of Deputies. Outside the court building there is a modern sculptural image of blind Justice and, standing at the center of the Plaza, a statue called The Two Candangos, the work of the Brazilian sculptor Bruno Giorgi, dedicated to the men and women who worked to build the city.

The government had to offer considerable incentives to civil servants to encourage them to move to Brasília, but the city planned for 600,000 people now has a population of 1.5 million, and Brasília's existence has done much to attract development to the heart of the country. It is a city likely to provoke strong feelings – both for and against – for many years to come.

Architecture as Sculpture

The sculptural qualities of Brasília's buildings are notable. Many were designed to create a dramatic silhouette against the sky and also to look striking when illuminated at night. Sometimes the symbolism is a little difficult to grasp. The cathedral, for example, has been variously described as representing a crown of thorns, a flower, and two hands raised heavenwards in prayer. Like much else, it is the design of Oscar Niemeyer, who worked with, and was influenced by, Le Corbusier. While homage to Le Corbusier's ideas is clear, Niemeyer developed his own distinctive and graceful style, well expressed in the harmonious proportions of the Ministry of Foreign Relations building, also known as Itamaraty Palace. Here the combination of gardens, a pool, and delicate arches reflected in water is particularly pleasing.

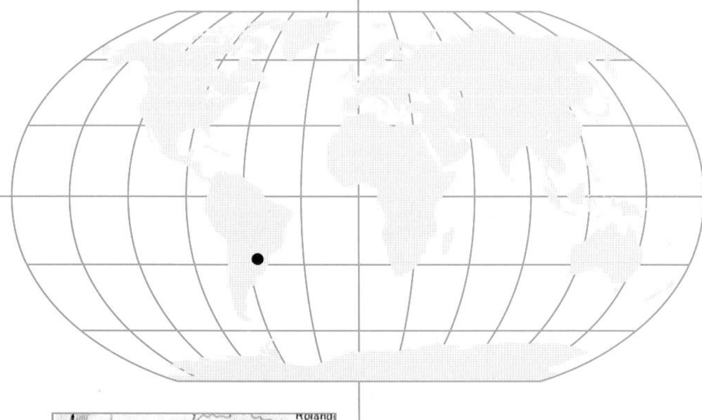

1982 Brazil

ITAIPU DAM

The most powerful hydroelectric plant in the world has harnessed the waters of the Mother of the Sea.

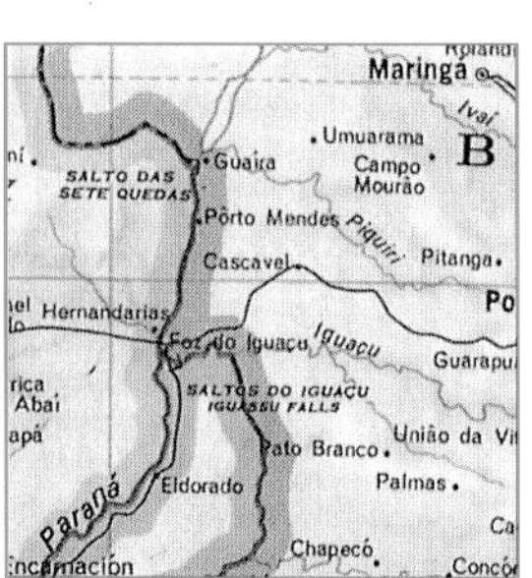

The Brazilian tourist base for both the Itaipu Dam and Iguaçu Falls is the town of Foz do Iguaçu, which has an airport. Flights from Rio, Asunción, Buenos Aires. Buses from Rio and São Paulo. By car, Foz do Iguaçu is on BR 277, some 930 miles (1,500 km) from Rio or 650 miles (1,050 km) from São Paulo.

On October 13, 1982, in the first operation of its kind on a river of this size in history, 12 great gates driven by hydraulic power descended until they rested on the bottom of the diverted channel of the Parana River. The operation took precisely eight minutes. For 14 days the pent-up water of the frustrated river mounted behind the massive concrete dam to a height 328 feet (100 m) above its normal level. At that point it began to pour through a specially constructed spillway 1,280 feet (390

Above: the water of the Parana foams and spumes in the spillway of the giant dam.

Right: the dam under construction. Part of a huge hydroelectric development jointly owned by Brazil and Paraguay, it has the most powerful generators in the world.

Facing page: a view of the Iguaçu Falls, which lie to the south of the dam.

m) wide at a rate of over 2.1 million cubic feet (60,000 cu m) of water per hour.

The Parana River (the name means Mother of the Sea) rises in Brazil and has a total length of more than 3,000 miles (4,830 km). It runs southwest to the town of Guaira, and for 118 miles (190 km) it forms the border between Brazil and Paraguay, running down to the spectacular Iguaçu Falls and the point where Brazil, Paraguay, and Argentina all meet. The Parana forms the border between Paraguay and Argentina for a stretch and then flows south across Argentina to Buenos Aires and the Rio de la Plata (Plate River).

Huge engineering projects to exploit the power potential of the Parana and its tributaries are under way in Brazil. More than 30 hydroelectric power plants – completed, under construction, or planned – will produce a total of 25 million kilowatts. This figure does not include the great Itaipu power plant itself, which is rated at 12.6 million kilowatts, the highest figure for a single power plant in the world. Although the Itaipu project was planned before the dramatic rise in oil prices in 1973, the rise caused the Brazilian government to plan to cut oil consumption and harness the country's abundant water reserves to create electric power.

The power station is operated by a company called Itaipu Binacional, founded in 1973 and jointly owned by Brazil and Paraguay, which share the power produced. The poetically named Itaipu means the "singing" of the river as it pours and ripples over rocks. The monster concrete dam (it is five times the size of the Aswan High Dam) is 12 miles (20 km) north of Foz do Iguaçu. It is almost 5 miles (8 km) long and rises to a height of 738 feet (225 m), or about the height of a 75-story building. The river at this point is 1,300 feet (400 m) wide and 200 feet (60 m) deep. A canal 1¼ miles (2 km) long and 490 feet (150 m) wide was blasted and hewn out of the rock to divert the river while the dam was being constructed. This was ready in 1978. The riverbed dried out and the building of the dam began in January 1979. The power station's generators are the largest in the world, rated at 700,000 kilowatts each.

The dam has created a lake covering an area of 520 square miles (1,350 sq km). Archaeological remains dating as far back as 8,000 years ago were rescued from some 300 sites before the inundation began, and thousands of animals were caught and then released in nature reserves on the banks of the lake, where 20 million trees are being planted. The dam and the lake are already attracting visitors to the tune of 700,000 a year.

The Devil's Throat

THE Iguaçu (or Iguassu) Falls are among the most spectacular and awe-inspiring sights in the world. Lying in a horseshoe shape are 275 separate falls, which hurtle 236 feet (72 m) into an abyss to create huge sheets and clouds of spray and a gorgeous irridescence of rainbows. The thunderous roaring of the water can be heard from miles away. Immediately above the falls, the Iguaçu River is some 2 miles (3 km) broad.

The name Iguaçu simply means "great waters" in the local Indian language. According to legend the great waterfall was created in an outburst of rage by the god of the Iguaçu River, who lived in a particularly wild and violent area of the downpour called the Garganta do Diablo (Devil's Throat). A daring boat trip offers a closer look at this area, and there are also helicopter flights, which give unforgettable views. The falls are close to the point where the Iguaçu and the Parana rivers join and the boundaries of Brazil, Argentina, and Paraguay converge. The countries are linked by two bridges: the Amizada (Friendship) Bridge between Brazil and Paraguay, and the Tancredo Neves Bridge between Brazil and Argentina.

AUSTRALASIA & OCEANIA

Perhaps they were figures of gods or ancestors, but the Easter Island statues were already an enticing mystery when the first Europeans arrived.

COVERING an area of approximately 64 million square miles (166 million sq km), the Pacific Ocean is larger than the entire land area of the globe. Scattered about it, mere specks of land in the vastness of the heaving sea, are more than 10,000 volcanic and coral islands. This was the last part of the earth to be settled by human beings, the last to be discovered and colonized by Europeans, the last to be freed from colonial dependence.

The Pacific islanders rank among the greatest long-range seafarers of all time. They sailed their outrigger canoes confidently over enormous distances of empty ocean, navigating by the sun, stars, and currents, by the swells and the flight of birds. They were perfectly capable of making headway against prevailing winds and adverse currents. Over many centuries they populated all the habitable islands of Oceania.

THE FAR VOYAGERS

The first human beings in Australia arrived from the southeast of Asia perhaps as long as 40,000 years ago. They were the ancestors of the Australian Aborigines who, when the first European colonists arrived, are thought to have numbered about 300,000.

It is believed that the earliest people to begin settling Oceania – maybe 20,000 years ago – were also of southeast Asian origin. Most of the main island groups in the western Pacific had been occupied by the first century A.D. Between the 5th and 10th centuries groups moved eastward across the Pacific to settle the islands there. They sailed in canoes tied together to form rafts, taking with them pigs, bananas, and breadfruit to rear and plant in their new homes.

It was at this stage that New Zealand and Hawaii were occupied, and perhaps Easter Island. Over several centuries between about A.D. 1000 and 1600, the Easter Islanders created one of the world's great enigmas by carving enormous statues – 12 or 15 feet (3.7 to 4.6 m) tall, or even taller – and setting them up on platforms to gaze out over the Pacific. No one knows why they did this, or why they stopped doing it and left statues unfinished in the quarry. By the time the European explorers arrived, the Easter Islanders either no longer knew or were not telling.

Mystery also clings to the so-called Venice of the Pacific at Nan Madol in the Caroline Islands, where a dynasty of rulers built about a hundred artificial stone islands, with sea walls up to 30 feet (9 m) high, linked by canals. It looks as if this was primarily a religious site, with temples and tombs, and there is another complex of the kind at the island of Leluh.

The mask is the head of the "living" Maori meetinghouse in Poverty Bay.

PARADISE LOST

Ferdinand Magellan and his crew were the first whites to round Cape Horn and sail out into the Pacific, which Magellan named. Other European venturers followed in search of a route to the Far East and hoping to find legendary treasures. One of them named the Solomon Islands, because he thought King Solomon's fabled diamond mines might be there.

The Dutch discovered Australia in the 17th century and called it New Holland. Abel Tasman discovered Fiji and touched at New Zealand, where the Maoris gave him a hostile reception. In three great voyages between 1768 and his death in 1779, Captain James Cook opened up more of the Pacific and claimed both Australia and New Zealand for Britain. He was killed in a minor skirmish in Hawaii.

In 1788 a small British settlement was established at Sydney Cove in Australia. The settlers were some 750 convicts, sentenced to transportation for crimes from murder to sheep-stealing to prostitution. Shiploads of convicts were sent to Australia far into the 19th century. They and their descendants and successors have built one of the world's most dynamic and successful democracies – and, in the Sydney Opera House, one of the most beautiful buildings of modern times.

All the native peoples of Australasia and Oceania were still in the Stone Age when the first Europeans encountered them. Travelers sent back idyllic reports from the Pacific of paradise islands, blue lagoons, coral reefs, palm trees, white sandy beaches, lovely and complaisant maidens. These paradises were then destroyed, by European economic exploitation and conquest, European religion, European diseases. Today's mass tourism is completing the job.

A purple dusk gathers romantically around the beautiful Sydney Opera House.

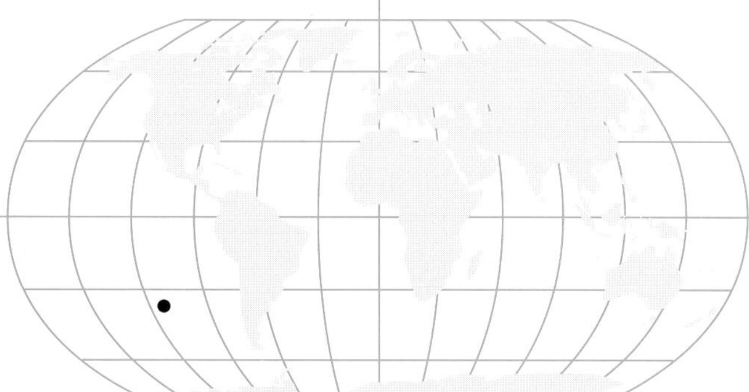

11th to 16th Century

EASTER ISLAND

Silent and enigmatic, the huge statues contemplate the Pacific.

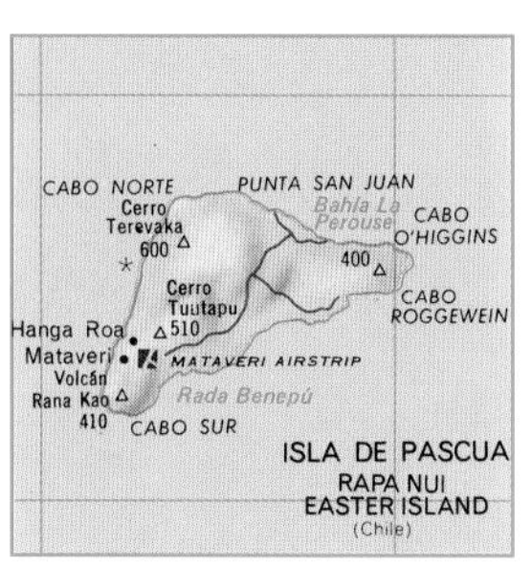

Easter Island is now visited by many tourists. It lies 2,000 miles (3,220 km) southwest of the Galapagos Islands and 2,600 miles (4,200 km) west of Valparaiso in Chile, the country by which it was annexed in 1888. Visitors can travel by air from Chile, but this is an expedition that requires careful planning.

EASTER Island offers convincing evidence that truth can be stranger than fiction. A volcanic island, roughly triangular, measuring 10 by 11 by 15 miles (16 by 18 by 24 km), it lies in the Pacific Ocean thousands of miles from any other habitation. When the first Europeans approached it on Easter Sunday in 1722, they saw that the island was ringed with massive statues gazing bizarrely out to sea. The inhabitants, however, appeared welcoming, and they lit fires encouraging the visitors to come ashore. When they did so, Captain Roggeveen and his Dutch crew observed three different races among the islanders, some dark, some with a reddish skin, and some strikingly pale-skinned with red hair. Some of these people had curiously extended earlobes, into which large discs were fitted, and these were the ones who seemed to show particular reverence for the giant statues. Apart from a tendency to steal anything they could lay their hands on, the people were friendly. But very few women were seen, and a large part of the population kept out of sight, probably hiding in underground caves.

In 1770 a Spanish expedition from Peru made similar observations. The people were still friendly and the land well cultivated, but Captain Cook, reaching the island only four years later, encountered a very different scene. The land had become neglected and barren, the people were listless and demoralized, and, while before there had been no sign of weapons or any warlike tendencies, they now carried wooden clubs and spears. The huge statues had been overturned, and no one seemed to worship them any more. In the 19th century, the island became a target for slave traders, and a massive Peruvian slave raid in 1862 proved appallingly destructive.

After coming close to destroying the Easter Islanders, the Western world finally began to study the people and their culture. Christian missionaries worked to convert the surviving population from their existing beliefs in a god called Make-Make, and in doing so discovered miniature idols that were kept in the people's homes, but apparently nor worshipped with any great ceremony. When wooden tablets carved with hieroglyphic signs were discovered, it became clear that this had been a society that had known how to write. Some of the tablets were destroyed as instruments of paganism, but a few survived. Known as *rongo-rongo* tablets, they were written from left to right and then right to left in alternate lines, but the meaning

Ancestral Voyagers

THE Norwegian archaeologist and anthropologist Thor Heyerdahl has carried out extensive research into the mysteries of Easter Island. His experiments sailing the balsa-wood raft *Kon-Tiki* and the reed boat *Ra II* have demonstrated without doubt that communication across vast distances could be achieved by ancient and supposedly primitive civilizations. Connections between the pre-Inca society at Tihuanaco, near Lake Titicaca in Bolivia, and Easter Island have been observed, and there also seem to be links with Peru, where

Above: a majestic line of statues contemplates the ocean. They may have been dragged from the quarry on sledges and then hauled upright with ropes and long wooden levers.

Facing page: tradition has it that a war between the Long Ears and the Short Ears put an end to the making of the statutes.

of the symbols remains a mystery that contemporary islanders cannot solve.

The most fascinating aspect of Easter Island, however, is its huge statues, about a thousand of them, which the islanders call *moai.* Many of them stand about 12 to 15 feet (3.7 to 4.6 m) high and weigh about 22.5 U.S. tons (20.3 metric tons). Some are bigger, up to 32 feet (9.8 m) tall and a weight of 101 U.S. tons (91.5 metric tons). They have exaggeratedly large heads, with jutting chins and elongated ears. Some have "hats" of red rock on top of their heads. Unfinished statues have been found in a quarry.

There has been much speculation about how the islanders managed to move these bulky figures (local tradition fiercely insists that the statues walked). Investigation has shown that the figures have a low center of gravity and that a team of 15 people can heave one along with ropes at a surprising speed. The statues have no legs, and, intriguingly, the Easter Island language has a verb that means to inch along without the use of legs.

There is no mystery any longer about how the statues were made and how they were moved into place. But unanswered questions remain. Why? What were they for? Do they represent gods or ancestors? Why do they stare out to sea? The statues remain silent.

the Spanish conquerors encountered tales of an island territory a long way to the west. Reeds found on Easter Island by some of the first explorers, and vegetables such as the sweet potato and the yuca, are native South American species. Easter Island tradition speaks of the Long Ears, who came from the east, and the Short Ears, who came from the west later. This suggests original settlers from pre-Inca Latin America (where ear extension is known to have been practiced) followed by Polynesians, who later overthrew the religiously minded Long Ears.

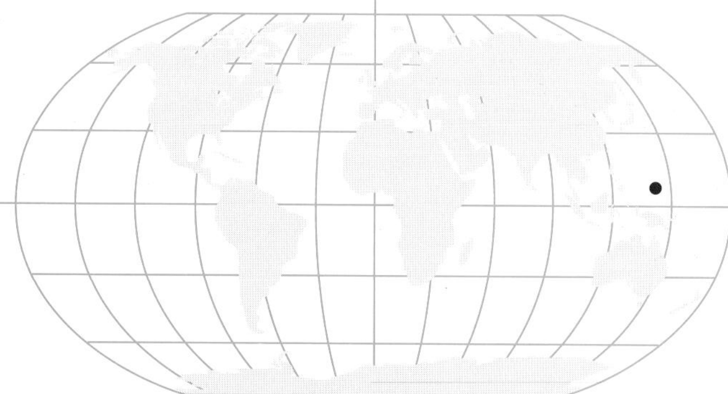

12th Century Caroline Islands

NAN MADOL

The Venice of the Pacific – an ancient stone city with a network of canals.

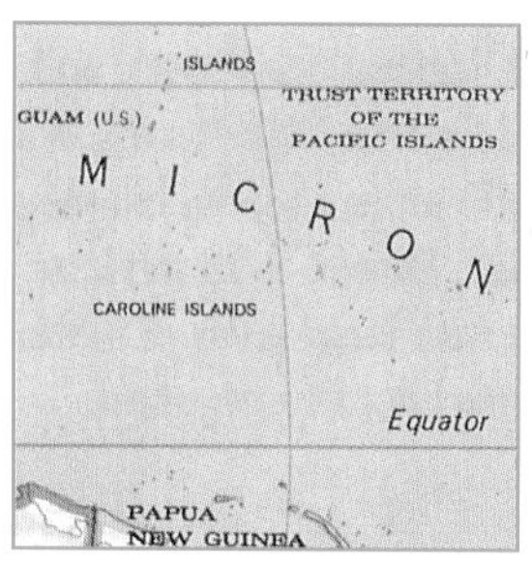

Honolulu is a good starting point from which to pick up Continental Air Micronesia's island-hopping service, which stops at Pohnpei in the Caroline Islands. It is also possible to fly to the island of Guam from a number of countries, including Japan, Indonesia, and Hong Kong, and to fly on from Guam to Pohnpei. Nan Madol is on the southeast edge of the island and should be visited by boat at high tide. Air Micronesia also serves Kosrae.

Leluh Island

LELUH Island is linked by a causeway to Kosrae, the place from which the conquerors of Nan Madol are believed to have come. The arguments for a connection between Ponhpei and Kosrae become more persuasive when the ruins on Leluh Island are taken into account.

Here, too, the people knew how to build up artificial islands: part of Leluh is man-made, and it became the site of a large, walled city, much of which can still be seen. Again there are sacred areas, tombs, canals, and royal quarters protected by walls, and again

Right: ruins of buildings on artificial islands line a complex of canals in what seems to have been primarily a religious center.

Facing page: supposedly haunted today, Nan Madol was built by the rulers of a lost but highly sophisticated civilization.

POHNPEI (known until recently as Ponape) is a volcanic island of great beauty in the Caroline archipelago. One of over 2,000 Micronesian islands scattered across millions of square miles of the Pacific Ocean between the equator and the Tropic of Cancer, it is about 130 square miles (337 sq km) in area and home to some 25,000 people. There are many natural attractions – not least the volcanic landscape and lush vegetation created in a climate where rain can measure 330 inches (838 cm) a year – but Pohnpei is particularly noted as the site of an extraordinary settlement known as Nan Madol.

Nan Madol, a complex of about a hundred small, artificial islands linked by canals, has been called the Venice of the Pacific. At some time in the distant past, probably during the 12th century, a dynasty of rulers called the Saudeleurs began to create these islands and construct buildings on them. Their building material was black basalt, a type of stone that occurs naturally on Pohnpei in curious hexagonal column formation.

The people who built Nan Madol were capable not only of moving great quantities of this stone without breaking it up, but also of using it in ingenious ways. The artificial islands have elaborate sea walls, up to 30 feet (9.1 m) high, built up out of layers of basalt columns. These walls sheltered buildings, also of black basalt, and the remains that can be seen today suggest that this was a community where religious ceremony was an important feature of life. Evidence of domestic arrangements is scant, but temples, tombs, and what seem to be administrative headquarters have all been found.

A thunder god was worshipped here (hardly surprising, in view of the heavy rainfall), and various sea creatures seem to have been kept in sacred pools. A holy eel was featured in one ceremony, and it is said to have been fed a great delicacy, cooked turtle. The Nan Dowas compound was the site of some elaborate tombs. There were four separate mausoleums here protected by high walls, and this compound is the largest surviving structure to be seen. A number of buildings have fallen into a state of decay, giving no indication of their original height.

Nan Madol may have taken as long as 300 years to build. The heavy basalt columns were transported from a quarry on Pohnpei to the site on the southeastern edge of the coast (presumably water transportation was used as much as possible). As the Micronesian islands have no sources of metal, all the cutting and shaping of the stone must have been done without the aid of metal tools.

At some stage the ruling Saudeleurs were driven out. What exactly happened is not clear, but legend and folklore speak of the thunder god's involvement, and there is a suggestion that Nan Madol was captured by people from Kosrae, another island lying to the southeast. By the time the Europeans and Americans started to explore the area in the 19th century, Nan Madol had been abandoned. Today, although it is not difficult to arrange a boat tour along some of the canals to inspect the surviving buildings, there is a belief among some of the islanders that this is a place haunted by ghosts.

the characteristic building material is basalt rock, although coral is also used. Some walls still stand at a height of 20 feet (6 m). The site has a small museum, which casts light on the history of the settlement.

Foreign Involvement in Micronesia

POHNPEI and the other Caroline Islands have recently been working toward self-government and terms of Free Association with the USA, following several decades as United States Trust Territories. Foreign involvement in the area has ranged from virtual indifference after the first European explorations in the 16th century, to rivalry for possession, when the natural resources of copra (dried coconut meat yielding coconut oil) began to be exploited during the 19th century. After German domination at the end of the 19th century, the Caroline Islands were occupied by the Japanese in 1914. When their strategic importance became obvious after the Japanese bombing of Pearl Harbor in 1941, American forces seized control and later had the territory recognized as a strategic area by the United Nations.

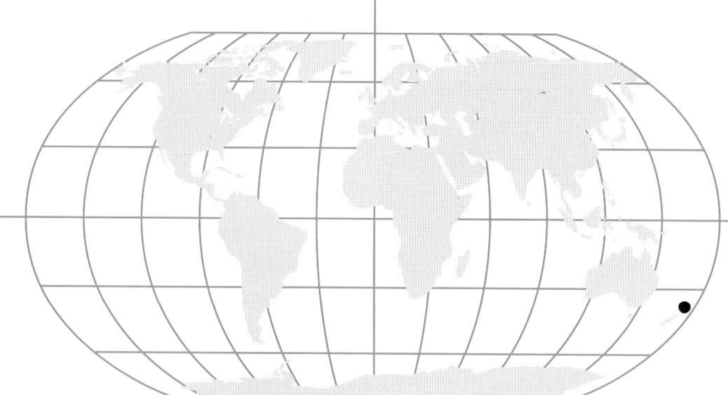

From 1880 New Zealand

ROTORUA

Maori traditional art flourishes among erupting geysers and boiling mud pools.

There are guided tours of the main attractions and boat trips on the lake. Rotorua is on the North Island, 150 miles (240 km) south of Auckland, which has an international airport with connections to Los Angeles, Vancouver, London, Tokyo, Hong Kong, Singapore, etc. Air, rail, and bus services from Auckland to Rotorua.

Not much more than a hundred years ago, the Rotorua area was a wasteland of swamp and scrub, pockmarked by hot springs and geysers shooting scalding water into the air at intervals, all overlaid with steam and a sulphurous smell. Today, pleasantly green and wooded, it is one of New Zealand's favorite playgrounds. The city of Rotorua has a population approaching 60,000 and attracts 10 times that number of visitors.

The Arawa tribe of Maoris lived in this area for centuries before the Europeans arrived, and it is still the pre-eminent center of traditional Maori culture. The Arawa supported the British in the Maori Wars and were attacked by other tribes in consequence. The warm springs and their assumed health value aroused European interest in the area, and in 1880 the New Zealand government reached agreement with the Arawa to build a spa on the shore of Lake Rotorua. The spa is the nucleus of today's city.

Ohinemetu, the original Maori village here, has a fine meetinghouse constructed in the 19th century and covered with elaborate carving. Woodcarving was the most highly regarded of the Maori traditional crafts. It was a religious art, which gave visible form to the tribal myths and so renewed and perpetuated them. The craft was confined strictly to men. Women were not allowed even to watch a carver at work.

A meetinghouse was the spiritual center of each Maori village. It was thought of as being a living thing, with the interior its belly, the ridgepole its spine, and the mask directly beneath the gable its head. Meetinghouses are richly ornamented with carvings and paintings, which depict gods, ancestors, and events of the past, so making a history of the tribe and an expression of its spirit.

Maori carvers also brought their skills to bear on Christian buildings, like Ohinemetu's Church of St. Faith, a half-timbered construction of 1910, which is lavishly endowed with carvings and woven wall hangings. A window depicts Jesus in a Maori chief's feathered cloak, walking on the water of Lake Rotorua. Outside, the tombs of Maori chieftains are raised above the ground for protection against steam.

Young craftspeople today are taught the

Right: a meetinghouse at Rotorua. Tribal meetinghouses were regarded as living creatures and the carvings and paintings with which they were ornamented constituted a visible history of the tribe.

Facing page: one of the Rotorua geysers blasting off. The local Maoris used to cook over the hot steam rising from the ground.

traditional skills at the Maori Arts and Crafts Institute in the Whakarewarewa area (Whaka for short), where carvers and weavers can be seen at work. The Institute is in the Maori village, which is fenced off in the old way with a high palisade and entered through an imposing gateway, carved with grotesque animal figures and heads and figures of two lovers from a local legend. Maori traditional dances and chants are performed in native costume in the meetinghouse here. There are numerous geysers, springs, and seething mud pools here as well, and demonstrations of the old Maori way of cooking with the circumambient steam.

The center of the European spa is Tudor Towers, the original main bathhouse in elaborate mock-Tudor style. Set in attractive gardens with bowling greens and croquet lawns, it all appears quintessentially British – until you notice a pool boiling merrily at 100°C.

National Bird

ONE of Rotorua's attractions is a kiwi house, where visitors can see New Zealand's national bird and symbol. Kiwis, nocturnal and unobtrusive, are not often seen in normal circumstances. They are peculiar creatures, about as unlike a bird as it seems possible for a bird to be. A kiwi cannot fly, has only rudimentary wings, and has no tail. It is the only bird that hunts its prey by smell. It has nostrils at the business end of its long bill, which it pokes into wet ground to sniff for worms, larvae, insects, and roots.

About the size of chickens, kiwis are almost blind. They live in burrows underground, where they lay eggs of massive dimensions, one or two a season, each weighing up to a pound (450 g), about 25% of the female kiwi's body weight. In proportion to the size of the bird, the eggs are the largest of any species. The male incubates the eggs, while fast asleep in the burrow; after nearly three months, the chicks hatch out fully feathered.

Maoris considered all birds sacred as children of the god of the forests. Kiwis were particularly sacred. Only chiefs were allowed to eat kiwi meat, and the birds' feathered skins were worn by chiefs as cloaks. The kiwi is descended from the much bigger moa, also flightless, which finally died out in the 18th century. One type of moa stood 12 feet (3.7 m) tall and was the largest bird ever recorded.

THE MAORIS IN NEW ZEALAND

Maori warriors fought fiercely but in vain for their land.

Wood carving was a sacred Maori craft, restricted entirely to men.

According to Maori tradition, their ancestors came to New Zealand from an island in the Pacific called Hawaiki. (Hawaiki was not Hawaii, but may have been in the Society Islands, near Tahiti.) They came in seven long canoes and their leader was Tama Te Kapua, in whose honor the meetinghouse in Ohinemetu is named. With them they brought the dog and the rat, which had not been known in New Zealand before. This happened somewhere about A.D. 1350.

Archaeologists have discovered that Polynesians had crossed the Pacific wastes to New Zealand long before, by the 8th century if not earlier. It is from the "great fleet," however, that most Maoris today trace their ancestry.

CANNIBAL FEASTS

Before the arrival of Europeans, the Maoris were divided into 40 or 50 tribes, with many subtribes, led by hereditary chiefs. They lived in fortified villages of thatched houses, ringed by palisades and ditches. They grew a variety of sweet potato, hunted the great flightless moa birds, and were expert fishermen (women were not allowed to fish). They used stone tools and made clothes of flax.

This was a strongly male-dominated warrior society, whose values were courage, loyalty, and honor. There were constant intertribal wars, fought with swords and clubs of stone and wood. Many of those who were defeated – men, women, and children – were killed and eaten by the victors, who thereby absorbed their life energy and spiritual force.

Maori warriors loved fighting, fine talk, and the savor of revenge. They were heavily and painfully tatooed, with whorl patterns cut into the skin all over their faces and coloring matter rubbed into the cuts.

Maori chiefs were surrounded by a powerful and dangerous aura of sacredness. If a chief's shadow fell on a storehouse of food, for instance, the storehouse and all it contained would have to be destroyed. The man who cut the chief's hair was not allowed to use his hands for anything else for a time and had to be fed like a baby.

THE MAORI WARS

New Zealand and the Maoris remained unknown to Europeans until 1642, when the North Island was sighted by the Dutch explorer Abel Tasman, the first man to sail around Australia. Some of his men were killed by Maoris and he sailed away. It was the Dutch who gave the place the name Nieuw Zeeland. In 1769, Captain Cook appeared and claimed the territory for Britain.

Now a trickle of whites came to New Zealand. Whaling stations were set up at points on the coast. Sealers ruthlessly hunted their prey almost to extinction. With no white government and legal system, the country became a refuge for wanted men and outcasts. The newcomers sold the Maoris liquor and firearms, which they used to lethal effect in their tribal wars. They also died from European diseases like measles, against which they had no resistance.

Christian missionaries turned their attention to New Zealand, but the Maoris paid little heed at first. With lawlessness unchecked, the British government eventually intervened and sent Captain William Hobson to take control as governor. In 1840 he signed with 45 Maori chiefs the Treaty of Waitangi, which was meant to provide for European settlement while protecting Maori rights. Maoris now began to be converted to Christianity in rapidly increasing numbers.

Inevitably, with European settlers moving in to farm the land, tension with the Maoris mounted. Disputes flared into fights and skirmishes. Maori chiefs went on the rampage on the North Island in the 1840s, but were put down by the colonists under the governor, Sir George Grey. Between 1860 and 1872, in a series of hard-fought wars, British troops and gunboats had to be brought in to defeat the Maori warriors. Some of the North Island tribes chose a king, Potatau I, in 1857 and rose in arms in 1863. The Hauhau resistance movement (named after its warcry) fought with fanatical courage. In 1868 a new guerrilla movement called Ringatu was formed, combining Maori tradition and Christian beliefs.

Maori bravery was no match for superior white technology. The wars ended in 1872 with the Maoris having lost enormous areas of their ancestral territory. They regarded the land not as belonging to anyone, but as being held by one generation in trust for the next. Maori traditional society was destroyed by the coming of the Europeans and the introduction of Christianity, but the issue of the white "land grab" in the 19th century still causes resentment among Maoris today.

On the other hand, Maoris have integrated into European society far more successfully than the Australian Aborigines. There has been much intermingling and intermarriage. Very few full-blooded Maoris are left, and most New Zealanders today are partly of Maori descent.

The richly carved and decorated interior or "belly" of a Rotorua meetinghouse.

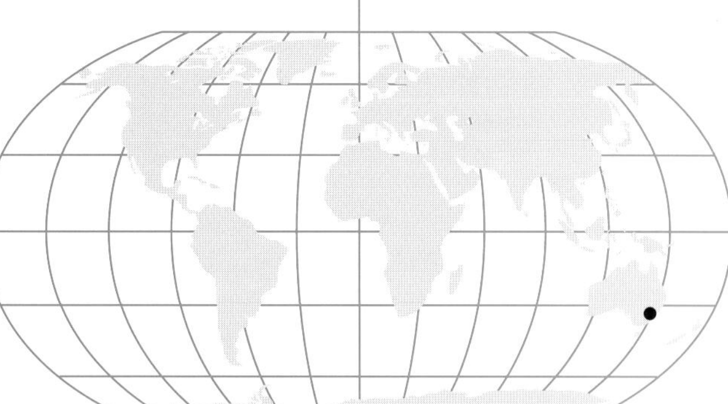

1973 Australia

SYDNEY OPERA HOUSE

Like a giant surrealist swan, this fantasy in steel and concrete seems poised to fly.

Sydney Opera House is on Bennelong Point on the south side of the harbor, close to Harbour Bridge, Sydney, New South Wales. Can be reached by bus or train to Circular Quay. Guided tours of the building. Harbor cruises from Circular Quay.

IN 1959 the competition to design an opera house for Sydney attracted 222 entries from 32 countries. The winner was an almost unknown Danish architect in his early 40s, named Joern Utzon. Like many of the other entrants, he had never seen the site and worked from photographs. His design was inspired partly by the idea of the sails of yachts on Sydney's immense and beautiful harbor, and partly by Maya and Aztec temples he had seen in Mexico.

Technically, Utzon's was the most difficult

Right: the opera house is splendidly illuminated at night, against the dark waters of Sydney's magnificent harbor, and with the lights of the city in the background.

Facing page: the intriguing visual relationship between the opera house, the harbor whose yachts inspired its "sails" and the curve of the Sydney Harbour Bridge, whose place as the city's visual symbol the opera house has usurped.

design to realize, though by far the most unusual and exciting. Both the appearance of the proposed building and the escalating cost of it aroused heated feelings. Cab drivers came to blows in Sydney's streets over its merits. It was supposed to open in 1963 and cost $7 million. It actually took 10 years longer and cost over $100 million. Most of the extra money was raised by lotteries.

Somehow the project kept moving forward amid incessant argument and violent storms of hostility. Utzon resigned in disgust in 1966. The beautiful concrete shells or "sails" – elliptic paraboloids in the jargon – proved impossible to construct as originally conceived and the design had to be modified. Thousands of hours of computer time went into solving the difficulties, and the final building is as much a triumph of Ove Arup's engineering as of Utzon's design.

The opera house was formally opened by Queen Elizabeth II on October 20, 1973. It has a strong claim to be classed as the most beautiful major building raised anywhere in the world since the Second World War, and one of the most beautiful of all time. It is seen at its best from the waters of the harbor, where it suggests a titanic white swan that might be about to take to the air. Floodlit by night, it is seraphically lovely.

The building stands beside the harbor on a site called Bennelong Point, named after an Australian Aboriginal friend of the first governor of the colony. There was once a fort here, and later a streetcar depot. The complex covers an area of 4½ acres (1.8 hectares). The roof shells weight 177,000 U.S. tons (161,000 metric tons) and are supported by 217 miles (350 km) of cables. On the sails are more than a million Swedish antifungal ceramic tiles, which glint in the sun and never need cleaning.

Inside, the effect has been labeled Space Age Gothic, with steel ribs and concrete fans and 67,000 square feet (6,225 sq m) of tinted glass. The building boasts the biggest theater curtains in the world, in wool, each covering close to 1,000 square feet (93 sq m) and needing six men to lift it. Woven in France in the Aubusson manner, they were designed by an Australian, John Coburn, as "curtains of the sun and moon." The concert hall organ is the world's biggest mechanical organ and has 10,500 pipes. There are five different performing halls, a movie theater, and two restaurants. The opera hall seats 1,550 people, the concert hall 2,700. The Sydney Symphony Orchestra, the Sydney Philharmonia Choir, and Sydney Theater all give performances in a building that has felicitously been called "a white swan in a land of black swans."

The Coathanger

Close to the opera house and making intriguing resonances with it is Sydney Harbour Bridge, which was the city's best-known landmark until the opera house came along. Functional in gray steel, its curving arch – locally nicknamed "the Coathanger" – has strength and a certain elegance. It was designed by an Australian railroad engineer, John Job Crew Bradfield, who was born at Sandgate in Queensland. The greatest moment in his life came on March 19, 1932, when the bridge was formally opened. The road across the bridge, which also carries trains, was named Bradfield Highway in his honor. The actual construction work was done by the British firm of Dorman Long, whose engineer tried to claim the credit for the design.

The demand for a bridge over the harbor, previously crossed only by ferries, goes back almost to Sydney's earliest days, and there were also those who called for a tunnel. Approval was eventually given to Bradfield's design, and work went on from 1923 to 1932, through the Depression (hence the gray paint, which was the cheapest available).

The bridge has a total length of 3,770 feet (1,150 m), the single main span being 1,650 feet (503 m) long. The crown of the arch is 439 feet (134 m) above the water of the busy harbor. The walkway along the eastern side commands excellent views of both the harbor and the city.

INDEX

The Automobile Association would like to thank the following photographers, libraries and associations for their assistance in the preparation of this book.

B & C ALEXANDER PHOTOGRAPHY 230&1 Nan Madol Ruins.

J ALLAN CASH PHOTO LIBRARY 8 Parthenon, 23 Vaulting Diocletian's Palace, 43 St Peter's Latium, 49 St Vitzus Cath. door, 58/9 Pont Cysyllte Aqueduct, 73 Baikal & Peking Expresses, 75 Pompidou Center, 101 Angkor Wat, 108 Meenakshi Temple, 109 Shree Meenakshi Temple, 120 Chandigarh, 125 Lalibela, 133 Ruins, 137 Courtyard, Fez, 141 Lalibela church, 143 Suez Canal, 158 Old Church of the Virgin of Guadalupe, 159 Painting, 171 Panama Canal.

ARCHITECTURAL ASSOCIATION SLIDE LIBRARY 121 High Crt. Justice, Chandigarh (F L Winter).

JANET & COLIN BORD/WALES SCENE 59 Pont Cysyllte Aqueduct, Plas Newydd.

ROBERT HARDING PICTURE LIBRARY 79 Hisham's Palace ruins, 100 Angkor Wat.

INTERNATIONAL PHOTOBANK LTD 14/5 Parthenon, 23 Diocletian's Palace, 41 Cath. of Assumption, 54/5 Iron Bridge, Coalbrookdale, 55 Iron Bridge Gorge.

JAPAN INFORMATION & CULTURAL CENTRE 122 Seto Ohashi Bridge.

JAPAN NATIONAL TOURIST ORGANIZATION 122 Seto Ohashi Bridge.

T MORRISON'S AMERICAN PICTURES 146 Basalt Atlantes Statue, 160 Golden Man of Calima, 161 L Guatavita, Gold Masks, 200 L Titicaca, 202 Valley of the Statues, Stone God, 203 Tomb & Platform Stone Gods, 204 Nazca Lines, 205 Monkey figure, Pot-eyed God, 211 Inca Road, Knotted Recording Device, 214 Inca gold mask, 215 Inca pot, Inca fortress, 216 Quito Church, 217 Quito Church int., Quito Blue Dome, High Altar, 219 Obelisk, B. Aires, 221 Christ the Redeemer detail, 222 Brasília int. Cathedral, Statue of the Warriors, 224 & 5 Itaipu Dam.

P RYLEY'S AMERICAN PICTURES 210 Inca Trail

SPECTRUM COLOUR LIBRARY *Back cover* Pyramids, Giza, 1 Stonehenge, 2/3 Five Pyramids, 9 Pompidou Center. 13 Avebury, 15 Frieze, Parthenon, 17 Maison Carree, Nîmes, 24 Bell, Leaning Tower of Pisa, 25 Leaning Tower of Pisa, 26 Alhambra Courtyard, 27 Alhambra courtyard decoration, 29 Chartres Cathedral, Royal Portal, 34/5 Meteora monastery, 35 Rousanou monastery, 39 House of Boatmen, Brussels, 40/1 Kremlin, 44 Carriage & Hofburg, Spanish Riding School, 45 The Hofburg, 50/1 Versailles Palace, 51 Versailles Palace, 52/3 Petrodvorets Great Palace, 64 Sacré-Coeur, 68 Parc Guell, Barcelona, 74 Pompidou Center, 76 Persepolis, Iran, 76 Meenakshi Temple ceiling, 77 Lion, Beijing, 79 Mosaic, Jericho, 80/1 Persepolis, 81 Sculpture reliefs, 85 Grt Wall of China watch tower, 86/7 Terra-Cotta figures, 91 Nemrut Dağ, 92 Göreme Valley, 93 Göreme churches, Painting, 96/7 Todaiji Temple, 97 Kasuga shrine, Buddha, 102/3 Toru gate, 112 Taj Mahal, 114 Tiles Topkapi Palace, 117 Pearl Mosque, 119 Potala Palace, 124 Stat. of Ramses, 125 Temple wall Grt Zimbabwe, 128 Karnak Temple, 132 Baths, Carthage, 134/5 Meroe Pyramids, 135 Meroe Temple, Pyramids, 138/9 Temple entrance, 139 Temple wall, 144/5 Aswan Dam, 150/1 Pyramid of the Sun, 157 Cliff dwelling, 159 Shrine, High Altar, 182 & 3 Hoover Dam, 190 N. Mus. Chapultepec, 191 Tula Statue, 193 Gateway Arch, 195 Sea World, 196 Louisiana Superdome, 207 L Titicaca, 208/9 Templo Adorato, 209 Birds & Fishes Wall, 212/3 Machu Picchu, 225 Iguacu Falls, 227 Maori Meeting Hse, 228 Easter Island statues, 234 Maori carving, 235 Maori Meeting Hse, 237 Sydney Opera Hse.

THE ANCIENT ART & ARCHITECTURE COLLECTION 28/9 Chartres Cathedral, 42 St Peter's, Rome, 78 The Round Tower Jericho.

THE SLIDE FILE 10 & 11 Newgrange.

USSR PHOTO LIBRARY 72 Yaroslavl Station, 72/3 Trans Siberian Express.

WORLD PICTURES *Front cover* Taj Mahal, *back cover* Neuschwanstein Castle, Golden Gate Bridge, 16/7 Pont du Gard, 19 Colosseum, 21 Hadrian's Wall, 33 Kapell Bridge, 36/7 Venice Grand Canal, 47 Library ceiling, Escorial, 48/9 Golden Lane, 53 Petrodvorets Great Cascade, 61 Guardsman, Windsor Castle, 63 Linderhof Palace, 65 Sacré-Coeur, 66 Parliament Buildings, Budapest, 69 Sagrada Familia, Barcelona, 71 Eiffel Tower, 84 Grt Wall of China, 89 Grt Wall, 94 Dome of the Rock, 95 Wailing Wall, 98/9 Buddhist shrine, 99 Borobudur Temple, 104/5 Gate of Supreme Harmony, 105 Temple of Heaven, 106/7 Topkapi Palace, 110 & 111 Blue Mosque, 112/3 Taj Mahal, 115 Taj Mahal, 116 Red Fort, 127 Giza Pyramids, 129 Karnak, 130 Valley of Kings Tomb, 131 Temple of Isis, 137 Arch of Caracalla, 142/3 Suez Canal, 145 Temple of Rameses II, 147 Kennedy Space Center, 148 Tikal Grt Plaza, 149 Temple One, 151 Teotihuacàn, 154 Chichén Itzá, 155 Grt Temple, 156 Cliff Palace, Colorado, 157 Court Hse Wish, 162 Jefferson's House, 164 Mormon Temple, 166 C P Railroad, 167 Train, 169 Statue of Liberty, 173 Californian coast, 174 Lincoln Mem, 175 Lincoln Statue, 177 Mnt. Rushmore, 180 World Trade Center, 181 John Hancock Center, Dallas skyline, 184 & 185 Golden Gate Bridge, 187 Las Vegas, 188 & 189 Kennedy Space Center, 191 Aztec Rain God, 194 Disney World, 195 Epcot Center, 198 & 199 C N Tower, 227 Sydney Opera Hse, 232 Maori Meeting Hse, Geyser N I.

ZEFA PICTURE LIBRARY UK LTD 6/7 Chichén Itzá, 18/9 Colosseum, 22 Diocletian's Palace, 32 Kapell Bridge, 37 Gondola, 38/9 Le Grande Place, Brussels, 46/7 Escorial, 60 Windsor Castle, 62/3 Neuschwanstein Castle, 67 Parliament Building, Budapest, 70 Eiffel Tower, 82 Petra, 83 Petra Mausoleum, 85 Grt Wall of China, 87 Terra-Cotta soldiers, 88 Han Dynasty Tomb Painting, 90/1 Gods of Commagenes Tombs, 105 Throne, 107 Topkapi Palace, 107 Mosiacs, 118/9 Potala Palace, 126 Sphinx, Pyramid, 136 Fez, 140 Lalibela Rock church, 141 Bet Mariam church, 152/3 Tula Pyramid remains, 153 Atlantes figures, 168 & 169 Statue of Liberty, 170/1 Panama Canal, 172/3 San Simeon, 173 Int. San Simeon, 176/7 Mt. Rushmore, 179 Empire State Building, 186/7 Las Vegas, 187 Caesars Palace, 189 Space Shuttle, 192 St Louis skyline, 195 Paddle steamer, 197 French Quarter, N Orleans, 199 Toronto, 201 Itamaraty Palace, 213 Hitching Post of the Sun, 218 Teatro Colon, B Aires, 220/1 Christ the Redeemer, 221 Rio de Janeiro, 223 Congress Building Brasília, 226 Easter Island statues, 229 Easter Island, 236 Sydney Opera Hse.